40.00

C9

MEDIEVAL FRONTIER SOCIETIES

Medieval Frontier Societies

Edited by
Robert Bartlett
and
Angus MacKay

CLARENDON PRESS · OXFORD
1989

Oxford University Press, Walton Street, Oxford OX2 6DP
Oxford New York Toronto
Delhi Bombay Calcutta Madras Karachi
Petaling Jaya Singapore Hong Kong Tokyo
Nairobi Dar es Salaam Cape Town
Melbourne Auckland
and associated companies in
Berlin Ibadan

Oxford is a trade mark of Oxford University Press

Published in the United States
by Oxford University Press, New York

British Library Cataloguing in Publication Data
Medieval frontier societies.
1. Europe. Frontier regions, to 1453
I. Bartlett, Robert II. MacKay, Angus
940.1
ISBN 0-19-822881-3

Library of Congress Cataloging in Publication Data
Medieval frontier societies / edited by Robert Bartlett and Angus MacKay.
p. cm.
Bibliography: p.
Includes index.
1. Civilization, Medieval—Congresses.
2. Europe—Boundaries—Congresses.
3. Europe—Ethnic relations—Congresses.
4. Europe—Historical geography—Congresses.
I. Bartlett, Robert. II. MacKay, Angus, 1939–
CB353.M42 1989   940.1—dc20   89-9350
ISBN 0-19-822881-3

Set by Hope Services, Abingdon
Printed and bound in
Great Britain by Biddles Ltd,
Guildford and King's Lynn

PREFACE

The papers published in this volume were originally delivered at a conference held in Edinburgh in September 1987. The theme of that conference was 'Medieval Frontier Societies' and the nature and scope of this book can best be explained by referring to the intentions of those who organized and participated in the conference. Clearly one premiss behind the undertaking was that areas of medieval Europe which were geographically widely separated and culturally and politically diverse could be fruitfully compared and contrasted. Another premiss was that the underlying experience which made such comparisons possible could be identified or symbolized by the concept 'frontier'.

In the event, terminological or definitional debate about the nature of the frontier did not take up much time at the conference and does not feature prominently in the pages that follow. The essay by Professor Burns refers to and seeks a partial vindication of the Turner thesis, but most contributors were happy to pursue empirical issues and allow the frontier element in their analysis to speak for itself. This has resulted in a certain diversity in the frontiers analysed. They range from the almost purely political frontier discussed by Professor Barrow, who argues that the Anglo-Scots border in the twelfth and thirteenth centuries was simply a line of demarcation between two kingdoms with few, if any, social, geographical, or cultural correlatives, through the sharp religious and political cleavage represented by the Christian–Muslim frontier in Spain, to the non-linear, cultural frontier between the indigenous peoples of eastern Europe and the German immigrants who settled among them in the High Middle Ages. Each of these frontiers thus had a different form and significance.

Recurrent themes did, however, emerge in many of the papers presented and the discussion which followed them. One such was militarization, the social and political response to the endemic warfare of hostile frontiers. Not all frontiers were hot—as has been pointed out, the Anglo-Scottish frontier was not a militarized zone in the period before the Scottish Wars of Independence—but they often were, and cool frontiers could heat up, as Mr Goodman demonstrates in the case of the Anglo-Scottish frontier in the later

Middle Ages, where institutions, expectations, and even local family structures seem to have been the product of an environment of long-term and ubiquitous fighting. Professor Davies, Professor López de Coca, and Dr Frame provide detailed analyses of the kind of institutions that a violent frontier tended to generate. On the one hand there was need for a machinery of military mobilization, be it the partly feudal, partly tax-based system of the fourteenth-century lordship of Ireland or the urban militias of medieval Christian Spain. On the other hand a variety of devices for mediation, arbitration, and negotiation also developed. As one reads about the professional ransomers active in Andalusia and Granada in the later Middle Ages or the intricate conventions of the Welsh March, one is struck by the way that precarious transactions were accomplished, persistently if not always smoothly, even in the most violent or divided worlds.

The frontier societies which were investigated were thus often highly militarized and this sometimes made them different from their neighbours—Ireland and Wales are contrasted by Dr Frame and Professor Davies with the experience of medieval England— but an even more essential and distinctive feature of these societies is that they were areas of cultural contact and cultural clash. In virtually every paper we see the interaction of different religions, laws, languages, and mores. On two frontiers, the Christian–Muslim frontier described by Professors López de Coca, González Jiménez, and MacKay, and that between Germans and Wends in the twelfth century, as analysed by Professor Lotter, the critical issue was religious. In both these regions Latin Christians confronted societies predicated on alien faiths; in both, Christian military effort was eventually given the legal framework of the crusade (in passing, it may be pointed out that any study of medieval frontier societies has to decide whether to exclude the eastern Mediterranean crusades or risk being swamped by them— we chose the former course).

There is ample evidence that frontier societies could witness hostility and segregation. Professor MacKay describes some of the violence to be found in Christian–Moorish relations. The Czech writers discussed by Dr Thomas were animated by a defensive animus to the German settlers in their midst; they were not happy about seeing Bohemia colonized and reacted vigorously at the prospect of it becoming a 'frontier society'. But cultural interaction

preface="" vii

also took place. In her intriguing study Dr Simms explores the poetry written by Irish bards for patrons of Anglo-Norman descent. These poets, writing in Ireland, showed a certain frontier flexibility: 'in the foreigners' poems we promise that the Irish shall be driven from Ireland; in the Irishmen's poems we promise that the foreigners shall be routed across the sea.'

Each one of the individual areas studied in these papers witnessed the immigration of outsiders during the Middle Ages, and the story of their settlement is integral to the experience of the medieval frontier. Professors González Jiménez, Knoll, and Bartlett each contribute discussion of this topic, the first providing a synthesis of settlement in Spain consequent upon the 'Reconquest', the second a study of the impact of Germans in the Polish towns of the twelfth and thirteenth centuries, the last a comparative look at the way new aristocracies put down roots in conquered lands.

In summary, then, these papers represent the varied perceptions of a group of medievalists who all turned their attention to regions whose medieval history was characterized by the movement of peoples, contact and often confrontation between cultures, violence which was sometimes endemic, and the social consequences which flowed from this. Most of the participants in the conference, it is fair to say, seemed to think that this comparative juxtaposition of different frontier societies had served a purpose; persistent readers will, of course, judge for themselves.

ACKNOWLEDGEMENTS

Grateful thanks are due to the Economic and Social Research Council, the Institute of Advanced Studies in the Humanities, Edinburgh, and the University of Chicago.

CONTENTS

LIST OF MAPS AND TABLES

ABBREVIATIONS

BL	British Library, London
Cal. Just. Rolls	*Calendar of the Justiciary Rolls . . . of Ireland*
DKR Ire.	Reports of the Deputy Keeper of the Public Records of Ireland
EHR	*English Historical Review*
IMC	Irish Manuscripts Commission
ITS	Irish Texts Society
MF	Mitteldeutsche Forschungen
MGH	*Monumenta Germaniae historica*
MPH	*Monumenta Poloniae historica*
NLI	National Library of Ireland, Dublin
NLW	National Library of Wales, Aberystwyth
NS	New Series
PRIA	*Proceedings of the Royal Irish Academy*
PRO	Public Record Office, London
PROI	Public Record Office of Ireland, Dublin
RIA	Royal Irish Academy, Dublin
RS	'Rolls Series' (*Rerum Britannicarum medii aevi scriptores*, 251 vols., London, 1858–96)
RSAIJn.	*Journal of the Royal Society of Antiquaries of Ireland*
SRG	*Scriptores rerum Germanicarum in usum scholarum (MGH)*
SS	*Scriptores (MGH)*
TRHS	*Transactions of the Royal Historical Society*
VCH	*Victoria County History* (London)

LIST OF CONTRIBUTORS

Professor Geoffrey Barrow, Department of Scottish History, University of Edinburgh

Professor Robert Bartlett, Department of History, University of Chicago

Professor Robert I. Burns, Department of History, University of California, Los Angeles

Professor Rees Davies, Department of History, The University College of Wales, Aberystwyth

Dr Robin Frame, Department of History, University of Durham

Professor Manuel González Jiménez, Departamento de Historia Medieval, University of Seville

Mr Antony Goodman, Department of History, University of Edinburgh

Professor José Enrique López de Coca Castañer, Departamento de Historia Medieval, University of Málaga

Professor Friedrich Lotter, Seminar für mittlere und neuere Geschichte, Göttingen University

Professor Paul Knoll, Department of History, University of Southern California

Professor Angus MacKay, Department of History, University of Edinburgh

Dr Katharine Simms, Department of Medieval History, Trinity College, Dublin

Professor Alfred Thomas, Department of Classical and Modern Languages, Rutgers University

Part I
SETTLEMENT

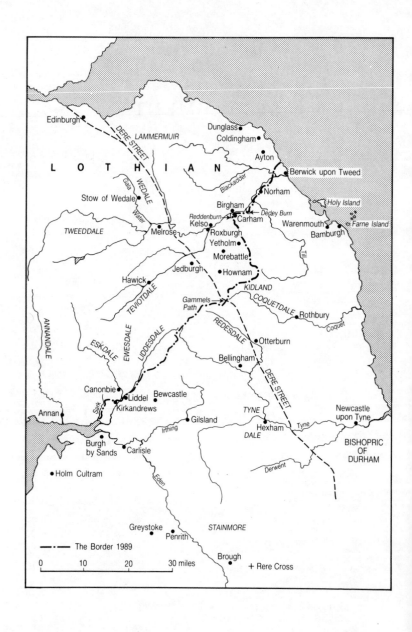

Map 1. The Anglo-Scottish Border

Frontier and Settlement: Which Influenced Which? England and Scotland, *1100–1300*

GEOFFREY BARROW

The frontier between Scotland and England, long known simply as 'the Border', began to take shape during the tenth century, when a resurgent West Saxon monarchy found itself drawn northward ineluctably by the collapse of the Danish kingdom of York, while an equally aggressive Scottish monarchy, with a hundred years' experience of governing the old kingdom of Picts, found itself challenged in the south-west by a still vigorous Brittonic Cumbria and in the south-east by a Bernician (Anglian) noble family sometimes called the 'House of Bamburgh'.[1] Between *c.*950 and 1018 the West Saxon rulers and their Danish supplanters were unable to push the boundary of their power further north than the Westmorland fells on the west and one or other of the three rivers Tees, Tyne, and Tweed on the east. Correspondingly, the kings of Scots failed to establish effective authority beyond the Tweed, even though they might from time to time harry and terrorize the country as far south as the Tyne or even the Tees. On the west they were for long thwarted by a line of independent rulers of Brittonic-speaking Cumbria, who it can scarcely be doubted viewed both Scots and West Saxons as a menace and played the one off against the other. The last king of this dynasty, Owain son of Dyfnwal, died about 1018 when the new Danish ruler of England, Canute, was preoccupied with other problems. King Malcolm II of Scotland seized his opportunity and successfully asserted Scottish control throughout Cumbria as far south as Stainmore Common on the boundary between Yorkshire and

[1] For the historical background of the Anglo-Scottish Border see Geoffrey Barrow, *The Kingdom of the Scots* (London, 1973), 139–61; D. P. Kirby, 'Strathclyde and Cumbria: A Survey of Historical Development to 1092', *Transactions of the Cumberland and Westmorland Antiquarian and Archaeological Society*, NS 62 (1962), 77–94. For the actual demarcation of the Border on the ground the indispensable guide is James L. Mack, *The Border Line* (rev. edn., Edinburgh and London, 1926).

Westmorland. From a long-term standpoint, the decisive period
came between 1092 and 1157. In the former year the second
Norman king of England, William Rufus, fixed the north-western
boundary of his kingdom at the line of Solway Firth and River
Esk, just north of Carlisle. Forty-five years later the Scots king,
David I, restored the pre-1092 situation and the restoration
remained effective for twenty years. In 1157, however, Henry II,
even more powerful than William Rufus, compelled the youthful
King Malcolm IV to surrender Cumberland and Westmorland,
and the border reverted once again, this time permanently, to the
Rufus line. On the east the border had run along the Cheviot
watershed and then down the midstream line of the River Tweed
to the sea throughout the crucial period from 1092 to 1157, as it
had almost certainly done since the later tenth century.

   To that extent, therefore, the Border was an artificial creation,
the product of a series of compromises or bargains negotiated with
seemingly little regard for either the inhabitants or even the
geography of the region through which its line was patiently
drawn. There had, after all, been some geographical sense in the
old kingdoms or tribal territories of Bernicia on the east and
Cumbria on the west. The former consisted essentially of land
drained by rivers flowing eastward from the 2,000 foot (650 m)
plateau marking the northern end of the Pennine backbone and
from the massif, averaging between 2,000 feet and 2,500 feet
(800 m), usually known as the Cheviot Hills and the middle
Southern Uplands. Inland, north–south communication is difficult,
even although the first-century Roman engineers showed what
could be done by constructing Dere Street linking York with
Edinburgh.[2] The coastal strip presents few problems, and the sea
was probably always the easiest route. From the coast access to
almost any inland area is relatively straightforward by using the
river valleys and a few ridgeway routes in between. It is easy to
understand how the country from Wear to Forth was occupied by a
single tribe, the Votadini, and how after the initial leap-frogging
coastal settlements the Angles made a single kingdom of Bernicia
out of this country, with its centre of gravity in the Tweed–

   [2] Ivan D. Margary, *Roman Roads in Britain* (rev. edn., London, 1967), 427–30,
439–41, 476–88; Lawrence Keppie, *Scotland's Roman Remains* (Edinburgh, 1986),
99–113.

Bamburgh district rather than in Lothian or on the River Tyne.[3]

Cumbria could never have possessed a comparable physical unity—as is demonstrated, indeed, by the use today of the two names Cumbria, now applied to the country south of Solway, and Strathclyde, referring primarily to the Clyde river system. Nevertheless, Cumbria at its greatest extent embraced three major river systems, Clyde, Solway, and Kent–Lune, between which communication, although not easy, was far from impossible. If you stand on the summit of Hart Fell on a clear day, you may at least fancy a certain Cumbrian unity as your eye takes in Ben Lomond close to the northern Brittonic boundary, the peaks of Arran in the west, Criffell on the Solway shore, and, to the south, the mountains of the English Lake District. But in contrast with Bernicia, the territory of a single tribal group or at most of two if the Selgovae of Selkirk Forest are included, Cumbria was evidently made up of at least four tribal homelands, the Damnonii of Alclut or Dumbarton, the Novantae of 'Rheged'—Galloway and the north Solway shore—the obscure Carvetii of the Eden valley, and the warlike Brigantes of the Pennine dales.[4] It seems to have been rare for these peoples to coalesce into an effective political unit. As the Romans discovered in the second century AD, through harsh experience, there are other ways of dividing the island of Britain.

For the medieval frontier had its roots in geology, which has given the northern counties of England a different underlying structure from that of southern Scotland, and to some extent a different soil. It is true that the carboniferous limestone which forms the basis of northern Cumberland and of so much of Northumberland swings round in a great arc to re-enter Scotland along the Berwickshire plain ('the Merse'). It is also true that the granite intrusion of the Cheviot and the vast deposits of andesite lavas surrounding it are shared almost equally by Scotland and England. But to the north and west layers of sandstones and

---

[3] Ian A. Richmond (ed.), *Roman and Native in North Britain* (Edinburgh and London, 1958); P. Hunter Blair, *Roman Britain and Early England* (Edinburgh and London, 1963). The essential information, both historical and geographical, is of course to be found in Bede's *Ecclesiastical History of the English People*, ed. Bertram Colgrave and R. A. B. Mynors (Oxford, 1969).

[4] Richmond, *Roman and Native in North Britain*; Steuart N. Miller (ed.), *The Roman Occupation of South-Western Scotland* (Glasgow, 1952); A. L. F. Rivet and Colin Smith, *The Place Names of Roman Britain* (London and Princeton, 1979).

greywacke some thirty miles across push into the limestone arc and give the valleys of Teviot and Tweed a green fertility and vegetation which are in sharp contrast with the bleak uplands of Tyne and Wear to the south. No wonder that for the English kings the northern counties always remained distant, unprofitable, and largely unvisited, whereas for the rulers of Scotland the country between the Firth of Forth and the Cheviot Hills was one of the richest and most frequented regions of their realm.

The geological contrast was not enough to impose completely different agricultural systems north and south of the Border. A pastoral way of life predominated throughout the frontier region and indeed from northern Yorkshire and the Pennines to the furthermost parts of Scotland.[5] Cattle, sheep, pigs, and goats provided the bulk of the population with its living, just as cheese, milk, oatmeal, and the flour obtained from bere, the six-rowed barley of the north, formed the staple diet of all but the wealthiest nobles and merchants. That is not to say that cereal crops were unimportant, rather that, save along the coastal strip and in a few well-favoured inland valleys such as around Hexham, in the vale of Whittingham, or around Jedburgh, Melrose, and Hawick, corn would not be grown to provide an exportable surplus but essentially to tide humans and beasts over the winter. Archaeological research, and especially intensive aerial photography in recent years, has made it impossible to doubt that the climate was more favourable for cereal cultivation than it is today: we have abundant traces of regular ploughing on ground which no modern farmer would dream of turning over even under the stimulus of huge barley or oil-seed rape subsidies, and at heights above sea level at which it is very doubtful if any modern varieties would ripen.[6] These archaeological findings are particularly interesting

---

[5] For the pastoral background in general see Gaillard Thomas Lapsley, *The County Palatine of Durham* (Cambridge, Mass., 1900); id. in *VCH Durham*, i (1905), 269–302; Geoffrey Barrow, 'Northern English Society in the Early Middle Ages', *Northern History*, 4 (1969), 1–28; A. J. L. Winchester, *Landscape and Society in Medieval Cumbria* (Edinburgh, 1987), esp. chs. 1, 2, 4, and 5; William Kapelle, *The Norman Conquest of the North* (Chapel Hill, 1979), esp. chs. 3 and 6; Barrow, *Kingdom of the Scots*, esp. chs. 1 and 9; M. L. Parry and T. R. Slater (eds.), *The Making of the Scottish Countryside* (London, 1980); R. A. Dodgshon, *Land and Society in Early Scotland* (Oxford, 1981); R. N. Millman, *The Making of the Scottish Landscape* (London, 1975).

[6] Aerial photographs covering several areas of southern Scotland are to be found in the National Monuments Record for Scotland maintained by the Royal

because they abundantly corroborate surviving documentary evidence which showed that many Border parishes now drastically depopulated possessed large acreages of arable which must have required a sizeable number of inhabitants to be cultivated and harvested. For example in the old hill parish of Mow south of Kelso, long suppressed for want of population and merged with Morebattle, itself largely depopulated, the charters preserved by the abbeys of Kelso and Melrose provide evidence of substantial numbers of small freeholders and lesser peasantry, husbandmen, cottars, etc., from the later decades of the twelfth century through to *c*.1300.[7] Although sheep and cattle pasture looms large in these documents, charter after charter refers to acres, rigs, and furlongs; and Professor Denis Harding of Edinburgh University and his colleagues have photographed many of these long-lost arable fields from the air. Similarly at Minto north-east of Hawick in 1248 a married couple were forced by financial hardship to sell the wife's 'terce' or dower, which consisted of rigs and parcels of arable lying in no fewer than ten different furlongs, and though we are told that some parcels were arable and some were meadow, there is no mention of animals or pasture.[8]

And yet we must recognize from overwhelming evidence, as yet documentary rather than archaeological, that horn prevailed over corn, that cattle and sheep constituted the primary source of livelihood, including exportable surpluses of hides, wool, and woolfells which paid the king's taxes and allowed a modest import of necessities and luxuries. The basic pastoralism of northern England and of most of Scotland other than the eastern coastal plain is of course in no sense peculiar to the medieval period; it must go back far into prehistoric times and still obtains today. The current sheep population of Scotland, 8.8 million, is said to be the highest ever recorded. We have no way of calculating the medieval total at all accurately, but flocks of 500 or 1,000 breeding ewes and

Commission for the Ancient and Historical Monuments of Scotland, 54 Melville Street, Edinburgh.

[7] These documents are conveniently brought together in *Liber sancte Marie de Melros*, ed. Cosmo Innes (2 vols., Bannatyne Club, Edinburgh, 1837), i, nos. 134–48, 292–8, 345–7, pp. 125–39, 257–63, 307–10, and *Liber sancte Marie de Calchou*, ed. Cosmo Innes (2 vols., Bannatyne Club, Edinburgh, 1846), i, nos. 146–79, pp. 113–49; ii, no. 406, p. 314.

[8] 'North Country Deeds', in *Miscellanea*, 2 (Surtees Society 127, 1916), 107–29, at 124–5, relating to Minto Kames in Minto, Roxburghshire.

similar numbers of wedders (castrated rams) are not uncommonly recorded. On the upland manor of Otterburn, for example, just south of the Border, there was pasture in 1245 for over 1,100 ewes and 1,400 acres of cattle pasture, as well as a valuable stud of stallions and brood mares at Cottonshope, where only hill ponies could be kept today.[9] At Romanno in Peeblesshire in the same period the canons of Holyrood and the Cistercian monks of Newbattle kept flocks of 1,000 ewes each.[10] On the moors about the headwaters of the Whiteadder in Berwickshire the Cistercians of Melrose ran three flocks each of 500 wedders.[11]

South of the Border, we may note the prevalence on the Northumberland Lay Subsidy Roll (1296) of occupational descriptions denoting the keeping of animals: herd, shepherd, hogherd, calfherd, cowherd, neatherd, oxherd, queyherd, stotherd (cf. the Scots surname Stoddart), and swineherd.[12] In this part of our region the most abundant evidence is to be found in the archives of the bishopric and cathedral monastery of Durham, and here as elsewhere the overriding importance of sheep and cattle rearing throughout St Cuthbert's Land—i.e. modern County Durham plus Bedlingtonshire, Islandshire, and Norhamshire—is apparent in the record of the majority of component estates—indeed, the cereal specialization of a number of County Durham manors only serves to emphasize the point. To the west of the Pennine–Cheviot watershed, in Cumberland, Furness, and Westmorland on the English side of the Border, as well as in western Roxburghshire, Dumfriesshire, and Lanarkshire in Scotland, the pastoral way of life was if anything even more dominant than on the east. Just as today this country forms one of the leading regions for beef and dairy products in the entire United Kingdom, so clearly in the earlier Middle Ages cattle were the mainstay of an overwhelmingly rural economy.[13]

[9] *Calendar of Documents Relating to Scotland*, ed. Joseph Bain (4 vols., Edinburgh, 1881–8), i, no. 1667, p. 350; *Liber de Calchou*, ii, nos. 325–9, pp. 261–3.

[10] *Liber cartarum Sancte Crucis*, ed. Cosmo Innes (Bannatyne Club, Edinburgh, 1840), no. 22, p. 18; *Registrum sancte Marie de Neubotle*, ed. Cosmo Innes (Bannatyne Club, Edinburgh, 1849), no. 130, pp. 97–8.

[11] *Liber de Melros*, i, no. 56, pp. 45–6.

[12] *The Northumberland Lay Subsidy Roll of 1296*, ed. Constance M. Fraser (Society of Antiquaries of Newcastle-upon-Tyne Record Series 1, 1968), p. xix and *passim*, most occupational epithets being noted in the index. A quey is a heifer, a stot is a bullock.

[13] Winchester, *Landscape and Society in Medieval Cumbria*, ch. 5.

Society in this frontier region was, at least in the twelfth and thirteenth centuries, no more differentiated by or at the line of the Border than were the crops, herds, and flocks which were raised to support its existence. From Yorkshire northward to beyond the Forth the greater and lesser secular magnates, earls, barons, and knights, and the prelates of the Church, bishops, abbots and priors, and cathedral chapters, presided over and were maintained by lordships most if not all of which had been formed by the deliberate hiving off of a once all-pervasive royal lordship.[14] North and south of the Border these great landowners held for the most part by military service, although we must note one fundamental difference in that no ecclesiastical estate in Scotland, whether of bishopric or of monastery, owed knight service or castle ward, but only the universal duty of 'common army'.[15]

The quotas of service seem to have been on a similar scale in England and Scotland, a striking fact when one bears in mind that Northumberland and Cumberland were poor and peripheral by English standards whereas, as I have said, the Scots kings regarded their southern sheriffdoms as the very heartland of their realm. Thus, of the tenancies-in-chief listed by the late Percy Hedley in his *Northumberland Families*,[16] only Alnwick, held by the de Vesci family, owed as many as twelve knights; most owed one, two, or three knights, although the leading families of Umfraville, Balliol, Bolebec, and Bertram had *servicia debita* of five or six. For Scotland we lack anything to compare with the *cartae baronum* of 1166, the replies to Henry II's questionnaire; but we may note that the Stewart owed only one knight's service for Birkenside, Legerwood, and Mow combined;[17] that the de Morvilles probably rendered six knights' service for Lauderdale;[18] and that for the whole vast lordship of Annandale de Brus owed only ten knights, two fewer than were due from Alnwick.[19]

---

[14] Barrow, *Kingdom of the Scots*, 19–68; Glanville R. J. Jones, 'Basic Patterns of Settlement Distribution in Northern England', *Advancement of Science*, 71 (1961), 192–200; id., 'Early Territorial Organization in Northern England', in Alan Small (ed.), *The Fourth Viking Congress* (Edinburgh and London, 1965), 67–84.

[15] Geoffrey Barrow, *The Anglo-Norman Era in Scottish History* (Oxford, 1980), esp. 161–6.

[16] William Percy Hedley, *Northumberland Families*, i (Newcastle upon Tyne, 1968), 21.

[17] *The Acts of Malcolm IV, King of Scots, 1153–65*, ed. Geoffrey Barrow (*Regesta regum Scottorum* 1, Edinburgh, 1960), no. 183, p. 224.

[18] Barrow, *Anglo-Norman Era*, 72.   [19] Id., *Kingdom of the Scots*, 281.

The duty of guarding or warding the king's castles was well
established in all parts of the region by 1200. In England it must
have dated from the 1080s or 1090s in respect of Newcastle and
Carlisle, and perhaps somewhat later in the case of Warkworth,
Bamburgh, and Norham. On the Scottish side the system
doubtless began with David I, and the earliest castles to have been
garrisoned in this way would have included Berwick, Roxburgh,
Jedburgh, and Selkirk, with Dumfries following *c*.1170. The
administrative device of dividing the northernmost English counties
into wards seems to have originated in the system of castle guard,
but we do not know when it was introduced.[20] It was functioning
by the thirteenth century, and it is to be noted that in Scotland the
sheriffdoms of Roxburgh and Lanark also had wards.[21] It seems
impossible to say whether this was imitation or a simultaneous and
independent response to identical stimuli.

Royal castles—indeed, castles of any status—were comparatively
uncommmon in the frontier region, their rarity emphasizing the
fact that the actual Border line was remarkably unmilitarized. The
English kings had Carlisle in the west and Newcastle in the east,
but nothing at all to guard the Tyne gap. Newcastle was unusual
among northern English strongholds in being built north of its
river crossing. Although formidable, it was sixty miles south of the
Border. Warkworth, founded by the Scots, was subinfeudated in
1158, as soon as Henry II recovered it.[22] The English kings
maintained Bamburgh indefinitely but it lay so far to the east that
it could easily be bypassed. King John tried to build a castle at
Tweedmouth, but abandoned the plan when it aroused violent
Scottish opposition;[23] the idea was never revived. The bishop of
Durham, standing in for the king, had a first-rate fortress at
Norham from 1121, often a thorn in the Scots' side, but in general
English magnatial castles—Wark on Tweed, Alnwick, Harbottle,
Mitford, Morpeth, and Prudhoe—cannot be regarded as unduly

[20] Robert Surtees, *The History and Antiquities of the County Palatine of Durham*
(4 vols., London, 1816–40); *History of Northumberland* (15 vols., London and
Newcastle upon Tyne, 1893–1940); Joseph Nicolson and Richard Burn, *The
History and Antiquities of Westmorland and Cumberland* (2 vols., London, 1777).

[21] *Memoranda de Parliamento, 1305*, ed. Frederic W. Maitland (RS, 1893), 180–
1; *Macfarlane's Geographical Collections*, iii, ed. Arthur Mitchell and James T.
Clark (Scottish History Society 53, 1908), 131.

[22] Hedley, *Northumberland Families*, i. 160–2.

[23] *The Acts of William I, King of Scots, 1165–1214*, ed. Geoffrey Barrow
(*Regesta regum Scottorum* 2, Edinburgh, 1971), 18–19.

numerous for the territorial area involved.[24] Wark on Tyne actually belonged to the king of Scots, while in Cumberland the density of baronial castles was less, if anything, than in Northumberland, although Appleby, Cockermouth, and Egremont were doubtless quite formidable, while in the earliest phase of castle-building the de Vaux motte at Brampton, and Liddel Strength, built probably by the Fleming Turgis Brundis, were obviously intended to deter attack from the north.[25]

In Scotland, castle-building by those feudal barons whose fiefs lay along the Border seems to have been on a markedly smaller scale than in the corresponding parts of England. The motte phase (c.1120–c.1190?) saw the construction of Hawick by the Lovels, Mote of Liddel by the de Soules, Staplegordon by the Conisbroughs, and Annan and Lochmaben by the de Brus family.[26] There must surely have been more than this, but the absence of either documentary record or physical remains makes it quite certain that if and wherever they existed they cannot have been of the first rank. In the later stone castle phase the erection of Hermitage by Nicholas de Soules and of Caerlaverock by John or Aymer de Maxwell in the 1240s was so exceptional that it induced in the English king, Henry III, a fit of paranoia which nearly pitched him into all-out war.[27] In the same period two great Scots lords, John Comyn later lord of Badenoch and David Lindsay of Crawford, commissioned strongly fortified hall-houses for themselves in

[24] A useful general view of Northumberland castles is provided by Robert Hugill, *Borderland Castles and Peles* (Newcastle upon Tyne, 1970). See also Cadwallader Bates, *The Border Holds of Northumberland* (Newcastle upon Tyne, 1891).

[25] Hugill, *Borderland Castles and Peles*, 147–9; R. Donaldson-Hudson, 'Liddel Strength in Cumberland', *History of the Berwickshire Naturalists' Club*, 37/1 (1965), 50–3; J. F. Curwen, *The Castles and Fortified Towers of Cumberland, Westmorland and Lancashire North-of-the-sands* (Cumberland and Westmorland Antiquarian and Archaeological Society, extra series 13, 1913); T. H. B. Graham, *The Barony of Gilsland* (Cumberland and Westmorland Antiquarian and Archaeological Society, extra series 16, 1934).

[26] G. G. Simpson and Bruce Webster, 'Charter Evidence and the Distribution of Mottes in Scotland', *Château Gaillard* (1972), 175–92, at 177–8; Geoffrey Barrow, 'The Pattern of Lordship and Feudal Settlement in Cumbria', *Journal of Medieval History*, 1 (1975), 117–38, at 132; id., *Kingdom of the Scots*, 281; id. *Anglo-Norman Era*, 101, 184.

[27] Matthew Paris, *Chronica majora*, ed. Henry Richards Luard (7 vols., RS, 1872–83), iv. 380; Walter Bower, *Scotichronicon*, ed. Walter Goodall (2 vols., Edinburgh, 1759), ii. 74. The castles referred to, respectively in 'Lothian' and 'Galloway', were evidently Hermitage and Caerlaverock.

North Tynedale, at Tarset and Dally respectively.[28] But the very fact that these small castles, like nearby Wark, were in England, like the fact that the first Warkworth Castle was built by a Scottish prince, Henry son of David I, only underlines how vain it would be to assess the twelfth- or thirteenth-century Border as though it were a fully defensive international frontier.

And yet it would be quite wrong to see the Border as merely symbolic. It functioned as a true frontier, punctuated by recognized crossing points at which tolls were regularly levied. In times of emergency it was capable of being guarded. An elaborate but distinctly archaic system of rules for pursuit of thieves and suppression of violence was freshly promulgated by an Anglo-Scottish commission in 1249 as the 'Laws of the Marches'.[29] A common or reciprocal legal code for the frontier emphasized, in effect, the separate identities of Scots and English jurisdictions—neither was adequate, of itself, to right a wrong or bring a malefactor to justice.

Such a frontier, long evolved, obdurately customary, the outcome of much hard bargaining, could scarcely fail to affect the lives of those who dwelt within its ambit. The feudal class in particular adapted to constraints which the Border inevitably imposed. Until 1328 there was nothing to hinder a person who already owned land in one kingdom from acquiring property in the other. This was evidently true at all levels of society, but naturally it had its most significant and permanent effects among families of barons and knights. To put an extreme case, a man or woman who held land for knight service in the army of the king of Scots, who owed garrison duty at Roxburgh or Berwick to defend the realm against English attack, was obviously in difficulty if he or she also held a fief on similar terms in one of the English border counties whenever a state of war or even of alert was proclaimed. Such a person had to make a choice and by and large this choice would be determined by the place of habitual or chief residence.

A letter written in 1286 by the Guardians of Scotland to the Guardian of England (the king of Scots had died and the king of

---

[28] *Close Rolls of the Reign of Henry III, 1242–7* (London, 1916), 221 (Tarset); *Cal. of Docs. Relating to Scotland*, v, supplementary vol., ed. G. G. Simpson and J. D. Galbraith (Edinburgh, 1986), no. 12, p. 136 (Dally).

[29] Ed. Thomas Thomson and Cosmo Innes, *Acts of the Parliaments of Scotland*, i (Edinburgh, 1844), 413–16 (red); trans. George Neilson, *Miscellany of the Stair Society*, i (Stair Society 26, 1971), 11–77.

England was in Gascony)[30] declared that whenever a woman holding land of the Crown in chief in both realms was due to be married she would be allowed to marry by leave of the ruler and king of whichever realm she was dwelling in at that period of her life—in other words, her marriage would not depend on her obtaining permission from both her feudal superiors.

This was surely a common-sense arrangement, and although we have no explicit evidence on the point we may assume that much the same principle was applied over the question of military service. For lengthy periods before 1296 the issue was hardly very serious but under war conditions there could easily be grave crises of personal loyalty. With the outbreak of war in the spring of 1296 the castle of Wark on Tweed (or Carham), built on the south bank of the river whose midstream line formed the Border, came under immediate attack from the Scots. Its lord was Robert de Ros, who not only held an estate of the Scottish crown (in upper Tweeddale?) but was in love with a Scotswoman. Because of this he helped the Scots to seize his own castle and hold it briefly against the English.[31] One month later, the wife of Earl Patrick of Dunbar— she is said to have been a daughter of Alexander Comyn earl of Buchan—held the castle of Dunbar in the name of the king of Scots against the invading English army, despite the fact that her husband had repudiated King John and had attached himself to King Edward.[32] The earls of Buchan were landowners in Leicestershire but Earl Alexander was one of the chief men of the Scottish realm and preoccupied with the defence of Scotland. Earl Patrick was likewise one of the greatest Scottish landowners, but he held estates in north Northumberland by very ancient pre-feudal tenure.[33] It was certainly not the case that the Border did not exist for such persons as de Ros, Comyn, or the earl and countess of Dunbar; rather that in times of crisis they had to come down on one side or the other.

For lesser folk the challenge of divided loyalties would seldom have been so pressing. For the peasantry, winning their livelihood

[30] *Documents Illustrative of the History of Scotland*, ed. Joseph Stevenson (2 vols., Edinburgh, 1870), i. 26–7.

[31] Geoffrey Barrow, *Robert Bruce and the Community of the Realm of Scotland* (rev. edn., Edinburgh, 1982), 98–9; Hedley, *Northumberland Families*, i. 229.

[32] James Balfour Paul (ed.), *The Scots Peerage*, (9 vols., Edinburgh, 1904–14), iii. 262–4.

[33] Hedley, *Northumberland Families*, i. 238.

involved hill grazing and transhumance, which must often have led
to cattle and sheep transgressing the Border line. For the whole
population trade was vital, and here again the Border must have
been crossed constantly as a matter of course. On the West March
there was no Scottish trading centre to compare with Carlisle and
it is no surprise to learn that the inhabitants of Wauchopedale near
Langholm (in Scotland) were in the habit of travelling to Carlisle
to exchange their produce for the necessities and luxuries which
could be obtained only in an urban market.[34] Similarly northern
Northumberland (despite the bishop of Durham's efforts to build
up Norham) had no towns to equal Roxburgh and Berwick.[35] It is
clear that both these Scottish burghs not only served as major
markets (or in Berwick's case as a major export outlet) for wool
producers and others in north-east England, but also contained
appreciable numbers of burgesses and others who originated (or
whose forebears originated) in England, including the English
Border area.[36]

The broad stratification of the population below the level of
knight and baron was universal throughout the frontier region,
indeed throughout north midland and northern England and most
of southern and eastern Scotland. In no sense can this stratification
have been produced by the Border. It underlay the Border and
feudal organization and must consequently have antedated both,
probably by many generations if not centuries.

A ministerial minor nobility or gentry characterized the four
northern counties of England and much of southern Scotland,
especially on the east. This class held its estates heritably but by
tenures not so strongly entrenched legally as those enjoyed by
knights and barons.[37] The commonest generic terms applied to

[34] *Cal. of Docs. Relating to Scotland*, iii, no. 1096, p. 197.

[35] Constance M. Fraser, 'The Pattern of Trade in the North-east of England,
1265–1350', *Northern History*, 4 (1969), 44–66, at 44, lists markets in 1293 at Wark
on Tweed, Norham, Wooler, Chatton, Bamburgh, Embleton, Alnmouth, Alnwick,
Warkworth, Rothbury, and Harbottle. With the exception of Alnwick, Bamburgh,
and Norham, these must have been very small places.

[36] A list compiled many years ago by the present writer shows persons settled in
the border burghs of Scotland whose names suggest origin in the following places in
northern England: Belford, Beverley, Durham, Filey, Goswick, Grindon, Howtel,
Menston, Mindrum, Ravenser, Rennington, Richmond, Rothbury, Scremerston,
Selby, Tritlington, York.

[37] For this see generally Barrow, *Kingdom of the Scots*, 19–35; id., 'Northern
English Society', 9–17; Kapelle, *Norman Conquest*, ch. 3; J. E. A. Jolliffe,
'Northumbrian Institutions', *EHR* 41 (1926), 1–42.

members of this important class were thane (*thegn*) and dreng. At the upper end of the social scale, emphasizing the particular connection which linked a thane to a recognized administrative district or 'shire,' the Old English word sheriff (*scir-gerefa*) might be used of certain leading thanes—for example the early twelfth-century sheriffs of Bamburgh, Norham, Teviotdale (Roxburgh?), Lauderdale, Hexham, and Copeland. In other contexts it seems that thanes or drengs might be entitled serjeants (*servientes*), responsible for the fulfilment of specialist offices connected with the forest or with peace-keeping.[38] Neither 'thane' nor 'dreng' was a strict term of art, for at the lower end of the scale thanes might overlap or be confused with drengs. Their essential characteristic lay in their being ministers or officers acting as estate managers for the kings and greater lords.

It is noteworthy that the rise of the Border in no way affected the survival or even the indispensability of this obviously numerous group, which clearly formed the backbone of the class of petty nobles and freeholders both north and south until the later decades of the twelfth century. Thanes and drengs seem to have faded more rapidly in England than in Scotland, perhaps because military feudalism was more insistent and demanding in the south, more adaptable in the north. In any event, the semantic change may well have been more conspicuous than the social reality. The class of small to middling freeholders, grouped into 'surnames' on both sides of the Border, who in the later medieval period (fourteenth–sixteenth centuries) built the typical small tower houses, peles, and bastles and sturdily survived the vicissitudes of a more turbulent era cannot have differed fundamentally from the thanes and drengs of an earlier age, who must in numerous instances have been their ancestors.[39]

Apart from this ministerial cadre, servants to their lords, whether kings or earls, bishops or barons, but obviously very much masters in their own communities, the settled population was largely composed of husbandmen ('bonders'), cottars, and gresmen or gersemen, that is grazing tenants. The classical husbandman, secure in his holding of twenty-six acres of arable with corresponding

---

[38] Ronald Stewart-Brown, *The Sergeants of the Peace in Medieval England and Wales* (Manchester, 1936).

[39] Thomas I. Rae, *The Administration of the Scottish Frontier, 1513–1603* (Edinburgh, 1966).

shares of grazing and other easements, does seem to have existed in real life, not merely in the textbooks. Certainly in southern Scotland the 'husbandland' of two thirteen-acre bovates or oxgangs is widely evidenced from the earlier twelfth century through to the fourteenth. Unfortunately, I have not had the opportunity to discover whether this was equally true for Cumberland or Northumberland. Boldon Buke (1183) shows that at Horncliffe, just south of the Tweed near Berwick, the eighteen husbandmen (*villani*) each held two oxgangs—i.e. one husbandland[40]—and that the same situation prevailed at Boldon itself and at the many other townships in the Palatinate which were said to be like Boldon;[41] so it looks as though the two-oxgang husbandland was probably the norm in English Northumbria generally.

Cottars and gresmen seem to have been as essential as husbandmen in the region's agrarian economy. Many individuals would not be able to cope, financially, physically, or merely in terms of farming skill, with the labour and responsibility of a full husbandland. Many others, in a period of steady population growth, would not get the chance of a husbandman's holding. Yet others would try their luck with beasts at pasture, squatting on the outer fringes of an established settlement or turning a summer shieling into a permanent homestead. Such must have made up the bulk of the cottar and gresmen population, which from the lord's point of view—more especially from the point of view of the lord's resident thane or dreng—would provide an essential source of seasonal and casual labour. The activities of the gresmen in particular would put pressure on the common grazing allocated since time immemorial to every township. Traditionally, this grazing was exploited by transhumance or the shieling system, under which the women, youngsters, and perhaps some of the older folk moved to a stretch of moor or hill ground from May to the end of August (or even later), taking with them the milking cows and ewes and their followers, and accumulating supplies of cheese and perhaps some butter for the winter. To extend the traditional grazing further and further into the hills, as would inevitably happen if small communities of gresmen attached themselves to estate after estate, would encroach on the 'waste' of

---

[40] *Boldon Book: Northumberland and Durham*, ed. D. Austin, supplementary vol. to *Domesday Book*, ed. John Morris (Chichester, 1982), 35.

[41] Ibid., 13, 15, 17, and elsewhere.

the Northumbrian and Cumbrian hills and the Southern Uplands.
Much of this waste on both sides of the Border was forest, that is,
hunting reserve, and much surviving record, of the thirteenth
century especially, is concerned with the resulting conflict not
necessarily between game-loving lords and pastoral tenants or
between rival lordships but between two opposing interests or
purposes within one lordship. It does not appear that there were
markedly different ways of dealing with this situation on the two
sides of the Border. The only broad contrast was provided by the
fact that the forest laws were noticeably less harsh and severe in
Scotland than in England.

Of the steady advance of human settlement into the uplands
there can be no doubt. The change of land use since the Middle
Ages in a big modern conurbation has scarcely been more drastic
than in the area of north-east Cumberland, north-west Northumberland, and southern Roxburghshire, where over the past
half-century the Forestry Commission has brought into existence
the largest unbroken stretch of man-made woodland—virtually all
of it rapid growing spruce and fir—in the British Isles. We have to
make a determined effort of imagination to see the slow but sure
advance of pastoral colonization on either side of the Border line.
In England we have the barony of Liddel reaching eastward up
the Kershope Burn; a chapelry at Falstone far up the North
Tyne where Emmethaugh (now drowned) and Kielder were
already settled in the mid-twelfth century;[42] outlying townships
of Alwinton in Upper Coquetdale such as Linshiel, which was a
permanent taxable habitation by 1336, not a mere summer pasture
station;[43] and further permanent homesteads by 1296 well into the
College valley under the shadow of the Cheviot.[44] Indeed, the
Northumberland Lay Subsidy Roll for 1296 provides startling
evidence of thirteenth-century congestion to contrast with modern
depopulation.

[42] *VCH Cumberland*, i (1901), 305; Geoffrey Barrow, 'A Note on Falstone',
Archaeologia Aeliana, 5th ser., 2 (1974), 149–52; *Pipe Roll, 22 Henry II* (Pipe Roll
Society 25, 1904), 139.

[43] *Northumberland Lay Subsidy Roll*, 183. Since a chapel was founded at
Linshiel in 1317 and the place formed a feudal tenement in 1242, its history clearly
goes back well before 1336.

[44] Ibid. 118 (Trolhop is Trowup in the College Valley), 126 (Hethpool). For
Hethpool and Trowup in the mid-13th century see also *Liber de Melros*, i, nos.
305–8, pp. 267–72.

On the Scottish side we may adduce the vanished communities of Carruthers, Half Morton, and Wauchope in Dumfriesshire; the chapelry of Wheelkirk dependent on an obviously well-peopled parish of Castleton or Liddesdale—even the site of the chapel of Wheelkirk would now be very difficult to locate, still more to visit;[45] the heavily depopulated though still just surviving parishes of Hobkirk and Southdean; the hill sheep farm of Penderleith where a substantial lordship is evidenced from the earlier thirteenth century;[46] and the much denser settlement of the obsolete parish of Mow which I have already referred to.

All this was going forward in the period between 1100 and 1300 and was at no point deterred by the existence of the Border. But the colonization of unpromising hill ground was by no means the only, nor indeed even the most important, social phenomenon observable in the Anglo-Scottish frontier region. The period saw the rapid growth, almost from scratch, of the city of Carlisle and the burghs of Roxburgh, Jedburgh, and Berwick, backed up by a cluster of smaller market towns. In Scotland the famous Border abbeys grew up in this period. Several of these, such as Canonbie, Jedburgh, Kelso, and the Benedictine daughter-house of Durham functioning at Coldingham from the 1130s, and the nunneries of Eccles, Coldstream, and Berwick, were sited on or very close to the actual Border line. Most of the corresponding religious houses in northern England were set further back, but bearing in mind that this was not a naturally rich country monasteries were not noticeably scarce. Durham maintained a sister-house of Coldingham on Holy Island; there were nuns at remote Holystone to whom the great King David I was a benefactor; the Premonstratensian Order had an abbey at Alnwick which was Dryburgh's mother-house; there were Cistercian abbeys at Newminster beside Morpeth and Holm Cultram on the Solway; there were Augustinian canons at Lanercost on the Irthing, at Hexham where the South and North Tyne rivers meet, and at Brinkburn on the Coquet; and finally (though the list is not exhaustive) there were Black Monk priories,

---

[45] Ian B. Cowan, *The Parishes of Medieval Scotland* (Scottish Record Society 93, Edinburgh, 1967), 209; G. Watson, 'Wheel Kirk, Liddesdale', *Transactions of the Hawick Archaeological Society* (1914), 20–2, at 20.
[46] *Origines parochiales Scotiae*, ed. Cosmo Innes *et al.* (2 vols. in 3, Bannatyne Club, Edinburgh, 1850–5), i. 392; *Cal. of Docs. relating to Scotland*, iii, nos. 1641, 1670, pp. 298–9, 308.

dependent upon southern parents, at Wetheral east of Carlisle and at Tynemouth east of Newcastle.

All this investment in the religious life, with its corollary of large-scale stone buildings and very extensive estates composed of village communities, arable, woodland, and hill grazing, speaks of sustained prosperity and growing confidence. New monasteries, new parishes, new trading towns and harbours, new lines of export in wool, cattle, silver, lead, and even coal, were all of a piece and took little account of the frontier's existence. Even communication routes were not fundamentally affected. It is true that the Irthing–Tyne route between Carlisle and Newcastle was particularly favoured and running as it does east and west it looks superficially like the interior lines of a defensive system. In fact it is due to an accident of geography or even geology; and by another such accident there is nothing to compare with the Tyne Gap in Scotland save the distinctly less practicable Tweed–Clyde route well north of the Border, or even the Inveresk–Biggar route exploited by the Romans, which of course is so far north that its relevance for the Border is virtually nil. Contemporary record tells us at least as much of the roads runnning north and south, linking England and Scotland by the Northumberland–Berwickshire plain or by the Fords of Solway between Annan and Bowness, as of roads (important though they must have been) which linked east and west. King Henry I, at least, was not favourably impressed even by the Tyne Gap when, in one of the twelfth century's rare distortions of administrative geography, he allocated Alston and Nenthead, around the head waters of the South Tyne, to Cumberland instead of Northumberland because the immensely valuable Pennine silver mines were safer under the control of a sheriff of Carlisle more or less within reach rather than of a sheriff of Newcastle who was unacceptably remote.

It remains to be seen whether or not we can suggest an answer to the question embodied in the title of this paper. Did the Anglo-Scottish frontier in the twelfth and thirteenth centuries influence the pattern and character of human settlement, or did that settlement influence the nature and perhaps even the location of the frontier? That there was *some* influence in both directions can hardly be denied. The pattern of Northumbrian and Cumbrian castles, almost all of them built on the south side of a river crossing, the great bridgehead of Newcastle upon Tyne and the forbidding promontory fortress at Tynemouth serving as the exceptions to prove the rule, cannot be due to accident. They were certainly planned in the knowledge that the Border lay only a short distance to the north and was a mere line which could be crossed at will. A similar pattern may be discerned in Scotland, though it is not so sharply marked. Berwick upon Tweed, Roxburgh, Jedburgh, Peebles, and Hermitage all stood on the north side of the river crossings they guarded, Roxburgh and Peebles making good use of the angle between two streams. But the early mottes of Liddel, Annan, and of course Dumfries were all built on the English side of their respective rivers, and the inference seems inescapable that in the period before *c.* 1160 an attack from Galloway was more to be feared—and expected—than one from the south. Ralph Lovel's motte at Hawick, built around 1140–50, seems to be a law unto itself: it occupies rising ground between the north-east flowing Teviot and its tributary the Slitrig Water which flows north on the east side of the castle mound—a Scottish castle in an oddly Anglo-Saxon attitude, or at least a Northumbrian one. The overall pattern of fortification, and consequently of early burghs or trading towns, seems to have been shaped to some extent at least by awareness of the Border.

As for the influence in the reverse direction, the Laws of the Marches, which regulated cross-border disputes and intercourse until the long war of 1296 to 1328 heightened international tension, reflect a pastoral society throughout the region, a society much occupied with sheep, cattle, and horses and the possibility— nay, the strong probability—of their straying or being stolen. In other words, the Laws of the Marches were not international law as it would be understood in later times, that is a code according to which whole nations can resolve their differences, but rather a way of enforcing the kind of law already familiar and acceptable to individuals north and south of the Border when, because of that Border, the individuals' customary courts lacked the competence to act.

It is not, I think, fanciful to see the choice of frontier line, as it solidified in the twelfth century, being to some extent determined by the facts of settlement. Not, it is true, along the Tweed from the sea to the Redden Burn, where the whole valley forms an agreeable unity. The kings of Scotland must often have yearned for the broad acres of Norhamshire—but could take only the half-moon meadow beside Wark, anomalously Scottish since time immemorial, though south of the river;[47] the bishops of Durham must likewise have coveted the fair fields of the Merse, but were allowed only the tiny parish of Upsettlington, anomalously in Durham not St Andrews diocese, though north of the river.[48] Nor, for that matter, along the Esk and Liddel from Kirkandrews up to Castleton, where again the valley must always have formed a unity in terms of settlement. But can we seriously doubt that the great hump of hill ground stretching eastward from the Kershope Burn to the northern offshoots of the Cheviot, hostile to all but the hardiest, most marginal of colonists, appealed to the plain common sense of kings, bishops, and others who were the historic Border's chief architects? Here, surely, settlement, or rather the absence of it, governed the location of the longest section of the frontier. These considerations apart—and none of them is of fundamental significance—it has to be said that between 1100 and 1300 the Anglo-Scottish border and settlement throughout the region through which that border ran coexisted without either of them exerting much influence upon the other. We must remember that for these two centuries relations between the kings of Scotland and England were in general either friendly or at least peaceful. Only on three occasions, indeed, between 1093 and 1296—in the late 1130s, in 1173–4, and in 1215–16—did outright conflict lead to large-scale devastation of northern England or southern Scotland. The society I have depicted could recover from the kind of war experienced on these occasions, provided it was not waged for more than a year or two. Here, as in so many other respects, it was the long-drawn-out war fought between English and Scots from 1296 to 1328 and again from 1333 to 1357—and, of course, far, far beyond—which engendered a fundamental change, affecting in course of time both human settlement and the frontier itself.

[47] Mack, *The Border Line*, 292–4.
[48] Cowan, *Parishes of Medieval Scotland*, 204–5.

2

Colonial Aristocracies of the High Middle Ages
ROBERT BARTLETT

Between the eleventh and the thirteenth centuries the political map of Europe and the Mediterranean was transformed by a series of conquests which established, more or less securely, new ruling classes in countries as distant and diverse as Ireland and Palestine, Andalusia and Prussia. In these places a new military and landed élite of foreign origin—a colonial aristocracy—intruded into and was imposed upon the indigenous society. The geography, climate, and prior economy and culture of the colonized regions varied enormously from the wealthy and civilized Islamic communities of the valley of the Guadalquivir to the pre-literate pagan world of the cold Baltic coasts, but the common circumstance of an intruded aristocracy tempts comparison. Moreover, beyond this comparability of situation is the fact that the alien aristocracies all shared certain traditions of Latin and Frankish origin.

Thus, when one analyses the changes brought about by the partial Anglo-Norman conquest of Ireland or the creation of the Mark of Brandenburg on formerly Slav terrain or the establishment of Outremer, the crusader colony in the Middle East, one is struck, simultaneously, by the contrasts between these different areas and by the common cultural and political baggage brought by the invaders. Charters from the crusader kingdom are clearly kindred to those from the lordship of Ireland or those introduced into colonial Brandenburg. Feudal law, of various forms but common underlying pattern, was introduced by the Anglo-Normans in Ireland, the Germans east of the Elbe, and the crusaders in Palestine and Syria. In the case of Spain, too, the conquerors participated in this wider culture. The saints whose cults were brought to Valencia and Seville in the thirteenth century were also prayed to in Riga and Acre.

In addition to those regions which experienced invasion and settlement at the hands of hostile French, German, or Spanish knights, there were other areas where foreign aristocrats came to settle, but at the invitation of native ruling dynasties. In Scotland, in the West Slav principalities of Pomerania, Mecklenburg, and Silesia, and, to a lesser extent, elsewhere, knights of French or German stock were encouraged to take up fiefs and castles, for the military power they could offer and as a counterweight to the native aristocracy. Thus in the twelfth and thirteenth centuries the Scottish royal family surrounded itself with Anglo-Norman incomers and endowed them with landed wealth in every part of the kingdom. The Piast dynasty of Silesia effectively Germanized itself and its retinue in the thirteenth century. Again, if we read the charter of 1243 by which Barnim I of Pomerania granted Magdeburg Law to the town of Stettin (Szczecin), we find that this Slav prince has among the witnesses his 'knights and vassals' (*milites et vassalli nostri*), who bear the following names: John of Berlin, marshal, Dietrich of Bertekow, Albrecht of Insleben, Gerhard of Uchtenhagen, Frowin of Drensen, and Goswin of Stettin.[1]

There is a case for considering these new invited aristocracies as colonial too, though we must use the word 'colony' here in the sense of a new plantation of outsiders and avoid the modern connotation of political dependence on a foreign state. Indeed, the phenomenon we are discussing should not be too closely tied to views about relations between states. Although these processes of conquest and colonization often involved the territorial extension of existing lordships or the creation of new ones, their outcome was very rarely the permanent subordination of one political entity to another, the usual colonial relationship of modern times. Colonial aristocracies, in the sense employed here, were alien military landed élites intruded upon native societies.

As we contemplate the colonial aristocracies of the High Middle Ages, there are some big questions which spring immediately to mind. What is the explanation of this aristocratic diaspora? Could it be in that change in aristocratic family structure recently hypothesized by some German and French historians?[2] How did

---

[1] *Pommersches Urkundenbuch*, i, ed. Klaus Conrad (2nd edn., Cologne and Vienna, 1970), no. 417, pp. 496–8.

[2] Karl Schmid, 'The Structure of the Nobility in the Earlier Middle Ages', in Timothy Reuter (ed.), *The Medieval Nobility* (Amsterdam, etc., 1978), 37–59 (and the comments of Reuter and Leopold Genicot, ibid. 6 and 27); Georges Duby, *The*

the new aristocracies relate to the native ruling classes they found in possession? These big questions are, naturally, compelling, but perhaps it may be a while before answers to them are convincing. The history of the medieval aristocracy is a history of families, so a clearer picture of the patterns of recruitment and integration of the colonial aristocracies of the High Middle Ages will only be possible after a great deal of painstaking genealogical work. The pioneering studies of another contributor to this volume[3] provide an exemplary model. But, in the absence of such systematic work, it may still be worth venturing some interim remarks based upon a sampling of the evidence and preliminary impressions. Ireland provides an example of a region where, although much has been done, much remains to be done, and it is to Ireland I now wish to turn.[4]

One primary tool for an analysis of the Anglo-Norman aristocracy is provided by the charters these aristocrats issued, received, or witnessed.[5] The documentary sources of the late twelfth and early thirteenth centuries record the names of hundreds of donors, recipients, and witnesses of grants of lands or rights in Ireland. These names can be supplemented, and sometimes fleshed out, from the narrative sources or from English documentary records. Such are the tools for a prosopography of the early colonial aristocracy in Ireland. Our big questions have to be answered from such sources or not at all.

The most obvious thing that the charters provide is a list of names and this itself is useful information about the composition of the new aristocracy. The first point to strike one about the

---

Chivalrous Society (London and Berkeley, 1977), 68–75, 101–2; Karl Leyser, 'The German Aristocracy from the Ninth to the Early Twelfth Century: A Historical and Cultural Sketch', *Past and Present*, 41 (1968) 25–53, esp. 32–6, repr. in his *Medieval Germany and its Neighbours* (London, 1982), 161–89; see also James Holt, 'Feudal Society and the Family in Early Medieval England, i: The Revolution of 1066', *TRHS*, 5th ser., 32 (1982), 193–212, esp. 199–200.

[3] Geoffrey Barrow, *The Anglo-Norman Era in Scottish History* (Oxford, 1980); id., *The Kingdom of the Scots* (London, 1973), chs. 10–12.

[4] For general orientation on Anglo-Norman Ireland see Goddard H. Orpen, *Ireland under the Normans, 1169–1333* (4 vols., Oxford, 1911–20); A. J. Otway-Ruthven, *A History of Medieval Ireland* (2nd edn., London, 1980); Robin Frame, *Colonial Ireland 1169–1369* (Dublin, 1981); Art Cosgrove (ed.), *New History of Ireland*, ii: *Medieval Ireland, 1169–1534* (Oxford, 1987).

[5] The conclusions advanced below are the by-product of a project (which is still in progress) of calendaring and indexing the earlier of these charters (to *c.*1210).

hundreds of names mentioned in these early charters is the vast
preponderance of names of northern French provenance. Geoffrey,
Henry, Richard, Robert, and William, the names of the Norman-
Angevin royal house, form a considerable proportion, rivalled by
such common names of the Norman magnate class as Gilbert,
Hugh, Ralph, Raymond, Roger, and Walter. Of course, by the
late twelfth century the fact that an individual from England or
Wales bears a French name is no evidence of ultimately French
descent, but a group of hundreds of names is a different matter.
For, even though these French names were gradually becoming
common among all classes, the enormous preponderance of such
names still, in the later twelfth century, suggests a group
containing many aristocrats of French stock.

Of secondary, but not insignificant, rank are those biblical
names coming into increasing popularity in the twelfth century,
names such as Adam, John, Phillip, and Simon, or the glamour
names like Alexander. In many cases when a particular descent
can be traced for men with these biblical names, that descent is
French. John de Courcy, conqueror of Ulaid, had an impeccable
Norman genealogy, John Poer bore a surname with the possible
meaning of 'the Picard' and had a father with the French name
Robert, while a Simon fitz William or an Alexander fitz Hugh
mark that moment in a family's history when the traditional
repertoire of names was leavened by new fashion. Nevertheless, it
may often be the case that the men with names of this ethnically
neutral nature were of English origin and thus represent a non-
French element in the colonial aristocracy established in medieval
Ireland. We know that one of the knights of Bury St Edmunds at
the time of King Stephen bore the name Adam, but turns out to be
the son of a Leofmaer,[6] so it may well be the case that early
settlers in Ireland such as Adam of Rattlesden, a Suffolk follower
of Theobald Walter, John Hundethin ('Dogstooth'?), found in
the region of Cork, or Alexander of Hadstock (in Essex) were
successful representatives of that group of men of English descent
who, by cultural adaptation and military usefulness, mingled with
the aristocratic *Francigenae* to produce a new hybrid ruling class,
fit and able for further conquest and expansion. Contemporary
documents reveal that what happened in Ireland after 1169 could

[6] James Holt, 'Feudal Society and the Family in Early Medieval England; ii:
Notions of Patrimony', *TRHS*, 5th ser., 33 (1983), 193–220, at 193–8, 218.

be described not only as the *adventus Francorum* but also the *conquisicio Hibernie ab Anglicis*.[7]

Other linguistic groups left a clear mark too. Adam fitz Morgan, or, as we should probably say, ap Morgan, David Walensis, Howel the clerk—perhaps, if fortunate, the same man as Howel *magister*—and (if not a scribal error) Mark Tudor show the importance of native Welsh as well as Norman-Welsh incomers. The Flemish settlers from Pembroke are represented by fitz Godeberts, Prendergasts, and a range of men with the cognomen Flandrensis.

This somewhat eclectic repertoire of names should be no surprise. It is reminiscent of a similar variety in the cultural and geographical background of the participants in the so-called Norman Conquest of England in 1066: a dominant north French group with a large penumbra of varied origin. Nor is there any good reason, in twelfth-century circumstances, why anything like a racial test should have been applied before recruiting retinues and undertaking *razzias*: qualities other than *limpieza de sangre* were so obviously more important. Thus, after the mixed French, Welsh, and Flemish mercenaries of the years 1169–71 had made their initial inroads into Ireland, an expansion of the enterprise, under the aegis of the monarchy, brought in magnates and knights from every part of the realm. What is surprising, however, is the tiny proportion of Irish names to be found in these charters.

It is perfectly patent that the early Anglo-Norman adventurers in Ireland fought in the service of or, later, in alliance with native Irish rulers. There are also some well-known, though not perhaps very numerous, cases of intermarriage between Norman magnates and women from high Irish royal stock. Nevertheless, the picture that emerges from the charters of this period is of an exclusively alien social environment. Among all the hundreds of charters of the years, say, 1170–1210, only a handful were issued by native Irish laymen. The O'Brien kings of Thomond issued some and these, naturally, contain Irish witnesses.[8] The family of Mac-

---

[7] *Calendar of the Charter Rolls, 1226–1516* (6 vols., London, 1903–27), i. 230–1; *Dignitas decani*, ed. Newport B. White (Dublin, 1957), no. 111, 112–13, and *Crede mihi*, ed. John T. Gilbert (Dublin, 1897), no. 74, p. 67; cf. *Register of the Abbey of St Thomas Dublin*, ed. John T. Gilbert (RS, 1889), no. 118, p. 102.

[8] In general, see Marie-Thérèse Flanagan, 'Monastic Charters from Irish Kings of the Twelfth and Thirteenth Centuries' (Unpublished MA thesis, University College, Dublin, 1972).

Gillamocholmog also issued charters but this was a very rare, perhaps unique, instance of an Anglicized Irish ruling kindred.[9] Even as early as the 1190s Dermot MacGillamocholmog's grants mention more immigrant than native witnesses. Indeed, over the course of the next four generations the family nomenclature successively abandoned the Irish 'Dermot' for the neutral 'John' and then that in turn for the boldly assertive 'Ralph'. When, in the later thirteenth century, Ralph fitz John issued his charters, witnessed by men called Robert fitz Richard and John fitz Robert, cultural and social assimilation was complete.

But grants by families like the MacGillamocholmog alias fitz Dermots, the very occasional charter of an Irish king, or, a more common occurrence, the presence of native Irish ecclesiastics, in their Latin guise, as grantors or witnesses, do not amount to very much. Especially if we exclude the clerics, the world of the charters is an immigrant world.

The deductions one makes from the fairly bare evidence of charters must be advanced cautiously. The only certain conclusions are that, first, the Anglo-Normans were very much more familiar with the process of issuing charters and did so far more frequently than the native Irish: the surviving charters of Strongbow alone, for example, outnumber those of all the Irish kings of the twelfth and thirteenth centuries. Secondly, and this is more curious, when Anglo-Norman aristocrats issued charters, they virtually never invited or expected native Irish testators. Irish names occur in these charters only when Irish ecclesiastics witness them or when there is mention of Irish *antecessores*, former and dispossessed holders or tenants. Just as many Anglo-Saxon thegns survive only in the terse record of Domesday Book—'in the time of King Edward Alfer held it'—so many Irish landowners are mentioned only when their lands were granted to Anglo-Norman immigrants: 'know I have granted to Alard fitzWilliam', says John, lord of Ireland, 'the land by Wexford which was Uccranethan's and Ubrenan's.'[10] Now it may be wrong to leap from this fact to a

---

[9] Charters of the MacGillamocholmog family will be found in *Chartularies of St. Mary's Abbey Dublin*, ed. John T. Gilbert (2 vols., RS, 1884–6), i, nos. 4–11, pp. 31–7; *Register of St Thomas*, no. 212, pp. 179–80; *Register of the Hospital of St John the Baptist Dublin*, ed. Eric St J. Brooks (Dublin, 1936), nos. 362–3, p. 239.

[10] Dublin, NLI D 8, calendared in *Calendar of Ormond Deeds*, ed. Edmund Curtis (6 vols., IMC, Dublin, 1932–43), i, no. 7, pp. 3–4; it seems likely that

picture of real social exclusivity in the entourage. As has been pointed out to good effect in the study of necrologies and memorial books, association, or lack of it, for one purpose need not imply association, or lack of it, for all other purposes.[11] Perhaps the attestation of a charter was an occasion when a very particular social or ethnic exclusivity came into operation. Perhaps because of their relatively charter-less society, the Irish were regarded as inappropriate participants in this process. If this were so, it would itself be interesting. But perhaps the exclusion went beyond this and really does reflect a world in which the immediate entourage of the Anglo-Norman landholder would be entirely Anglo-Norman or immigrant and the native Irish, with the exception of the occasional ecclesiastic, would figure only as auxiliary troops, labouring bondsmen, or barbarous allies—not groups one would wish to act as witnesses to the most formal transactions.

This situation is very different from that in Mecklenburg, Pomerania, Silesia, or, for that matter, Scotland. In those regions where a native dynasty encouraged and presided over the settlement of an immigrant aristocracy, charter witness lists reflect the mixed composition of the new ruling class. Thus, when, in 1261, Henry and Władysław, the dukes of Silesia, endowed Wrocław with Magdeburg Law, the witnesses of comital status included John of Würben, Janos, Stosso, Berthold, and Konrad the Swabian, a group roughly equally Polish and German.[12] This is a kind of ethnic equilibrium we do not find in Ireland.

The nature of the documentary evidence available for Ireland thus means that it will tell us a great deal more about the immigrant aristocracy than about the native aristocracy or about relations between the two, though this itself is a fact about the relationship. If we turn to the use we can make of this material for understanding the immigrants, there are two areas which it obviously illuminates: the relations between and stratification among members of the new aristocracy; and the related question of the pattern of their recruitment and origins.

'Uccranethan' and 'Ubrenan' are Uí Chremthannáin and Ua Bráenáin, allies of Dermot MacMurrough: Cosgrove, *New History of Ireland*, ii. 27.

[11] Leyser, 'German Aristocracy', 34 (repr., 170).

[12] *Schlesisches Urkundenbuch*, iii, ed. Winfried Irgang (Cologne and Vienna, 1984), no. 373, pp. 241–2.

The immigrant venture in Ireland in the twelfth century obviously underwent two quite distinct stages. The first was short, from 1169 to 1171, but intense and very important for the future. In this stage the patterns were ecological. Norman, Welsh, and Flemish frontiersmen from south Wales, within sight of Ireland, seized an opportunity to intrude there in the pursuit of wealth. The Irish Sea, that Mediterranean *in parvo*, linked rather than divided. In the second stage, however, beginning in 1171, the intervention of the English Crown transformed the situation. The new men in Ireland relied upon *Königsnähe*, nearness to the king, not nearness to Ireland, as the basis of their Irish involvement. Being a *familiaris* of Henry II or of John rather than a rugged south Welsh upbringing was now what mattered: hence the arrival of Suffolk men in the entourage of Theobald Walter, a close associate of John and well endowed by him in Ireland. The ecological aspect was being overshadowed by the purely political.

The difference between the two stages is also clear in the motives of the new aristocrats and the basic framework within which they settled. The early arrivals were a political out-group: Robert fitz Stephen, with his divided loyalties, the suspect figure of Strongbow, 'a man greater in family than estates'.[13] Like the Normans who went to Sicily in the eleventh century, these men were partly squeezed out by the hostility of a centralizing lordship. In these cases, at least, the creation of conquest states on the periphery of Latin Christendom was a consequence of intensified political control in its core. Like the Normans in Sicily, too, the first arrivals were mercenaries, invited in by Dermot MacMurrough, Dermot 'of the Foreigners', Dermot 'the modernizer',[14] Dermot the failed counterpart of David I of Scotland.

The contrast between the two strata of immigrant aristocrats could hardly be sharper. In the first case, a political out-group; in the second royal favourites. In the first, mercenaries, who came to fight and hoped for land; in the second, recipients of wide lands by

[13] Gerald of Wales (Giraldus Cambrensis), *Expugnatio Hibernica*, 1. 12, ed. A. B. Scott and F. X. Martin (Dublin, 1978), 54.
[14] See F. X. Martin, *No Hero in the House: Diarmait Mac Murchada and the Coming of the Normans to Ireland* (Dublin, 1976), 6, 21; also Cosgrove, *New History of Ireland*, ii. 43–79, *passim*, and cf. Francis J. Byrne, *Irish Kings and High Kings* (London and New York, 1973), 272–4.

royal charter, who, nevertheless, might have to fight to make their parchment estates a reality. The tension between the two groups is volubly reflected in the pages of the notorious Gerald of Wales, whose family was a classic instance of the disgruntled early adventurers.[15]

Since the work for a comprehensive statistical analysis and prosopography of the early Anglo-Norman aristocracy in Ireland is not yet complete, it may be worth while to take one case-study to explore questions of recruitment, stratification, and assimilation in more detail.

The most spectacular beneficiary of royal patronage in Ireland was Hugh de Lacy, who, in 1172 , was granted 'the land of Meath with all its appurtenances'.[16] Hugh had been a loyal servant of the Angevin kings, especially in their military needs, and was a major baron with holdings concentrated in the border counties between Wales and England. His family had been fighting the Welsh since the 1060s and so Hugh was no stranger to the peculiar requirements of the frontier. His elevation in Ireland, however, was not the result of any direct frontier links but a consequence of royal favour, a reward for past service, and a stimulus to future loyalty. Hugh's acquisition of Meath, one of the historic 'fifths' of Ireland, is a classic example of the opportunities that frontier societies offered; his decapitation by a lithe Irishman in 1186 a reminder that opportunities were accompanied by risks.

Although the name is Irish and it was granted to Hugh de Lacy 'as Murrough O'Melaghlin best held it', the de Lacy lordship of Meath is best regarded as a quite new political entity. The terms on which it was held—the service of fifty knights—involved the application of an imported Anglo-Norman feudalism. Similar feudal principles governed its distribution to vassals. Its boundaries were created by the exercise of military power and did not exactly mirror those of any single earlier political unit. As was clearly

---

[15] See the present writer's *Gerald of Wales 1146–1223* (Oxford, 1982), 20–5.

[16] Orpen, *Ireland under the Normans*, i. 285–6; *Calendar of the Gormanston Register*, ed. James Mills and M. J. McEnery (for RSAI, Dublin, 1916), 177; H. J. Lawlor, 'A Calendar of the *Liber Niger* and *Liber Albus* of Christ Church, Dublin', *PRIA* 27 C (1908–9), pp. 1–93, no. 121, p. 65; James Ware, *De Hibernia et antiquitatibus ejus disquisitiones* (2nd edn., London, 1658), 197; Richard Butler, *Some Notices of the Castle and of the Ecclesiastical Buildings of Trim* (Trim, 1835), 260–1; *Calendar of Archbishop Alen's Register*, ed. Charles McNeill (RSAI, Dublin, 1950), 1.

recognized, the lordship was a 'conquest'.[17] It was new on the map. One reason for this is that it was open-ended. While the more densely settled regions in the valleys of the Boyne and Blackwater had clearly defined boundaries with adjacent Dublin, Leinster, and Uriel, in the western part of the lordship the frontiers were open. Here was a land of intermittent but endemic warfare, where new castles marked each extension of de facto control, where Irish client kings were maintained, and where speculative grants extended the prospective horizon of the lordship. Like the early American colonies of Massachusetts and Virginia, with their claims extending to the Pacific, the de Lacy lords of Meath cherished the indefiniteness of their western frontier.

In practice such grandiose pretensions were unrealizable. The actual occupation of the land involved a slow process of putting down local roots. What the de Lacys had to do, in the words of the contemporary *chanson de geste* which describes the early days of Norman Ireland, was 'plant' their land—'terre herberger'.[18] The same source, summarizing Hugh de Lacy's activities in Meath, presents a clear picture of what such planting involved:

> Know you all, thus was the land planted
> With castles and cities and keeps and
>   strongholds.
> Thus well rooted (*ben aracinez*) were the
>   noble renowned vassals.[19]

The three main elements mentioned here—castles, towns, and vassals—are plotted on Map 2. It covers the period 1172–1210, from the initial enfeoffment of Hugh de Lacy with Meath to his son Walter's temporary dispossession by King John. It thus represents the activities of the first generation of colonizers. Perhaps it would be truer to say it represents the minimum level of their activity, because it is based only on written sources. There are, for example, around one hundred mottes in the area of the lordship,[20] some of which must date from this early period. The

[17] *Chartularies of St. Mary's*, i, no. 254, p. 275; cf. *Irish Cartularies of Llanthony prima and secunda*, ed. Eric St J. Brooks (IMC, Dublin, 1953), no. 75, pp. 87–8.
[18] *Song of Dermot and the Earl*, ed. Goddard H. Orpen (Oxford, 1892), l. 2941.
[19] Ibid. ll. 3202–7.
[20] Brian Graham, 'The Mottes of the Anglo-Norman Liberty of Trim', in

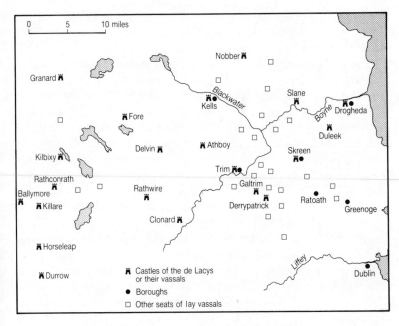

Map 2. The De Lacy Lordship of Meath 1172–1210

castles mapped, however, are those which occur in the written record, an occurrence which reflects either their importance or their involvement in some noteworthy event: Durrow, the site of Hugh de Lacy's killing, is a good example.

Some of the castles of the middle and lower Boyne date to the 1170s. At Trim, which was the de Lacy *caput* in Meath, Hugh de Lacy 'fortified a house . . . and threw a trench about it and then enclosed it with a stockade'[21] at a time when, it seems, the ink was still drying on Henry II's charter of enfeoffment. This privileging of a site as an enduring administrative centre, reinforced by the erection of a castle, was another innovation in the human geography of the area. Throughout Europe in the eleventh, twelfth, and thirteenth centuries the building of castles had, as one of its consequences, the disruption of older territorial divisions and the creation of new ones organized around the recently constructed

Harman Murtagh (ed.), *Irish Midland Studies: Essays in Commemoration of N. W. English* (Athlone, 1980), 39–56.

[21] *Song of Dermot*, ll. 3223–5.

fortress. The Anglo-Norman 'castelries' found in Louth[22] or the castle-centred lordships, like the thirteenth-century liberty of Trim itself, fit into this pattern.

Castles were also, of course, instruments of conquest and it is possible, by mapping the castles of the 1170s, like Trim, those of the 1180s, further west, and the frontier line of the 1190s, to trace the effective military expansion of the lordship. It is worth remembering, however, the vulnerability as well as the strength of the castle. Castles could, indeed, enable small bodies of knights to survive in hostile terrain, but most of them, in this period, were makeshift in the extreme. A castle was a wooden tower on top of a mound of earth. It could be burned; it could be stormed; and many were. Killare, for example, which Hugh de Lacy built in 1184, was burned and sacked by the Irish only three years later: 'They carried away their accoutrements, arms, shields, coats of mail and horses, and slew two knights.'[23]

Perhaps a more solid token of enduring foreign presence was another innovation of the early years of the lordship, the borough. Towns, in the sense of relatively densely populated settlements with an elaborate division of labour and an important role for exchange, already existed in Ireland. What seems to have been new was the legal model or blueprint provided by the chartered town. This model itself was clearly an importation. Three charters issued by Walter de Lacy for his towns of Meath survive, for Trim, Kells, and Drogheda, and in each case the burgesses were granted the *lex Britolli* or *Bristolli*.[24] Whether we wish to translate this as 'law of Breteuil' or 'law of Bristol'[25]—a case can be made for either—there is no doubt that the avowed template for municipal law in Meath was of English or French origin.

[22] *Register of St Thomas*, no. 3, p. 9; no. 44, p. 43.
[23] *Annals of the Kingdom of Ireland by the Four Masters*, ed. John O'Donovan (7 vols., Dublin, 1848–51), iii. 79, *s.a.* 1187.
[24] Best editions in Gearóid MacNiocaill, *Na buirgéisí* (2 vols., Dublin, 1964), i. 74–5, 124–5, 172–3.
[25] Mary Bateson, 'The Laws of Breteuil', *EHR* 15 (1900), 73–8, 302–18, 496–523, 754–7; 16 (1901), 92–110, 332–45, established the importance of the urban privileges originally associated with the Norman town of Breteuil in shaping the internal arrangements of many towns in the west of England, Wales, and Ireland. However, given the fact that 'the law of Bristol' was also used as a model for Irish towns (e.g. Cork was granted the customs of 'Bristou en Engleterre', MacNiocaill, *Na buirgéisí*, i. 158) and the danger of basing too much on the presence or absence of a single 's' in enrolments of the fourteenth or seventeenth centuries, it would be wise not to be too dogmatic as to which town was being invoked as a model.

The rights Walter granted to his burgesses were quite stereo-typical: freedom from toll, use of wood, pasture, and water passage, a grant of three acres of arable with each burgage, a fixed annual rent of twelve pence. In addition the burgesses of Kells were granted the right to be impleaded only within their hundred. This institutional framework was quickly given a social reality. Shortly after Walter de Lacy's expulsion from Meath in 1210 we learn that there was a *prepositus* in Drogheda named Roger of Hampton, who witnessed a document along with some other presumed burgesses of Drogheda with characteristic names like Daniel of Taunton, Peter White of Bristol, and Herbert of Chester.[26] The introduction of English legal forms was matched by the immigration of English burgesses.

Of more immediate importance to the de Lacys than the embarkation of Peter White of Bristol, however, was the provision of a network of military tenants, men to garrison the castles and engage in the endless raids and rustling of medieval warfare. We know the names of many of these men from the narrative sources and the charters already mentioned. Some are simply ghostly testators, Robert fitz Richards and Richard fitz Roberts, who flit briefly and enigmatically through the documentary records. Others we can know a little more about.

Actual charters of enfeoffment are rare, but we do have the complete or partial texts of three granted by Hugh de Lacy to his followers in Meath,[27] and they show the kinds of lands granted and the terms on which they were held. In one, dating to the years 1184–6, Hugh bestowed upon William Petit (*Parvus*) and his heirs the land of Magheradernon in western Meath to be held in fee by the service of one knight for every thirty carucates to be performed at the castle of Killare. Here we have the characteristic mixture of old and new: the land or *terra* bears an Irish name and can be granted as a unit, without reference to boundaries, because it is a familiar part of the landscape; on the other hand, it is now measured in carucates, held by feudal service, and orientated

---

[26] *Irish Cartularies of Llanthony*, no. 99, pp. 100–1 (1214).
[27] Petit: London, BL Add. MS 4792, fo. 159^v (a 17th-century transcript), ed. Orpen, *Song of Dermot*, 310; de Nugent: Butler, *Trim*, 252–3 ('from Sir William Betham's collections'); William Lynch, *A View of the Legal Institutions . . . in Ireland . . .* (London, 1830), 150 (trans.); Hose: Ware, *De Hibernia*, 197; there is also a charter of Hugh de Lacy, enfeoffing Hugh Tyrell with Castleknock, for the area outside Meath.

toward one of Hugh's brand-new castles. It is rather like Hugh's own tenure of Meath—the geography was familiar but negotiable. The two other surviving records of enfeoffment by Hugh de Lacy reinforce this point. Gilbert de Nugent was granted 'Delvin which the O'Phelans held in the time of the Irish (*in tempore Hibernicorum*)' and Hugh Hose or Hussey 'all the land of Deece which MacGillaSeachlainn held', thus both receiving named Irish territorial units with named Irish *antecessores*. Yet Nugent held Delvin for five knights' service and both he and Hussey had new castles, at Delvin and Galtrim, within a decade of these grants. Irish *terrae* had become castle-centred fiefs.

William Petit, Gilbert de Nugent, and Hugh Hussey were among the very top stratum of vassals, men of wealth and power, the 'barons of Meath'. Petit, for example, was a successful military leader, close to John, lord of Ireland, both before and after he became king, justiciar of Ireland in the early 1190s, and steward of Meath between the de Lacy forfeiture in 1210 and his own death in 1213.[28] Below this class of great tenants, who numbered perhaps a dozen in all, stood a numerous class of lesser knights and military tenants. Obviously, the lower one goes in the social scale the less forthcoming the sources are. But this level can still be investigated.

It would be wrong to picture this class as recruited from a pool of landless wanderers. The completely free-floating atomistic individual was a great rarity and not usually a successful one. Wandering landless knights were more common in literature than reality, but we can occasionally glimpse the precarious existence of a genuine example. Matthew Paris gives the instructive story of a certain Ralph, one of the paid knights of Frederick II of Hohenstaufen, who left his lord in pique at not receiving adequate rewards and went to Lyons 'having no fixed residence and seeking

---

[28] *Song of Dermot*, ll. 3134–7; Gerald of Wales, *Expugnatio* 2. 35, p. 235; *Chartularies of St. Mary's*, i) no. 121, pp. 143–4 (the ghost of the supposed 'joint justiciarship' of Peter Pipard and William Petit should be laid: the manuscript (Oxford, Bodleian Library, MS Rawlinson B 495, fo. 50ᵛ) reads 'tunc justic' not 'tunc justiciariis' as printed and is perfectly explicable as a singular applying to Petit, the last named witness); *Rotuli chartarum in turri Londinensi asservati (1199–1216)*, ed. T. D. Hardy (London, 1837), 133; *Rotuli litterarum patentium in turri Londinensi asservati (1201–1216)*, ed. T. D. Hardy (London, 1835), 39; *Rotuli litterarum clausarum in turri Londinensi asservati (1204–27)*, ed. T. D. Hardy (2 vols., London, 1833–44), i. 106, 186; 'The Irish Pipe Roll of 14 John, 1211–12', ed. Oliver Davies and David B. Quinn, *Ulster Journal of Archaeology*, 4, Supplement (July 1941), 20; *Chartularies of St. Mary's*, ii. 312.

a lord under whom he might serve more usefully as a paid knight'. When he was later asked if he had found such a master, he replied 'No, because I am not known here (*Non, quia ignotus sum*)'.[29] The crucial factor was 'being known' and this implied being known not only by name, or even by record, but also as a member of a family or the dependant of a lord. It was such social location that acted as a check on the individual's drift towards true atomism, the extreme positions such as hermit or—where the unfortunate Ralph found himself—outlaw.

Recruitment of the lower strata of military tenants, then, usually took place through the intermediary structures of kinship or lordship or both, and it will be worth looking at a few examples to see the characteristic ties and extent of such connections.

Hugh de Lacy certainly counted as a good lord. There was, indeed, more doubt about whether he counted as a good vassal, and Henry II, perhaps regretting his earlier generosity to Hugh, was supposed to have been very gratified by the news of his death,[30] but for his own men he made good provision. Two case-studies will show the forms and the varieties of good lordship in a conquered land.

The family of Feipo offers a classic example of those who flourished through colonial ventures.[31] In 1166, before the Irish enterprise, Adam de Feipo was a household knight of Hugh de Lacy, described as one of a group of retainers who held less than a hundred shillings' worth of land. 'They hold . . .', reported Hugh, 'without any fixed service . . . some live with me and I find their necessities, some are in my castles in Wales and I find their necessities.' The opportunities which soon thereafter opened up in Ireland transformed Adam's situation. Hugh de Lacy granted him substantial holdings in Meath, centred at Skreen, not far from the Boyne, and, in the early 1180s, built him a castle there. So Adam de Feipo was transformed from a virtually landless follower,

---

[29] *Chronica majora*, ed. Henry Richards Luard (7 vols., RS, 1872–83), iv. 605 (1247).
[30] William of Newburgh, *Historia rerum Anglicarum*, 3. 9, ed. Richard Howlett, *Chronicles of the Reigns of Stephen, Henry II and Richard I* (4 vols., RS, 1884–9), i. 240.
[31] For the following paragraph see *Red Book of the Exchequer*, ed. Hubert Hall (3 vols., RS, 1896), i. 283; *Song of Dermot*, ll. 3156–7; Gerald of Wales, *Expugnatio*, 2. 23, p. 194; *Chartularies of St. Mary's*, i, nos. 66–7, 69, 71–2, 73–6, pp. 91–9; ii, p. 21; Orpen, *Ireland under the Normans*, ii. 85.

serving in his lord's castles, to a baron of Meath, with his own
substantial vassals, his castle, and wealth and land sufficient to
permit generosity to religious houses, like the Cistercians of
St Mary's, Dublin, as well as the support of his own dynasty,
which continued in the male line down to the fourteenth century.

The story of the Escotot family has no such simple thread.[32]
Members of the family were, already by the time of the Irish
enterprise, important in the de Lacy entourage. Its head in 1166
was Richard de Escotot, who held three knights' fees in Herefordshire and Shropshire with a seat at King's Pyon, only three miles
from the Lacy castle at Weobley. Richard also, however, had a run
of less well-provided relatives, Roger de Escotot, holding one fee,
and Anketil and William de Escotot, who were numbered, like
Adam de Feipo, among the household knights. In short, this
evidence from 1166 presents a fairly prolific family, of impeccably
Norman nomenclature, in the service of a great magnate, whose
older members were reasonably well endowed with land but whose
junior members survived as stipendiaries.

The first striking thing about the Escotot family and the
establishment of the de Lacy interest in Ireland is that it was the
well-endowed main line of the family that profited. Richard de
Escotot, who was a witness to the charter whereby Walter de
Lacy, Hugh's heir, granted urban liberties to Drogheda in 1194,
held lands at Donaghmore and Trevet in modern County Meath
and he and his son and heir, Walter de Escotot, made grants from
these estates to the Augustinian abbey of St Thomas, Dublin, late
in John's reign and early in the next. The colonial ventures of the
twelfth and thirteenth centuries did not always neatly soak up
younger sons or landless cousins. There is also the law, 'Unto him
that hath, it shall be given'.

For a knightly family, however, the effective exploitation of a
colonial estate offered some problems. In this respect, an
agreement made by Walter de Escotot is revealing. In a document
of around 1214 Walter leased to St Thomas's, Dublin, his land in
Donaghmore for five silver marks per annum. The money was to

---

[32] For the following three paragraphs see *Red Book of the Exchequer*, i. 282–3;
W. E. Wightman, *The Lacy Family in England and Normandy 1066–1194* (Oxford,
1966), 2, 139, 155, 198, 211; 'Irish Pipe Roll', 30 (the editor's note here is
inaccurate); Dublin, RIA MS 12 D 2, fo. 66ʳ; *Register of St Thomas*, nos. 4, 6, 9–
13, 16–17, 52, 307, pp. 9–10, 12–13, 15–20, 22–4, 48, 261–2.

be paid in St Augustine's church, Bristol, each Michaelmas. The arrangement made good sense. The sea route between Dublin and Bristol was a busy one, even though subject, as the charter itelf carefully points out, to 'contrary winds, storms at sea and the malignity of pirates'. Both St Thomas's and St Augustine's belonged to the Victorine congregation of the Augustinians and the Bristol house had lands in Ireland and thus had to arrange its own remittances. For a landowner in the Severn valley, like Escotot, Bristol was a natural focus. Indeed, this document was itself issued 'in the full hundred of Bristol' and was witnessed not only by Irish bishops and the sheriff of Dublin but also by the mayor of Bristol.

What is clear from this transaction is that it was simpler for Walter de Escotot to make his ties with Ireland purely economic and to abandon all expectation of political or social weight as a Meath landowner than to maintain the constant personal contact that would be required of a truly Anglo-Irish lord. It was, it seems, particularly men of this status who faced such a dilemma. Great magnates, like the de Lacys, could establish large, quasi-autonomous estate administrations that would run their Irish lordships while they were in England and their English lordships when they were in Ireland. Much lower down the scale, the de Feipos had nothing much to lose in England and could quite happily forget about the stipends doled out to them in Hugh de Lacy's draughty castles and transplant themselves to their new life as barons of Meath. The difficulties were encountered by those in the middling stratum of the aristocracy, men with a few knights' fees in England who also picked up a few knights' fees in Ireland. The difficulties were manifold. It was not easy to prosecute one's lawsuits effectively while over the sea. In 1190, for example, William fitz Mathew, a Gloucestershire landowner, was in Ireland; while he was there, he sent his servants into a disputed estate in Gloucestershire to establish seisin; on his return from Ireland four years later he found himself facing a charge of robbery because of the hay his servants had taken from that estate.[33] The slow pace of communications was also, of course, a complicating factor. In 1222 Gilbert de Kentwell, a substantial Suffolk landowner, had to request royal letters to the justiciar of Ireland, since 'Peter,

---

[33] *Rotuli curiae regis (1194–1200)*, ed. Francis Palgrave (2 vols., London, 1835), i. 36.

bishop of Ossory, disseised him of the land of Kilfane (County Kilkenny), which he held from the bishop, because it was reported that Gilbert was dead. As Gilbert is in good health in the king's service, the king commands the justiciar to give him seisin of the land . . .'[34]

The Escotot interest in Meath, which we have followed down to 1214, can be traced for another generation, to Walter de Escotot's daughters and co-heiresses, Hawisia and Isolde, who married into the local Herefordshire gentry and litigated energetically with each other.[35] Each of the sisters had inherited half of the five marks' income specified in the agreement of 1214. Eventually both branches of the family found it more convenient to cash in this income. Late in the reign of Henry III Isolde's husband sold his interest for 25 marks to Henry de Stratton, an important royal official in Ireland. In 1262, in her widowhood, Hawisia granted her revenue from Donaghmore to a Meath landowner and appointed attorneys 'in all her business affairs concerning Ireland' to put him in seisin. This last document was issued at Chipping Campden in Gloucestershire. In the space of three or four generations we have gone from landless knights in the castles of great barons on the look-out for the fruits of overseas conquest to an elderly female *rentier* in Gloucestershire. There was clearly more than one way of being a colonial aristocrat.

Ireland was an Outremer, a non-contiguous conquest lordship, and the Escotot case shows how this situation could produce a class of transmarine magnates and offer wonderful opportunities for poorly endowed members of the fighting classes; it also, however, created problems for gentry with moderate interests in each country, problems that included the provision of effective legal representation in both regions, the remittance of revenue, pirates, bad weather, spurious reports of death, and, we can add, the sceptical attitude of the two exchequers involved.

One last remarkable fact about the ties between the de Lacys and the Escotots is their durability.[36] The name Escotot apparently

[34] *Rotuli litterarum clausarum*, i. 499.

[35] For the following paragraph see *Register of St Thomas*, nos. 70–80, pp. 62–71; *Book of Fees* (3 vols., London, 1920–31), ii. 804, 809, 812, 817, 1479; *Roll of the Shropshire Eyre of 1256*, ed. Alan Harding (Selden Society 96, 1981 for 1980), cases 193, 363, pp. 76, 148 (this case was continued in the Northumberland eyre of the same year).

[36] For the following paragraph see Lewis C. Loyd, *The Origins of Some Anglo-*

derives from the village of Ectot in the Calvados, only eleven miles from Lassy, ancestral home of the de Lacys. In 1085 a Richard de Escotot witnessed a charter of Roger de Lacy. In 1110 Gilbert de Escotot and Robert his son granted St Peter's, Gloucester, land in Gloucestershire for the soul of Walter de Lacy 'their lord'. We thus see a relationship of presumably mutual profit between a magnate dynasty and a loyal and successful knightly family extending over two centuries, more than five generations, four countries, and two seas, a relationship forged in the struggle for retinues in eleventh-century Normandy and finding its dying fall in the widows of the West Country gentry in the 1260s. Whatever their difficulties in getting their rent from Meath, the squabbling sisters Hawisia and Isolde owed it to de Lacy patronage.

At the same time that the de Lacys were establishing their conquest principality, another family was building one too, over 800 miles to the east. The conquest principality of Brandenburg was constructed from the same network of castles, military vassals, and chartered towns as the lordship of Meath.[37] From their base in the Altmark, west of the Elbe, which they acquired in 1134, the margraves of the Ascanian dynasty gradually extended their power eastward. Brandenburg itself fell into their hands definitively in 1157 and by the end of the century was not only a margravial castle but also the seat of a margravial *advocatus*, the chief territorial officer, and a newly founded chartered town. Spandau and Fahrland also had margravial advocates by 1197. In 1214 Margrave Albert II built the castle of Oderberg 'on the Oder against the Slavs',[38] probably, in this case, the Pomeranians. Thus, in the space of three generations the margraves of Brandenburg extended their lordship about 150 miles eastward.

Such a lordship was, however, initially only a skeleton or framework. It needed to be filled out and made robust by the settlement of knights, burgesses, and peasants. Just like the de

---

Norman Families, ed. C. T. Clay and D. C. Douglas (Harleian Society Publications 103, 1951), 39; *Historia et cartularium monasterii sancti Petri Gloucestriae*, ed. William Henry Hart (3 vols., RS, 1863–7), i. 73.

[37] For general orientation see Eberhard Schmidt, *Die Mark Brandenburg unter den Askaniern (1134–1320)* (MF 71, Cologne and Vienna, 1973); Johannes Schultze, *Die Mark Brandenburg*, i: *Entstehung und Entwicklung unter den askanischen Markgrafen (bis 1319)* (Berlin, 1961).

[38] *Cronica principum Saxonie*, ed. O. Holder-Egger, *MGH, SS* 25 (Hanover, 1880), 472–80, at 478.

Lacys, the Ascanians had to 'terre herberger'. The most active members of the family in this respect were the brothers John I and Otto III, whose period of joint rule covered the years 1220–66:

> After they had grown to be young men they lived together harmoniously as brothers should, the one deferring to the other. This concord enabled them to crush their enemies, raise up their friends, increase their lands and revenues and grow in fame, glory and power. They obtained the lands of Barnim, Teltow and many others from the lord Barnim [of Pomerania] and purchased the Uckermark up to the river Welse. In *Hartone* they acquired castles and advocacies. They built Berlin, Straussberg, Frankfurt, New Angermunde, Stolp, Liebenwalde, Stargard, New Brandenburg and many other places, and thus, turning the wilderness into cultivated land, they had an abundance of goods of every kind. They were also careful to support religious services, had many chaplains and settled Dominicans, Franciscans and Cistercians within their territories.[39]

Here, in the words of a contemporary, are the chief components of the new principality of Brandenburg: the acquisition of land and castles, the construction of new towns and extension of cultivated land, the introduction of the new religious orders. Equally significant was the creation of a landed aristocracy.

The knightly aristocracy planted in the lands between the Elbe and the Oder by the margraves of Brandenburg had some distinctive features.[40] It was composed almost entirely of *ministeriales*, that is, knights who were technically unfree. Their origins lay in the retinue of the margrave and many of them had been enfeoffed in the Altmark, the old settled area west of the Elbe, before they were granted lands further east. Their path can be traced through the witness lists of the margraves' charters and from the evidence of place-names of villages east of the Elbe borrowed from those in the Altmark. The ministerial family of von Kerkow, for example, had a seat at Kerkau in the Altmark. It was a successful family, producing justices and bishops and being endowed with substantial estates east of the Elbe sometime before 1271. Here their villages bore the names Neuendorf, Neuhof, and

[39] *Cronica principium Saxonie*, ed. O. Holder-Egger, *MGH, SS* 25 (Hanover, 1880), 472–80, at 478.
[40] For the following see Hans K. Schulze, *Adelsherrschaft und Landesherrschaft: Studien zur Verfassungs- und Besitzgeschichte der Altmark, des ostsächsischen Raumes und des hannoverschen Wendlandes im hohen Mittelalter* (MF 29, Cologne and Graz, 1963).

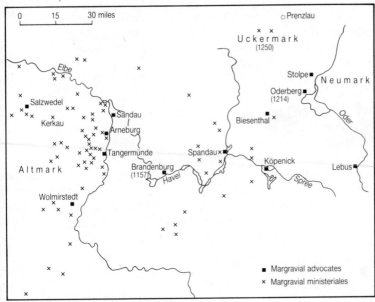

Map 3. The Mark of Brandenburg under John I and Otto III 1220–1267 (*Source*: Schulze)

Kerkow, unmistakable evidence for new settlement and an Altmark connection.[41]

Around one hundred members of this ministerial class are mentioned in the charters of John I and Otto III and they are the men who formed the new landed aristocracy of the central part of the Mark of Brandenburg. The late Michael Wallace-Hadrill remarked perceptively, about a much earlier period, 'War bands are tribes in the making';[42] in the twelfth and thirteenth centuries magnate retinues are landed aristocracies in the making.

East of the Oder the situation was somewhat different. One reason for this is that Brandenburg, like Meath, was an open-ended conquest principality. While it had a definite and well-controlled core, it also had, as one went further from this core, indefinite boundaries capable of expansion when conditions were propitious. The contrast between the densely settled and reasonably secure area around Trim in the valley of the Boyne and the

---

[41] Ibid. 156–8.
[42] *Early Germanic Kingship in England and on the Continent* (Oxford, 1971), 11.

precarious dominion over western Meath is paralleled by that
between the populous Altmark and the relatively unsettled and
insecure Neumark, east of the Oder. Both principalities had
starting-points or foundations, Meath at its eastern extremity,
Brandenburg at its western, and both extended, in reality or
speculatively, ever further westward or eastward respectively.

This had consequences for the structure of the aristocracy.
While fiefs and manors in the settled areas were obviously more
desirable in that they were predictably profitable, they tended to
be smaller and more subject to the authority of the lord of the
land. Grants on the open frontier of the lordship, however, while
often speculative donations of unsettled lands, tended to involve
more extensive lands and concede greater autonomy. Thus, in the
case of Brandenburg, one can contrast the many small knightly
vassals of the Altmark and the Mittelmark with the great, quasi-
princely dynasties of the Neumark, like the von Wedels.[43]

The purpose of wandering from the Boyne to the Oder in this
cavalier fashion is twofold. The first is the traditional rationale of
the comparativist approach, the hope that light will be shed and
understanding increased by the juxtaposition of two things that are
at once similar and different. Let me offer two explicit comparisons
between the two areas, one highlighting the common, one the
distinctive, experience.

The Anglo-Norman lordships in Ireland and the transElbian
parts of the Mark of Brandenburg shared some common features
by the very fact of being conquest principalities created at the time
they were. One such feature was that in both regions the estates of
the military aristocracy were held exclusively by feudal tenure.
This was a direct result of the circumstances of conquest. In Meath
and Leinster and the Mittelmark a great *dominus terre* had been in
a position, when settling tenants, to apply a reasonably systematic
concept of enfeoffment as practised in his homeland at the time of
the conquest. In Brandenburg, the effect was sharpened by the
contrast with the old-settled core: as one travelled from the
Altmark eastwards across the Elbe, one left a land where allodial
holdings were, at least in the twelfth century, fairly common, to a

---

[43] Helga Cramer, 'Die Herren von Wedel im Lande über der Oder: Besitz und
Herrschaftsbildung bis 1402', *Jahrbuch für die Geschichte Mittel- und Ostdeutschlands*,
18 (1969), 63–129.

land where the local aristocracy consisted entirely of knights holding fiefs. In Ireland the greater Anglo-Norman lordships had been granted out on feudal terms with fixed *servitia debita* and it is thus possible to indulge in the engaging occupation of calculating knights owed and knights enfeoffed, of identifying fiefs and holders, as one does for England. This is not surprising: Anglo-Norman Ireland was settled by men from a conquest state who themselves had fairly sharp notions of feudal tenure and practically no experience of allodial property.

There is some truth, then, to the idea that Western Europe in the High Middle Ages consisted of a central area where feudal and allodial property coexisted, fringed by newer conquest territories of a highly feudalized nature. This fact reflects, in part, the chronology of conquest. It has been pointed out that one of the reasons for the difference between the highly autonomous power of the Marcher lords of Wales and the more restricted position of the Anglo-Irish magnates is the growth of royal law in England, the country from which the Marchers came, in the century or so between the initial conquests in Wales and Ireland.[44] The prevailing conditions in the colonizing region could thus be very important in determining results in the colonized countries. Just so, the settlement of the Mittelmark by a knightly class with a castle-holding élite reflects the situation in late twelfth- and early thirteenth-century Germany without any admixture of the institutions of the past, like allodial property. Colonial regions can thus offer pure, even exaggerated, versions of the social arrangements current at the time of their creation in the core or metropolitan areas.

Despite such common features, there are also divergences in the historical development of the conquest principalities established in Ireland and those east of the Elbe and one of the most important is that the former always remained conquest principalities while the latter gradually ceased to be so. By about 1300 Brandenburg was one of a group of political units east of the Elbe, some ruled by dynasties of Slav origin, some by dynasties of German origin, all inhabited by a mixed Slav and German population. The social organization of these various principalities no longer exhibited remarkable contrasts. To take an example: in 1250 the margraves

---

[44] A. J. Otway-Ruthven, 'The Constitutional Position of the Great Lordships in South Wales', *TRHS*, 5th ser., 8 (1958), 1–20, esp. 1.

of Brandenburg acquired the Uckermark from Pomerania, along
with its chief town, Prenzlau. It is worth noting what kind of place
Prenzlau was. It had had a mint since the late twelfth century; a
parish priest was mentioned in 1187; nearby was the Premonstratensian house of Gramzow, with a monastic body partly,
perhaps mainly, German in composition. In the year 1235 Barnim
I of Pomerania had granted the town Magdeburg Law and
entrusted it to eight *promotores*, who had German names and
some of whom came from Stendal in the Altmark. Thus, when the
Ascanians acquired this slice of Pomerania in 1250 they found a
town whose population was Christian and, probably, German-
speaking, ruled by an oligarchy drawn from the Mark of
Brandenburg itself, where coins were minted and German law
prevailed.[45] By the later thirteenth century, then, the political
frontiers east of the Elbe and south of the Baltic no longer
corresponded to boundaries between different societies. Mecklen-
berg, Pomerania, Great Poland, Silesia, Brandenburg, and the
Wettin lands were endemic rivals but not different social or
cultural worlds. In Ireland the process of homogenization never
produced a comparable outcome. The division between the
English and Irish parts of Ireland was always much more than a
simple issue of political control. Irish kings did not mint coins or
endow towns with the *lex Britolli*.

The juxtaposition of these different conquest lordships forces us
to ponder such contrasts. Clearly, the process of cultural assimilation
consequent upon the establishment of the new colonial aristocracy
took very different paths in Ireland and east of the Elbe. It may be
that the crucial variable was that Anglo-Norman Ireland was an
'Outremer', not a contiguous territory, and that this placed limits
on immigration by non-aristocrats of the same culture as the
immigrant élite. In the eastern Baltic and in Syria comparable
Outremers existed, regions where the secular and ecclesiastical
aristocracy and the burgess class formed alien minorities among
native majorities. There may be other explanations. But, clearly,
the comparative approach is one way to focus the questions asked.

The second purpose of this juxtaposition of Ireland and
Brandenburg is, however, non-comparativist. Indeed, it is rather
to suggest that there is some sense in which these two ventures of

---

[45] Dietmar Lucht, *Die Städtepolitik Herzog Barnims I. von Pommern* (Cologne
and Graz, 1965), 9–13.

conquest, settlement, and cultural change form not two stories that can be fruitfully compared, but one story. The intrusion of the heavy cavalry and castle-builders of the post-Carolingian world, often in alliance with the shrill Gregorians of the newly remodelled Church, bringing in their train new peasant settlers and burgesses with clear ideas of their legal aspirations, was one of the major forces that shaped the history of high medieval Europe. In Ireland and east of the Elbe very different societies were touched by this expanding world; but that expanding world had its inner unity.

3

Frontier and Settlement in the Kingdom of Castile (1085–1350)

MANUEL GONZÁLEZ JIMÉNEZ

INTRODUCTION

In the history of the medieval Iberian kingdoms, the frontier played a primordial role: there were internal political, religious, and cultural frontiers, but there were also important 'external' frontiers, particularly that with Islam. This latter frontier, which was the expression of a constantly changing reality, reflected the history of a country which was in the process of a lengthy transformation. In this sense it is interesting to note that this frontier ceased to exist at the very moment when the kingdom of Castile reached its maturity of formation after the reconquest of Granada by the Catholic Kings.

But the frontiers of the Christian kingdoms with Islam constituted far more than a political and military boundary, because the frontier was related to a projected ideal which was never abandoned during the Middle Ages: the Reconquest, that is, the slow recovery by the northern Christians of a country which had been conquered and occupied by Muslims at the beginning of the eighth century.[1] In this sense, the idea of Reconquest, which was something more than the mere process of conquest of the lands controlled by the Muslims, was kept alive, as is well known, by an ideology which considered that the Muslim occupation was illegitimate. From this we can deduce a fundamental point about the medieval history of Spain: all the frontiers with Islam, even those which were the most lasting, were regarded as being impermanent because of this ideology—frontiers which, at some point, would cease to exist. Thus, for example, during the later Middle Ages no permanent or long-lasting frontier agreements were drawn up between the

---

[1] The bibliography relating to the Reconquest is extensive. See the latest synthesis, which also analyses the ideological aspects of the Reconquest phenomenon, by Derek W. Lomax, *The Reconquest of Spain* (London, 1978).

kingdoms of Castile and Granada like those agreements which were drawn up with Portugal (Treaty of Alcañices, 1297) or with Aragón (Peace of Torrellas, 1304), but simply short-term peaces or truces. Consequently, if the frontier was by definition impermanent, and if the Moor was *the* enemy—the 'Other' as Ron Barkai would put it[2]—who had to be defeated and whose lands would sooner or later be reconquered, the society which had to undertake the task had to be, in the words of Elena Lourie, a society 'organized for war', as we shall see later on.[3]

From the conquest of Toledo (1085) onwards, Castile consciously took over the ideology of the Reconquest, which had slowly been formulated during the previous centuries, and which was now strengthened by the crusading idea. This is not the place to discuss the implication of the concept of the Reconquest, which continues to be a matter of polemic among Spanish historians.[4] But we should remember that the idea of the Reconquest reached its stage of maturity during the late eleventh century, for these were years during which Spain was definitively 'opened up' to the rest of Europe. Evidently, the idea of the Reconquest preceded the crusading ideal,[5] but it was nevertheless influenced by the latter concept of Holy War which was promoted by the papacy, Frankish warriors, and Cluniac monks—all three latter parties enjoying great influence at the court of Alfonso VI. In any case, the crusading ideal helped to reinforce the concept of Reconquest with religious arguments, the Reconquest already being a war which was justified by political and ideological motives.

This paper will attempt to give an overall vision of the frontier settlement phenomenon, as it occurred between 1085 and 1350. During this period of almost three hundred years the Castilian-Leonese frontier with Islam gradually moved southwards until it stabilized itself in a form which would remain almost unchanged

[2] Ron Barkai, *Cristianos y musulmanes en la España medieval: El enemigo en el espejo* (Madrid, 1984).

[3] Elena Lourie, 'A Society Organized for War: Medieval Spain', *Past and Present*, 35 (1966), 54–76.

[4] See Manuel González Jiménez, 'Reconquista y repoblación del Occidente Peninsular (siglos XI–XIII)', in *Actas del II Congreso Luso-Español de Historia Medieval*, ii (Oporto, in press). See also Lomax, *Reconquest*, 38–41.

[5] The influence of the crusading ideal on the Reconquest is at present being investigated by my research student Francisco García Fitz. An old study which is still useful is that by Carl Erdmann, *A ideia de cruzada em Portugal* (Coimbra, 1940).

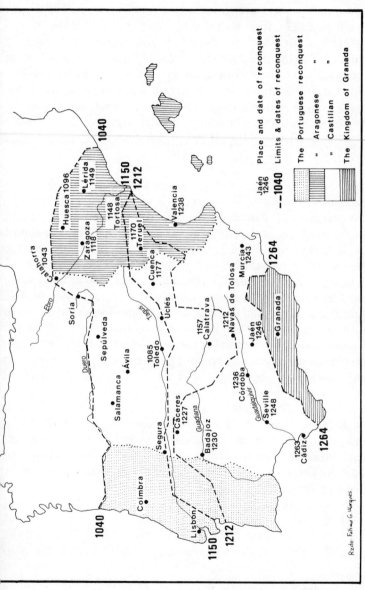

Map 4. The Reconquest

Legend:

Jaén — Place and date of reconquest
1246

- - - — Limits & dates of reconquest

The Portuguese reconquest

" " Aragonese "

" " Castilian "

The Kingdom of Granada

Places and dates shown on map:

1040

Calahorra 1043
Huesca 1096
Lérida 1149
1150
1212
Zaragoza 1118
Tortosa 1148
Valencia 1238
Teruel 1170
Cuenca 1177
Soria
Sepúlveda
Uclés
Murcia 1243
Salamanca
Ávila
Toledo 1085
Calatrava 1157
Navas de Tolosa 1212
1264
Granada
Jaén 1246
Segura
Cáceres 1227
Córdoba 1236
Seville 1248
Badajoz 1230
Coimbra
Cádiz 1263
1264
Lisbon
1040
1150
1212

Rivers: Ebro, Duero, Tagus, Guadiana, Guadalquivir

Rzdo Fahad G. Warques

until the end of the Middle Ages. Each of the different phases of settlement (*repoblación*) coincided with a new frontier, once the old frontier of the Duero river, which for centuries had separated Castile and León from al-Andalus, came to an end between 1076 and 1085. But, and this is the interpretation which will be maintained in the present paper, the creation of each new frontier during these centuries was accompanied by the same mentality, although the manifestations that resulted were not always the same. In a word, what was attempted at each stage was the creation of effective institutions which would guarantee at the same time the defence of the land and its settlement.

THE BIRTH OF THE FRONTIER

The conquest of Toledo by Alfonso VI signified an important move forward, in both territorial and qualitative terms. For almost the first time the Christians succeeded in controlling a large Muslim city. Up to this point Christian advances had taken place in lands where the Muslims were not effectively in control. In effect the settlement which had timidly begun round about 800 had spread like an ink stain through the territories located to the south of the Cantabrian mountains, until it reached the banks of the Duero between the years 850 and 900. There a first frontier was established and consolidated during the rest of the century and a half—a frontier supported by both an impressive system of defensive strongholds such as Zamora, Toro, and Simancas, and a network of castles and fortresses. The next jump southwards would take time to occur. Al-Andalus continued to be a formidable enemy, as the Christians were to find out by blood and tears during the late tenth century. Thus the various attempts to cross the Duero had to be abandoned when al-Mansur began his terrifying campaign against the Christian north.[6]

The death of al-Mansur in 1002, the fall of the caliphate of Córdoba thirty years later, and the fragmentation of al-Andalus into numerous taifas or 'Party-Kingdoms'[7] radically changed the political context. Al-Andalus was no longer a permanent threat to

---

[6] See Lomax, *Reconquest*, 46–8.

[7] See David Wasserstein, *The Rise and Fall of the Party-Kings: Politics and Society in Islamic Spain, 1002–1086* (Princeton, 1985).

the continuing existence of the Christian kingdoms, and became instead a fabulous source of wealth in the form of booty and tribute payments or *parias*,[8] as well as becoming a land ready to be affected by the long-desired Christian expansion.

Nevertheless the Castilians would still take time in beginning their reconquest operations. But once their internal problems had been resolved, Ferdinand I of Castile and León (1035–64) occupied the Portuguese sector between the Duero and Mondego rivers, that is the towns of Lamego, Viseu, and Coimbra. The political crisis resulting from the terms of Ferdinand I's last will and testament entailed another delay. His son Alfonso VI (1072–1109) would once again take the initiative by repopulating or reorganizing Sepúlveda in 1076, and by undertaking a series of campaigns which would culminate with the taking of Toledo in 1085. At one stroke the Christians had moved from the Duero to the Tagus, leaving behind them a vast and practically unpopulated region, called the Extremaduras.

But Toledo was too vulnerable, and so the future of this Toledan bridgehead, located in the very body of al-Andalus, an al-Andalus which had recovered its menace after the arrival of the Almoravids in 1086, lay in the settlement of the Extremaduran rearguard. This systematic process began in 1087 with the settlement of Ávila by the French Count Raymond of Burgundy, son-in-law of Alfonso VI. During the following years the settlement of Segovia (*c.*1088), Salamanca (*c.*1100), and Soria (*c.*1110) would be carried out.

In this way the Extremaduras witnessed the first systematic attempt to create an authentic frontier society organized for war. The settlement of this large region was carried out on the basis of new criteria.[9] Up to this point, popular initiative had, to a large extent, characterized the settlement of the plains and valleys of León and Old Castile. At the best of times the king had simply limited himself to blessing or stimulating the settlement initiatives

[8] On the system of *parias*, see José M. Lacarra, 'Aspectos económicos de la sumisión de los reinos de Taifas (1010–1102)', in *Homenaje a Jaime Vicens Vives*, i (Barcelona, 1965), 255–77.

[9] On the repopulation of the Extremaduras, and especially the region of Ávila, see Ángel Barrios García, *Estructuras agrarias y de poder en Castilla: El ejemplo de Ávila (1085–1320)* (2 vols., Salamanca, 1983–4). See also the study by Luis-Miguel Villar García, *La Extremadura castellano-leonesa: Guerreros, clérigos y campesinos (711–1252)* (Valladolid, 1986).

undertaken by individual magnates, bishops, monasteries, and by groups of more or less organized free peasants.[10] Now, however, settlement was controlled by the king from the very first moment, and he delegated the settling of colonists, the initial organization of lands, and the resolution of conflicts between settlers to nobles of such outstanding importance as Count Raymond of Burgundy. The fact is that the settlement at this time, as against that of previous periods, was not simply a matter of occupation of lands which would then be put into cultivation, but was an essential part of a policy of establishing and defending a formally constituted frontier system.

This new strategic and military policy can be clearly discerned in the settlement of the Extremaduras. In the first place, the kings were deliberately interested in establishing human settlements capable of effectively participating in both offensive and defensive warfare.[11] For this task mere peasants were not sufficient—what was needed was fighting men skilled in war. This factor explains those clauses of the *fuero* of Sepúlveda (1076) which allowed the town to become 'a refuge for assassins, adventurers, and outlaws',[12] whose crimes were forgiven by the mere fact that they took part in the settlement of the area.[13] We will return to this point later. But alongside these violent settlers, the other colonists who came to the Extremaduras were essentially free men who from the start appear grouped into two categories—*caballeros* or *milites*, and *peones* or *pedites*. These categories were not so much a reflection of social distinction as of economic opportunities which allowed some to fight on horseback while others fought on foot.[14] But access to the group of knights was open to everybody, provided they had horses—and this is perhaps one of the unique features of

[10] The fundamental work on repopulation during the 9th and 10th centuries continues to be that by Claudio Sánchez-Albornoz, *Despoblación y repoblación del valle del Duero* (Buenos Aires, 1966). See also the more recent interpretation by José A. García de Cortázar *et al.*, *La organización social del espacio en la España medieval: La Corona de Castilla en los siglos VIII a XV* (Barcelona, 1985), 43–83.

[11] José M. Lacarra drew attention to this aspect years ago when he pointed out that 'il était donc indispensable de trouver des colons qui fussent capables à la fois de participer à leur propre défense et d'assaillir l'ennemi pour leur propre compte', 'Les Villes-frontières dans l'Espagne des xie et xiie siècles', *Le Moyen Âge*, 69 (1963), 205–22, at 206.

[12] Ibid. 207.

[13] *Fueros de Sepúlveda*, ed. Emilio Sáez (Segovia, 1953), 45 (clauses, 10, 11, 13, 17, 18).

[14] See Lacarra, 'Les Villes-frontières', 211.

this frontier society, as Professor Powers has repeatedly pointed out.[15]

Secondly, the new settlements were established in easily defended places. With the solitary exception of Salamanca, which came to life again within the remains of a Roman town, all the other towns were natural strongholds which were almost impossible to destroy. This fact can easily be seen in the case of Sepúlveda and Segovia. The former, located more than 1,000 metres high, occupied a narrow plateau flanked by the deep ravines of the Caslilla and Duratón rivers. The example of Segovia is not so spectacular, but like Sepúlveda the site of the town was flanked by two rivers (the Clamores and the Eresma). To such natural defences were added massive stone walls, which are most typically illustrated by those of Ávila.

Thirdly, the military condition of the settlements located in the Extremaduras can be clearly seen in their municipal laws or *fueros*, especially in the late *fuero* of Cuenca, and in the chronicles of the period. In effect, this society of warrior-shepherds and militant peasants made of war one of the basic elements of their economy. This is reflected in the laws which minutely regulate the military obligations of the *vecinos* or citizens, the organization of *cabalgadas* (that is, military expeditions against the Moors in order to obtain wealth), and the sharing out of booty.[16] The renown of these men was so great that the Muslim geographer al-Idrisi affirmed that the men of the Extremaduras 'stood out in war, being bold, full of initiative, and hardy';[17] and the *Chronica Adefonsi imperatoris* gives a detailed account of the predatory incursions of the men of the Extremaduras into al-Andalus.[18] For this reason Professor Gautier-Dalché does not exaggerate when he states that 'war was

[15] James F. Powers, 'The Origins and Development of Municipal Service in the Leonese and Castilian Reconquest, 800–1250', *Traditio*, 16 (1970), 91–113; id., 'Townsmen and Soldiers: The Interaction of Urban and Military Organization in the Militias of Medieval Castile', *Speculum*, 46 (1971), 641–55.

[16] The *Fuero de Cuenca*, ed. Rafael de Ureña y Smenjaud (Madrid, 1935), deals at length with the regulations concerning *cabalgadas*. See also the curious text entitled *Fuero sobre el fecho de las cabalgadas*, which is derived from the *Fuero de Cuenca* and falsely attributed to Charlemagne, in *Memorial histórico español*, 2 (1851), 437–506.

[17] Al-Idrisi, *Geografía de España*, ed. Antonio Ubieto Arteta (Valencia, 1974), 146.

[18] *Chronica Adefonsi imperatoris*, ed. Luis Sánchez Belda (Madrid, 1950)], no. 119, pp. 92–3.

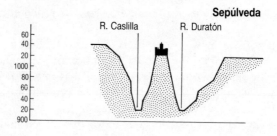

Sepúlveda

R. Caslilla   R. Duratón

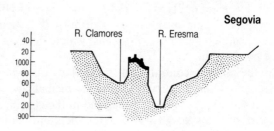

Segovia

R. Clamores   R. Eresma

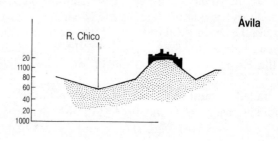

Ávila

R. Chico

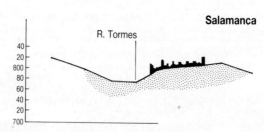

Salamanca

R. Tormes

Map 5. The Strategic and Military Nature of the Frontier Towns of the Extremaduras. Figures refer to metres above sea-level.

an industry which afforded a living, either directly or indirectly, to most of the population' of the region.[19]

Finally, there were the military obligations of the settlers. The *fueros* and other legal texts of the towns of the Extremaduras and New Castile are full of regulations on this matter. J. F. Powers has given a detailed analysis of the military services required of the *vecinos* of frontier towns:[20] the *fonsado* or offensive expedition led by the king or by a noble in his service; the *fonsadera*, the equivalent of English *scutage*; the *hueste*, or expedition similar to the *fonsado*; and other services such as the *apellido*, or obligation of military defence. But in any case what is important is to emphasize that all the colonists were obligated to participate, as *caballeros* or *peones*, both in offensive and defensive warfare. In the case of an offensive expedition such an obligation only affected some of the *caballeros*,[21] since the rest of them had to stay in the town to guarantee its defence. But in all cases what was at issue was a personal obligation from which no one could be excused unless they were old or ill.[22]

In this way the process of settlement succeeded in establishing stable communities of warriors and peasants capable of restoring economic life, of themselves defending the land against the enemy, and, if necessary, of participating in punitive raids or expeditions of conquest.

The most characteristic element of these urban militias was the cavalry. We are faced here with 'popular' knights whose origin and significance are well known thanks to an outstanding series of studies;[23] a group of knights which was open to all those with enough money to buy a horse and the relevant accompanying weapons, or into which men with a certain level of wealth were forced to enter.[24] If a man lost his horse during a military

[19] Jean Gautier-Dalché, *Historia urbana de León y Castilla (siglos IX–XIII)* (Madrid, 1979), 389.

[20] Powers, 'Origins and Development of Municipal Service', *passim*.

[21] According to the *Fuero* of Uclés (1179), 'quando fuerit fonsato de rege cum castella atmonitonem, vadant de vobis tercia pars de militibus in fonsato.' See M. Rivera Garretas, *La encomienda, el priorato y la villa de Uclés en la Edad Media (1174–1310)* (Madrid and Barcelona, 1985), 235.

[22] Lacarra, 'Les Villes-frontières', 210.

[23] For an up-to-date bibliography on this topic see Manuel González Jiménez, 'La caballería popular en Andalucía (siglos XIII–XV)', *Anuario de estudios medievales*, 15 (1985), 315–29.

[24] In León this form of 'popular knighthood' had a compulsory character which

expedition, he was compensated for the loss by money or goods from the booty collected, the system thus maintaining the essential existence of the important group of knights.[25] The originality of this system was that the *caballeros villanos*, as they were known, had access to social status similar to that of the knightly nobility by means of the continuous exercise of knightly functions. Thus towards the end of the thirteenth century, according to Elena Lourie, 'many non-noble knights had come to enjoy all the concrete privileges of nobility'.[26] But well before this happened the *caballeros villanos* stood out as the socially and economically dominant group within the frontier towns. Their specialized military function, their continuous participation in the benefits derived from war, and their control of municipal institutions all helped to make them into a kind of urban oligarchy which almost monopolized the exercise of power.

Another outstanding feature of this system, apart from its military and juridical aspects, was the way in which settlement was organized. The frontier towns were established in the midst of huge territorial regions, which had two clearly distinguishable sectors: the town or *villa*, that is the urban nucleus which was the centre of power and administration, and which was a fortress and market at the same time; and the dependent territory or *tierra*, often densely covered with villages and hamlets.

The town, the place where the colonists first settled, dominated the surrounding countryside with its walls. Inside, urban areas were sometimes differentiated according to the various places of origin from which the initial settlers had come: Castilians, Mozarabs, Galicians, Franks, and Portuguese, as was the case, for example, in Salamanca.[27] Divided up into parishes or *collaciones* the urban space was contained by the town walls. A considerable size of urban space was often involved: Ávila, 76.5 acres; Soria, 247 acres; Salamanca, 272 acres. Inside these urban areas there

is not apparent in Castilian *fueros* until a much later date: see José M. Pérez Prendes, 'El origen de los caballeros de cuantía y los cuantiosos de Jaén en el siglo XV', *Revista española de derecho militar*, 9 (1962), 111–75.

[25] See Carmela Pescador del Hoyo, 'La caballería popular en Castilla y León', *Cuadernos de historia de España*, 33–4 (1961), 121–2.

[26] Lourie, 'A Society Organized for War', 72.

[27] Manuel González García, *Salamanca: La repoblación y la ciudad en la Baja Edad Media* (Salamanca, 1973), 19–26.

were 'vast open spaces which were not to be covered with houses for many centuries'.[28]

On the other hand, the land or *tierra* constituted the world of the villages and of large or small peasant holdings. In many cases we are talking about small settlements of no more than half a dozen families. These settlements were indeed numerous. Thus, according to a document published by Esther Jimeno, about 1270 there were in the *tierra* of Soria no less than 238 villages or *aldeas*.[29]

The relationship between the towns and their villages, as we have already seen, was dominated by the tight dependency of the latter upon the former. The town was the holder of a collective lordship of its lands, and, through its town council, it organized not only the defence of its region but the settlement by colonists, the sharing out of land among the new settlers, a wide variety of aspects of economic life, and the collection of taxes. The *villa* was also a commercial centre, the distribution centre for artisanal commodities, and a centre of consumption of agricultural and pastoral products. The town not only received agrarian surpluses in the form of produce for sale by the peasants, rents owed to the urban oligarchy, and tithes payable to the bishop and cathedral, but also the taxes owed by the inhabitants of the villages to the urban council. A document of 1283 provides us with information about the numerous taxes which affected the villagers of the *tierra* of Ávila.[30] In theory such taxes belonged to the municipal finances. But some of them were shared out among the *caballeros*. Thus in Sepúlveda the proceeds of the *montazgo* tax (a pastoral tax) belonged to the *caballeros villanos*.[31] Perhaps this situation did not reflect the original reality but, rather, a date closer to the beginning of the thirteenth century, when two concepts of knighthood were being differentiated: knights with a certain pedigree, who controlled the town council, and the new knights, mostly rich artisans and merchants, who were obliged to perform military service because of their wealth. In any case, this is an early example of the contempt which knights, who owned lands and cattle, displayed towards manual labour.

[28] Lacarra, 'Les Villes-frontières', 216.
[29] Esther Jimeno, 'La población de Soria y su término en 1270', *Boletín de la Real Academia de la Historia*, 142 (1958), 207–74 and 365–494.
[30] Hilda Grassotti, 'Un abulense en Beaucaire', *Cuadernos de historia de España*, 43–4 (1967), 133–53.
[31] *Fueros de Sepúlveda*, Fuero extenso, clause 6, p. 63.

THE FRONTIER OF TOLEDO

The frontier system of the Extremaduras was a resounding success. The proof of this is that not one of the many and mighty attacks by the Almoravids or Almohads was even capable of reaching, let alone penetrating, this frontier. This was so partially because the reconquest of Toledo had in reality created a new frontier line based on the Tagus, against which all the Muslim attacks foundered despite the fact that this new frontier was not a strong one.

The weaknesses of this frontier were due to its advanced and exposed nature, and above all because from its very beginnings there had been no time to organize and repopulate it properly before it was subjected to an endless number of attacks by the Almoravids.[32] In effect, between 1090 and 1137, the Toledan region was attacked, invaded, and sacked on at least ten occasions. And during the second half of the twelfth century, between 1171 and 1211, the Almohads subjected the whole region to a ferocious and pitiless pressure. In reality this second frontier, based, to begin with, on the Tagus and later on the Guadiana river, was a very insecure and dangerous area, which had little attraction to would-be settlers, right down to the great Christian victory of Las Navas de Tolosa (1212). And it was precisely this permanent insecurity which helps to explain the main features of New Castile and other regions, such as the present-day Extremadura or the Portuguese Alemtejo. The outstanding features were as follows:

1. There was a shortage of population, both Muslim and Christian, to the south of Toledo. Few Muslims remained in the region, and some areas, such as La Mancha, were still scarcely populated at the beginning of the thirteenth century.[33]

2. This depopulation in part explains the ranching orientation of the region's economy, as Professor Bishko has demonstrated in a seminal article.[34]

---

[32] See Julio González, *Repoblación de Castilla la Nueva* (2 vols., Madrid, 1975–6), i. 86–108.

[33] See Emilio Cabrera Muñoz, 'Del Tajo a Sierra Morena', in García de Cortázar *et al.*, *La organización social del espacio*, 123–61, at 132–5.

[34] Charles J. Bishko, 'The Castilian as Plainsman: The Medieval Ranching Frontier in La Mancha and Extremadura', in Archibald R. Lewis and Thomas F. McGann (eds.), *The New World Looks at its History: Proceedings of the Second*

3. The frontier nature of this region is shown by the remarkable spread in it of the *fueros* of the Extremaduras, which would now reach their peak of development in the *fuero* of Cuenca.[35]

4. Lastly, nothing illustrates the harsh nature of the frontier better than the birth of the military orders of Calatrava (1158), Santiago (1170), and Alcántara (1176) in this region during the second half of the twelfth century.[36]

The struggle for control of the lands of New Castile and the Transierra (present-day Extremadura) was long and bitter. At the end of the eleventh century the Christians controlled a large area of the territory to the north of the Tagus between Talavera and Medinaceli. By the mid-twelfth century the frontier had moved to the Guadiana river, on whose banks was located the advanced castle of Calatrava, held by the order of the same name. Leonese advances in Extremadura were checked in 1179 when the Almohads regained Cáceres. Only the conquest of Cuenca in 1177 could compensate for the many reverses suffered by the Christians.

In these circumstances the settlement of the region depended on the creation of solid military structures capable of ensuring defence. To the north of the Tagus, where the major part of the population was for long concentrated, towns and urban councils, modelled on those of the Extremaduras, were created and located upon the basis of previously existing Muslim towns. Most of these were royal towns, although some belonged to the sees of Toledo and Sigüenza. All these towns used *fueros* from the Extremaduras. And even in Toledo itself, which had a different *fuero*, the basic military organization of its colonists was not dissimilar to that of the Extremaduran towns.

But the main feature of the region was the remarkable growth of lordships. In this respect Professor J. González has demonstrated the difference between the Toledo area and the Extremaduras,[37] the latter region only witnessing the growth of lordships at a much

International Congress of Historians of the United States and Mexico (Austin, 1963), 47–69.

[35] See n. 16. The importance of the *Fuero* of Cuenca was due to the remarkable way in which it spread throughout the eastern part of la Mancha and throughout upper Andalusia.

[36] On the military orders, see Lomax, *Reconquest*, 107–11. For further bibliographical information, see Derek W. Lomax, *Las órdenes militares en la Península Ibérica durante la Edad Media* (Salamanca, 1976).

[37] González, *Repoblación de Castilla la Nueva*, ii. 16–36.

later date. The difference is to be explained by the fact that the Tagus frontier was the first line of defence. Nevertheless, the first appearance of lordships in the region was not due to any necessity of defence against the Almoravids but rather to the need to endow the Toledan archbishop and cathedral chapter with land and vassals. And thus, between 1086 and 1099, the Church of Toledo received a series of lordships, some of which were of considerable importance. This situation changed radically from the reign of Alfonso VII (1126–57) onwards. Defensive preoccupations provoked this king to involve the nobility in the task of settlement. Despite this, the Church also received important towns, such as Alcalá de Henares (1129) and Sigüenza (1138). But there is no doubt that the principal beneficiaries were the great nobility and royal vassals, such as Count Manrique de Lara, who received the town of Molina, and Count Ponce de Minerva, to whom the king granted the strategic town of Zorita.

From the second half of the twelfth century this picture of lordships changed because lordships were now mainly granted to the new military orders, given royal recognition of their military capacity on the frontier.[38] The most important order, that of Calatrava, occupied the most dangerous frontier sector of the Guadiana, as well as all the deserted and vast lands adjoining it, and some of the rearguard towns, such as Zorita. Just behind this Calatrava sector the Order of the Hospitallers received the lordship of Consuegra, and in the eastern sector the Order of Santiago was given a long territory which included important towns such as Uclés, Mora, Oreja, and Ocaña.

The presence of the military orders on the frontier was absolutely vital for the defence and settlement of the lands to the south of the Tagus. The highly centralized nature of these orders, as well as their military specialization, contributed to the con-solidation of the Christian presence on a frontier which only managed to maintain itself during the difficult years of Almohad attacks thanks to the efforts and heroism of these warrior-monks. Their well-deserved prestige allowed them to increase their influence and lands, after the battle of Las Navas de Tolosa, in the regions of Extremadura and Andalusia.

To the north of the Tagus and in most eastern parts of New

---

[38] González, *Repoblación de Castilla la Nueva*, ii. 30.

Castile large urban centres predominated. These were very well-fortified towns which sometimes contained an interior fortress or *alcázar* which was the most important defensive point. The outstanding example is that of Toledo, almost completely surrounded by the Tagus and protected by a virtually impregnable wall. But the military strongholds which were most physically similar to the Extremaduran towns were Guadalajara and Cuenca. The former, located on a narrow *meseta*, was flanked by two deep ravines and by the Henares river. Cuenca, for its part, was situated between the deep course of the River Júcar and the River Huécar, and the northern part of the town, the part most difficult to defend, was reinforced by a castle.

On the other hand, the lands to the south of the Tagus were those of the great castles. Only a few centres close to the river had surrounding walls. The reason for this is simple: when the Christians took these lands they found no important towns, but only rural settlements. But, in addition, when the huge region to the north and south of the Guadiana river was properly repopulated, which was not to happen until well into the thirteenth century, the frontier had moved decisively into Andalusia, and it was no longer necessary to invest in such costly fortifications. Thus, what predominated in this area were the large castles, such as those of New Calatrava, Consuegra, and Uclés, and small fortresses and defensive towers where the population could find refuge in times of danger.

As in the Extremaduras, the population of New Castile and the Transierra was obliged to defend the frontier. This is more apparent to the north of the Tagus and in more eastern parts of New Castile than in La Mancha, which was mostly repopulated when the frontier had already moved south of the Guadalquivir. Nevertheless some *fueros* of this region, like that of Uclés, have the same legal structure as those of the towns of the Extremaduras. As in the latter towns, there was a marked degree of social mobility which made it possible for *peones* to enter the ranks of the knights. The *fuero* of Toledo clearly alludes to this possibility when, with respect to the *peones*, it states that 'quisquis ex illis equitare voluerit in quibusdam temporibus, equitet et intret in onores militum'.[39] Likewise in many *fueros* it is clear that the

[39] *Colección de fueros municipales y cartas pueblas de los reinos de Castilla,*

knights were socially dominant, were exempt from certain taxes, and monopolized the main urban offices.[40]

The last and most enduring frontier between Castile and Islam was established shortly after the conquest of Andalusia by Ferdinand III.[41] The defeat of the Almohads at Las Navas de Tolosa led to internal upheaval within al-Andalus and Morocco. The Christian kingdoms of Portugal, León, Castile, and Aragón profited from this opportunity, and in less than a quarter of a century were able to limit Muslim power to a few enclaves—that is, the kingdoms of Granada, Murcia, and Niebla, as well as the region of Cádiz–Jerez—all of which were under a Castilian 'protectorate'.

As far as Andalusia is concerned, Ferdinand III, in a series of successful campaigns, captured the most important cities in the area: Baeza (1227), Úbeda (1232), Córdoba (1236), Jaén (1246), and Seville (1248). Upon his death, he left his heir Alfonso X a large and united realm. But the task of organizing, repopulating, and defending the recently conquered lands still lay ahead.

In theory, and only in theory, as events would tragically prove in the following years, the Reconquest had come to an end. All the lands of al-Andalus were in Christian hands. Ferdinand III died convinced of this fact, as is shown by the words cited in the *Primera crónica general*, which the king addressed to his son Alfonso from his deathbed:

Son . . . I leave you the whole realm from the sea hither, that the Moors won from Rodrigo, king of Spain. All of it is in your dominion, part of it conquered, the other part tributary.[42]

In truth, the valley of the Guadalquivir river was virtually in Castilian hands, and the Christians had established their rule over the main cities and towns of the region. Yet, in the countryside large groups of *mudéjares*, or subjected Moors, remained on the

León, *Corona de Aragón y Navarra*, ed. Tomás Muñoz y Romero (Madrid, 1847), 565.

[40] González, *Repoblación de Castilla la Nueva*, ii. 156–9.

[41] Julio González, 'Las conquistas de Fernando III en Andalucía', *Hispania*, 24 (1946), 545–631.

[42] *Primera crónica general de España*, ed. Ramón Menéndez Pidal (2 vols., Madrid, 1955), ii. 772.

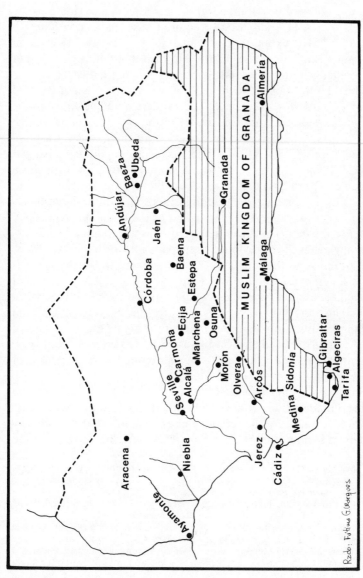

Rzdo: Fatima G.Warquos.

Map 6. Andalusia after the Thirteenth-century Reconquest

land under the rule of the king of Castile, has had been established by their surrender treaties.[43] Granada, Murcia, and Niebla also had the status of vassal-kingdoms: their rulers paid tribute to the king of Castile, and when required also gave *consilium et auxilium*.[44] The extant royal documents of the period are clear on this point, and the names of the Moorish kings appear, together with other important vassals, confirming royal privileges.

Thus the frontier, as such, did not yet exist or was not yet well defined. This was the case of the borders with the kingdom of Granada, and even more pointedly in the case of Murcia, where the main strongholds and fortresses were manned by Castilian forces from 1244. After 1264, however, conditions changed radically. The rebellion of the *mudéjares* of Murcia and Andalusia put an end to this state of affairs,[45] and forever finished the dream of a Muslim Spain which submitted itself with resignation to Castilian protection. After the defeat of the rebellion, Alfonso X expelled the *mudéjares* from some cities, as was the case of Jerez.[46] In many instances, the Moors, anticipating the order of expulsion, fled *en masse* to the kingdom of Granada and to North Africa. I ought to emphasize that this also meant the end of any dreams of peaceful coexistence between conquerors and conquered, between Christians and Moors. Consequently, the new political and military realities, made more acute after 1275 by the incursions of the Marinids, forced the Castilians to undertake important new military efforts and to attempt a new and complete restructuring of the frontier.

So after the first conquests in the mountainous region of the upper Guadalquivir, a new frontier emerged, which was to be defended jointly by the archbishop of Toledo[47] and the military orders of Santiago and Calatrava.[48] However, the situation in the

---

[43] See Manuel González Jiménez, 'Los mudéjares andaluces (siglos XIII–XV)', in *Actas del V Coloquio de Historia Medieval Andaluza* (Córdoba, in press).

[44] *Primera crónica general*, ii. 746.

[45] On the revolt of the *mudéjares*, see *Historia de Andalucía*, ii (Madrid and Barcelona, 1980), 107–10 (Manuel González Jiménez).

[46] *Libro del repartimiento de Jerez de la Frontera: Estudio y edición*, ed. Manuel González Jiménez and Antonio González Gómez (Cádiz, 1980), pp. lxxxi–lxxxiii.

[47] The archbishop of Toledo received a lordship of some 2,000 square kilometres which would later be known as the *Adelantamiento* or March of Cazorla: see María del Mar García Guzmán, *El Adelantamiento de Cazorla en la Baja Edad Media* (Cádiz, 1985).

[48] On the lordships of the military orders, see José Rodríguez Molina, 'Las

plains of the middle and lower Guadalquivir was quite different. After the reconquest of Córdoba and Seville the towns and castles of the area surrendered almost immediately, and consequently little attention was given to their defence. This explains the fact that few garrisons were set up along the frontier with the kingdom of Granada.

However, after the uprising of the *mudéjares* in 1264 and the attacks of the Granadans and Marinids, Alfonso X reinforced the entire defence system along the frontier of Seville and Córdoba. And so the military orders were once again brought in to take charge. Thus the Order of Santiago was given the stronghold of Estepa;[49] the Order of Calatrava was given Osuna and Cazalla;[50] the Order of Alcántara was given Morón and the castle of Cote;[51] and finally the newly founded Order of Santa María de España was given the task of defending Medina Sidonia and Alcalá de los Gazules.[52] What is more, in order to reinforce the defence system of the area, several new lay lordships were held by members of the royal family,[53] and others were held by prominent knights of the region.[54]

I must make it clear, though, that the defence of the frontier and the reconquered lands was primarily the responsibility of the settlers. They had been given houses and lands by the king on the condition that they settled in Andalusia and defended the territory. None of this was new. From the time of the reconquest of Toledo land-settlers were something more than just simple colonists. On the other hand, it was also a way of guaranteeing that people would stay on the land won back from the Moors. And

órdenes militares de Calatrava y Santiago en el Alto Guadalquivir (siglos XIII–XV)', *Cuadernos de estudios medievales*, 2–3 (1974–5), 59–83.

[49] For this grant, see *Diplomatorio andaluz de Alfonso X*, ed. Manuel González Jiménez (in press).

[50] Ibid.   [51] Ibid.

[52] Juan Torres Fontes, 'La Orden de Santa María de España', *Miscelánea medieval murciana*, 3 (1977), 75–118 (and, for the grant of Medina Sidonia and Alcalá de los Gazules in particular, 110–13).

[53] The Infante Don Juan, Alfonso X's brother, received the lordship of the towns of Baena, Luque, and Zuheros: see Manuel González Jiménez, *En torno a los orígenes de Andalucía: La repoblación del siglo XIII* (Seville, 1980), 132 n. 173.

[54] Ibid. 136. Thus the Portuguese knight Gonzalo Yáñez do Vinhal received the lordship of Aguilar de la Frontera, and Sancho Martínez de Jódar, who had been *Adelantado* of Andalusia in 1253–4, became lord of various frontier areas in the 'kingdom' of Jaén.

so, in Andalusia and in Murcia as well, the old socio-military categories of knights and foot-soldiers once again appeared. The entire population of settlers fitted into one or other of these categories. However, the exact terminology used was somewhat different as befitted new times and new ways. The terms included those of *caballeros de linaje* or *caballeros hidalgos*, who were knights belonging to the lower ranks of the nobility;[55] *caballeros ciudadanos*, who were city-dwelling knights, equivalent to the *caballeros villanos*; and finally the *peones* or foot-soldiers.

After 1264, these categories became more numerous in some frontier towns and reflected the degree of military specialization of the inhabitants. Thus in the *repartimiento* of Jerez[56] we find that there were *caballeros hidalgos*, who were referred to in other documents of the time as *caballeros del feudo* because they received a *feudo* of 200 *maravedíes* annually from the king to defend the city of Jerez.[57] We also find *caballeros ciudadanos* and, of course, *peones*. But within these latter groups other military categories are mentioned—for example, the *ballesteros* or crossbowmen; the *arqueros* or archers; the *adalides*, who were the captains of the hosts; the *almocadenes*, who were in charge of the infantry groups; and the *almogávares*, who were infantry soldiers specialized in frontier warfare. The *repartimiento* of Jerez goes still further and mentions forty *arqueros del rey* or king's crossbowmen, who were a highly specialized group of mounted soldiers. Yet another *repartimiento*, that of Vejer de la Frontera, a town located near Tarifa, distinguishes between on the one hand *caballeros hidalgos*, *escuderos* or squires, and *adalides*, who were of the ruling class, and on the other hand *caballeros ciudadanos*, *ballesteros*, and *almocadenes*, and finally *peones* or foot-soldiers.[58]

In some frontier towns of great strategic value the regulations concerning the defence of the territory are much more explicit

---

[55] On the origins of the lower nobility in Castile-León, see Salvador de Moxó, *Repoblación y sociedad en la España cristiana medieval* (Madrid, 1979), 411–13. On the lineage knighthood of Portugal, see José Mattoso, *Identificação de um país: Ensaio sobre as origens de Portugal, 1096–1325*, i (Lisbon, 1985), 133–4.

[56] *Libro del repartimiento de Jerez*, pp. lii–liii.

[57] For the text of Alfonso X's privilege, see ibid. 199–201.

[58] See Miguel Ángel Ladero Quesada and Manuel González Jiménez, 'La población en la frontera de Gibraltar y el repartimiento de Vejer (siglos XIII–XIV)', *Historia, instituciones, documentos*, 4 (1977), 199–316, esp. 285–305.

than usual. This can be seen, for example, in the royal charter or *carta-puebla* given by Alfonso X to Alcalá de Guadaira.[59]

The town of Alcalá is located about twenty kilometres south of Seville on the Guadaira river. From the castle on the top of the hill it dominates an extensive, fertile plain. Around the middle of the thirteenth century the town was divided into two sectors which were separated by an inside wall. There was the *villa* or town where, from 1247 onwards, the first Christian settlers set up their dwellings, and the *arrabal* or suburb outside the main walls, where the *mudéjar* population was confined after its surrender. Protected by its walls and fortress, Alcalá controlled the main road leading into Seville from Granada and from the area of Jerez. The strategic value of the town was enormous, especially if we take into account the fact that the land to the south of Alcalá and as far as the frontier was practically unpopulated.

Because of its importance, the town was initially dependent on the city council of Seville. But, in 1258, it was conceded to the chapter of the cathedral. The significance of Alcalá in the defence of the city was fully proved, when, in the summer of 1275, the Marinids began a series of attacks on the area. The cathedral chapter was unable to meet the heavy military costs, and ceded the town and castle once again to Seville. It is almost certain that the population of Alcalá had greatly diminished at this time, and so the city of Seville had to undertake the upkeep of the garrison there. In order to rectify this situation, Alfonso X issued the town with a royal charter in 1280 and undertook a second and definitive settlement.

The first part of this text contains donations made by the king to the 150 new settlers. They were given land which was to be divided among them in family lots. They were also given a series of tax exemptions, which was a common practice in newly settled frontier towns. But the most interesting part of this document is that which deals with the very detailed military obligations of the colonists. For example, the townspeople of Alcalá were responsible

---

[59] The original privilege has disappeared. In the early nineteenth century the Municipal Archive of Alcalá possessed a copy of it which was published by Leandro José de Flores in his book *Memorias históricas de la villa de Alcalá* (Seville, 1833; new edn. Alcalá, 1983). I have published the reconstructed text of the *carta-puebla* in Manuel González Jiménez, 'Alcalá de Guadaira en el siglo XIII: Conquista y repoblación', in *Actas de las I Jornadas de Historia de Alcalá de Guadaira* (Alcalá, 1987), 45–52, at 51–2.

for keeping night watch in the castle and in the *arrabal*, in 'those places where it was customary to keep watch'; they also had to guard the fortress during the day. According to the text, and to ensure that these obligations were correctly undertaken, the settlers had to dwell 'in the castle with their bodies'. If they wanted to sell their property they had to do so to people who would comply with these regulations. If anybody from the town fell captive to the Moors, he was allowed to sell his land in order to pay the ransom, but he had to sell it to someone who would live in the town and who was prepared to comply with his military obligations.

I have referred above to the tax exemptions that existed in the frontier towns. This was, in effect, the main way to attract new settlers. But there were other kinds of privileges granted to the settlers of frontier towns. And so, from the times of Alfonso X and on into the middle of the fourteenth century a whole new frontier legal system was drawn up, which I think is worth analysing.

1. *Tax exemptions*. The town of Medina Sidonia, which was repopulated in 1264, still preserves an interesting series of royal charters which clearly demonstrate how tax exemptions developed. Thus, in 1268, Alfonso X freed the town's foot-soldiers from paying tithes and other taxes to the king.[60] Some years later he exempted them from paying tolls within the whole kingdom.[61] Finally, in 1288, Sancho IV confirmed these exemptions and extended them to all types of taxes.[62]

Two important frontier towns—Tarifa, conquered by Sancho IV in 1292, and Gibraltar, occupied in 1309 by Ferdinand IV— enjoyed even wider exemptions. Thus, in 1295 Sancho IV abolished such taxes as tithes, tolls, the *alcabala* or sales tax, or any other tax 'on goods that they took or brought or sold by sea or by land anywhere in our kingdoms, or in places belonging to the military orders or lordships which are under our Lordship'.[63] And, in order to ensure adequate supplies and provisions for the town, he granted exemptions to Christian, Moorish, and Jewish merchants who brought arms and food to Tarifa. They paid no commercial tax and no anchor-tax or anchorage on their boats. Finally, the charter given to Gibraltar by Ferdinand IV in 1310 includes an

[60] Ladero Quesada and González Jiménez, 'Población en la frontera', 225.
[61] Ibid. 230.   [62] Ibid. 231–2.   [63] Ibid. 232–3.

extensive range of tax exemptions, which, I believe, covers all the
known taxes of the time.[64]

2. *Military privileges*. The military duties of the inhabitants of
the frontier towns were mainly defensive, as we saw in the charter
of Alcalá de Guadaira. Nevertheless, other documents of the time
refer to their obligation to take part in any royal expeditions that
were carried out between the Guadalquivir river and the sea.[65] In
time, even this relatively limited duty was abolished, as can be
seen in the royal charter given to Gibraltar.[66] This document also
provides us with details about other military features of the
Andalusian frontier towns, which lasted down to the modern
period. In the first place there was the status of the inhabitants as
soldiers, which meant that they received corresponding payments
from the king. For example, the charter granted to Gibraltar
stated:

in order that the town of Gibraltar may be better protected, we order that
there should be 300 *vecinos* there . . . and that all those who live there . . .
should have their service-payments . . . the *ballestero de monte*,[45]
maravedíes; and the *ballestero de estribera*, 40 *maravedíes*; and the *peón*,
35 *maravedíes*; and if he is an *almocadén*, 50 *maravedíes* . . . And if any of
these men should perform guard-duty on the walls of the town of
Gibraltar, then they are to have 10 *maravedíes* each for this watch-duty
over and above their service-payments.[67]

Secondly, and in accordance with their military status, these
soldier-settlers also received annual payments of grain for their
subsistence. This system, which was to be amply extended during
the second half of the fourteenth century, seems to have been
devised during the reign of Alfonso XI (1312–50). One of the
earliest references to it is to be found in the privilege granted in
1335 to the settlers of the castle of Tíscar in the 'kingdom' of
Jaén.[68] And by 1345 the king was providing supplies of grain to the
inhabitants of a whole series of recently conquered towns, such as
Alcalá la Real, Priego, and Rute.[69]

[64] Ladero Quesada and González Jiménez, 'Población en la frontera', 238.

[65] Ibid. 225.

[66] For the complete text of this document, see ibid. 237–9.

[67] Ibid. 238.

[68] *Colección diplomática de Quesada*, ed. Juan de Mata Carriazo Arroquia
(Jaén, 1975), 42.

[69] *Colección diplomática de Baeza*, ed. José Rodríguez Molina (Jaén, 1983),
doc. 52, pp. 137–8.

3. *The privilege of the 'homicianos'*. This privilege of asylum was undoubtedly one of the most characteristic privileges that existed in the frontier towns. For example, the charter of Gibraltar, in which this privilege first appeared, gave the right of 'asylum' 'to all who went to Gibraltar and who became citizens or residents, be they bandits or thieves or assassins, or any other men no matter what wrong they may have done, or to any married woman who may have abandoned her husband . . . that they may be defended and guarded from death'.[70] This right of 'asylum' existed as far back as 1076, where we find it in the *fuero* of Sepúlveda, but it had fallen into disuse until it was introduced again by Ferdinand IV in 1310. The reappearance of this privilege can only be explained by the pressing need to attract settlers of any condition to frontier towns, which were the most unattractive places to settle in. The privilege only makes exceptions in the case of particularly serious crimes, such as treason, or the surrender of castles to the enemy, or the breaking of truces or the king's peace, or the abduction by vassals of the lord's wife.

The privilege of the *homicianos* enjoyed an extraordinary diffusion along the whole frontier. In 1323 Alfonso XI granted it to the settlers of the castle of Alcaudete in the 'kingdom' of Jaén.[71] In 1327 the town of Olvera, which was the first to be reconquered by the young king,[72] received the same privilege, and in 1333 he granted it to Tarifa, because the town 'is very near the Moors and needs many people to defend it'.[73] From this point on almost all the towns of the frontier were to receive the same privilege.

As in the case of Gibraltar, the pardon affected all types of crimes and wrongdoing—homicides or *muerte de omes*, robbery, etc.—with the sole exception of the crimes of *alevosía* (the breaking of the feudal oath), treason, and other similar faults. But there was one important change in the privilege granted by Alfonso XI—for crimes to be considered legally proscribed it became necessary to live on the frontier for 'one year and one day'. In some cases, as in Olvera, the town could also provide

[70] Ladero Quesada and González Jiménez, 'Población en la frontera', 237.
[71] *Colección de privilegios, franquezas, exenciones y fueros*, vi, ed. Tomás González (Madrid, 1833), 237–8.
[72] R. F. Escalona, *Historia del real monasterio de Sahagún* (facsimile edn., Madrid, 1982), 652–3.
[73] Ladero Quesada and González Jiménez, 'Población en la frontera', 241.

temporary refuge—for four years—to those who were being pursued for debt.

In spite of these many privileges, great difficulties were encountered in resettling the frontier. In 1367, Medina Sidonia, which had been repopulated over and over again,[74] had no more than 150 citizens or householders.[75] In many frontier towns the only inhabitants were groups of *homicianos* or delinquents availing themselves of the right of asylum, and settler-soldiers who received from the Crown annual payments of money and quantities of grain supplied by the inland towns.

But the scarcity of population affected not only the frontier towns. In fact the problem existed to a lesser or greater degree in the whole of Andalusia. There were vast uncultivated and uninhabited tracts of land between the inland towns and the frontier. Obviously this lack of population added greatly to the insecurity of the frontier, which was already inadequately defended by a remote front line of fortresses. The inland towns were similarly affected. So it was of prime importance to repopulate the countryside because this was the only means of guaranteeing not only the security of the frontier itself, but that of the whole territory. By the end of the thirteenth century the military orders had become so immersed in the administration of their enormous properties that they had lost that interest and vigour in war which had been so characteristic of them at the beginning, and they could no longer be called on for this undertaking. Consequently, it was to the nobles of the region that the task was given, which explains the reason for their enormous rise to power from then on. So it was that between 1280 and 1350 the great noble families, such as the Pérez de Guzmán, Ponce de León, Fernández de Córdoba, Aguilar, and others, became firmly rooted in Andalusia.[76]

In many cases, castles and towers were built near the frontier, and as a result tiny lordships appeared, as happened in the lowlands of Seville.[77] They existed, as can be seen in some royal

---

[74] On the successive repopulations of Medina Sidonia, see *El libro del repartimiento de Medina Sidonia: Estudio y edición*, ed. A. M. Anasagasti and L. Rodríguez (Cádiz, 1987).

[75] Ladero Quesada and González Jiménez, 'Población en la frontera', 248.

[76] See *Historia de Andalucia*, ii. 239–40.

[77] For the formulation of these small lordships, see Manuel González Jiménez, *La repoblación de la zona de Sevilla durante el siglo XIV* (Seville, 1975), 71–4.

charters by Alfonso XI, 'to defend our land and this frontier from
the enemies of our faith'.[78]

Let me conclude by saying something about the structure of the
defence system along the Andalusian frontier. As has been
pointed out recently,[79] the defence system set up by Castile in the
late Middle Ages was comprised of three lines of frontier
fortresses.

The first of these, situated on the very frontier itself, controlled
the roads and passes through which the Moors might enter. Its
main purpose was not to stop the enemy, but rather to watch his
movements and, in case of peril, to raise the alarm by means of
visual and smoke signals. This line consisted of observation points,
watch-towers, and some castles, like, for example, the castle of
Cote near Morón.

This first line was backed up and defended by a second line of
strongholds, built on high ground and surrounded by a complex
system of walls and fortresses. Arcos de la Frontera is a very good
example of this type of town. It is built on the top of a sheer cliff
and is surrounded below by the River Guadalete. Estepa is
another good example of a second-line stronghold, and was, right
up to the end of the Middle Ages, like many other Andalusian
towns, a frontier town where the entire population lived huddled
within the shelter of its walls.

Finally, the third line of defence was formed by a number of
castles whose main functions were that of giving protection to the
peasants, and that of liaison between the frontier and the inland
towns, where the campaigns against the enemy were planned and
organized.

[78] Seville, Archivo Ducal de Medinaceli, Sección Alcalá de los Gazules, *legajo*
59, no. 9: *Carta-puebla* of Torre del Bao (3 Mar. 1336).
[79] See Manuel García Fernández, *Andalucía en tiempos de Alfonso XI*
(microfiche edn., Seville, 1987).

Part II
INSTITUTIONS

4

Frontier Arrangements in Fragmented Societies: Ireland and Wales

REES DAVIES

From the late eleventh century onwards—in other words from the period of 'the awakening of Europe' and 'the making of the Middle Ages'—Ireland and Wales may appropriately be regarded as two of the western frontier zones of medieval Europe. They stood at one of the peripheries of the area of feudal imperialism associated with Norman conquest and colonization and indeed seemed to slow down and even to frustrate its apparently remorseless advance. They were also frontierlands in cultural terms, where a new, confident, aggressive, north-western European, Latin- and French-dominated aristocratic and ecclesiastical culture came into contact, and often confrontation, with native cultures profoundly different from it in their economic configuration, political assumptions, ecclesiastical norms, social customs, and literary and artistic traditions.[1]

It is appropriate, therefore, to consider Ireland and Wales, for all their differences, alongside each other as frontier societies. They certainly shared many common features. In both countries the process of domination, conquest, and settlement by the Anglo-Normans was slow, spasmodic, and long drawn out. In Wales it began virtually on the morrow of the battle of Hastings, but for much of the twelfth and thirteenth centuries its progress was uncertain and it was only with the two major royal campaigns of 1276–7 and 1282–3 that it was eventually and suddenly brought to a triumphant conclusion. The saga of the Anglo-Norman penetration of Ireland began in 1169, almost exactly a century later than that of Wales. After making rapid and impressive initial progress, it was already clearly faltering by the second half of the thirteenth

---

[1] This theme is explored, through the writings of Gerald of Wales, in Robert Bartlett, *Gerald of Wales 1146–1223* (Oxford, 1982). See also Huw Pryce, 'In Search of a Medieval Society: Deheubarth in the Writings of Gerald of Wales', *Welsh History Review*, 13 (1986–7), 265–81.

78 *Rees Davies*

century. Thereafter the English government and English settlers in
Ireland had gradually to come to terms with the painful truth that
the conquest of Ireland was, and was to remain, piecemeal,
uncertain, and incomplete. Consequently Ireland in the fourteenth
century—like Wales in the twelfth and for much of the thirteenth
century—was a country of halves, half under native and the other
half under Anglo-Norman rule.[2] The boundary between these two
halves—or whatever other more sophisticated fractions we may
care to employ—was one of the obvious frontier zones of medieval
Wales and Ireland.

The two countries shared a further common experience: English
settlement within them was very uneven in its geographical
distribution and density. Parts of the eastern borderlands, river
valleys, and southern coastal lowlands of Wales and much of
southern and eastern Ireland were intensively settled and became
proudly and defiantly English in customs, language, place-names,
law, agriculture, social structure, and so forth. But rarely did these
alien settlements form extensive consolidated blocs which can be
neatly and confidently represented on a map. More often were
they fairly small and more or less isolated enclaves, separated from
each other by mountains, estuaries, forests, or bogs and interspersed
with large native districts where English settlers had scarcely
penetrated and where English governance was frequently skeletal,
nominal, or non-existent.[3] Thus to travel the few miles from the
thoroughly Anglicized lowlands of Radnor into the uplands of
Maelienydd, from the security of Pembroke to a frontier fortress
such as Cilgerran, from Dublin into the treacherous fastnesses of
the Wicklow mountains, or from Thurles and Tipperary into the
Irishry of Ely O'Carroll was to enter a different world and to cross
a frontier, or rather frontiers, all the more profound for not being
neatly delineated on a map. Civil and ecclesiastical administrators
might attempt to acknowledge the fact by defining the respective

[2] The concept of Ireland as 'a country of halves' has been explored in Robin
Frame, *English Lordship in Ireland, 1318–1361* (Oxford, 1982), 25, 53–4, 80. See
also Map 7, below.
    [3] Rees Davies, *Lordship and Society in the March of Wales 1282–1400* (Oxford,
1978), 303–6; C. A. Empey, 'Conquest and Settlement: Patterns of Anglo-Norman
Settlement in North Munster and South Leinster', *Irish Social and Economic
History Journal*, 13 (1986), 5–31; id., 'The Norman Period, 1185–1500', in William
Nolan (ed.), *Tipperary: History and Society: Interdisciplinary Essays on the History
of an Irish County* (Dublin, 1985), 71–92; Art Cosgrove (ed.), *New History of
Ireland*, ii: *Medieval Ireland, 1169–1534* (Oxford, 1987), 221–5.

districts as Englishries and Welshries or as *inter Anglicos* and *inter Hibernicos*; but their categories could hardly begin to do justice to the complexity of the situation. This uneven pattern of conquest, control, and settlement meant that both Wales and Ireland in the medieval period were societies of multiple and highly localized frontiers (in the loose sense of that term) where two peoples met, overlapped, and confronted each other. This highly fragmented and fluid situation was the very reverse of the definitiveness and clarity which characterized the frontier between the realms of England and Scotland (disputed lands and march districts notwithstanding).[4]

The contrast between Scotland on the one hand and Wales and Ireland on the other likewise stands out in another direction. In Scotland the Anglo-Norman settlers were introduced into the country by invitation and were, on the whole, readily and smoothly assimilated into Scotland's society, while subtly transforming it. In Ireland and Wales, however, alien settlement came largely, though not exclusively, in the wake of conquest and the English settlers entrenched their position in the host society by institutionalizing the separation between themselves and the native peoples. So it was that the governmental terminology of Wales and Ireland from at least the thirteenth century predicated a duality in the peoples and institutions of both countries: English and Welsh, *Gaedhil* and *Gaill*, *pura Wallia* and *marchia Wallie*, 'land of war' and 'land of peace', native law and customs and English common law and mores, and so forth. Such a duality— 'distinction and diversity' as the Act of Union of England and Wales in 1536 called it—sanctioned and promoted a mentality of separation and discrimination which in its turn begat a profound psychological frontier within both countries. A deep and officially sanctioned fissure of race and culture ran through the societies of medieval Wales and Ireland; the attempts, conscious or unconscious, either to deepen or to bridge that fissure were one leading motif in the histories of both countries in the later Middle Ages.[5] Both societies were, in that respect, truly frontier societies.

---

[4] Geoffrey Barrow, *The Kingdom of the Scots* (London, 1973), ch. 4, 'The Anglo-Scottish Border'; Denys Hay, 'England, Scotland and Europe: The Problem of the Frontier', *TRHS*, 5th ser., 25 (1975), 77–93.

[5] For Ireland see James F. Lydon, 'The Problem of the Frontier in Medieval Ireland', *Topic: A Journal of the Liberal Arts*, 13 (1967), 5–22 and P. J. Duffy, 'The Nature of the Medieval Frontier in Ireland', *Studia Hibernica*, 22–3 (1982–3),

Wales and Ireland shared yet another common experience which profoundly shaped their histories: they were, governmentally and politically, deeply fragmented countries. Deep as was the conviction of ultimate cultural, linguistic, and legal unity in both countries,[6] it is the intensely regional character of loyalties, politics, religion, and power which is the dominant feature of the native, pre-Norman histories of both countries. As the Anglo-Normans pushed forward their conquest of Wales and Ireland, they became the heirs of this particularism and indeed seemed to exult in it, adjusting the forms, formal and especially informal, of their authority to the pre-existing patterns and geography of power.[7] Countries in which the units of political power and governance are multiple and which lack a central, stable, unchallenged supervisory source of jurisdiction and power have their own internal complex frontiers and have to devise their own working solutions for dealing with the problems raised by such frontiers. Such were both medieval Ireland and Wales, both in the pre-Norman and Anglo-Norman periods.

Wales and Ireland may, therefore, be considered as countries of plural frontiers, none of which exactly coincided with one another, notably the frontiers of conquest, settlement, peoples, culture, and units of power. One reflection of the community of experience and problems shared by the two countries was the prominence of the word 'march' (or 'marches') in the vocabulary of authority and in the geography of power in both countries. 'Marches' are not, of course, peculiar in any way to these two countries. They were a common feature of border districts within and at the boundaries of medieval Europe. Some of the problems they posed—especially in terms of feudal loyalties and fiscal and jurisdictional status—have been closely studied by historians.[8] Nevertheless marches and

21–38; for Wales, Rees Davies, 'Race Relations in Post-Conquest Wales', *Transactions of the Honourable Society of Cymmrodorion* (1974–5), 32–56.

[6] Donnchá Ó Corráin, 'Nationality and Kingship in Pre-Norman Ireland', in T. W. Moody (ed.), *Nationality and the Pursuit of National Independence* (Historical Studies 11, Belfast, 1978), 1–35; Rees Davies, *Conquest, Coexistence and Change: Wales 1063–1415* (Oxford, 1987), 15–20.

[7] See esp. for Wales, David Walker, 'The Norman Settlement in Wales', in R. Allen Brown (ed.), *Proceedings of the Battle Conference on Anglo-Norman Studies*, i (Woodbridge, 1978), 131–43 and, for Ireland, Robin Frame, 'Power and Society in the Lordship of Ireland, 1272–1377', *Past and Present*, 76 (1977), 3–33; Cosgrove, *New History of Ireland*, ii. 37, 311–12.

[8] Jean-François Lemarignier, *Recherches sur l'hommage en marche et les*

their associated institutions figure particularly prominently in the histories of medieval Ireland and Wales. That this was so was largely a consequence of the hesitant and faltering character of Anglo-Norman conquest in both countries and the need, accordingly, to develop and institutionalize a vocabulary which reflected that uncomfortable fact. That seems to have happened in Wales from the later twelfth century, as the prospect of the total subjugation of the country receded ever further beyond the immediate political and military horizon. Hitherto the term 'march' or 'marches' seems to have been used in a loose geographical sense to describe the borderlands of Wales.[9] It is, apparently, only from *c.*1200 that the phrases 'March of Wales', 'law of the March', and 'barons of the March' enter regularly as official and fairly precise categories into English governmental vocabulary.[10] The adoption of such a vocabulary reflected the acceptance of the fact that there was an extensive area between native-controlled Wales on the one hand and the kingdom of England on the other which was intermediate in its status, laws, and governance and had its own recognizable and recognized habits and institutions. The March of Wales, therefore, was an extensive frontier zone shaped by the character and chronology of the Anglo-Norman penetration and conquest of Wales. Likewise in Ireland in the thirteenth century the term 'marches' came to be used regularly to describe the areas which lay between Gaelic-controlled and English-dominated areas, and soon terms such as 'marchers' and 'law of the march' became part of the common vocabulary of Irish life.[11]

Significant and illuminating as are such similarities between Ireland and Wales, the differences between the two countries are equally striking. A cursory examination of the terminology soon alerts us to some of those differences. In Wales the term 'March'

frontières féodales (Lille, 1945); J. Balon, 'L'Organisation judiciaire des marches féodales', *Annales de la société archéologique de Namur*, 46 (1951), 5–72.

[9] e.g. *Domesday Book*, ed. Abraham Farley (2 vols., London, 1783), i, fo. 186[v] ('in Marcha de Walis'); *Welsh Assize Roll 1277–84*, ed. James Conway Davies (Cardiff, 1940), 237 ('quinque villas de Marchia', 1167–75).

[10] *Littere Wallie*, ed. John Goronwy Edwards (Cardiff, 1940), p. xlvii; Davies, *Conquest, Coexistence and Change*, 213, 272, 287–8.

[11] Cosgrove, *New History of Ireland*, ii. 240, 270, 272–3; Robin Frame, 'War and Peace in the Medieval Lordship of Ireland', in James F. Lydon (ed.), *The English in Medieval Ireland* (Dublin, 1984), 118–41, esp. 133–5.

(or 'Marches') was regularly and consistently used from the thirteenth to the sixteenth centuries to describe a large collection of lordships which had gradually been brought under Anglo-Norman rule—ultimately some forty or so in number and extending over more than half of the surface area of Wales. Before the Edwardian conquest of 1282–3 this March was contrasted with native Wales, *pura Wallia* or simply *Wallia*; after the conquest with the royal or principality lands in north and west Wales.[12] In other words in Wales the March by the end of the thirteenth century was an area well defined in geographical terms and institutional status. In Ireland, on the other hand, there was no single march; rather 'marches' were those districts of uncertain control which lay between 'the land of peace' (under English rule) and 'the land of war' (under Irish control); as such they were often associated with violence and danger.[13] In Wales the law of the March, *lex Marchie*, was accorded from at least *c*.1200 an official status alongside native Welsh law and English common law; its official acceptance as an identifiable body of law was sanctioned by no less august a document than Magna Charta (clause 56).[14] In Ireland, on the other hand, the law of the march was regarded as a perversion, an unofficial and regrettable concession to the customs of the Irish by those who lived cheek by jowl with them. It was officially classed with brehon law as 'not law but bad custom' and was even more dramatically condemned by others as being synonymous with 'the law of the devil'.[15] In Wales the process of Anglo-Norman conquest which had initially brought the March into being was complete by 1283; thereby the military *raison d'être* of the March was extinguished. In Ireland, on the contrary, the process of English conquest was stalled by the late thirteenth century and thereafter went into retreat. War continued to be a normal and recurrent feature of life in Ireland; the institutions and conventions of

---

[12] See Map 8.
[13] See e.g. *Cal. Justic. Rolls (1295–1303)*, 199 ('the marches outside the land of peace'); Goddard H. Orpen, *Ireland under the Normans, 1169–1333* (4 vols., Oxford, 1911–20), iv. 42 ('in the land of war or in the marches'); John A. Watt, *The Church and the Two Nations in Medieval Ireland* (Cambridge, 1970), 93 n. 4 ('in pessima namque marchia et periculosa inter Anglicos et Hibernicos').
[14] Rees Davies, 'The Law of the March', *Welsh History Review*, 5 (1970–1), 1–30.
[15] *Statutes . . . of the Parliament of Ireland: King John to Henry V*, ed. Henry F. Berry (Dublin, 1907), 388–9, 436–7; Cosgrove, *New History of Ireland*, ii. 343.

a military frontier were thereby perpetuated long after they had become historical memories in Wales.

The contrasts between Wales and Ireland are, therefore, as suggestive as the similarities. By studying the two countries together it may be possible to see how frontier institutions and conventions shaped to deal with the experience of war in a fragmented and partially conquered society could be adapted to cope with the assumptions of peace in a similarly fragmented but fully conquered society. It is to the former type of society—and therefore more particularly to the Irish evidence—that we turn first.

Medieval Ireland was a society habituated to war. It had been so in pre-Norman times; it remained so throughout the later Middle Ages.[16] The parties to warfare might change with confusing complexity; the methods and technologies employed altered over time; but the essential assumptions, practices, and purpose of war remained largely unchanged. They have been brilliantly characterized by Dr Katharine Simms and Dr Robin Frame.[17] Raids and counter-raids were almost seasonal in their occurrence; the taking and distribution of preys and plunder were central to the economy and power of native chieftains; military prowess of the most bloodthirsty variety was still at a priority, as might be demonstrated, for example, by the compliments paid to, and charges levelled against, Piers Bermingham (d. 1308);[18] military obligations remained meaningful, particularly from 'those who are nearest to the marches there'.[19] 'The Irish', as one observer remarked wearily, 'are more often at war than at peace.'[20] The same in truth could likewise have been said of the Anglo-Norman settlers, who quickly adopted the native idiom of warfare and who were more often than not at odds among themselves as well as at war with the

---

[16] Phrases such as 'when through general war the land is untilled' are common in the legal documents of the period, e.g. *Dowdall Deeds*, ed. Charles McNeill and A. J. Otway-Ruthven (IMC, Dublin, 1960), no. 43, pp. 20–1.

[17] See esp. Katharine Simms, 'Warfare in the Medieval Gaelic Lordships', *Irish Sword*, 12 (1975–6), 98–108; Robin Frame, 'The Justiciarship of Ralph Ufford: Warfare and Politics in Fourteenth-century Ireland', *Studia Hibernica*, 13 (1973), 7–47; id., 'English Officials and Irish Chiefs in the Fourteenth Century', *EHR* 90 (1975), 748–77; id., 'War and Peace'.

[18] Cosgrove, *New History of Ireland*, ii. 267–8.

[19] Quoted in Frame, 'War and Peace', 135.

[20] *Calendar of Documents Relating to Ireland (1171–1307)*, ed. H. S. Sweetman (5 vols., London, 1875–86), v, no. 335, p. 117.

native Irish. Ireland was indeed *terra guerre*, a land of war—or rather wars.

The situation had not been very dissimilar in Wales for much of the twelfth and thirteenth centuries. During that period it also was a country where the eventuality of war or wars seemed more certain than the prospect of peace.[21] Native princes and Anglo-Norman *conquistadores* alike resorted to war between and among each other as a regular and accepted way of promoting their ambitions and rearranging their relationships. Local raids and 'private' wars were common in their occurrence—such as the 'war' between William Vescy and Morgan ap Hywel in Caerleon or the dispute, conducted with banners displayed, between Fitzwarin of Whittington and Fitzalan of Oswestry.[22] Such a militarized society generated its own etiquette on issues such as the proper display of banners, the exchange of prisoners, and the division of booty.

Societies where power is essentially decentralized and wars frequent and local soon devise mechanisms to contain such wars, to provide a breathing space in the calendar of hostility, and to introduce a measure of peace in the feud. So it was that the institutions and conventions of a military frontierland were created in Wales and Ireland. The evidence is richer (and later) for Ireland, but there are clear hints that the situation had once been not dissimilar in Wales.

The most immediate need was for procedures to bring hostilities to an end, however temporarily. Ecclesiastics no doubt played a crucial role as intermediaries: two leading churchmen in twelfth-century Wales were appropriately commemorated as 'a mediator between Gwynedd and Powys' and as 'a peaceful arbitrator between various peoples'.[23] But others might also play the role of go-between: an Irish source provides a fascinating glimpse of an O'Toole woman who went on regular missions to the mountains, where she stayed with other women, in order to recover stolen goods and cattle carried off by her kinsfolk.[24] Sooner or later,

[21] Rees Davies, 'Kings, Lords and Liberties in the March of Wales, 1066–1272', *TRHS*, 5th ser., 29 (1979), 41–61 at 45.

[22] *Close Rolls of the Reign of Henry III (1247–51)* (London, 1922), 136; *Calendar of the Close Rolls (1296–1302)* (London, 1906), 495; Robert W. Eyton, *Antiquities of Shropshire* (12 vols., London, 1853–60), xi. 40.

[23] *Brut y Tywysogyon: or, The Chronicle of the Princes, Red Book of Hergest Version*, ed. Thomas Jones (Cardiff, 1955), 111, 121.

[24] *Cal. Justic. Rolls (1305–7)*, 480–1. For the fate of this female go-between, see Cosgrove, *New History of Ireland*, ii. 261 n. 5.

however, the parties at war or hostility would have to enter into
direct negotiations or parleys. Many such parleys were, doubtless,
informal and unofficial, arranged simply to mend fences and to
end recriminations so that life could continue more or less
normally. Anglo-Norman lords conducted such parleys with native
Irish or Welsh leaders in order to bring them, or to bring them
back, into a framework of acknowledged dependence, however
loose and fragile. So it was that Maurice fitz Thomas, the future
earl of Desmond (d. 1356), defended his right to negotiate (*ad
parliamentandum*) with certain Irish on the grounds that other
lords in Ireland did the same.[25] The government in Dublin might
fulminate against such unlicensed parleys in a desperate attempt to
keep alive its pious hope of 'one peace and one war',[26] but behind
the theoretical aspiration and legislative bluster, it had to come to
terms with a world which lay largely beyond its control. English
families were given permission to treat with the attackers 'in the
manner of marchers',[27] while the justiciar himself resorted to raids
and parleys alternatively and complementarily to try to deal with
the intractable problem of the native Irish.[28] Parleys could be used
to defuse feuds between local parties, as was the case in the parley
between the O'Carbraghs and the Barrys in 1307.[29] But equally
they might be arranged to try to terminate frontier disputes of
much graver political import, as in the parley between the Welsh
princeling Maredudd ab Owain and the vassals of the earl of
Pembroke in 1244 or that between Llywelyn ap Gruffudd, prince
of Wales, and the earl of Gloucester called to settle an explosive
dispute over control of upland Glamorgan in 1268.[30] Such a useful
device naturally developed its own conventions: fixed places were
appointed where parleys might be held;[31] covenants might be
entered into to ensure that the parties attended;[32] and so regular

---

[25] Quoted in Frame, *English Lordship*, 39.
[26] *Statutes . . . of Ireland*, 204–5, 278–81.
[27] Quoted in Geoffrey J. Hand, *English Law in Ireland 1290–1324* (Cambridge, 1967), 35–6.
[28] For a good example see the roll of expenses of the justiciar John Sandford, 1288–90: *Cal. of Docs. Relating to Ireland*, iii, no. 559, esp. 265–6, 271–2.
[29] *Cal. Justic. Rolls (1305–7)*, 385.
[30] *Calendar of Ancient Correspondence Concerning Wales*, ed. John Goronwy Edwards (Cardiff, 1935), 48; *Littere Wallie*, 101–3; J. B. Smith, *Llywelyn ap Gruffudd: Tywysog Cymru* (Cardiff, 1986), 241–2.
[31] Mills and bridges seem to have been particularly favoured venues for parleys.
[32] *Cal. Justic. Rolls (1305–7)*, 385.

were such parleys that, like attendance at the host, they were
regarded as a common obligation of marcher life.[33]

The success of parleys was, of course, not guaranteed. They
might be abused: under the cover of a parley at the bridge of
Carmarthen the Welsh, 'throwing off their tunics and sounding a
horn', attacked the army of the earl of Pembroke in 1233, just as
the author of *Caithréim Thoirdhealbhaigh* (*The Triumphs of
Turlogh*) noted indignantly that it was 'a fundamental principle of
that specious rascal, Thomas de Clare, to make peace when he had
just been preyed, but to prey others at once upon ratification of
peace'.[34] In such circumstances a parley might end in a bloodbath,
such as that in 1335 when thirteen of the family of Archdeacon
were slaughtered.[35] But a parley could also terminate hostilities
and pave the way to a truce or even a peace. Submissions might be
made; hostages surrendered or exchanged; herds of cows given as
compensation for past depredations; and promises made for the
future.[36] But parleys were more likely to be about mutual
concessions than unilateral submission. Accordingly a settlement
often involved the appointment of mutually acceptable arbitrators:
when the English of Louth struck an agreement with the
MacMahons the compensation was to be determined 'by the
consideration and ordinance of the natives of their marches, as
well English as Irish, to be chosen for the purpose', just as
the treaty between the earl of Ormond and Rory O'Kennedy
involved the establishment of a panel of arbitrators, four from
each side.[37] As such examples indicate, a parley could on occasion
lead to the drawing up of a formal public instrument by a public
notary.[38] Arrangement might also be made for future breaches of
such truces to be amended by mixed juries, drawn equally from

---

[33] *Cartae et alia munimenta . . . de Glamorgan*, ed. George T. Clark (6 vols.,
Cardiff, 1910), ii. 360 ('non permittatis venientes ad parliamentum vel exercitum
hospitari vel comedere'), 550.

[34] *Calendar of Ancient Correspondence*, 34; *Caithréim Thoirdhealbhaigh*, ed. and
trans. Standish H. O'Grady (2 vols., ITS 26–7, London, 1929), ii. 17–18.

[35] John Clyn, *Annals of Ireland by Friar John Clyn and Thady Dowling*, ed.
Richard Butler (Dublin, 1849), 26.

[36] *Cal. Justic. Rolls (1295–1303)*, 61.

[37] *Cal. Justic. Rolls (1304–14)*, 161; *Calendar of Ormond Deeds*, ed. Edmund
Curtis (6 vols., IMC, Dublin, 1932–3), ii, no. 34, pp. 21–2.

[38] Such as that concluded between Donal O'Hanlon and the community of
Louth in 1337: James F. Lydon, *Ireland in the Later Middle Ages* (Dublin, 1973),
50. Cf. the agreement between Llewelyn ap Gruffudd and the earl of Gloucester,
Littere Wallie, 101–3.

both parties, at a day of parley (*dies parliamenti*). Such at least is the implication of one notable example from Glamorgan.[39]

Mediation, parley, arbitration, and truce were among the mechanisms whereby two warring and militarized societies attempted to contain and curtail their own aggression in partly conquered countries. They are the frontier institutions of a society at war. Two other observations may be briefly made about these institutions. First, they were essentially local in character. Conquest in Wales and Ireland had been and remained largely 'private' and unco-ordinated; so, therefore, by definition was peace-making. Marcher lords in Wales could and did conclude their own peace treaties with native Welsh lords and princes.[40] They could ask to be, and were, exempted from any general peace into which the king of England might enter with native Welsh princes.[41] In Ireland the king in theory claimed that he alone had the right to make general peace and war and to license parleys; but in truth the situation on the ground was very different. It is little wonder that the lord of Trim claimed that he could conclude 'private' truces with the Irish who were against the king's peace, so long as the justiciar was not actually out on campaign against them.[42] Peace-making, like war, in a fragmented society was largely devolved into the hands of local *potentes*.

Secondly, it is as well to place the institutions of the frontier in the context not only of a warring society but also of two peoples who, in spite of and indeed through war, were having to come to terms with each other. The habits of the frontier—especially of frontiers which were so fluid, local, and slow in the making—make for give and take. However much central directives might preach the necessity of uniformity with metropolitan norms and the desirability of the separation of peoples, a fusion of the practices and outlook of two contiguous and overlapping societies was bound to take place. In Wales part of that fusion was formally

[39] *Cartae . . . de Glamorgan*, ii. 550.

[40] e.g. Ranulf earl of Chester concluded a peace with Llywelyn ab Iorwerth in 1218 and Roger Mortimer of Wigmore with Llywelyn ap Gruffudd in 1281: *Annales Cestrienses*, ed. Richard C. Christie (Lancashire and Cheshire Record Society 14, 1887), 50–1, *s.a.* 1218; *Littere Wallie*, 99–100.

[41] *Close Rolls of the Reign of Henry III (1231–4)* (London, 1905), 568–9; *Littere Wallie*, 54–8; John Goronwy Edwards, 'The Normans and the Welsh March', *Proceedings of the British Academy*, 42 (1956), 155–77, at 171–2.

[42] *Calendar of the Gormanston Register*, ed. James Mills and M. J. McEnery (Dublin, 1916), 181–2.

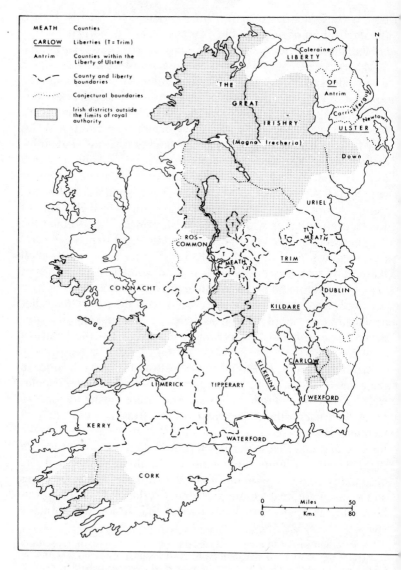

Map 7. Ireland in the Late Thirteenth Century
(*Source*: K. W. Nicholls's map in *New History of Ireland: Medieval
Ireland 1169–1534*, ed. Art Cosgrove (Oxford, 1987), p. 174.)

acknowledged in that capacious phrase 'the laws and customs of the March'; the rest can be documented in the hybrid institutions and practices so characteristic of Marcher life.[43] In Ireland the theoreticians legislated and fulminated, but recent research increasingly emphasizes that 'the differences in any region between the lordships of Anglo-Norman and of Gaelic surname . . . appeared imperceptible' and that 'the position of the Gaelic Irish chiefs' approximated ever 'closer to that of their neighbours, the Anglo-Irish barons'.[44] The habits of war and the mechanisms of peace in a fragmented frontier society are but part of a larger process of confrontation and accommodation between two societies and two cultures.

In Wales, unlike Ireland, the process of conquest was eventually completed by the end of the thirteenth century. To that extent Wales ceased to be a military frontierland. With the exception of the native revolts of 1287, 1294–5, and 1316 and of localized 'private' wars between Marcher lords (of which the Gloucester–Hereford dispute of the 1290s and the Despenser war of 1321 are the best known examples), Wales henceforth enjoyed a remarkable period of peace. Nevertheless Wales still retained for the remainder of the Middle Ages many of the features of a frontier zone. It was a conquered country where two cultures and peoples met, confronted, and adjusted to each other; it was also a country where the distinction between native and settler, Welsh and English—however artificial it often was on the ground—still remained basic in the governance of the country. Wales also still retained the vestiges of its former frontier status in the way it was ruled. After the final Edwardian conquest of 1282–3, Wales was not integrated within itself institutionally nor was it assimilated into the body politic of England. The recently conquered lands in north and west Wales were, it is true, shired after the English fashion; but no attempt was made to dismantle the virtually

---

[43] Davies, *Lordship and Society*, 443–56.
[44] Kenneth Nicholls in Cosgrove, *New History of Ireland*, ii. 422 (cf. the comments of James F. Lydon, ibid. 269); Katharine Simms, *From Kings to Warlords: The Changing Political Structure of Gaelic Ireland in the Later Middle Ages* (Woodbridge, 1987), 30. For two studies of particular topics see Gearóid MacNiocaill, 'The Interaction of Laws', in James F. Lydon (ed.), *The English in Medieval Ireland* (Dublin, 1984), 105–17, and C. A. Empey and Katharine Simms, 'The Ordinances of the White Earl and the Problem of Coign in the Later Middle Ages', *PRIA* 75 C (1975), 161–87.

independent collection of lordships in southern and eastern Wales which had been forged out of the slow process of Anglo-Norman conquest. These lordships were now known collectively as the March of Wales. They stood as the fossilized mementoes of an earlier age, monuments to the previous particularism of power in Wales and to the uncoordinated and piecemeal way in which the country had been gradually conquered by the Anglo-Normans. Their continued survival as units of lordship and power until the sixteenth century perpetuated the fragmentation of Wales; it also allows us to glimpse how virtually sovereign lordships regulated their frontier relations with each other in an age of peace as they had once done in an age of war.[45]

In the later Middle Ages the March of Wales consisted of forty or so lordships arranged in a solid bloc from north-east Wales, down the eastern border, and along the whole extent of the southern coastline. Some of these lordships were very old and had been in the making for centuries; others, especially in the north-east, were recent creations called into being by the territorial grants made by Edward I in 1282–3. Yet regardless of age and size, they all shared—and came to be regarded in the period itself as sharing—certain distinctive and, by English standards, extra-ordinary features which may be briefly itemized. They were territorially concentrated lordships; all land within them, other than church land, was held immediately or mediately of their respective lords.[46] Administratively, they were self-contained units of govern-ance, at least in their relation with the king's administration. Powers of governance within them lay in the hands of officials appointed by the lord and answerable exclusively to him. There were no coexistent, alternative, or superior sources of authority; no royal sheriff, judge, escheator, or tax-collector exercised his office within them. It is little wonder that a later commentator referred to Marcher lords as 'soveraigne governors of their tenantes and people'.[47] So indeed they were. Fiscally, likewise,

[45] Davies, *Conquest, Coexistence and Change*, 285–8, 391–4. The evidence on which the remainder of this essay is based is reviewed more fully in Davies, *Lordship and Society*, esp. ch. 11; but I have revised some of the opinions expressed there and added some new evidence.

[46] As the earl of Gloucester put it in 1290, 'all lands and tenements within the land of Glamorgan are of his demesne': *Rotuli Parliamentorum* (6 vols., London, 1767–77), i. 43.

[47] George Owen, *The Description of Pembrokeshire*, ed. Henry Owen (4 vols., Cymmrodorion Record Series 1, 1892–1936), iii. 140.

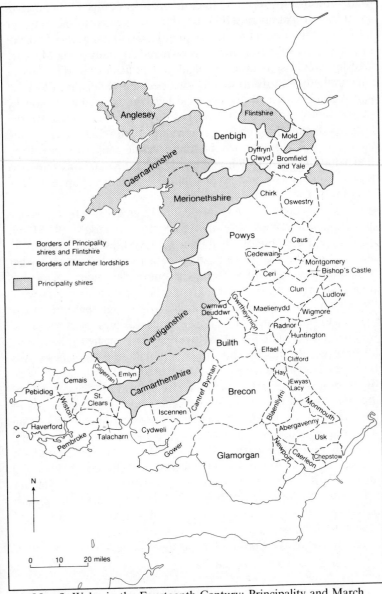

Map 8. Wales in the Fourteenth Century: Principality and March (*Source*: Rees Davies, *Conquest, Coexistence, and Change: Wales 1063–1415* (Oxford, 1987), 393

Marcher lordships were in effect independent units. Only once, in 1292, was a royal tax raised in the March; for the rest, the Marcher lords taxed their own tenants frequently and under a whole host of pretexts, but exclusively for their own ends. Finally, each Marcher lordship was a self-sufficient legal and judicial unit. The law of each individual lordship was its own peculiar amalgam of English and Welsh law, feudal practice, and local custom.[48] Jurisdictionally the immunity of the March from royal justice was expressed in the lawyer's dictum that the king's writ did not run there; but equally important is it to emphasize that there was no common supervisory judicial authority between and above the individual lordships, no jurisdiction in error, and no possibility (normally) of appeal other than to the lord's own council.

Utter fragmentation and the jealously guarded self-sufficiency of each of its lordships were, therefore, the hallmarks of the March of Wales. The men of neighbouring lordships were known as aliens, *extranei*, and treated as such. Each lordship was regarded as an autonomous unit in terms of commercial policy, economic organization, and the labour market, and vigorous measures were taken to try to preserve this autarchy.[49] A strong sense of loyalty to one's lord, lordship, and fellow tenants was promoted and those who dared to deviate from that loyalty were punished. Thus in the lordship of Bromfield and Yale a penalty of 100 marks was threatened against anyone who prosecuted a fellow tenant outside the lordship, since such behaviour was 'contrary to the customs of the country and the royal liberties and franchises of the lords of Bromfield'.[50] Such an approach was not grounded solely in seignorial jealousy and protectionism. It drew also on a very long tradition of particularism within native Welsh society and on intense and often vicious communal rivalries between neighbouring districts.[51] It was in the pursuit of such rivalries and as a defiant expression of their regality that Marcher lords in the thirteenth century vigorously defended their right to resort to 'private' wars against their neighbours to settle their disputes.

The March of Wales, therefore, is the area *par excellence* within

---

[48] Davies, 'Law of the March', esp. 10–12.

[49] Davies, *Lordship and Society*, 233–7.

[50] NLW Peniarth MS 404 D. fo. 103. For other comparable proclamations and for actual fines imposed in pursuit of such a policy, see Davies, *Lordship and Society*, 238–9.

[51] Davies, *Lordship and Society*, 241–2.

the British Isles where the uninhibited character of seignorial power and the fragmentation of authority can be most clearly studied. The problems posed by such a situation and the abuses to which it could give rise were manifold. Wanted men fled from one lordship to another to avoid prosecution; tenants in arrears with their rent or anticipating a heavy seignorial fine drove their herds and flocks to neighbouring lordships to avoid distraint; men were abducted from one lordship to another and only released on payment of a ransom; a man charged with murder might defend his refusal to reply in court simply by asserting that he was a stranger and had not been caught red-handed; while a chaplain's exemption from the jurisdiction of a Marcher court could be bluntly explained in these terms: 'he is not to reply between the two lands (viz. the lordships of Maelienydd and Clun) for any felony . . . because he is not in our jurisdiction.'[52] The March seemed to be a criminal's paradise, a land of multiple bolt-holes and loopholes. The basic procedures of medieval law-keeping—distraint, outlawry, and pledging—were subverted by the frag-mentation of judicial authority, while communal raids could be, and were, undertaken under the cloak of Marcher immunity. Indeed one might almost say that the abuses of judicial frag-mentation and immunity were institutionalized in the March by two practices. The first, disclaimer, was the practice whereby a man charged with an offence in court could disclaim the lordship of the lord of the court and thereby terminate proceedings on the grounds that the court and its lord had no jurisdiction over him.[53] The second practice, avowry, was a complementary one, whereby a lord avowed a man—in other words accepted him into his judicial protection—for a nominal sum, often no more than fourpence a year, even though he was not one of his tenants.[54]

These practices were on occasion loudly condemned by English parliaments,[55] and were eventually to be cited as a pretext for the

---

[52] *Calendar of the Patent Rolls (1327–30)* (London, 1891), 80, 82; Shropshire Record Office 552 (Clun Court Rolls) 1/10, m. 12; 1/3, m. 3.

[53] Thus a man hauled before the earl of Stafford's court in the lordship of Caus was challenged to declare whether he disclaimed the earl's lordship in full court in the presence of the steward. He did so and was promptly handed over to the bailiff of the earl of March: NLW Peniarth MS 280 D, fo. 71.

[54] For the practice of avowry in Ireland, Cosgrove, *New History of Ireland*, ii. 298.

[55] See esp. *Rotuli Parliamentorum*, iii. 508, 615–16.

abolition of Marcher franchise. Such condemnations need, however, to be placed in perspective. The abuses diagnosed in the March of Wales are those which confront any society where power and governance is dispersed and where there is no single supervisory or appellate authority. They are not a pathological condition peculiar to the March of Wales. Indeed given the essentially decentralized character of power and governance in the Middle Ages and the proliferation and vigorous defence of immunities and franchises, it is surely the evolution of a unitary 'national' jurisdiction and of a single common law which is the phenomenon which demands an explanation. In other words on a broad perspective, geographical and historical, it may well be that it is the kingdom of England rather than the March of Wales which should be classified as the exception.

Furthermore the morcellement of the March was no more than a continuation of the fragmentation of authority already prevalent in native Wales. Native Welshmen, princes and communities alike, had already addressed themselves to the problems posed by such fragmentation. So much is suggested by the use of the vernacular term *cydfod* (literally 'coexistence') to describe agreements between communities and lordships in the later Middle Ages and by the survival of texts of such agreements (*cydfodau*) in Welsh antiquarian manuscripts.[56] So much is suggested also by references in pre-Edwardian conquest documents to 'accustomed places on the borders of those parts' where disputes might be settled between neighbouring jurisdictions and to the practice whereby Welsh magnates hold pleas in the borders of their lands 'in the manner of parliaments'.[57] But it is in the fourteenth and fifteenth centuries, under the rule of English lords, that we can study in detail the procedures adopted to cope with the fragmentation of authority and jurisdiction in Wales. The evidence testifies to the existence of what is virtually an international law of the March.

There was, first, a great deal of correspondence and meetings between stewards of neighbouring lordships to defuse quarrels, exchange information, and co-ordinate action; if problems proved intractable the councils of the two lords might meet to try to sort

[56] J. B. Smith, 'Cydfodau o'r Bymthegfed Ganrif', *Bulletin of the Board of Celtic Studies*, 21 (1965–6), 309–24; 25 (1972–4), 128–34.
[57] *Calendar of Ancient Correspondence*, 95; *Calendar of Various Chancery Rolls 1277–1326* (London, 1912), 206.

them out. Through such mechanisms fines might be respited or cancelled, cases deferred, and sealed copies of a judgement given in the court of a neighbouring lordship produced as evidence.[58] A letter of 1359 from the steward of Denbigh to his colleague in the neighbouring lordship of Dyffryn Clwyd illustrates what a close working relationship could be achieved through such arrangements: lists of wanted men were exchanged and such of them as could be arrested in a neighbouring lordship were bound over to appear at the next court of the march to face the prospect of extradition.[59]

Such mutual policing and exchange of information clearly helped to counter some of the fragmentation of authority in the March, but even more important were some of the formal mechanisms commonly employed to deal with the problem. One of the most prominent of these was the letter of the march, *littera marchie* or *littera de kedevot*.[60] Its operation is best illustrated by an example: when John Bowyer appeared before the justices of the duke of Lancaster at Monmouth in 1413 he produced letters of the march from Sir John Skidmore, steward of the neighbouring lordship of Goodrich Castle, asking that he be handed over as a tenant of Lord Talbot of Goodrich Castle. Accordingly he was released into the custody of Lord Talbot's bailiff and the case against him was deferred to the next day of the march, *dies marchie*.[61] The procedures followed on this occasion were common form throughout the March. So well established was the letter of the march as a legal instrument that an exemplar of it was copied into a contemporary formulary, and parchment was bought on the assumption that several such letters would be written annually.[62] Even case-law had developed to define the occasions when a letter of the march was not admissible, notably when an offender was caught red-handed or a claimant could be proved to be a serf or holding customary land.[63] Side by side with letters of the march—

[58] All these measures can be fully documented from the Dyffryn Clwyd court rolls in the PRO.

[59] PRO Court Rolls (SC 2) 281/7, m. 22 schedule.

[60] For this alternative name PRO SC 2/219/2, m. 24, m. 29; 219/4, m. 10; 219/5, m. 9.

[61] PRO Justices Itinerant (JI) 1/1152, m 18. Cf. T. B. Pugh (ed.), *The Marcher Lordships of South Wales 1415–1536: Select Documents* (Cardiff, 1963), 59, 65.

[62] BL Royal MS A xi, fo. 11; PRO Duchy of Lancaster, Ministers' Accounts (DL 29), 633/10317 Hay.

[63] BL Royal MS A xi, fo. 11; PRO SC 2/222/5, m. 16ᵛ; Pugh, *Marcher Lordships of South Wales*, 65.

which were normally delivered in court by an accredited seignorial official rather than by the defendant—should be placed letters of safe conduct granted to Marcher tenants about to embark on a journey outside their lordship in search of stolen cattle or goods.[64] Both safe conducts and letters of the march were genuine and well-established devices to deal with some of the problems posed by the fragmentation of authority and to discriminate between those who abused such fragmentation for their own ends and bona fide tenants, travellers, and litigants.

The successful production of a letter of the march normally required a defendant to appear at the next day of the march (or love day, *dies amoris*, or day of composition, *dies composicionis*, as it was alternatively called). Such days of the march can be documented for virtually every part of the March of Wales. Indeed in the case of three lordships—Dyffryn Clwyd, Caus, and Brecon—the evidence makes it clear that march days were held with *all* their respective contiguous lordships. The only lordships which were theoretically not included in such arrangements were those of the king, for it was held that, just as the king could not perform homage to any of his subjects, so 'he could not have a march with anyone'.[65] Even that prohibition was overlooked in practice for documentary evidence makes it clear that arrangements closely akin in form and substance to days of the march were entered into by some of the communities of the royal lands in Wales.[66] Days of the march were in fact a common and regular way in which relations between the fragmented units of late medieval Wales were organized. They were held at established venues or landmarks on the borders between lordships;[67] attendance at them was obviously considered to be so regular that it could be included among the list of obligations of local burgesses; while a letter on how to claim goods at a court of the march was of such

[64] For an example of such a safe conduct see Northumberland Record Office, Swinburne (Capheaton) Collection 1/99. I owe this reference to Mr D. A. L. Morgan.

[65] *Calendar of Ancient Correspondence*, 93; *Calendar of Various Chancery Rolls*, 336; *Rotuli Parliamentorum*, i. 397; *Calendar of Ancient Petitions Relating to Wales*, ed. William Rees (Cardiff, 1975), nos. 12708, 12780, pp. 425–6, 430–1.

[66] J. B. Smith, 'The Regulation of the Frontier of Meirionnydd in the Fifteenth Century', *Journal of the Merioneth Historical Society*, 5 (1965–6), 105–11.

[67] Fords (Welsh, *rhyd*) and passes (Welsh, *bwlch*) seem to have been favourite venues.

common form that it was included in a contemporary formulary.[68] Another negative indication of how central and regular a mechanism they were in frontier relations in Wales was the fact that their suspension was regarded as tantamount to a declaration of hostilities.[69]

Days of the march were not, of course, an exclusively Welsh or even frontier phenomenon. They were one of the devices employed in medieval society generally to reduce tension and settle quarrels by arranging 'extra-curial' arbitrations and mediations.[70] In Wales the most immediate antecedents of days of the march may be found on the one hand in a well-established native tradition (referred to above) of meeting at fixed places to sort out inter-regional disputes, on the other in the practice of encouraging feudal lords (*pares*) to hold pleas on the boundaries of their fiefs instead of resorting to arms. Such indeed is the context of some of the earliest references to a day of the march in Wales: for the earl of Gloucester in 1290, as for the earl of Arundel in 1293, it was an acknowledged way of terminating discord between two lordships through the judgement of 'neighbours and mutual friends who are, as it were, justices' in the matter. It was as such an expedient for settling frontier disputes in Wales that days of the march were fully sanctioned even by Edward I.[71]

By the fourteenth century, however, days of the march were not reserved merely for such inter-lordship disputes; instead they had become a regular feature of the dispensing of justice for ordinary litigants whose homes lay in different lordships. Nevertheless they were still regarded as one of the regalities of Marcher lords and as such the right to hold them was not to be usurped by lesser men.[72]

---

[68] Cardiff Free Library, Brecon Documents, 2 (rental of May, 1340); BL Royal MS A xi, fo. 12ᵛ.

[69] See the younger Despenser's letter of Mar. 1321 in *Calendar of Ancient Correspondence*, 260.

[70] See, most recently, Michael T. Clanchy, 'Law and Love in the Middle Ages', in John Bossy (ed.), *Disputes and Settlements: Law and Human Relations in the West* (Cambridge, 1983), 47–69.

[71] T. B. Pugh (ed.), *Glamorgan County History*, iii: *The Middle Ages* (Cardiff, 1971), 592 n. 140; *Placitorum abbreviatio* (Record Commission, London, 1811), 231; *Welsh Assize Roll*, 309.

[72] Pugh, *Glamorgan County History*, iii. 307; J. B. Smith, 'Marcher Regality: *Quo Warranto* Proceedings Relating to Cantrefselyf in the Lordship of Brecon', *Bulletin of the Board of Celtic Studies*, 28 (1978–80), 267–88, esp. 251, 285; *Cartae de Glamorgan*, iii. 992 ('salvis similiter querelis que die marchie inter terrras vicinas de consuetudine terminari debent').

Their official status, as part of the machinery of Marcher governance, was further indicated by the fact that the delegation to the day of the march was normally led by one or more of the lordship's major officials—the steward or his deputy, the constable, the receiver, or a local bailiff. But the occasion was one for assuaging communal tensions as well as for sorting out official problems. So it was that the officials were accompanied by some leading tenants, *probi*, from whose ranks were chosen the mixed juries—normally six jurors from each lordship—who decided cases at the day of the march.[73] For the day of the march was to all intents and purposes a court. It is regularly referred to as such, *curia marchie*, and the judicial records make it clear that it dealt with a whole range of matters judicial (both civil and criminal) and administrative.

So firmly established were mechanisms such as letters and days of the march that it comes as no surprise to learn that written codes of agreement were drawn up to determine what general issues could be dealt with in inter-lordship meetings and how they should be treated. No contemporary record of such an agreement— known as *convencio* in Latin, *cydfod* in Welsh—survives; but the range of issues covered by such an agreement can be guessed at from entries in contemporary court rolls and from later copies of such agreements preserved in antiquarian collections. They include matters such as the treatment of fugitives, extradition of wanted men, action on distrained goods, the status of safe conducts and letters of the march, arrangements for safeguarding the status of *bona fide* migrants, and so forth. It is clear that in north Wales at least such agreements were concluded between most lordships, often at the initiative of the steward and for fixed but renewable periods.[74]

The frontier arrangements and institutions of the March of Wales in the later Middle Ages were more sophisticated, complex, and regular than those of any other part of the British Isles. This should not occasion surprise. Governmentally and judicially, Wales was much more fragmented even than English Ireland, for though there were major liberties in Ireland they were, at least in theory, subsumed under the ultimate jurisdictional authority of Dublin, bound by obedience to the English common law, subject

---

[73] For references, which could be readily extended, see Davies, *Lordship and Society*, 245–6.

[74] Smith, 'Cydfodau'; Davies, *Lordship and Society*, 247, esp. n. 70.

to common taxation, and politically answerable to a single parliament. In the March of Wales, however, there was not even the veneer of unity; rather was it a collection of virtually autonomous lordships. Each lord, as one aggrieved litigant put it, was 'virtually king and justiciar' within his lordship.[75] Only through a mutual acknowledgement of the problems and dangers that such utter fragmentation posed could solutions to them be found and accepted. How far mutual necessity was the mother of frontier institutions in the March is sometimes revealed in the records with disarming frankness: a wanted man will be handed over to the steward of Denbigh provided that in similar cases in the future the lord of Dyffryn Clwyd is guaranteed like treatment for his men; a defendant agrees to appear in his lordship's court once the plaintiff has put in an appearance in his own court; a case from Clun involving men from Knighton is deferred until it is learnt how the men of Clun were treated in the courts of Knighton.[76] Such a tit-for-tat approach may appear petty (if familiar enough from our own international relations today); but from it were eventually woven the more permanent and institutionalized mechanisms of inter-lordship relations in the March of Wales.

Those mechanisms served to establish a workable, if fragile, relationship not only between neighbouring lords and their officials but also between neighbouring communities. Much of the cross-border tension in the March, as in so many frontier societies, was born out of communal rivalries generated by issues such as cattle-rustling, disputes over grazing rights, disagreements over boundaries, or vendettas prompted by a murder and fed by a tradition of enmity. If such rivalries were to be curbed the leaders of the communities would have to be involved in the negotiations. So indeed they were. Some of the inter-lordship agreements were in fact concluded by leading representatives of the communities, not by the lords.[77] At other times lords, officials, and tenants would co-operate (as indeed they did at days of the march). Thus it was by the counsel of the earl of Arundel and the lord of Stapleton

---

[75] *Cartae . . . de Glamorgan*, ii. 554.
[76] PRO SC 2/216/4, m. 34; 219/3, m. 10; 220/1, m. 15; Shropshire Record Office 552/1/19, m. 1.
[77] See the *cydfodau* published in Smith, 'Cydfodau', or the agreement of 1451 between 'the gentlemen, tenants, commoners and residents' of Elfael and Aberedw on the one hand and Hay, Blaenllyfni, and associated lordships on the other, NLW, Kentchurch Court, no. 1027.

and with the consent of the tenants that an inter-lordship feud, triggered by a vicious murder, was terminated in Clun by a *concordia* in 1401.[78]

It is this fumbling search for a *modus vivendi*, between units of power as well as between natives and settlers, which is one of the major motifs in the histories of medieval Wales and Ireland. The histories of both countries sit uneasily with some of the basic presuppositions of English historiography, notably its centralist point of departure in documentation and approach and its bias (all the stronger for being unspoken and unexamined) in favour of strong government, legal uniformity, and direct and clear lines of command and authority. Such a historiography finds it difficult to come to terms with societies which are institutionally fragmented, fluid in their frontiers, multiple in their loyalties, cultures, and laws, and normally well beyond the reach of the practical authority of metropolitan government. Such, however, are most medieval frontier societies. What we witness in Ireland are the frontier conventions devised within such a society to cope, however imperfectly, with the almost intolerable tensions of a bloody, piecemeal, and uncompleted conquest. In Wales similar institutions were eventually regularized and refined to cope with the problems of a fragmented society in an age of peace. It may, therefore, be not altogether inappropriate to hope that the evidence from both countries may have more than a local interest and that it might contribute to an understanding of medieval frontier societies in general.

[78] Shropshire Record Office 552/1/34, m. 4. In 1451 the steward of Brecon was ordered to compel the tenants of Hay to make restitution to their neighbours of Whitney and Eardisley 'with ye advise and help of other gentlemen of both countreis that rest and peace may be had between our lordships', NLW Peniarth MS 280 D, fo. 50.

5

Military Service in the Lordship of Ireland 1290–1360: Institutions and Society on the Anglo-Gaelic Frontier

ROBIN FRAME

The English king's Lordship of Ireland in the Middle Ages was a land of constant, small-scale war.[1] This was a characteristic inherited from the Irish past, where tribute-warfare was endemic, and perpetuated because of the incompleteness of the conquest and the limited effectiveness of the Dublin government. The pastoral emphasis of Irish rural society ensured that cattle-raiding was a chief feature of the military life. It was a way of pursuing local disputes; on a grander scale, it was a means by which Gaelic Irish and Anglo-Irish magnates asserted their power by exacting submission and hostages and imposing services. The 'official' wars, with which this paper is concerned, were mostly of a similar type: the normal aim of the king's ministers who conducted them was not so much to occupy or (as was more to the point in the later Middle Ages) reoccupy land, as to exercise lordship.[2]

There is a precious, and still neglected, means of entry into this world of frontier warfare. At the start of the present century voluminous records of the medieval Dublin government still survived. They were destroyed in 1922 at the beginning of the Irish civil war, when the Four Courts in Dublin were set ablaze. Ironically, no small proportion of the parchment that went up in smoke was filled with commissions, payments, accounts, and other

[1] I am indebted to Professor Michael Prestwich for helpful comments on an earlier version of this paper.
[2] For Irish warfare in the context of Gaelic society, see Katharine Simms, 'Warfare in the Medieval Gaelic Lordships', *Irish Sword*, 12 (1975–6), 98–108; ead., *From Kings to Warlords: The Changing Political Structure of Gaelic Ireland in the Later Middle Ages* (Woodbridge, 1987), chs. 7–8; and, in the context of the Lordship of Ireland, Robin Frame, 'English Officials and Irish Chiefs in the Fourteenth Century', *EHR* 90 (1975), 748–77; id., 'War and Peace in the Medieval Lordship of Ireland', in James F. Lydon (ed.), *The English in Medieval Ireland* (Dublin, 1984), 118–41. Compare also the comments of Rees Davies in this volume.

types of material relating to the military activities once directed from Dublin Castle: war had helped to generate the records it was later to consume. But not everything was lost. Some records had been published; some had been transcribed or calendared in manuscript between the sixteenth century and 1922; some can be recovered thanks to bureaucratic processes that deposited duplicate copies at Westminster. The years from about 1290 to about 1360 are specially rich in surviving material. This period also has a more natural unity, in that the Dublin government was faced by a continual military challenge but was left, by kings who were preoccupied by campaigns in Scotland and France, to conduct warfare from shrinking Irish resources; from 1361 to 1399, by contrast, English-financed expeditionary forces were sent to Ireland, to some extent altering military goals and possibilities.[3]

As maps 9 and 10 show, Dublin's military arm stretched reasonably wide. If it did not embrace the whole island, it reached far beyond a cramped eastern 'Pale'. Moreover, even districts where government rarely intervened directly lay within the orbit of Anglo-Irish magnates who were normally reliable. The distribution of military activity arose from a combination of factors, among them the interplay of physical and political geography: the frequent royal expeditions in Leinster, for example, reflect the closeness of Dublin to the predominantly Irish uplands of Wicklow and midland bogs. It might be argued, of course, that documents left by a colonial government, operating along English administrative lines and charged with upholding English law, can cast only a distant and uncertain light on Ireland's complex society. But perhaps the amount they do disclose is the more striking for that very reason. Moreover in Ireland as elsewhere the military sphere is one of the most revealing areas where men consorted together, conventions arose, and institutions were shaped.[4] Its significance is apparent if we look in two directions: towards England, from

[3] See Philomena Connolly, 'The Financing of English Expeditions to Ireland, 1361–76', in James F. Lydon (ed.), *England and Ireland in the Later Middle Ages: Essays in Honour of Jocelyn Otway-Ruthven* (Dublin, 1981), 104–21; James F. Lydon, 'Richard II's Expeditions to Ireland', *RSAIJn.* 93 (1963), 135–49.

[4] See e.g. Robert I. Burns, *Islam under the Crusaders: Colonial Survival in the Thirteenth-century Kingdom of Valencia* (Princeton, 1973), chs. 12–14; and, for a general perspective, Robert Bartlett, 'Technique militaire et pouvoir politique, 900–1300', *Annales: Économies, sociétés, civilisations*, 41 (1986), 1135–59.

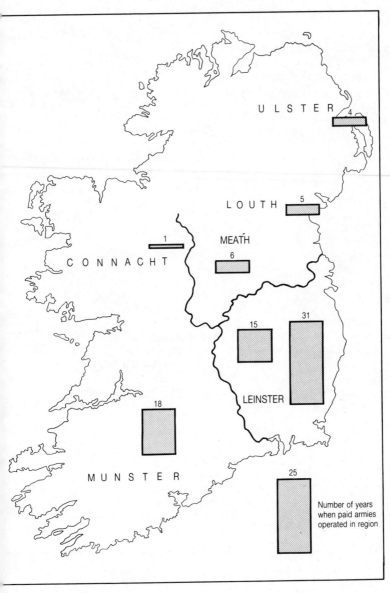

Map 9. Expeditions by Paid Armies in Ireland 1295–1360

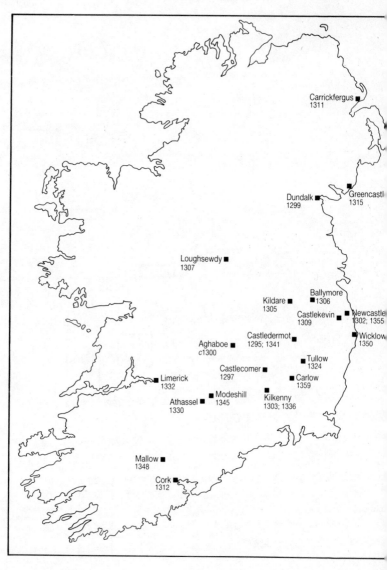

Map 10. Summonses of the Knight Service in Ireland 1295–1359
(*Source*: based on A. J. Otway-Ruthven, Royal Service in Ireland',
RSAIJn. 98, (1968), 43–4)

where the Lordship of Ireland derived its formal institutions; and then towards the culturally mixed world of the Irish frontier itself.

Ireland had been apportioned to its aristocratic conquerors in return for knight service. The circumstances and timing of this development were crucial. It occurred under the firm control of the English monarchy, and at a period—roughly 1170–1240—when English custom had hardened. As a result, the scheme of tenures and obligations in Ireland mirrored that of England almost exactly.[5] The two countries continued in step owing to the insistence of thirteenth-century kings that English law was to be observed in their new Lordship. Ireland was an overseas territory to which the metropolis exported its institutions, and did so self-consciously at least from the time of King John.[6] But when we move away from legal forms and look instead at the military importance of feudal obligations, contrasts are at once apparent. The sharpest is also the most simple: in England feudal service and its monetary equivalent, scutage, were to all intents and purposes obsolete after 1327; in Ireland the knight service was summoned frequently throughout the thirteenth and fourteenth centuries, and beyond.[7] The chief reason for the divergence is scarcely mysterious: it lies in the incidence of warfare within Ireland. Feudal service, for all its limitations, was of value in internal war; and there could be no doubt about men's duty to contribute towards operations that were near at hand and unambiguously defensive in purpose. Ireland experienced neither the friction caused by royal attempts to exploit feudal obligations for overseas campaigns, nor the

[5] A. J. Otway-Ruthven, 'Knight Service in Ireland', *RSAIJn.* 89 (1959), 1–15, is the classic study. For a particular case-study see the chapter by Robert Bartlett in this volume.

[6] See Geoffrey J. Hand, *English Law in Ireland 1290–1324* (Cambridge, 1967), 1–5; Paul Brand, 'Ireland and the Literature of the Early Common Law', *Irish Jurist*, NS 16 (1981), 95–113.

[7] A. J. Otway-Ruthven, 'Royal Service in Ireland', *RSAIJn.* 98 (1968), 37–46; Steven G. Ellis, 'Taxation and Defence in Late Medieval Ireland: The Survival of Scutage', *RSAIJn.* 107 (1977), 5–28. Cf. N. B. Lewis, 'The Summons of the English Feudal Levy, 5 April 1327', in T. A. Sandquist and M. R. Powicke (eds.), *Essays in Medieval History Presented to Bertie Wilkinson* (Toronto, 1969), 236–49; Michael Prestwich, 'Cavalry Service in Early Fourteenth-Century England', in John Gillingham and James C. Holt (eds.), *War and Government in the Middle Ages: Essays in Honour of J. O. Prestwich* (Woodbridge, 1984), 147–58, at 148–52; J. J. N. Palmer, 'The Last Summons of the Feudal Army in England (1385)', *EHR* 83 (1968), 771–5.

drastic reductions in *servitia debita* that took place in England
during the thirteenth century, making knight service of little value
to the Crown.[8]

In Ireland the feudal obligation undoubtedly on occasion
produced troops. In 1288 the justiciar summoned the military
tenants of the four lordships of Leinster to serve against the Irish
of Offaly and Leix. The service, which as in England was owed for
forty days, arrived at Kildare on 9 September. Each contingent,
under its seneschal, was assigned a sector of the marches to guard.
The justiciar was then called away to deal with a crisis further
south, and had to rush back in order to reach Leinster before the
feudal service ended. He arrived in time, and by 21 October had
replaced the levies with paid guards.[9] In Ireland as elsewhere
customary restrictions curtailed the value of knight service; none
the less in a land of localized and spasmodic war it had its uses.
Although in the early fourteenth century the government may
have taken some services entirely in money,[10] corporal service did
not die out. A writ calling the knight service to Limerick in 1332
ordered the exchequer to levy it in cash—but only 'from those who
do not come there, as the custom is'.[11] A Dublin tenant and some
of the Leinster forces made the journey and were exempted from
scutage.[12] Indeed on this expedition such service may have been
crucial: the paid force did not rise above 79 men, a tiny number
even for an Irish army; yet annals talk of a major campaign
involving the earl of Ormond and other lords.[13] It is probable that

[8] James C. Holt, *The Northerners* (Oxford, 1961), 88–92, 98–102; Michael
Prestwich, *War, Politics and Finance under Edward I* (London, 1972), 75–7; Ivor J.
Sanders, *Feudal Military Service in England* (Oxford, 1956), 59–90. Cf. Otway-
Ruthven, 'Knight Service', 4. The position in Ireland regarding the latter question
needs further study (Otway-Ruthven, 'Royal Service', 39 and n. 17).

[9] *Calendar of Documents Relating to Ireland (1171–1307)*, ed. H. S. Sweetman
(5 vols., London, 1875–86), iii, no. 559, pp. 265–7.

[10] PROI EX 2/1, p. 67; *Rotulorum patentium et clausorum cancellariae Hiberniae
calendarium* (Dublin, 1828), p. 9, nos. 106–7, p. 11, nos. 410–11.

[11] *Parliaments and Councils of Mediaeval Ireland*, ed. H G. Richardson and
G. O. Sayles (IMC, Dublin, 1947), 10. The summons in 1355 was in similar form
(NLI MS 2, fo. 237).

[12] *DKR Ire.* 43 (1912), 46; 44 (1912), 21; A. J. Otway-Ruthven, *A History of
Medieval Ireland* (London, 1968), 103 and note.

[13] *DKR Ire.* 43 (1912), 56; John Clyn, *Annals of Ireland by Friar John Clyn and
Thady Dowling*, ed. Richard Butler (Dublin, 1849), 24. Evidence from 1348, 1355,
and 1384 confirms that the assembly-points continued to have a real military
significance (PRO E 101/241/16; *Rotulorum patentium . . . calendarium*, p. 57, no.

a feudal summons, accompanied by a general call to arms, mobilized a sizeable force, but one that scarcely troubled the exchequer. The vitality of the tradition of personal service is hardly surprising. The knights and esquires of Ireland inhabited a warlike environment and were likely to fight on one basis or another. When a campaign was accompanied by a feudal summons, the active military tenant may well have preferred to serve rather than to pay scutage. In 1342 a parliamentary assembly at Kilkenny complained to Edward III about royal ministers who 'compound in money for the services that ought to be done in person, to the great oppression of the people'.[14] There may in fact have been a drift towards personal service in the years after 1315, when military emergency coincided with economic hardship.

It would be misleading, however, to dwell too much on the evidence of corporal service, for there is no doubt that feudal summonses chiefly meant money. We still lack a thorough study of Irish scutages in this period. But two things seem clear. The first is the close connection of scutages with specific campaigns. It is true that in the thirteenth and early fourteenth centuries the proceeds of the knight service might be awarded to magnates; but such grants were related to real, though devolved, military under-takings, and anyway they ceased around 1315.[15] The relationship between scutages and royal expeditions was becoming tighter in the fourteenth century. The second point is that scutages brought in sums that were not negligible in the context of Irish wars. A scutage proclaimed in 1307 raised £388; and if the average yield in the years 1320–60 was around £200, the fall was in step with the general decline in Dublin's collecting power at the same period.[16] To a historian of English military finance such sums will appear laughably small. But we must adjust our sights. Irish campaigns were usually brief affairs, involving paid forces that rarely rose above 1,000 men. £200 would have covered the cost of a modest expedition. The real inadequacy of scutage lay in the fact that

134, p. 59, no. 16, p. 62, no. 111; 'Lord Chancellor Gerrard's Notes of his Report on Ireland', ed. Charles McNeill, *Analecta Hibernica*, 2 (1931), 93–291, at 289–90).

[14] *Statutes . . . of the Parliament of Ireland: King John to Henry V*, ed. Henry F. Berry (Dublin, 1907), 358–61.

[15] See Otway-Ruthven, 'Knight Service', 7.

[16] PRO E 101/235/6, 15 (1307); E 101/238/15 (1324: £185); E 101/241/4 (1341: £214); E 101/241/17, 20 (1348: £216). Cf. H. G. Richardson and G. O. Sayles, 'Irish Revenue, 1278–1384', *PRIA* 62 C (1962), 87–100, at 93–5, 99–100.

there were so many more expeditions than scutages: over the period 1320–60, for example, there was scarcely a season without a campaign, but only one expedition in six saw a scutage. Presumably more frequent proclamations of the knight service would have been politically untenable.

The importance of the feudal obligation, whether as a source of manpower or money, should not be exaggerated. But it is an informative subject. Irish conditions ensured the survival of feudal service as an integral part of the Lordship's structure; they also gave it a distinctive quality. If the identity of English and Irish institutions here seems little more than skin-deep, the same is true in other areas of military and fiscal organization.

Alongside the feudal tradition existed the general duty of the king's subjects to serve in the defence of the Lordship. This was a version of something universal in the medieval West, but Ireland received it in its English guise. In England freemen aged between 15 and 60 were obliged to assist in local defence; they were also liable to be selected for service beyond their localities, normally at the king's wages. A succession of ordinances, from the Assize of Arms of 1181 to the Statute of Winchester of 1285, had established a schedule of arms, graded according to wealth in lands and goods, which men were expected to possess.[17] In Ireland the obligation rested on the same foundations; in 1333 the inhabitants of County Dublin were to be assessed to arms 'according to the ancient ordinance and to the Statute of Winchester'.[18] The Statute had been sent for observance in Ireland only in 1308.[19] But an Irish statute of 1297 had already stated that every man worth £20 in land was to have a barded horse together with the appropriate arms; its vagueness about the obligations of the less wealthy probably indicates, not that their duties were uncertain, but that they were well known.[20] This is confirmed by an ordinance of arms promulgated by Geoffrey de Geneville, lord of Trim in Meath from 1252 to 1307, which broadly follows the pattern of English writs of arms, showing the familiarity in Ireland of the detailed assessments that the 1297 statute takes for granted.[21]

---

[17] William Stubbs, *Select Charters* (9th edn., Oxford, 1913), 183–4 (1181), 362–5 (1242), 464–6 (1285); Michael Powicke, *Military Obligation in Medieval England* (Oxford, 1962), chs. 3, 5, 7–8, 10.
[18] PROI RC 8/17, pp. 359–60.
[19] *Statutes . . . of Ireland: John to Henry V*, 244–57.   [20] Ibid. 200–1.
[21] *Calendar of the Gormanston Register*, ed. James Mills and M. J. McEnery (for RSAI, Dublin, 1916), 182.

Views of arms and arrays of the type prescribed by the Statute of Winchester took place in the parts of Ireland responsive to royal authority. Initially the province of the sheriffs, in time they passed into the control of the *custodes pacis*, who were, at least from the 1340s, appointed regularly throughout the counties and liberties of Leinster, Meath, and Munster. These Irish keepers of the peace sprang from the same root as the English, who also enforced the Statute of Winchester. But differences are at least as striking as similarities. In England supervision of the local peace-keeping system came to be only one item in their much wider competence as they developed into justices of the peace. The Irish keepers too gained additional tasks, and were sometimes called justices in the fifteenth century. But at the centre of their activities remained assessments to arms and arrays, together with the exercise of a local military captaincy involving both leadership in war and powers of negotiation and truce-making: the separation that took place in England at an early date of quasi-judicial functions from those appropriate to wardens of the marches or conservators of truces did not occur in Ireland.[22]

The universal military obligation drew its significance from the priorities of the Irish frontier. It was fundamental to defence at local level. For instance in 1316, when there was serious unrest among the Irish of Wicklow, the government set about mobilizing the population in south Dublin. Commissioners were appointed to speed the levying of some thirty men in each vill between the River Liffey and the mountains and four or six from smaller districts. Those chosen were to serve at the cost of the rest. They were placed under the command of William Comyn, whom the Dublin annalist describes as a *custos pacis*.[23] Similar practices can be seen on other occasions, and the system seems clear: all (including the Gaelic Irish living within the Lordship[24]) were liable for assessment according to their wealth; a proportion would be chosen to serve

[22] Robin Frame, 'The Judicial Powers of the Medieval Irish Keepers of the Peace', *Irish Jurist*, NS 2 (1967), 308–26; *Historic and Municipal Documents of Ireland*, ed. John T. Gilbert (RS, 1870), 378; *Statutes . . . of Ireland: John to Henry V*, 378–81, 382–5, 448–9, 450–1, 454–5. Cf. Alan Harding, 'The Origins and Early History of the Keeper of the Peace', *TRHS*, 5th ser., 10 (1960), 85–109; Bertha H. Putnam, 'The Transformation of the Keepers of the Peace into the Justices of the Peace, 1327–1380', *TRHS*, 4th ser., 12 (1929), 19–48.

[23] *Historic and Municipal Documents*, 375–7; *Chartularies of St Mary's Abbey Dublin*, ed. John T. Gilbert (2 vols., RS, 1884–6), ii. 297, 350, 351–2.

[24] PROI RC 8/6, p. 186; PROI EX 1/1, m. 45.

with the financial support of the others.[25] There is, of course, nothing peculiar to Ireland in such arrangements. But familiar habits were adapted to a particular context of highly localized war.

Given the conditions that obtained in Ireland, we might also expect the general obligation to have been a main source of manpower for royal armies. Yet the presence of levies on campaigns is oddly hard to trace. In England there were two main elements in fourteenth-century armies: the retinues of the magnates, and the contingents of the shires and boroughs, both of which appear in the records of the exchequer and wardrobe. The accounts of paymasters in Ireland, however, usually list only retinues. The elusiveness of levies almost certainly springs from the fact that they were unpaid, or at least not paid by the central government. Their presence was brought about through summonses quite different from those of the knight service. In 1345, for example, it was proclaimed that 'all lieges of the lord king, whatever their status, should come before the justiciar at Cashel, to follow the king's banner and to hear and perform whatever else should be demanded of them on the king's behalf.'[26] By the mid-fourteenth century there is evidence of the discharge of the obligation through the provision of wages locally. In 1358 County Kilkenny undertook to pay for 272 men who were to join the justiciar on campaign and grants of a set number of troops for a set time were also made at the same period by other counties in both Leinster and Munster.[27] Towns also met their responsibilities in this form: in 1352–3 the city of Cork paid six months' wages for 160 troops serving on expeditions in south-west Ireland.[28] That the outlines of such arrangements were far from novel is shown by references in Edward I's time to aids granted by counties and liberties to help pay for armies operating in their vicinities.[29] It is

[25] As in south Dublin in 1355 (*Rotulorum patentium . . . calendarium*, p. 55, no. 29, p. 56, nos. 34–5, p. 57, nos. 132–3, p. 62, no. 108). The exact means by which the obligation was calculated and applied awaits thorough study.

[26] G. O. Sayles (ed.), 'The Legal Proceedings against the First Earl of Desmond', *Analecta Hibernica*, 23 (1966), 1–47, at 26. For similar summonses in 1289, 1342, and 1372, see *Cal. of Docs. Relating to Ireland*, iii, no. 559, p. 272; NLI MS 13, Part A, fos. 339–41; *Parliaments and Councils*, 50. Cf. the comments on the virtually cashless Scottish military system in Alexander Grant, *Independence and Nationhood: Scotland 1306–1469* (London, 1984), 34–5, 154–6.

[27] *Rotulorum patentium . . . calendarium*, p. 74, nos. 64–5. Cf. p. 65, nos. 41–2, p. 72, no. 10. [28] PROI RC 8/27, p. 27–9.

[29] e.g. *DKR Ire.* 36 (1904), 72, 74; 37 (1905), 28; 38 (1906), 101; 39 (1907), 24.

clear, in short, that the general obligation played an important role, and in a manner adapted to a land where internal war was endemic.

We have strayed across the, barely perceptible, border with a third aspect of the Lordship's institutional structure: taxation. Between the 1290s and the 1370s Ireland saw the development of parliamentary taxation, in the form of subsidies assented to by knights of the shire and burgesses of the chief towns. At first such taxes were related to the king's military needs in Scotland or elsewhere, but from the 1340s they were sought to fund the war-effort within Ireland. Despite some differences (the Irish subsidy was assessed on the ploughland rather than on movables, and representatives of the lower clergy continued to sit in Parliament in Ireland) the story might appear to have much in common with that of taxation in England at the same period.

Such a conclusion is, however, in important respects misleading. Those who have discussed taxation in medieval Ireland have all stressed that its most distinctive feature was the frequency and importance of taxes raised locally.[30] Paradoxically, and no doubt because concern with taxation has tended to be a by-product of interest in Parliament, the Irish local subsidy awaits its historian. Nevertheless it is clear that the divergence between England and Ireland was specially wide and significant in the fiscal area. England was unusual in the unity and uniformity of its fiscal system. By the reign of Edward III there was little likelihood of grants being obtained through separate negotiations with individual counties; military obligations too were being drawn within the matrix of national consent.[31] The closest approach to local taxation may be the informal arrangements made in the far north to buy off the Scottish raiders in the time of Edward II.[32] The kingdom was taxed as a whole (though the north might be

---

[30] H. G. Richardson and G. O. Sayles, *The Irish Parliament in the Middle Ages* (Philadelphia, 1952), 51, 114–18; Joseph R. Strayer and George Rudisill, jun., 'Taxation and Community in Wales and Ireland, 1272–1327', *Speculum*, 29 (1954), 410–16; James F. Lydon, 'William of Windsor and the Irish Parliament', *EHR* 80 (1965), 252–67, at 256.

[31] G. L. Harriss, *King, Parliament and Public Finance in Medieval England to 1369* (Oxford, 1975), 87–97, 383–400; W. N. Bryant, 'The Financial Dealings of Edward III with the County Communities, 1330–1360', *EHR* 83 (1968), 760–71.

[32] E. L. G. Stones (ed.), *Anglo-Scottish Relations 1174–1328* (Oxford, 1965), no. 37, pp. 288–91 [144–5]; Jean Scammell, 'Robert I and the North of England', *EHR* 73 (1958), 385–403, esp. 396–401.

exempted in practice[33]) and the taxation was directed towards the financing of war beyond its frontiers.

In Ireland too taxation and war were closely related. One root of the local subsidy was the translation of local defence obligations into monetary terms. A moment ago we encountered William Comyn as commander of a force composed of men selected in the south Dublin area, who were supported by the contributions of their fellows. Later in 1316 he appears leading a troop of 140 maintained by a subsidy assessed on County Dublin generally; the rate was carefully varied, so that the northern half paid 2s. a carucate, while the south (whose responsibility was greater) paid 3s. 4d.[34] An example from 1358 brings out the assumptions that lay behind this type of arrangement with special clarity. The government ordered the collection in County Kildare of a subsidy that had been granted by the earl of Kildare and the community of the county to pay the wages of a force of 624 raised to defend it against O'More of Leix. The troops were to serve initially for a fortnight, and after that for so long as necessity required. The cost was to be met by a levy, in cash or supplies, of 40d. a week on every ploughland and everyone with goods worth £6. Those actually serving in the force at their own expense were exempted.[35] Nine days later the collection of the subsidy was cancelled, since peace had been made with the O'Mores 'by assent of the said county and of the community of County Carlow'.[36] War taxation, and war and peace generally, were being handled at local level, though under central supervision; if we wished to be pompous, we might identify the doctrines of *necessitas* and *cessante causa cessat effectus* strutting upon this tiny Irish stage.

The smallness of the arena does not mean that the fiscal system lacked complexity. In 1306 an arrangement was made in the justiciar's court, involving John fitz Thomas, lord of Offaly and future first earl of Kildare, and his Irish client Fyn O'Dempsey. Fyn was to fight other Irish of the Kildare area and for this purpose John would provide him with ten horsemen for ten weeks, at a cost of £23. Half of this sum was to come from the proceeds of a

---

[33] James F. Willard, *Parliamentary Taxes on Personal Property 1290 to 1334* (Cambridge, Mass., 1934), 122–5.

[34] *Historic and Municipal Documents*, 380–3: the subsidy was said to be 'de assensu communitatis comitatus nostri Dublin' (381).

[35] NLI MS 3, fo. 26; *Rotulorum patentium . . . calendarium*, p. 75, no. 92.

[36] *Rotulorum patentium . . . calendarium*, p. 69, no. 57.

scutage proclaimed at Kildare in the previous year; the rest would be found by the community of Kildare. Six months later, when John and Fyn had succeeded in beheading O'Dunn and other 'Irish felons', the county assented to the payment of a reward of £40. John also received an additional grant to help him garrison his exposed castle of Geashill in Offaly. Part of the money was to come from the Dublin exchequer; part was to be assessed on the county, but the frontier areas of Carbury and Tethmoy, adjacent to Offaly, were to be exempted.[37] All this is the smallest of small beer; yet it is not without sophistication. Money was coming from the treasury, from feudal taxation, from impositions on the county with at least a measure of local consent. There was interaction between the lord and the county, between different areas of the county, between lord, county, and the Gaelic districts—and between all of those and central government.

The intimate relation between the habit of local taxation and the prevalence of regionalized warfare seems clear. Fiscal horizons were shaped by conditions which also imparted a distinctive emphasis to the institutions Ireland shared with England. This is an obvious point, but one that may still need to be stressed. Historians of the Lordship sometimes appear dazzled by the power and centralization of the English kingdom, and bowed down by the weight of English historiographical traditions. From the standpoint of the historian of the state, Ireland may indeed seem to have retained an antique feudalism and an underdeveloped system of taxation, but these characteristics need to be seen in their own military and political context, not measured against a model of acceptable development to which England conforms, but Ireland does not. My own comment that the Irish *custodes pacis* 'could not become justices of the peace in the normal [*sic*] sense . . . without losing their anachronistic [*sic*] military functions' seems, in retrospect, a perfect example of the pitfalls.[38]

It is no accident, despite the disparity in scale, that Ireland's military and fiscal structure is sometimes reminiscent less of England than of France, especially the war-torn and heavily regionalized France of the 1340s and 1350s.[39] It has recently been

---

[37] *Cal. Justic. Rolls (1305–7)*, 215–16, 271.
[38] Frame, 'Judicial Powers', 326.
[39] John B. Henneman, *Royal Taxation in Fourteenth-Century France: The Development of War Financing 1322–1356* (Princeton, 1971), 320–9; id., *Royal*

shown, too, how unitary fiscal arrangements within the small area of English Normandy a century later splintered in the face of disjointed border war.[40] The picture of an England with a single fiscal and military system is, of course, itself a caricature: a visitor to the north, or even to the coastal counties, during the 1340s would soon have been aware of the joins that could show under special stresses.[41] But in broad terms the comparison holds. England and Ireland offer the possibility of following the variant development over a long period of a common institutional inheritance in contrasting settings: on the one hand an ancient and unified kingdom geared for outward war; on the other a newer land, politically far less coherent, where military energies were expended locally, with profound consequences for government, lordship, and community.

This is to take a very lofty view. From a more mundane standpoint what we have been examining amounts to some of the ways in which expeditions were funded and armies topped up with manpower. Central to the government's military activities were paid forces, and evidence of their composition survives in abundance. Just as royal campaigns covered a fair proportion of Ireland, so the capacity to recruit ranged widely in both a geographical and a social sense. The dry-as-dust accounts of military paymasters offer a window through which many aspects of the Lordship may be glimpsed.

The accounts divide the troops into three main classes: men-at-arms (knights and other heavy cavalry); hobelars (spearmen with the small horses or 'hobins' for which Ireland was noted); and foot. The categories are precisely those found in English armies of the 1330s, after the hobelar had been adopted into English warfare by Edward I, and before he was displaced by the mounted archer in the early years of the Hundred Years War.[42] However,

Taxation in Fourteenth-Century France: The Captivity and Ransom of John II, 1356–1370 (Philadelphia, 1976), 283–90.

[40] C. T. Allmand, *Lancastrian Normandy 1415–1450: The History of a Medieval Occupation* (Oxford, 1983), 181–2.

[41] James Campbell, 'England, Scotland and the Hundred Years War', in J. R. Hale, J. R. L. Highfield, and Beryl Smalley (eds.), *Europe in the Late Middle Ages* (London, 1965), 184–216, at 192–3; Herbert J. Hewitt, *The Organization of War under Edward III 1338–62* (Manchester, 1966), ch. 1.

[42] Albert E. Prince, 'The Army and the Navy', in James F. Willard and William A. Morris (eds.), *The English Government at Work 1327–1336*, i (Cambridge, Mass.,

once more appearances are deceptive. Whereas in English retinues and armies of the central third of the fourteenth century heavy cavalry and mounted infantry tended to be roughly equal in number,[43] in Ireland, as Table 1 shows, hobelars outnumbered men-at-arms by anything from 2:1 to 10:1, the ratio being on average about 4.5:1. Although some armies did contain significant numbers of men-at-arms,[44] and nothing suggests that conventional military expressions of status were losing their hold on the upper classes,[45] there can be no doubt that hobelars were ideal for the cattle-rustling in rough country that accounted for so much of military action in Ireland. The Trim tariff of arms, which imposed the duty to own horses on men with only five marks in goods, hints at the importance of small mounts.[46]

Another marked difference was in the character of the infantry. Not until 1337 do archers (*sagittarii*) appear in the accounts.[47] Thereafter they remain few in number, are always distinguished from the ordinary foot, and often seem to have belonged (as the even scarcer mounted archers invariably did) to the retinues some justiciars brought from England with them. This cannot mean that the common foot-soldier knew nothing of archery. Bows and arrows were used by Anglo-Irish and Gaelic-Irish alike, and the Trim document insists that all with goods worth half a mark should have a bow and a sheaf of arrows.[48] The distinction was between longbowmen after the English fashion (who in the fifteenth century were scarce even in the eastern counties), and foot who

1940), 332–93, at 338–41; James F. Lydon, 'The Hobelar: An Irish Contribution to Medieval Warfare', *Irish Sword*, 2 (1954–6), 12–16.

[43] Albert E. Prince, 'The Strength of English Armies in the Reign of Edward III', *EHR* 46 (1931), 353–71, at 354–8, 360–2, 363–4, 367–8.

[44] As can be seen from Table 1. In 1317 the justiciar was able to muster 220 men-at-arms out of a total force of 920 (Robin Frame, 'Select Documents xxxvii: The Campaign against the Scots in Munster, 1317', *Irish Historical Studies*, 24 (1984–5), 361–72, at 364). The relative heaviness of 'heavy cavalry' in Ireland is a matter that requires further study, paying proper attention to region and period; the 14th-century Anglo-Irish man-at-arms in the south and east should not be confused with the bare-legged, saddleless horseman familiar from later sources.

[45] Robin Frame, 'Power and Society in the Lordship of Ireland, 1272–1377', *Past and Present*, 76 (1977), 3–33, at 31.

[46] *Calendar of the Gormanston Register*, 182.

[47] PROI RC 8/21, pp. 28–30; RC 8/22, pp. 63–6.

[48] *Calendar of the Gormanston Register*, 182. Cf. *Chartularies of St. Mary's*, ii. 340; *Annals of Connacht (Annála Connacht)*, ed. A. Martin Freeman (Dublin, 1944), 296–7; *Cal. Justic. Rolls (1295–1303)*, 171, 186, 228, 350–1, and *1305–7*, 43, 128, 136, 479, 489, 514.

TABLE I. *Some Paid Armies in Ireland 1308–1358*

		Men-at-arms	Hobelars	Foot	Mounted archers	Foot archers	Total
1308	Leinster	16	161	628	0	0	805
1329	Leinster	78	291	285	0	0	654
1329	Meath	89	217	72	0	0	378
1330	Munster	158	340	224	0	0	722
1332	Leinster	124	561	741	0	0	1,426
1338	Leinster	75	137	248	0	10	470
1342	Meath	24	164	359	0	16	563
1342	Leinster	14	120	347	0	14	495
1344	Leinster	89	166	228	128	77	688
1345	Munster	121	623	1,190	68	28	2,030
1348	Munster	34	103	401	26	50	614
1352	Munster	16	96	443	15	0	570
1353	Leinster	41	351	604	15	0	1,011
1354	Leinster	60	393	633	22	0	1,108
1358	Leinster	6	243	610	0	0	859

Sources: The table is based on: Philomena Connolly, 'An Account of Military Expenditure in Leinster, 1308', *Analecta Hibernica*, 30 (1982), 1–5, at 4–5; *DKR Ire.* 43 (1912), 28–9, 43–4, 54–5; PROI RC 8/15, pp. 473–7; NLI MS 761, pp. 35, 139–40; PROI RC 8/22, pp. 63–6, 297–304; *DKR Ire.* 53 (1926), 44–5, 45–6; Robin Frame, 'The Justiciarship of Ralph Ufford: Warfare and Politics in Fourteenth-Century Ireland', *Studia Hibernica*, 13 (1973), 7–47, at 44–7; PROI RC 8/24, pp. 456–64; PROI RC 8/26, pp. 349–53, 657–73; PROI RC 8/27, pp. 146–70, 388–93. Armies varied in size from day to day; the calculations are for a particular day when the force was at or near full strength. The high number of archers in 1344–5 is explained by the presence of a substantial English retinue serving

might have a short bow as well as cutting weapons among their equipment.[49]

These little armies depended to some extent on the most English groups in Ireland, from the justiciar's English retinue to the citizens of Dublin, or the knights and esquires of the later Pale counties who could raise contingents of up to twenty men.[50] But large, indeed often preponderant, elements of armies were drawn from outside such circles. In 1306 the justiciar John Wogan entered into a contract with Henry Roche, an esquire. Henry was retained of Wogan's household for his lifetime, along lines broadly familiar from English indentures of retinue. The document may be a rare survivor from among many since the terms are stated to be those that applied to the justiciar's other esquires and, when Henry became a knight, he was to have the same liveries as the other knights. The contract obliged him to serve in peace and war. In war he was to bring troops, both 'gentlemen' and others, to join Wogan, and arrangements for their support were specified.[51] The details are of interest, but more so for present purposes is Henry's identity: he was lord of the Rower in south-east Kilkenny, and head of one of the extended kins that were typical of the Irish counties and lordships, and particularly of their borderlands, in the later Middle Ages.[52] The Roches figure in the local Kilkenny

[49] *Statute Rolls of the Parliament of Ireland: Henry VI*, ed. Henry F. Berry (Dublin, 1910), 646–9; *Statute Rolls of the Parliament of Ireland: I–XII Edward IV*, ed. Henry F. Berry (Dublin, 1914), 292–3; *Statute Rolls of the Parliament of Ireland: XII–XXII Edward IV*, ed. James F. Morrissey (Dublin, 1939), 98–101; Kenneth Nicholls, *Gaelic and Gaelicised Ireland in the Middle Ages* (Dublin, 1972), 86. *Sagittarii* could be levied in Dublin and its hinterland in the 1350s (e.g. PRO E 101/243/6; *Rotulorum patentium . . . calendarium*, p. 60, no. 41, p. 62, no. 116); and the Statutes of Kilkenny of 1366, following an English enactment of 1363, prescribed archery practice for the king's subjects in Ireland (*Statutes . . . of Ireland: John to Henry V*, 438–9; Powicke, *Military Obligation*, 184).

[50] e.g. PROI RC8/16, pp. 300–6; 8/26, pp. 438–40; 8/27, pp. 162–3; *DKR Ire.* 54 (1927), 31; PRO E 101/243/6.

[51] PROI RC7/11, pp. 435–8. Cf. N. B. Lewis, 'The Organization of Indentured Retinues in Fourteenth-Century England', *TRHS*, 4th ser., 27 (1945), 29–39, at 34–8. A briefer contract made in 1310 between Wogan and a *valettus*, John son of William Butler of County Waterford, survives in *Rotulorum patentium . . . calendarium*, p. 16, no. 57. The knights who received liveries from the Irish exchequer in the 1270s included landholders from the southern counties (e.g. *Cal. of Docs. Relating to Ireland*, ii, no. 1294, pp. 234–41). I hope to return to the question of the *familia* on another occasion.

[52] For the family, see Eric St J. Brooks, *Knights' Fees in Counties Wexford, Carlow and Kilkenny* (IMC, Dublin, 1950), 150, 201. On the lineages in general,

annals of the Franciscan John Clyn, where they and their like
appear in the guise of disturbers of the peace and, in one of Clyn's
characteristic phrases, 'oppressors of the faithful'. In 1324 he tells
us that 'Arnold le Poer, the seneschal of Kilkenny, with others of
that county, maintained a large guard at Inistioge against the
Roches and strongly besieged them, compelling them to surrender
hostages for the observing of peace and fidelity in the future.'[53]
Wogan had harnessed in the king's service a lord of military habits
whose power lay eighty or more miles south of Dublin. The sense
of a significant connection is heightened by the fact that the
contract includes the provision that the duties are to be taken up
by Henry's heir in the event of his death.

No details of Henry Roche's service in war survive, but there is
evidence of the size and structure of a contingent led on a
campaign in Leinster in 1309 by the head of another branch of the
family, David son of Alexander, lord of Fermoy in Cork. After the
expedition a pardon was awarded to no fewer than 125 men of
David's following, 55 of whom bore his own surname.[54] The
Roches may have been an uncommonly polyphiloprogenitive lot[55]
but there can be no doubt that connections, whether or not the
subject of written contracts, with leaders of powerful Anglo-Irish
lineages enabled the Crown to draw upon a deep well of
manpower.

David of Fermoy also had with him 70 men who were not of his
surname, among them smaller family clusters including six
Barretts from Cork. Another unusual document raises the curtain
a little more. David served again on a Leinster expedition in 1313.
Afterwards he brought cases in the justiciar's court against two of
the Caunton family, alleging that they had failed to observe
contracts made with him. Patrick son of Robert Caunton was
convicted of breaking an agreement 'to serve David in warlike
undertakings throughout all Ireland when summoned at David's
will'. David also accused Robert son of Gregory Caunton of

see Nicholls, *Gaelic and Gaelicised Ireland*, 8–12, and Robin Frame, *English Lord-ship in Ireland, 1318–1361* (Oxford, 1982), 27–38.

[53] Clyn, *Annals*, 16–17; cf. 11, 37–8.
[54] *Cal. Justic. Rolls (1308–14)*, 199–200; Frame, 'Power and Society', 20.
[55] See Nicholls, *Gaelic and Gaelicised Ireland*, 12. The size of such lineages is partly explained by the adoption of permissive Irish marriage customs (ibid. 11); it also owed something to a social environment that favoured the maintenance of ties between distant kin.

neglecting to fulfil a contract, enshrined in letters patent which were produced in court, to take up arms on his behalf whenever required. In this case Robert mounted a successful defence on the grounds that he could not have served without peril because of the enmity that existed between him and other members of the Roche family who were going on the expedition.[56] It may be that written contracts were common among the lesser lords who, unlike two or three of the comital houses, have left virtually no records. But we gain only the occasional glimpse of the relationships that lay behind the impressive numbers some leaders could put in the field. It is a world where ties of kinship and clientage were interwoven, and where the retinues these helped to consolidate could be drawn into the official scheme of military organization, and over an impressive distance.[57]

Closely associated with these affinities were semi-permanent companies of troops, composed chiefly of foot-soldiers or 'kern', who took service with both Anglo-Irish and Gaelic Irish lords. In the midlands and south they were often led by men who themselves belonged to the Anglo-Irish lineages, and it is a mistake to try to draw the boundary between lords and captains too firmly. Shreds of gentility clung to the troops themselves, some of whom are described as 'armoured kern';[58] we hear of Geoffrey Christopher of Waterford gathering kinsmen around him, whom 'he began to make kerns'.[59] Retinues, or elements within them, thus might have a professional quality. The ambiguity of the role of the companies is often apparent. It is well caught in the financial accounts of Elizabeth de Clare, lady of extensive lands in Kilkenny and Tipperary. Her ministers hired the services of Henry de Valle and his kern for a year, and also paid Walter Carragh de Bermingham and his 180 men not to oppress the tenants of one of her lordships: the difference between these transactions was not perhaps very wide.[60] The official view of the companies can seem

[56] PRO I RC 7/12, pp. 145–7.
[57] Cf. Jenny Wormald, *Lords and Men in Scotland: Bonds of Manrent 1442–1603* (Edinburgh, 1985), ch. 5.
[58] PROI RC 8/27, p. 391.
[59] *Cal. Justic. Rolls (1305–7)*, 252. On kern, see Nicholls, *Gaelic and Gaelicised Ireland*, 85–7, and Simms, *From Kings to Warlords*, 93–4, 119–21, 125–6. As in the case of the cavalry, there is a danger of incautiously projecting Tudor images backwards.
[60] PRO SC 6/1239/16, 28.

decidedly hostile and Irish councils and parliaments constantly condemned the exactions of 'kerns and idlemen'.[61] But to the government such bands were not merely a nuisance and royal armies seem to have relied more and more on employing them directly as time passed. They had obvious advantages: they were cheap, since a kern's pay was one penny or, at most, three halfpence a day; and they came, so to speak, off the peg. Many captains, including Walter de Bermingham, found the king in the queue to hire them.[62]

The military system also mobilized in the Crown's service Gaelic Irish lords. To discuss them separately from the Anglo-Irish might be thought to perpetuate a false distinction. But the fact that the Anglo-Irish held their lands by English legal titles that were defensible in the courts, and the Irish in general did not, was a barrier, psychological as well as practical, whose importance should not be discounted at a time when royal government was still effective over large areas of Ireland. Nevertheless in cultural complexion and style of life Gaelic lords probably differed no more from their Anglo-Irish neighbours than some Anglo-Irish (or indeed some Gaelic) lords differed from others. Marriage and other bonds of alliance had long crossed and blurred national boundaries and loyalties were largely local and personal in a society marked by violent competition and feud. At the same time as David Roche's large retinue was pardoned in return for military service in 1309, so too were Henry O'Nolan and seventeen kinsmen who had taken the king's wages: Henry's very name seems to encapsulate the process of blending.[63] The numbers supplied by Irish lords could be considerable. Between 1332 and 1353 O'More of Leix served on campaigns with 180, 284, and (most impressively) 505 men.[64] Irish-led contingents at times made up a substantial proportion of the total force. In 1348 the justiciar had 617 men in pay in Munster, of whom 43 per cent were in the

[61] e.g. *Statutes . . . of Ireland: John to Henry V*, 202–5, 269, 282–5, 328–9, 376–9, 446–9. Idlemen (*ociosi*) were landless men of gentle birth or pretensions.

[62] e.g. PROI RC 8/27, pp. 267, 391, and 8/28, pp. 57–8.

[63] *Cal. Justic. Rolls (1308–14)*, 146. For another aspect of cultural blending see the chapter of Katharine Simms in this volume.

[64] *DKR Ire.* 43 (1912), 54–5; Robin Frame, 'The Justiciarship of Ralph Ufford: Warfare and Politics in Fourteenth-Century Ireland', *Studia Hibernica*, 13 (1973), 7–47, at 45; PROI RC 8/26, pp. 349–53.

retinues of Irish lords.[65] On another Munster campaign in 1353 Irish retinues formed 57 per cent of an army of 669 paid men.[66]

The usual practice was for Gaelic lords to join armies operating in their own regions. The dates of their arrival sometimes suggest that they had come to the king's banner after a campaign had started, aware of the availability of wages, and of the disadvantages of standing aside when a successful assertion of royal authority was taking place.[67] But the king's influence was not always haphazard. Especially when large military ventures were arranged, leaders could be pulled far beyond their normal spheres: MacMurrough, whose seat of power was in eastern Leinster, served in Munster in 1345 and 1352.[68] Now and then we can see the relationships that underlay such service. O'More was disciplined by a royal expedition in 1347. This was followed by a settlement, recorded in writing, that had among its terms the provision that he would serve in war at his own expense within his own districts, and at the king's wages beyond them.[69] Moreover from early in the fourteenth century there is evidence of Irish lords, mostly from eastern Leinster, receiving annual fees from the Dublin government. By mid-century, when such stipends appear more frequently, it is clear that they imposed on their recipients an obligation to perform military service. A typical formula involved the leader's agreement 'to remain with the king and serve him faithfully, and to go in force with the justiciar of Ireland against other Irish'. Ireland had long since seen some harmonizing of native and Anglo-Norman styles of warfare; it had also seen magnates and royal ministers become skilled at exploiting Irish segmentary disputes and at conducting the diplomatic dance that surrounded hostages. In the area of military service too there was an accommodation of a straightforward sort between the system of the Lordship of Ireland and patterns that had come to exist in Gaelic society, where fighting for an overlord outside home territory was done in return for pay, and the ceremonial gifts once given by an over-king

[65] PROI RC 8/24, pp. 458–63.
[66] PROI RC 8/26, pp. 666–70.
[67] e.g. Frame, 'Ralph Ufford', 33.
[68] Ibid. 46; PROI RC 8/26, p. 660.
[69] Genealogical Office, Dublin Castle, MS 192, pp. 53–5; Frame, 'English Officials and Irish Chiefs', 759–60. Fuller details of what follows in this and the next paragraph may be found in Frame, 'English Officials and Irish Chiefs', 759–76.

to the vassal-kings who submitted to him had been transmuted into wages of war.[70]

The partial absorption of the Irish lords who lived within Dublin's orbit is visible in other ways. Although Irish retinues were composed almost entirely of hobelars and foot, their leaders might take wages as men-at-arms and, in that sense at least, they were placed on a level with the lords who had English status.[71] There are some hints of fuller assimilation. During the 1350s John son of Taig O'Byrne, lord of the O'Byrnes of Wicklow, constantly switched between the parts of 'rebel' and government stipendiary; in the 1360s he appears to have been dubbed a knight in the European fashion.[72] These close military links are part of the background against which we can understand the role of the Crown in confirming the authority of Irish leaders amongst their own people: John's lordship over the O'Byrnes had been formally sanctioned in a session held before the justiciar in 1350.[73] The case of the MacMurroughs, descendants of the pre-conquest rulers of Leinster, is specially interesting. In 1328 Donal son of Art MacMurrough had tried to present himself as king of Leinster, an act of antiquarian bravado that saw him at once deposited in the dungeons of Dublin Castle. In 1335 he was serving Edward III in Scotland, drawing pay as a banneret. And in 1357 a successor, Art Kavanagh, was 'created MacMurrough' (that is, clan chief) by the royal government. This is part of the wider story, recently illuminated by Dr Katharine Simms, of the slow crumbling of Irish royal pretensions, and the growth, at times with official encouragement, of new styles of authority.[74] For the military sphere was, needless to say, inseparable from the political and social.

There can be no doubt, taking military service as the measure, that the Crown could bring its authority to bear in some detail over at least half of Ireland.[75] In the south-east it exercised an intensive lordship which embraced a heterogeneous society and found

[70] Frame, 'English Officials and Irish Chiefs', 765; the subject is now more expertly treated in Simms, *From Kings to Warlords*, 109–10.
[71] e.g. *DKR Ire.* 43 (1912), 54–5; Frame, 'Ralph Ufford', 45–6; PROI RC 8/26, pp. 349–53, 660.
[72] PRO E101/244/10.
[73] Edmund Curtis, 'The Clan System among English Settlers in Ireland', *EHR* 25 (1910), 116–20, at 116–17.
[74] *From Kings to Warlords*, ch. 3.
[75] For an attempt to outline the political geography of the period, see Frame, 'Power and Society', 5–18.

expression in a mixture of English and Irish modes. In Munster
royal lordship was patchier and more spasmodic, but there too
ministers could mobilize English and Irish in the king's interests.
When leading members of the small group of families of comital
rank were closely associated with government, it gained in range
and penetration. A dramatic example dates from 1308 when
William de Burgh, cousin of the earl of Ulster and his main agent
in his western lordship of Connacht, served briefly as deputy
justiciar. Direct royal influence around and beyond the Shannon
had been fading for two decades; it was scarcely to recover until
the Tudor period. Yet William's time in office saw a campaign in
Leinster fought by an army composed almost entirely of contingents
brought into pay by Gaelic lords from Connacht.[76] More significant than this transient episode is the way that magnate influence
deepened royal authority in areas where it was normally shallow.
The Butler earls of Ormond, with their clusters of land and
widespread influence stretching across south Leinster and east
Munster, provide the best illustration. Butler power, like that of
royal government in its own heartland, was articulated through
relationships with Anglo-Irish and Irish lords and lineages. Where
these are documented, they often include provisions for military
service akin to those in O'More's submission of 1347.[77] The earls
also had the capacity to mobilize bands of kern from Kilkenny and
Tipperary. It is no coincidence that during the 1350s, when the
second earl of Ormond was closely connected with the government,
contingents led by O'Kennedys of Ormond, who are not normally
found on royal expeditions, appear in the king's pay.[78] When the
earl was justiciar of Ireland in 1359–60, royal armies drew heavily
on companies led by cadet Butlers and members of other lineages
such as Howell, Marsh, de Valle, and Purcell, with some of
which Ormond had written contracts, as he also had with the
O'Kennedys.[79] The earl could mobilize an area almost as large as a

---

[76] Philomena Connolly, 'An Account of Military Expenditure in Leinster, 1308',
Analecta Hibernica, 30 (1982), 1–5, at 4–5.

[77] e.g. *Calendar of Ormond Deeds*, ed. Edmund Curtis (6 vols., IMC, Dublin,
1932–43), ii, nos. 35–6, 46, pp. 22–3, 28–30; cf. *Red Book of the Earls of Kildare*,
ed. Gearóid MacNiocaill (IMC, Dublin, 1964), no. 168, pp. 154–5. For an excellent
recent discussion see the comments of John A. Watt in Art Cosgrove (ed.), *New
History of Ireland*, ii: *Medieval Ireland 1169–1534* (Oxford, 1987), 325–9.

[78] PROI RC 8/26, pp. 349–53, 672; PRO E101/244/2; *Calendar of Ormond
Deeds*, ii, no. 48, p. 30.

[79] PROI RC 8/28, pp. 57–8, 478, 487; RIA, MS 12 D 10, p. 167; *Calendar of*

province, a fact that was sometimes recognized by the making out
of a commission of the peace covering several counties, in which
he stood first.[80]

If we are to find a 'frontier' in the sense of barrier, it might seem
reasonable to look for it in the area of English military organization
in Ireland, not least since the maintenance of English law, and by
the fourteenth century of Englishness generally, was explicitly a
function of royal government. Such a search is encouraged by the
language of royal documents, which talk of wars between 'the
king's faithful people' or 'the justiciar and the English', and 'Irish
enemies and rebels' or 'Irish felons and enemies'.[81] This jargon,
when enriched with a sauce of stereotyped images, can conjure up
a picture of an English government mobilizing an English settler
population against a threat that was alien and external. These
contemporary formulations and the perceptions that lay behind
them have their own claims to our attention, but they can be
treacherous. At the simplest level, it is necessary to recall that the
forces opposing the 'Irish enemies' contained large numbers of
Irish troops, some of them led by Gaelic lords indistinguishable
from those against whom expeditions were aimed, and others by
men of English status who were heavily influenced by Irish culture
and social habits. The act of assembling such armies implies a high
degree of involvement with that supposedly exterior scene.
Official statements in Ireland are reminiscent of the supercilious
grumbles of members of the late Roman élite, who were free to
voice them precisely because of the security they were afforded by
German manpower under German leaders who were pretty
thoroughly assimilated.[82] Later medieval Ireland, like other
frontier societies, had its share of ambiguities. The working of
practical relationships (a subject still very little studied) often

---

Ormond Deeds, i, no. 682, pp. 287–90, ii, nos. 33–4, 37–9, 46, pp. 19–22, 23–6,
28–30. The local military world of the 15th-century descendants of these lords and
captains is marvellously captured in *Poems on Marcher Lords*, ed. Anne O'Sullivan
and Pádraig Ó Riain (ITS 53, London, 1987).

[80] See Frame, 'War and Peace', 133–4.

[81] The vocabulary awaits detailed analysis; these examples are taken from PRO
E101/239/24; 240/13, 243/3 and 6. Some of the paradoxes are brought out in
P. J. Duffy, 'The Nature of the Medieval Frontier in Ireland', *Studia Hibernica*,
22–3 (1982–3), 21–38.

[82] See e.g. E. A. Thompson, *Romans and Barbarians: The Decline of the
Western Empire* (Madison, 1982), 231–2.

seems at odds with the attitudes of the Lordship's ruling groups as they appear in legislation or in formal messages to the king and Council in England. Even within the restricted and artificial scene we have been considering, 'the frontier' is to be understood as a process of interaction.

It also of course has a territorial connotation, since the military measures taken by royal ministers and by magnates tended to concentrate on districts where cultivable land and lines of communication bordered with upland or bog. In that sense Ireland may be said to have contained frontiers. Awareness of them is apparent in the contemporary vocabulary of 'land of peace', 'land of war', and 'march'. Historians have been much preoccupied with the expansion of the lands of war at the expense of the lands of peace during the fourteenth century, or, to put it another way, with the retreat of English forms of administration.[83] But it is equally true that the whole of Ireland was a frontier; the expeditions of justiciars might be regarded as part of an unending effort to manage a world that was everywhere to some degree a marcher one. This was a point that could escape officials recently arrived from England. In 1350 new ministers included amongst their recommendations to the king a scathing indictment of established military practice:

it seems good to arrange to conquer from the enemy some place occupied by them and to inhabit it with English; this could be done by God's aid without great expense, to the king's great profit. For the accustomed habit before this time was simply this: to spend all the revenues of the land on war without any conquest or profit.[84]

The irritation is understandable, and justified in the sense that vulnerable areas could no doubt have been more assiduously defended and exploited. But there is also a reluctance to admit that, in important ways, war and diplomacy *were* government.

Contemporary official rhetoric invites us to judge the government's military activities by dubious criteria: their success or failure in preserving English styles of authority immaculate, or (an equally impossible task in fourteenth-century conditions) in maintaining inviolate the boundaries of settled, arable zones.

[83] See Frame, 'War and Peace', 126–7.
[84] *Documents on the Affairs of Ireland before the King's Council*, ed. G. O. Sayles (IMC, Dublin, 1979), 193.

Ireland was a crucible which nobody and nothing could escape. Military and fiscal institutions familiar in England assumed a different shape and meaning across the Irish Sea. Alongside and intertwined with them lay a second set of relationships and conventions that amounted to an additional scheme of control. Government reached out and, in the king's interests, incorporated the warlike and culturally hybrid inhabitants of the Lordship. As it did so it spoke as though its purpose was to defeat and exclude them—as in some ultimate, illusory sense it was. The illusion may have been necessary; but to attend exclusively to such public words is to find our eyes deflected from a richer story, of mingling and of institutional adaptation.

6

Institutions on the Castilian–Granadan Frontier
1369–1482

JOSÉ ENRIQUE LÓPEZ DE COCA CASTAÑER

INTRODUCTION

This chapter attempts to evaluate the relationship between the Crown of Castile and the Nasrid kingdom of Granada from 1369 to 1482 by focusing attention on frontier institutions. The frontier between both polities remained virtually stationary during this period, although neither side was ready to recognize this fact: in the case of Castile because the ideology behind the Reconquest prevented finishing the war against the Moors until their final expulsion from the Iberian peninsula;[1] in the case of Granada because the Muslims were aware of this menace and, from time to time, reacted with a renewal of the spirit of the *jihād*. From the beginning Granada existed in a situation of constant tension which had a pronounced psychological effect on the Moorish population, which was composed mainly of refugees from previous Christian advances. Such a situation, as Henri Terrasse pointed out long ago, produced a siege mentality, and Holy War was popular both among the inhabitants of the Nasrid state and among the Berber mercenary troops and volunteers from North Africa, who were always an important element in the country.[2] To this end Ibn Hudhayl, a scholar from Almería, devoted the second chapter of his treatise on Holy War to the *ribat* or frontier convent, and he stressed that the defence of Granada against the Christians, both

---

[1] The *locus classicus* is José Antonio Maravall, *El concepto de España en la Edad Media* (3rd edn., Madrid, 1981), 249–95. For an excellent account of the military and political development of the *Reconquista*, see Derek W. Lomax, *The Reconquest of Spain* (London, 1978).

[2] Henri Terrasse, 'Le Royaume nasride dans la vie de l'Espagne du Moyen Âge: Indications et problèmes', in *Mélanges offerts à Marcel Bataillon* (*Bulletin hispanique*, 64 bis, 1962), 253–60, at 254–6.

on land and sea, was the most essential obligation imposed on believers.[3]

It may seem surprising, therefore, that the frontier remained so stable during the period in question. To understand this, it must be remembered that the Castilian monarchy had to face a long succession of internal problems. Peter I's defeat and murder in 1369 gave the throne to the new Trastamaran dynasty, but during the reigns of Henry II (1369–79) and John I (1379–90) little interest was shown in Granada except for the renewal of truces. The same 'paralysis' marked the first decade of Henry III's reign (1390–1406). All these monarchs were aware of the fact that relations with the Moors constituted only one element in more complicated internal and international political patterns. At different times during this period the real dangers were posed by the interventions in Castilian affairs of France, England, and Portugal. Thus the monarchy, by following a policy of relative stability on the Moorish frontier, attempted to prevent the opening up of yet another military front in time of crisis.[4] Thus when the master of the military order of Alcántara shocked all Spain in 1394 by ignoring royal truces and invading Granada as if he were a twelfth-century crusader, only to be defeated and killed at the frontier, Henry III apologized to the Nasrid Sultan Muḥammad VII.[5]

The pattern changed at the opening of the fifteenth century when Henry III displayed signs of an intention to resume the war on a grand scale. But his unexpected death in 1406 meant that the leadership of this project, as well as the regency for the young John II, passed into the hands of the Infante Ferdinand, who seized the fortress of Zahara in 1407 and the important stronghold

---

[3] In his work, there are frequent appeals to solidarity, ideological unity, and hatred of the ancestral enemy. See Dominique Urvoy, 'Sur l'évolution de la notion de "ǧihād" dans l'Espagne musulmane', *Mélanges de la Casa de Velázquez*, 9 (1973), 335–71, at 349–51.

[4] Angus MacKay, 'The Ballad and the Frontier in Late Medieval Spain', *Bulletin of Hispanic Studies*, 53 (1976), 15–33, at 19.

[5] Lomax, *Reconquest*, 168. To be sure, Martin Yáñez de Barbuda, a Portuguese exile, only shocked the king and the aristocracy because his private war was supported by Andalusian folk. The story of this unfortunate expedition, as it appears in Ayala's *Crónica de Enrique III*, can be envisaged as an example of 'popular crusade'. See José Enrique López de Coca Castañer, 'El reino de Granada, 1354–1501', in *Historia de Andalucia*, iii (2nd edn., Madrid, 1981), 327–497, at 345–6.

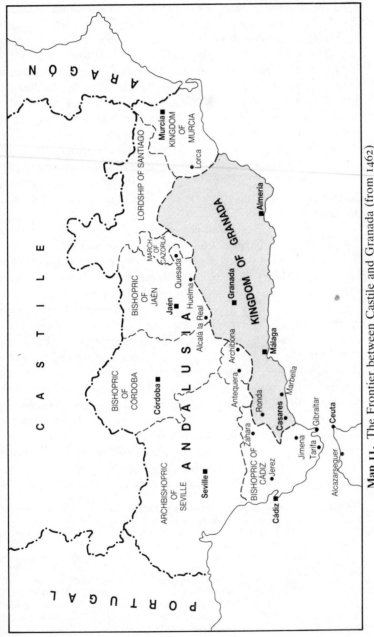

Map 11. The Frontier between Castile and Granada (from 1462)

of Antequera three years later. However, by the Compromise of
Caspe, Ferdinand became king of Aragón in 1412 and, in
consequence, he left Castile to its own devices. The Castilian
monarchy resumed the war in 1430, and John II won the battle of
La Higueruela just outside the Nasrid capital (1431). Thereafter it
was left to the men of the frontier to press the attack, and down to
the truce of 1439 several fortresses were gained on the eastern
frontier. But a new internal crisis allowed the Moors to recover all
these places from 1445 to 1450. Matters improved for Castile when
Henry IV (1454–74) ascended the throne. During his four
campaigns between 1455 and 1458 Christian armies were used for
short attacks on vulnerable points, and by the end of 1462 the
Castilians had secured strategic positions such as Archidona and
Gibraltar.[6]

To be sure, all these examples of an intermittent full-scale war
bringing kings and armies into serious combat were motivated by
reasons of internal policy. Even the Infante Ferdinand, as well as
John II and Henry IV, envisaged these sporadic and short-term
offensives as a means to secure internal peace.[7]

Yet, although the period 1369–1482 was characterized by only
twenty or twenty-five years of open war, can we talk about peace
during the rest of the period when the frontier witnessed endemic
petty hostilities? As a matter of fact 'peace', as we understand it
today, was a meaningless concept for the Christians and Moors,
especially for the latter. For it must be remembered that,
according to Islamic legal doctrine, the normal relationship
between both sides was not peaceful but warlike.[8] In this sense, it
would be useful to employ the concept of 'cold war' to understand
the main features of these ninety years—that is, to use a concept
which indicates that although relations were bad and warlike, they
were to some extent restrained and had not reached the point of

---

[6] There is a comprehensive account in Charles J. Bishko, 'The Spanish and
Portuguese Reconquest, 1095–1492', in Kenneth Setton (ed.), *A History of the
Crusades*, iii: *The Fourteenth and Fifteenth Centuries*, ed. Harry W. Hazard
(Madison, 1975), 396–456, at 439–47.

[7] Miguel Ángel Ladero Quesada, *Granada: Historia de un país islámico (1232–
1571)* (2nd edn., Madrid, 1979), 133.

[8] Anne K. S. Lambton, *State and Government in Medieval Islam: An
Introduction to the Study of Islamic Political Theory: The Jurists* (Oxford, 1981),
201–2; Charles-Emmanuel Dufourcq, 'Chrétiens et musulmans durant les derniers
siècles du Moyen Âge', *Anuario de estudios medievales*, 10 (1980), 207–25, at
209–10.

'hot war'.[9] Restraint was to some extent in the interests of both the Castilian and Granadan courts. If Castile had to face serious internal problems, the Nasrid state was troubled in a similar way.[10]

This chapter does not deal—except peripherally—with that side of the story; nor does it attempt to write the history of a roughly stabilized confrontation along the frontier. Such an effort is precluded both by the absence of substantial Muslim sources on the subject and by my own interests.[11] My focus is different. I want first to consider the nature of the truces which kings and sultans periodically signed. Then I will discuss the movement of people and trade across the frontier. Finally, I will examine peace-keeping mechanisms and trans-frontier arrangements.

TRUCES

We can distinguish between treaties where the sultan of Granada agreed to be a vassal of the king of Castile and the truces or mere suspensions of hostilities. The Nasrid polity had begun its historical existence as a Castilian vassal in the mid-thirteenth century. This vassalage had been a condition of survival, but it also meant that a basic contradiction was built into the fabric of the state. For a Muslim ruler to be the vassal of a Christian sovereign revolted every principle of Islamic law. And the vassalage of Granada was not only humiliating but onerous. It involved the

[9] Don Juan Manuel (1282–1348), a member of the Castilian royal family who was writing about the conflict between Christians and Muslims at that time, remarks that *hot* and *cold* wars are distinguished by, among other things, the manner in which they end: 'war that is very strong and very hot ends either with death or peace, whereas cold war neither brings peace nor gives honour to the man who makes it.' The discussion comes from his *Libro de los estados*, a dialogue in which a wise man, called Julio, gives moral advice to a young prince, Turin, on the conduct of warfare against the infidels. See Don Juan Manuel, *Obras completas*, ed. José M. Blecua (2 vols., Madrid, 1982–3), i. 357. See also Luis García Arias, *El concepto de guerra y la denominada 'guerra fría'* (Saragossa, 1956), 67.

[10] Luis Seco de Lucena Paredes, *Muḥammad IX, sultán de Granada* (Granada, 1978), *passim*; José Enrique López de Coca, 'Revisión de una década de la historia granadina, 1446–1455', *Miscelánea de estudios árabes y hebraicos*, 29–30 (1980–1), 61–90; id., 'Granada bajo la casa de Abū Naṣr Saʿd', in *Seis lecciones sobre la guerra de Granada* (Granada, 1983), 59–73.

[11] José Enrique López de Coca, 'Sobre historia económica y social del reino nazarí de Granada: Problemas de fuentes y método', in *Actas del I Congreso de Historia de Andalucía, 1–2: Andalucía medieval* (2 vols., Córdoba, 1978), ii. 395–404.

sultan's attendance at the Castilian court and the sending of military contingents to fight against fellow Muslims as well as Christians. Granada also had to pay large sums of money, known as *parias*, as annual tribute to Castile. In order to get the money the sultans taxed their Muslim population far more heavily than *sharī'ah* or religious law allowed.[12]

This humiliating situation disappeared during the second half of the fourteenth century when Castile was ruled by its first Trastamaran sovereigns, who were more worried about other dangers. Now Nasrid sultans renewed the truces without being obliged to pay any tribute, and without being linked to Castile by any feudal relationship. Meanwhile their subjects could trade almost freely across the frontier. It almost appears as if the two polities envisaged each other as equals. It was beyond doubt an atypical situation, and one which the Castilian rulers tried to correct from the beginning of the fifteenth century.[13] But, to tell the truth, they only succeeded with some Nasrid princes whom they supported in their claims or pretensions to the throne of Granada—Yūsuf ibn al-Mawl, Yūsuf ibn Aḥmad, and Sa'd ibn 'Alī. Only the latter made good his claim in 1455, but shortly thereafter he broke with his feudal lord, Henry IV.[14]

For their part, Granadan sultans wished to maintain the advantageous position secured by their fourteenth-century predecessors. But neither the Castilians nor the Muslims could attain their ultimate goals. Both sides were obliged to come to terms by

[12] Terrasse, 'Le Royaume nasride', 254. The contradiction has been pointed out in Jocelyn N. Hillgarth, *The Spanish Kingdoms, 1250–1516* (2 vols., Oxford, 1976–8), i. 320–1. The controversy about illegal taxes was common to other Islamic states, where 'men of religion' reacted from time to time for ideological reasons. See John F. Hopkins, *Medieval Muslim Government in Barbary until the Sixth Century of the Hijra* (London, 1958), 39–40. The novelty, in the case of Granada, was that *fuqah* supported the sultan's policy concerning taxes, claiming that it was motivated by the demands of 'public utility'; see José López Ortiz, 'Fatwàs granadinas de los siglos XIV y XV', *Al Andalus*, 6 (1941), 73–127, at 85.

[13] e.g. see the answer given by Prince Ferdinand to the Granadan ambassador in 1409: *Crónica de Juan II de Castilla*, ed. Juan de Mata Carriazo (Madrid, 1982), 268–9.

[14] The feudal contract between John II and Yūsuf ibn al-Mawl is published in Luis Suárez Fernández, *Juan II y la frontera de Granada* (Valladolid, 1954), 39–42; Sa'd ibn 'Alī won the throne with Castilian help. On his break with King Henry IV, see Lorenzo Galíndez de Carvajal, *Crónica de Enrique IV*, ed. Juan Torres Fontes, *Estudio sobre la 'Crónica de Enrique IV' del Dr. Galíndez de Carvajal* (Murcia, 1946), 67–543, at 98. See also López de Coca, 'Revisión de una década', 78–85; id., 'Granada bajo la casa de Abū Naṣr Sa'd', 61.

means of more or less lasting truces, in which Granada agreed to deliver up a certain number of Christian captives, as a *sign of service*, and to pay a tribute. All this happened, of course, when Castile was able to command respect from its opponent. Such a situation was not possible during the second half of Henry IV's reign and during the first years of that of the Catholic Kings, when Granada was freed from both these obligations.

The texts of eleven different truces from 1406 to 1481 are available in printed editions, apart from the truce of 1443, which I have recently discovered in the British Library. In the case of the truce of 1439 the negotiations preceding or leading up to the truce itself are also available, and they document the diplomatic efforts deployed by both sides, as well as the methods used to collect the *parias* in Granada and to organize the delivery of captives.[15] It appears that it was easier for the Nasrid sultans to pay a heavy tribute than to deliver up captives. In these negotiations Muhammad IX appealed to John II's generosity, claiming that he could not oblige his subjects to deliver up their captives without ransoms, because they were needed in order to exchange them for those of their relatives who were prisoners in Castilian territory. John II countered this by claiming that Muslims could more effectively have their relatives liberated if they concentrated on labouring in their fields and taking care of their cattle rather than raiding across the frontier.[16] The subsequent attempts to fulfil the agreement show that it was a difficult task to deliver up all the

---

[15] The truce of 1406 is summarized in Emilio Mitre Fernández, 'De la toma de Algeciras a la campaña de Antequera', *Hispania*, 32 (1972), 77–122, at 118–20. For the truce of 1410, see *Crónica de Juan II de Castilla*, 402–6. The truces signed in 1413, 1414, 1415, and 1424 have been published in Mariano Arribas Palau, *Las treguas entre Castilla y Granada firmadas por Fernando I de Aragón* (Tetuan, 1956), 47–56, 75–84, 85–94, 95–102. For the truce of 1439 and the previous negotiations, see José Amador de los Ríos, *Memoria histórico-crítica de las treguas celebradas en 1439 entre los reyes de Castilla y Granada* (Madrid, 1879), *passim*. The truce of 1443 is in BL Add. MS 9924, fos. 225–35 (it is an 18th-century copy). For the truce of 1472, see Juan Torres Fontes, 'Las treguas con Granada de 1469 y 1472', *Cuadernos de estudios medievales*, 4–5 (1979), 211–36, at 235–6. The truce of 1477 is in *Colección diplomática del Archivo Histórico Municipal de Jaén*, ed. José Rodríguez Molina (Jaén, 1985), 60–2; see also Juan de Mata Carriazo, 'Las últimas treguas con Granada', *Boletín del Instituto de Estudios Giennenses*, 3 (1954), 11–43, at 36–9. For the truce of 1481, see J. A. Bonilla and E. Toval, *El tratado de paz de 1481 entre Castilla y Granada* (Jaén, 1982), 29–32.

[16] Amador de los Ríos, *Memoria histórico-crítica*, 85, 90; see also Arribas Palau, *Las treguas entre Castilla y Granada*, 39.

prisoners demanded by the Christian authorities because Moors
hastened to conceal their captives.[17]

Each side was well informed about the other's internal situation.
This information was useful during diplomatic bargaining and it
helped to clarify the respective negotiating positions. For example,
after five months of exchanging messages and proposals in 1439,
John II was not prepared to admit any more bargaining from his
Muslim opponent. Accordingly, he sent the following order to his
representative at the negotiations, Íñigo López de Mendoza: 'You
must tell them that if we have an internal revolt, we know very
well that they are not very peaceful either.'[18]

Another characteristic aspect of these truces was that the
Granadan promises to pay *parias* and deliver up captives were not
inserted in the texts of the truces themselves, but were recorded in
other documents of a more private nature in which the Nasrid
sultans promised to fulfil these obligations, which are described as
gifts.[19] Why was this?

The Muslim legal doctrine, which received its basic shape during
the first century and a half of the Islamic era, admitted the
possibility of paying tributes to unbelievers under exceptional
circumstances. In fact under Ummayad rule several caliphs
concluded treaties with the Byzantines in which they paid tribute
in order to avoid being attacked while they were bedevilled by civil
wars. But later the majority of the jurists seem to have advised
against paying an annual tribute, although they saw no harm in
paying it for a short period.[20] In our case, it would appear that by
choosing to regard tribute and the freeing of captives as *gifts*, the
sultans and their legal advisers could justify the contractual
relationship with Castile as well as other agreements inserted in
the truces.

A truce could work only if it was adhered to by the authorities
on both sides of the frontier. In this sense, there were certain
features which are common to all the known surviving texts, and it
was these features which permitted the development of several

[17] Amador de los Ríos, *Memoria histórico-crítica*, 142–8. See also *Hechos del condestable don Miguel Lucas de Iranzo*, ed. Juan de Mata Carriazo (Madrid, 1940), 103.
[18] Amador de los Ríos, *Memoria histórico-crítica*, 109.
[19] Ibid. 140–2; BL Add. MS 9924, fos. 234ᵛ–35.
[20] Majid Khadduri, *War and Peace in the Law of Islam* (Baltimore, 1955), 215–17.

institutions which are examined below. These features were as follows:

1. Both sides recognized that captives could escape to their respective homelands. But if they crossed the frontier with stolen goods, the authorities on the receiving side were obliged to return these goods. In addition, both sides allowed the free movement of ransomers and other similar people performing such a humanitarian task.

2. Both Castile and Granada allowed merchants from the other side to enter their respective territories. Such merchants were obliged to pay customs taxes, and they were prevented from trading in certain goods and commodities which were traditionally forbidden.

3. Both sides agreed to deputize certain chosen individuals in order to settle trans-frontier quarrels. These deputies could act as judges, were able to prosecute delinquents, and could pass sentences. If these were not executed, the offended parties could appeal to their respective lords.

CAPTIVES AND THEIR REDEMPTION

Captivity was a result of war and frontier raids, and so although we are better informed about the fate of Christian captives in Muslim territory, it was undoubtedly a common occurrence in Andalusia and Murcia as well as Granada. The treatment to which captives were liable varied: they could be released on paying ransom or they could be exchanged with prisoners from the other side. According to Castilian propaganda Christian captives were forced to convert to Islam, but in fact this was not a common practice because Muslims wanted to retain a captive's economic value, which was usually lost, or at least considerably reduced, when a captive apostatized.[21]

---

[21] The ballad 'Río Verde, Río Verde' affords an example of this propaganda. The anonymous minstrel, who did not know the ultimate fate of Juan de Saavedra, supposed he had been killed because he refused to accept Islam. See Luis Seco de Lucena Paredes, 'La historicidad del romance "Río Verde, Río Verde"', *Al Andalus*, 23 (1958), 75–95; José Enrique López de Coca Castañer, 'De nuevo sobre la historicidad del romance "Río Verde, Río Verde"', in *Actas del I Coloquio de Historia Medieval Andaluza* (Córdoba, 1982), 11–19. Anyway, it must be borne in mind that Christian children captured in their early years usually converted and

Obviously bad conditions of captivity may have led prisoners to alleviate their position by means of conversion.[22] As far as we know, Christian captives lived under harsh pressure as convict workers. They were forced to replace the animals moving the chain-pumps for irrigation, to mill, or to work on the buildings of walls and fortresses. At night they were confined in underground gaols which were usually disused cisterns and silos.[23] An Andalusian tradition dating back to the sixteenth century reflects the special situation of Christian captives in Ronda, a Nasrid stronghold of the north-west frontier. The tradition refers to a staircase, called *La Mina*, which connected the rocky bed of the river Guadiaro to the town, which was located fifty metres above. The staircase was built in order to ensure a supply of water to the town, and Christian captives were employed in bringing it up. Hence the common saying still in force in Andalusia: 'May you die in Ronda carrying goatskins [of water].'[24]

Liberation for captives could arrive in different ways. It was recognized that they could attempt to escape, and this phenomenon must have been frequent in the central districts of the frontier where the Christian fortress of Alcalá la Real, located 300 metres above the neighbouring Granadan countryside, had a night-beacon to orientate Christian fugitives. In 1395, for example, the Crown spent 3,600 *maravedíes* on olive oil, wicks, and the beacon-keepers' salaries.[25] In addition, Christian captives could be

became *mamālik*—that is, warriors in the royal Nasrid guard. See Rachel Arié, *L'Espagne musulmane aux temps des Nasrides, 1232–1492* (Paris, 1973), 244–5.

[22] See e.g. the case of a young man from Jaén who, after four months in gaol, circumcized himself and said he wanted to be a Moor: Juan de Mata Carriazo, 'Relaciones fronterizas entre Jaén y Granada: El año 1479', *Revista de archivos, bibliotecas y museos*, 61 (1955), 23–51, at 29.

[23] Women and children worked as household slaves in private homes; they provided the necessities of the house by collecting firewood, tending livestock, cultivating the gardens, and breaking up rock to make lime. See José Maria de Cossío, 'Cautivos de moros en el siglo XIII: El texto de Pero Marín', *Al Andalus*, 7 (1942), 49–112.

[24] Pedro de Medina, *Libro de grandezas y cosas memorables de España*, ed. Ángel González Palencia (Madrid, 1944), 186. A British officer from Gibraltar, touring in the Serranía in the 1830s, had the chance to see this staircase: Charles Rochfort Scott, *Excursions in the Mountains of Ronda and Granada with Characteristic Sketches of the Inhabitants of the South of Spain* (2 vols., London, 1838), i. 141.

[25] Carmen Juan Lovera, 'Catálogo de la colección diplomática de Alcalá la Real', *Boletín del Instituto de Estudios Giennenses*, 91 (1977), pp. 9–45, docs. 42–3, p. 37.

liberated just after a truce had been signed, because the Muslims were usually obliged to release a certain number of them. But in normal circumstances liberation was the result of certain mechanisms of redemption which had been developed and perfected over the previous centuries.

During the twelfth and thirteenth centuries some Spanish towns developed a system of licensing professional ransomers known as *alfaqueques*. Some sources of this period refer to the rights and obligations of *alfaqueques* in the fulfilment of commissions of ransom. These individuals, who were appointed by the Crown or by town councils, were privileged men who travelled under safe conduct across the frontier between Muslims and Christians. They were usually merchants who maintained a more or less regular traffic with the Moors and who were charged with ransoming captives as well. For their services, these *alfaqueques* were paid 10 per cent of the ransom price. Although the obligations for providing the ransom money fell mainly on the captives or their families, there were other sources of funds as well. Some towns helped pay for the rescue of their citizens. Various brotherhoods also guaranteed their members that they would be ransomed if they were captured by the Muslims. Finally, at the beginning of the thirteenth century, two religious orders dedicated to the redemption of captives were instituted in Spain. The Order of the Holy Trinity was established in Aragón in 1201, and seventeen years later James I granted a charter to the Order of the Merced. Both orders subsequently established houses in Castile.[26]

Financing ransoms was easier with respect to important individuals captured by the Moors on the battlefield, because they enjoyed substantial help from the Crown. The case of Juan de Saavedra, who was taken prisoner after the defeat of Río Verde (1448), constitutes a good example. He remained in captivity for nearly two years before paying the 12,000 gold *doblas* which the Muslims demanded. As he could not afford this large sum, his brother Gonzalo, an official from Seville, persuaded both the town and King John II to contribute a third of the ransom.[27] Similarly eight

[26] Juan Torres Fontes, 'Los alfaqueques castellanos en la frontera de Granada', in *Homenaje a don Agustín Millares Carlo* (2 vols., Las Palmas, 1975), ii. 99–116, at 100–2.

[27] Seco de Lucena, 'La historicidad', 90–4.

years later, when the Moors captured Don Juan Manrique, count of Castañeda, Henry IV paid a third of the ransom.[28]

It was not so easy for common people to get the money they needed to release their friends and relatives. Alms and testamentary legacies were not enough for this purpose.[29] In addition, and in exchange, the Moors usually demanded the release of their co-religionists who were prisoners on the Castilian side of the frontier. In these circumstances, a Christian captive's relatives were obliged to try and reach an agreement with those persons who held Muslim captives. As a result, however, these owners could be tempted to try and sell their captives at a higher price. To avoid abuses, the authorities in the March of Cazorla in the early fifteenth century stipulated that every owner of a Moorish captive, who could be exchanged for an inhabitant of the March who was a prisoner in Granada, could only demand 30 per cent more than the price which he had originally paid for the Moor in question.[30] Later on, at the request of the Cortes, Henry IV confirmed this arrangement, which was extended to all the frontier. But it only applied in cases where Moors had been held captive by their owners for less than a year, because if they had been prisoners for a longer period of time, then the owners could only demand half the price they had originally cost. And, in addition, when Muslim prisoners were sold at auction, priority was given to those would-be buyers who needed them for ransoming a Christian captive.[31]

As regards ransoming procedures, eighteenth-century accounts are available about the activities of the Trinitarians and Mercedarians in Granada and the martyrdom suffered by several of the friars.[32] We also know something about the ransoming activity deployed by the Jeronymite monks of Guadalupe in the fifteenth century

---

[28] A. López Dapena, 'Cautiverio y rescate de D. Juan Manrique, capitán de la frontera castellana, 1456–1457', *Cuadernos de estudios medievales*, 12–13 (1984), 243–53.

[29] Tomás García Figueras, 'Relaciones fronterizas de Jerez y los musulmanes de las serranías de Cádiz y Málaga', in *Actas del Primer Congreso de Estudios Árabes e Islámicos* (Madrid, 1964), 277–84, at 282; Juan Torres Fontes, 'La frontera de Granada en el siglo XV y sus repercusiones en Murcia y Orihuela: Los cautivos', in *Homenaje a don José María Lacarra* (Saragossa, 1972), iv. 203; María del Mar García Guzmán, *El Adelantamiento de Cazorla en la Baja Edad Media* (Cádiz, 1985), 216.

[30] García Guzmán, *El Adelantamiento de Cazorla*, 214.

[31] *Colección diplomática de Jaén*, 28.

[32] Arié, *L'Espagne musulmane*, 326.

shortly after the destruction of the Murcian village of Cieza by Granadan troops.[33] But, curiously, there is no information about these activities in the contemporary Christian sources of the frontier towns, in spite of the existence of Trinitarian and Mercedarian convents in Murcia, Córdoba, Seville, and Jerez. How is this silence to be explained? It seems that all the money collected by these friars was administered from a central fund belonging to the main houses which both orders possessed in Castile—which were also the houses where the ransoming expeditions were organized.[34] But these practices disappointed the frontier people and provoked many complaints. For instance, in 1386 John I, after taking note of the grievances of Alcalá, wrote to the Trinitarian and Mercedarian headquarters warning them that all testamentary legacies collected in Alcalá for ransoming captives must only be employed in the redemption of its native inhabitants.[35]

In these circumstances, frontier people were more interested in making direct contacts with their Muslim neighbours in each frontier district. Town council records from Jaén and Jerez de la Frontera, which have been studied by Carriazo and Sancho de Sopranis, show that the activities of local *alfaqueques* constituted the best procedure for ransoming captives.[36] The different town councils appointed their own *alfaqueques*, whose missions, rights, and duties were regulated by the *Partidas*, the famous law code of Alfonso X. According to the *Partidas* a good *alfaqueque* combined the following characteristics: (1) he should be trustworthy; (2) he should not be a covetous person; (3) he should have a knowledge of Arabic; (4) he should possess diplomatic qualities; (5) he should be courageous and long-suffering; (6) he should be well-off and, in consequence, able to act as a guarantor for the payment of ransoms.[37]

The *alfaqueques* could enter the kingdom of Granada without hindrance if they obtained a special permission called the *amān* or safe conduct, which permitted them to travel or reside in Muslim

---

[33] These monks sold the silver lamps and other ornaments of the monastery in order to finance the rescue of fifty captives. See Torres Fontes, 'La frontera de Granada', 203–4.

[34] García Figueras, 'Relaciones fronterizas', 282.

[35] Juan Lovera, 'Catálogo de Alcalá la Real', doc. 31, p. 33.

[36] García Figueras, 'Relaciones fronterizas', 280; Carriazo, 'Relaciones fronterizas', 39.

[37] *Apud* Torres Fontes, 'Los alfaqueques castellanos', 102–3.

territory for a limited period. However, these *musta'min* or holders of *amān* were expected to respect the religious beliefs and practices of the Muslims and to abstain from saying or doing anything which might be construed as lack of respect for Islam. These provisions help to explain the martyrdom of several Mercedarians at different times. We know that they took advantage of their presence among the captives to say mass and administer the sacraments, although it is not clear whether this was done with the permission of the Granadan authorities or clandestinely.[38] Moreover, as far as the local *alfaqueques* were concerned, they did not enjoy complete liberty of movement. According to custom, they were obliged to travel by the main routes while displaying an *alfaqueque*'s flag and sounding trumpets.[39]

As these *alfaqueques* were above frontier hostility and enjoyed something akin to diplomatic immunity, they not only arranged for the liberation of captives, but they could also act as merchants, ambassadors, and spies—and not always on the right side.[40] All these reasons explain the royal interest in controlling their activities by means of an official known as the *alfaqueque mayor de tierra de moros*—that is, a sort of superior whose jurisdiction covered all the frontier. This office was first mentioned in the Cortes of Toro of 1371, but the Crown apparently did not name any person to hold it. As far as the fifteenth century is concerned, we know about these *alfaqueques mayores* from 1439 onwards, when the office was always held by members of the Saavedra lineage. The different royal appointments specified the rights and duties of this official, who was the only one who could organize the ransom of captives along the whole frontier from Tarifa to Lorca. In theory, all the existing urban *alfaqueques* had to be recognized and accepted by the *alfaqueque mayor*; but in practice the Saavedra were always quarrelling with the different municipalities, who were aware and jealous of their autonomy and privileges.[41]

How were these problems viewed from the Muslim side? We

[38] On the doctrine of *amān*, see Lambton, *State and Government*, 201.

[39] Torres Fontes, 'Los alfaqueques castellanos', 114; Hipólito Sancho de Sopranis, 'Jerez y el reino de Granada a mediados del siglo XV', *Tamuda*, 2 (1954), 287–308, at 305.

[40] MacKay, 'The Ballad and the Frontier', 24.

[41] Torres Fontes, 'Los alfaqueques castellanos', 104–9; José Enrique López de Coca Castañer, 'Esclavos, alfaqueques y mercaderes en la frontera del mar de Alborán, 1490–1516', *Hispania*, 38 (1978), 275–300, at 288–9.

know nothing about the living conditions of Muslim captives in Andalusia and Murcia, but the diplomatic negotiations show that the Granadan population felt very concerned about the fate of those who lived in captivity.[42] Ibn al-Khatib, the famous statesman and scholar of the fourteenth century, wrote about a fellow countryman, Muḥammad b. Aḥmad al-Dawsi (1270–1328), who exhorted the Muslims to collect funds for ransoming captives.[43] The patchy documents which have survived show that testamentary legacies were very important; but it appears that most of the money was obtained from the revenues of mosques, which were used both for feeding poor people and for ransoming captives.[44]

The activities of Muslim *alfaqueques* are ill documented, but it is clear that they were more numerous than their Christian counterparts. They paid ransoms with silk because Castilians often refused to accept Nasrid currency, which suffered a continuous depreciation of its value during the fifteenth century.[45] In this sense, a contemporary *fatwa* or juridicial opinion condemned an *alfaqueque* because, being obliged by the Christians to pay in Granadan currency a total which was double the amount previously agreed, he attempted to compensate for his losses by blackmailing the families who had engaged his services. The same *fatwa* accused other *alfaqueques* of making profits from the silk trade during their ransoming activities. According to it, these *alfaqueques* used to advance money against future supplies of silk, which was a practice considered as usury and thus condemned by *fiqh* or juridical doctrine.[46]

TRADE RELATIONS

Without an *amān* or safe conduct no exchange or ransom of captives was possible, because neither Christians nor Muslims

---

[42] Generally speaking, they appear as household slaves. See Luis Suárez Fernández, *Historia del reinado de Juan I de Castilla*, ii: *Registro documental, 1371–1383* (Madrid, 1982), 200; Torres Fontes, 'La frontera de Granada', 200–1.

[43] Arié, *L'Espagne musulmane*, 326 n. 4.

[44] A testament dated 17 Mar. 1487 was published in *Documentos arábigo-granadinos*, ed. Luis Seco de Lucena Paredes (Madrid, 1961), doc. 58, p. 101 (Spanish translation p. 109).

[45] For a contract of redemption dated 7 Aug. 1486, see ibid. doc. 57, p. 100 (Spanish translation p. 108).

[46] López Ortiz, 'Fatwàs granadinas', 94–5; Carriazo, 'Relaciones fronterizas', 40.

were allowed to enter or leave Castile and Granada. Such 'passports' regularized the crossing of the frontier and avoided illegal movements which would have aggravated the tension between the two sides. But the grant of these safe conducts during the periods of truce also facilitated trade relations.[47]

Trade was more essential for Granada than for Castile. Granadan agriculture was characterized by the intense exploitation of limited areas in order to support a relatively dense population. But the production of cereals was not enough for the demands of internal consumption. Cereals had to be imported and they were paid for by specialized crops (dried fruits), and by industrial products, especially silk and sugar. As far as we know, this was the pattern of maritime trade, where the Genoese played a very important role. But Granada was lacking in olive oil and cattle as well, and these commodities could be more easily obtained from across the frontier with Castile.[48] The customs tariff of Alcalá la Real of 1476 details the commodities that crossed the frontier in both directions: from Castile to Granada—young cattle, cows, clothes, friezes or woollen clothes, cowls, tunics, hose, olive oil, and honey; from Granada to Castile—sardines, silk, linen, dried fruits, sugar, burnooses, and Moorish veils.[49]

It is not possible to think in terms of a free trade because both ecclesiastical laws and Castilian civil laws prohibited the export of war material which might strengthen Granada against the Christians. Thus weapons and implements of war were considered as contraband, the sale of which was absolutely forbidden. Similarly horses, mules, and cereals were so useful in war that their sale was also prohibited. In order to avoid contraband and for tax purposes the Castilian Crown set up control centres on the frontier in order to inspect merchants. These centres were knowns as *puertos* and customs officials there levied the *diezmo y medio diezmo de lo morisco*, which was a 15 per cent tax on the value of commodities.

---

[47] The Egyptian scholar 'Abd al-Basít, who visited Granada in 1466, wished to benefit from a truce to go to Córdoba with Muslim merchants. See G. Levi della Vida, 'Il regno di Granata nel 1465–1466 nei ricordi di un viaggiatore egiziano', *Al Andalus*, 1 (1933), 307–34, at 324.

[48] José Enrique López de Coca Castañer, 'Comercio exterior del reino de Granada', in *Actas del II Coloquio de Historia Medieval Andaluza* (Seville, 1982), 335–77.

[49] Pedro A. Porras Arboledas, 'El comercio fronterizo entre Andalucía y el reino de Granada a través de sus gravámenes fiscales', *Baetica*, 7 (1984), 245–53, at Appendix I, p. 250.

There was of course a similar tax on the Moorish side, known as *magran.*[50]

The number and location of these *puertos* changed according to political circumstances and according to the different truces signed by kings and sultans. In the truce of 1406 Henry III only permitted trade through the *puerto* of Alcalá la Real, the shorter route to the Nasrid capital, but in the truces of 1439 and 1443 the *puertos* which were established were Alcalá la Real, Huelma, on the north-east frontier, and Zahara or Antequera in the western regions. Trade could also be subject to other restrictions. In the case of Alcalá la Real, for example, Muslim merchants crossing the frontier could go only as far as the little town of Alcaudete while their Christian counterparts had to stop at Puerto Lope.[51] Similarly the urban authorities of Jaén warned Christian merchants in 1417 that they could enter Muslim territory only on Mondays and Fridays. Their safe conducts were therefore useless on other days, and if they were robbed or attacked by the Moors, they would not be able to count on Christian reprisals as a means for compensation.[52]

In addition to the tax-collectors there were other officials in charge of preventing contraband—at least on the Castilian side of the frontier. They were called *alcaldes de las sacas* and their jurisdiction was divided into two zones. Members of the Saavedra lineage, already mentioned in their capacity as *alfaqueques mayores*, were also the *alcaldes de las sacas* in the archbishopric of Seville and the bishopric of Cádiz from 1445 onwards.[53]

However, there are many indications that there was considerable smuggling across the frontier. An interesting document from Alcalá la Real describes the predicament of a customs official in 1420 when, with the local authorities turning a blind eye, the whole population devoted itself to smuggling while he was confined to his house and even threatened with death.[54] Doubtless this was an exceptional case, but the contraband trade could take other forms. A written report sent to John II (c.1429) pointed out

[50] Miguel Ángel Ladero Quesada, 'Almojarifazgo sevillano y comercio exterior de Andalucía en el siglo XV', *Anuario de historia económica y social*, 2 (1969), 69–115, at 99.
[51] Mitre Fernández, 'De la toma de Algeciras', 118; Amador de los Ríos, *Memoria histórico-crítica*, doc. lxxx, pp. 133–7.
[52] Porras Arboledas, 'El comercio fronterizo', Appendix II, p. 251.
[53] Ibid. 248–50.
[54] Juan Lovera, 'Catálogo de Alcalá la Real', doc. 60, pp. 13–14, 42–3.

that frontier castellans tolerated smuggling because they were in league with the smugglers and received a share of the profits. And if this happened in frontier districts belonging to the Crown, the situation was worse in areas belonging to other lordships.[55]

As has already been noted, the export of horses and mules to Granada was forbidden. In order to enforce this prohibition John I stipulated in 1380 that all such animals located within twelve leagues of the frontier should be recorded along with such features as their ages, sizes, and colours. But the smugglers reacted to this challenge by crossing the frontier through a *puerto* in the company of Christian merchants, selling their beasts in Muslim territory, and recrossing the frontier at a different place as if they were merchants. This explains why in 1382 the same king ordered customs officials to record the movements of merchants on a 'round-trip' basis.[56]

Matters were not much different with respect to the licensed trade in other livestock. The problem here was that the Castilian authorities limited the number of heads of livestock that could be sent to Granada during the periods established by the different truces. But as the frontier zone was mainly a wilderness rich in pastures, there were cattle on the move on the Christian side during the whole year, and they could be slipped across the frontier on the sly. It is not surprising, therefore, that in 1479 the Catholic Kings ordered the recording of livestock grazing within ten leagues of the frontier.[57] But there was also another way of smuggling livestock which could be described as 'half-licensed'. On the south-west frontier, the Moors from the mountains and high plains of Ronda, Villaluenga, and Marbella used to rent their heavily forested hills to Christians from Gibraltar, Jimena, and Jerez by means of oral agreements. In this way Christians put sheep, cows, and pigs—but not horses—into Muslim territory. Normally, they then gave the Moors a certain number of sheep and cows, as well as olive oil, as rent (but not, of course, pigs). This pattern is documented for the last quarter of the fifteenth century. It appears that such practices were also common on the

---

[55] Miguel Ángel Ladero Quesada, *La Hacienda Real de Castilla en el siglo XV* (La Laguna, 1973), 333 and 343.
[56] Suárez Fernández, *Historia del reinado de Juan I*, doc. xliv, pp. 120–2.
[57] *Colección diplomática de Jaén*, doc. xliv, pp. 120–2.

north-east frontier, where the cattle from the Christian town of Lorca were led to pasture in the Muslim mountains of Huéscar.[58]

PEACE-KEEPING MACHINERY

The most common problems on the frontier in terms of 'official' truce were, generally speaking, those relating to kidnapping, robbery, cattle-rustling, and the consequent reprisals.[59] As a result, in truce negotiations between Castile and Granada considerable care was taken to set up trans-frontier administrative arrangements in order to avoid such incidents. The origins of this peace-keeping machinery pre-date the period under discussion. In the truce of 1310 both sides agreed to appoint some *boni homines* to deal with such problems. Later on, the biographer of the Marinid Sultan Abu'l-Hasan, Ibn Marzuq, described his own journey to the north-west frontier in 1333, where he stayed a long time 'at the frontier between the Christians and Muslims, listening to the complaints of people from both religions, maintaining the rights of all and sundry'.[60]

As it emerged, the Muslim institution of a judge was independent from its Christian counterpart. The Granadan judge, known as *al-qāḍi bayna-l-mulūk* or 'the judge between the kings', dealt only with Christian complaints about Muslim transgressions. His authority covered the whole frontier, although it is probable that he could appoint deputies for each district. This magistracy was in the hands of the same lineage throughout the fifteenth century— that of the Banū al-Amin, who were well known in Castile

[58] Manuel Acién Almansa, *Ronda y su serranía en tiempo de los Reyes Católicos* (3 vols., Málaga, 1979), i. 136–7; Miguel Rodríguez Llopis, *Señorío y feudalismo en el reino de Murcia* (Murcia, 1986), 230.

[59] The conflict across the frontier was facilitated by the nature of the terrain and the patterns of settlement. Ease of penetration was aided by the absence of permanent settlement in many parts, and the abundance of stock and lack of people helped to make raiding endemic. There were plenty of movable goods and few people to tend them. See María C. Quintanilla Raso, 'Consideraciones sobre la vida en la frontera de Granada', in *Actas del III Coloquio de Historia Medieval Andaluza* (Jaén, 1984), 501–19, at 508–9, 519.

[60] Andrés Giménez Soler, *La Corona de Aragón y Granada* (Barcelona, 1909), 167–70; Ibn Marzuq, *El 'Musnad': Hechos memorables de Abū l-Ḥasan, sultán de los benimerines*, ed. and trans. María J. Viguera Molíns (Madrid, 1977), 325–6.

because its members usually acted as the negotiators of truces.[61]

Compared to such a centralized institution, the Castilian equivalent presents itself as compartmentalized from the very beginning. There were *alcaldes entre los cristianos y los moros* (judges between the Christians and Moors), also known as *jueces de las querellas* (judges of complaints), in the region of Murcia, in the episcopal regions of Córdoba-Jaén, etc. In the case of Murcia these judges are documented from 1378 to 1403 and were always associated with the Fajardo family, who also provided the *adelantados* or wardens of that region.[62] In the case of Córdoba-Jaén, the office is more or less documented from 1381 to 1420, and it was attached to the lineage of the Fernández de Córdoba.[63] In dealing with frontier incidents these judges had at their disposal men who were not unlike scouts. Known as *rastreros* or *fieles del rastro*, they investigated cases within their own areas and, if the trail led across a municipal boundary, they handed on the task of detection and pursuit to their colleagues. These scouts did not depend on the judges but upon the local municipalities and they were paid by their own urban authorities. However, they could also be paid by an individual who had called on their services.[64] All the thirty *rastreros* of Jaén in 1479 were members of a closed corporation, and they were paid 200 *maravedíes* for each investigation, with the money being shared out between those who actually carried out the task.[65]

The institution of the 'judge of complaints' or 'judge between the kings' emerged in order to avoid the negative results of trans-frontier reprisals and vendettas. Both polities developed a system that, in theory, would prevent the escalation of violent incidents and would also provide a method of making quick reparations. But

---

[61] Luis Seco de Lucena Paredes, 'El juez de frontera y los fieles del rastro', *Miscelánea de estudios árabes y hebraicos*, 7 (1958), 137–40, at 139–40; id. 'Sobre el juez de frontera', *Miscelánea de estudios árabes y hebraicos*, 11 (1962), 107–9, at 109.

[62] Juan Torres Fontes, 'El alcalde entre moros y cristianos del reino de Murcia', *Hispania*, 20 (1960), 55–80; Suárez Fernández, *Historia del reinado de Juan I*, 72, 107.

[63] María C. Quintanilla Raso, *Nobleza y señoríos en el reino de Córdoba: La casa de Aguilar (siglos XIV y XV)* (Córdoba, 1979), 61; Juan de Mata Carriazo, 'Un alcalde entre los cristianos y los moros, en la frontera de Granada', *Al Andalus*, 13 (1948), 34–96.

[64] Juan Torres Fontes, 'Notas sobre los fieles del rastro y alfaqueques murcianos', *Miscelánea de estudios árabes y hebraicos*, 10 (1961), 89–105.

[65] Carriazo, 'Relaciones fronterizas', 33–4.

in practice things were quite different. As far as is known, judges' decisions were not always accepted and their sentences were not executed. In these circumstances people's complaints and grievances were only appeased by a system of controlled reprisals.[66]

In April 1428 representatives from all the places belonging to the *Adelantamiento* or March of Cazorla met at the little village of Santo Tomé to discuss what to do about the continuous Granadan raids despite the truce then in force. According to the 'use and custom of the March', they decided to call on the services of Christian raiders—but only to attack those particular territories from which the Muslim raids were launched. By the terms of the contract the Castilian raiders were to cross the frontier in order to seize hostages or livestock so that there would be something with which to bargain afterwards.[67] However, it should be noted that during this meeting no mention was made of the possibility of appealing to the judges. And this was not the only case. Professor Carriazo pointed out long ago that the institutionalized judges were in the long run useless. Both the Christian and Muslim judges, for example, are totally absent from the very detailed and practical frontier arrangements surviving in the municipal documentation of Jaén from 1479. Something similar happened in other frontier areas, as documents from Jerez for the same period demonstrate.[68]

As a rule the issues motivating conflicts were local and personal, with the result that there was a local search for stability and local arrangements evolved as one of the principal mechanisms which responded to the destabilizing effects of these conflicts. Two examples from the region round Gibraltar will illustrate the nature of this trans-frontier co-operation.

The first example concerns a case of kidnapping. One day in 1470 an individual named Gonzalo de Bollullos asked the castellan of Gibraltar, Pedro de Porras, for permission to go to the nearby Moorish village of Casares in order to sell a certain amount of olive oil. The castellan sent the local *alfaqueque* to the Muslims in order to arrange a meeting-place and the conditions of the

[66] For an example from Alcalá (1392), see Juan Lovera, 'Catálogo de Alcalá la Real', doc. 35, pp. 75–6.
[67] C. Sáez Rivera, 'El derecho de represalia en el Adelantamiento de Cazorla durante el siglo XV' (unpublished paper).
[68] García Figueras, 'Relaciones fronterizas', *passim*.

transaction. The Muslims agreed to meet Bollullos at the mouth of the River Guadiaro in two weeks' time. Then Bollullos publicly announced that he was going to Seville to get the olive oil and he set off. But, instead of going to Seville, he crossed the Straits to the Portuguese garrison of Alcazarseguer. Once there, he chartered a little galley with twenty-five *almogávares* or raiders and had several jars filled up with water with oil floating on the surface. They sailed to the meeting-place and, lying in ambush, they shortly thereafter seized six Moors who, as expected, had come from Casares to transact business. The captives were to be sold in the Portuguese town of Ceuta, on the opposite side of the Straits. The Muslim authorities appealed to Pedro de Porras, who reacted quickly. His letters to the count of Villarreal, governor of Ceuta, secured the release of five of the six Moors who had been abducted, but the sixth Moor had already been sold to a Portuguese from Berja (in the south of Portugal). For this reason Pedro de Porras arrested one of Bollullo's nephews and sent him to Casares as a hostage, while Bollullo's other relatives were charged with the task of ransoming the remaining Muslim.[69]

The second example reveals the fact that when a raid or an attack occurred, this did not necessarily prevent trans-frontier collaboration and help. Round about 1471–2 Christian castellans from Jimena and Gibraltar met up with Muslim castellans from Ronda, Casares, and Marbella by the River Guadiaro in order to adjust the boundary-line. But at this same time the famous Granadan aristocratic lineage of the Banū al-Sarrāŷ had revolted against the sultan, seized the town of Málaga, and announced that they were ready to attack Christian territory. However, the Muslim castellans mentioned above promised to warn the Christians if the rebels came to their region so that they could ensure the security of their livestock. Yet, later, when the Banū al-Sarrāŷ attacked the territories of Jimena and Gibraltar, they obtained a great deal of booty. What had happened? The Moorish castellan of Marbella, 'Alī ibn Kumāsa, was a member of the Granadan élite connected with the rebels, and he did not notify the Christians about the impending raid. But the Banū al-Ḥakīm, a local lineage which ruled Ronda and its district, were furious about this failure of collaboration. Moreover, the castellan of

<hr>

[69] Málaga, Archivo Catedral, file 62, books 10 and 38.

Casares apologized to the Christians of Jimena and Gibraltar and volunteered that, if the Christians wanted to retaliate by mounting an expedition against the lands of Málaga, Muslims from Casares would head the party.[70]

Such examples could easily be multiplied.[71] Do they reveal the existence of a sense of a common frontier identity? Scholars usually regard frontier societies as being peripheral due to the remoteness of the people from central government. And, precisely because they were remote from central authority, they had to create their own semi-formal patterns of behaviour and mutual collaboration in order to survive. A frontier society belonged to its central authority but, left to its own devices, it adapted to the opposing frontier society in different ways. Although marked by hostility, frontier societies also tended to become like each other; the violence was counterbalanced by a degree of acculturation, the use of peace-keeping mechanisms, and even a sense of frontier identity.[72]

However, although elements of all this can be glimpsed on the Castilian–Granadan frontier, the reality of the secular trend was quite different. According to González Dávila, the biographer of Henry III who wrote about these trans-frontier arrangements in the mid-seventeenth century, peace 'is not a serious proposition when different laws and religions are involved'.[73] In this sense, the best evidence is afforded by the aggressive behaviour which Christian frontier people displayed against their Muslim neighbours just after the Nasrid kingdom had been conquered by the Catholic Kings. Both in the south-west and in the north-east of the former Muslim kingdom, where Muslims remained after the conquest as *mudéjares*, the Christians removed landmarks and boundary-stones, and they cancelled the agreements concerning the use of

---

[70] Ibid. and book 12. Sometimes the quarrels of the kings had little effect on this area. See López de Coca, 'Revisión de una década', 81–2. See also the letter which the warden Per Afan de Ribera sent to the town council of Seville on 24 July, 1450: Seville, Archivo Municipal, Actas Capitulares 1450, fo. 97.

[71] Sancho de Sopranis, 'Jerez y el reino de Granada', 292–3; Juan Lovera, 'Catálogo de Alcalá la Real', doc. 33, p. 34; Carriazo, 'Relaciones fronterizas', 43; MacKay, 'The Ballad and the Frontier', 24.

[72] Owen Lattimore, *Studies in Frontier History: Collected Papers, 1928–1958* (London, 1962), 470; Carriazo, 'Un alcalde', 92; MacKay, 'The Ballad and the Frontier', 25–6.

[73] Gil González Dávila, *Historia de la vida y hechos del rey don Henrique III de Castilla* (Madrid, 1638), 181.

pastures. Such collaboration, they claimed, was not useful once the Moors had been finally defeated.[74]

EPILOGUE

In conclusion it should be emphasized that the conquest of Granada (1482–92) did not signify the disappearance of all the institutions which have been examined here. For example, the defunct frontier continued to exist for taxational purposes because the *diezmo y medio diezmo de lo morisco* was maintained for a short period, despite the protests of the Christian settlers who had just established themselves in the conquered lands. The vast majority of these colonists were dissatisfied with their living conditions, and as a result they began to resent a royal policy which tolerated the staying-on of Muslims. Influenced by the ideology behind the Reconquest, these settlers believed that they had gone to Granada to recover the inheritance of their ancestors, which had been wrested from them by the infidels long ago. Naturally they did not want to live alongside the vanquished enemy, and they took advantage of any opportunity to assert their rights as Christians.[75]

It must also be remembered that a new frontier appeared just after the conquest of the Nasrid state—a coastal frontier threatened by North African piracy, and to which many of the techniques and mechanisms of the land frontier were transferred. For example, the financing and organization of ransom procedures continued to exist, with the *alfaqueques* being appointed by the local town councils, and of course with the lineage of the Saavedras once again attempting to control these activities.[76]

[74] García Guzmán, *El Adelantamiento de Cazorla*, 122–6; Archivo General de Simancas, Cámara-Pueblos, file 22 (concerning disputes between Vélez and Lorca); José Enrique López de Coca Castañer and Manuel Acién Almansa, 'Los mudéjares del obispado de Málaga (1485–1501)', in *Actas del I Simposio Internacional de Mudejarismo* (Madrid and Teruel, 1981), 307–47, at 329.

[75] Christian people living in the Málaga area registered their disagreement, and supported their arguments in the following way: 'We are Christians, we feel like Christians and we pay the Church as all Christians do. *We are not Moors and our properties are not in Moorish territory.* We all belong to the same king, land and lordship.' See José Enrique López de Coca Castañer, 'Poblamiento y frontera en el obispado de Málaga a fines del siglo XV', *Cuadernos de estudios medievales*, 2–3 (1974–5), 367–407, at 387–8; id. 'Privilegios fiscales y repoblación en el reino de Granada, 1485–1520', *Baetica*, 2 (1979), 205–23, at 213–14.

[76] López de Coca, 'Esclavos, alfaqueques', 282–92.

7

Economic and Political Institutions on the Polish–German Frontier in the Middle Ages: Action, Reaction, Interaction

PAUL KNOLL

Nearly half a century ago, the distinguished American medievalist S. Harrison Thomson, who died in 1975, undertook to summarize a millennium of relations between the Czechs and the Germans. Thomson's perceptions of East Central European history had been formed by his memories of the First World War period, in his own experiences in the 1920s and 1930s in Czechoslovakia, and in the cauldron of European politics that had boiled over into the early stages of the Second World War. When he wrote in 1941, the outcome of that war was by no means certain. Thomson was regarded (with good reason) as a fervent Czech nationalist with little affection for Germany. Nevertheless Thomson, whose appreciation of historical perspective marked him as the European he claimed all Americans were whether they knew it or not, took a long view of the course of relations on the Czech–German frontier.

It was his observation that while there had, indeed, been many instances of conflict between the two groups, the history of these relations was not one of simple antagonism. Rather, he wrote, 'in politics, culture and economic status there has been a pendulum-like swing between dominance by Czechs and dominance by the Germans'.[1] He concluded that a much more appropriate matrix within which to understand the history of these relations was the tripartite one which would account for moments of Czech dominance and of German response; moments of German dominance and Czech response; and times where there was not division and opposition but genuine co-operation. Thus he talked

---

[1] S. Harrison Thomson, 'Czech and German: Action, Reaction and Interaction', *Journal of Central European Affairs*, 1 (1941), 306–24, at 308.

of the history of this relationship as being one of 'action, reaction, and interaction'.[2]

I begin with this observation about one way of looking at a different European frontier from the one considered here, because it seems to me to provide some helpful suggestions about ways of understanding the nature of the Polish–German frontier in the Middle Ages. We must recognize that the elements in the history of that frontier contain many components which will not fit into the simplistic formulations of earlier scholarship. For example, what is one to make of the dichotomy between these two roughly contemporary observations? The first comes from an anonymous French Dominican who commented that he had found there to be a natural enmity (*odium naturale*) between the Poles and the Germans.[3] The second comes from an interpolation in the *Chronicle of Great Poland* and states that the Germans and the Slavs live together in partnership and that there are no other peoples in the world who are as courteous and friendly towards one another (*communes* and *familiares*) as the Slavs and the Germans.[4] Rather than try to reconcile these two opposing views, it seems to me that one should instead seek to understand how both could express differing aspects of the larger whole of relations on the German–Polish frontier in the Middle Ages.

In this study what I wish to attempt therefore is a description of certain developments within the Polish community and their relation to the fact that Poland stood on the eastern side of a frontier which was, in very many ways, influenced from the German lands to the west. We shall have reference, in roughly

[2] S. Harrison Thomson, 'Czech and German: Action, Reaction and Interaction', *Journal of Central European Affairs*, 1 (1941), 313 and 316; see also 323–4. Thomson's more fully developed views on Czech history, and on Czech–German relations in particular, are expressed in his *Czechoslovakia in European History* (2nd edn., Princeton, 1953), in which the article cited above in this note and n. 1 appears in revised form as ch. 7 (130–58). For an analysis of Thomson's views and of his historiographical contribution, see Lubomyr R. Wynar, *S. Harrison Thomson: Bio-bibliography* (University of Colorado Bio-bibliographical Series 1, Boulder, Colo., 1963); and the comments of Gray Boyce *et al.*, 'S. Harrison Thompson', *Speculum*, 51 (1976), 578–80.

[3] 'Quod naturale odium est inter eos et Teotonicos', *Anonymi descriptio Europae orientalis*, ed. Olgierd Górka (Cracow, 1916), 56.

[4] 'Nec aliqua gens in mundo est sibi tam communis et familiaris veluti Slaui et Theutonici. Sic eciam per Latinos ducz a quo Theutonici et Slaws a quo Slawi, germani qui et fratres sunt appellati', *Chronica Poloniae Maioris*, ed. Brygida Kürbis, *MPH*, NS 8 (Warsaw, 1970), 6–7.

chronological order, to aspects of economic structure and the changing fortunes of Polish state forms. Necessarily we will touch at times upon concerns which are relevant to the themes that constitute the subjects addressed by others in this volume, but our focus will be primarily upon institutions and the varying impact upon them from the western side of our frontier.

The early state of the Piasts was one which coalesced around the person of the duke, a military and political leader who was, with the coronation of Bolesław Chrobry in 1025, elevated to the status of king. The emergence of the duke was based in a social transformation which had superceded the older tradition of small tribal assemblies of freemen presided over by elders. In these, issues had been decided by consensus and by deferring to the wisdom and experience of the elders. Such military leaders as had been necessary had been chosen by the group and given limited authority.

   By the eve of Poland's entry into the historical consciousness of Christian Europe in the tenth century, these military leaders had successfully transformed their tenuous political control into something more substantial by attempting to secure wealth and office for themselves and their heirs. They extended their authority over the surrounding territory, often from fortified settlements which the Polish historian Witold Hensel has called 'incipient towns'.[5] They were supported in this by military retainers. Eventually a new political aristocracy emerged which was able to reduce some of the peasantry to servitude and to obtain tribute from the remainder of the free population. From among the many regional, though small-scale, territorial organizations, the state of the Polanes in the Warta river valley based in Gniezno was ultimately successful in dominating the others. It was this entity that the Saxons came in contact with in 963.[6]

[5] Witold Hensel, *Anfänge der Städte bei den Ost- und Westslawen* (Bautzen, 1967), 29–30; id., 'The Origins of Western and Eastern European Slav Towns', in M. W. Barley (ed.), *European Towns: Their Archaeology and Early History* (London, 1977), 373–90, at 375. His views, as expressed in these publications in Western languages, are more fully developed in his *Słowiańszczyzna wczes-nośredniowieczna: Zarys kultury materialnej* (4th edn., Warsaw, 1987), ch. 3, 393–525.
[6] The early history of the Polish tribes ('prehistory' in the sense that written records are not available) has been studied in masterful detail by Henryk Łowmiański, *Początki Polski* (6 vols., Warsaw, 1964–85); for the period to the middle of the 10th century, see vols. i–iv especially. His work, while it may be

154 *Paul Knoll*

This early Polish state was characterized by a system of governance in which the duke and his representatives (who were eventually called castellans) organized the economy of the countryside in order to support their own social, military, and nutritional requirements. Though a majority of the populace was theoretically free, with hereditary rights to the land, they were subject to the demands of the duke and his representatives. These included taxes paid in kind, and sometimes in money, as well as a range of specific services which were rendered to the duke, his court, and his local administrators. This system (the precise nature and significance of which has been hotly disputed in Polish historiography) has come to be known as the *ius ducale*.[7]

Between the tenth and the twelfth centuries the system of the *ius ducale* generally functioned effectively. As the needs of the state increased, however, correspondingly heavy burdens were laid upon the populace. Nor was it only the duke (and later the king) and his administration who imposed these. An institution like the Church, not yet itself heavily endowed and not yet having established its own immunities, co-operated closely with the ruler, with whom it had been reciprocally associated since Duke Mieszko's conversion to Christianity in the 960s.[8] To fulfill the

challenged in details, is now the standard treatment of the topic. A brief introduction to these issues is provided in my entry on 'Poland' in Joseph R. Strayer (ed.), *The Dictionary of the Middle Ages*, ix (New York, 1987), 716–31, at 716–17.

[7] The literature on this controversial topic is enormous. Among the most important recent contributions are Tadeusz Lalik, 'Organizacja grodowo-prowincjonalna w Polsce XI i początków XII wieku', *Studia z Dziejów Osadnictwa*, 5 (1967), 5–51; Karol Buczek, 'Z badań nad organizacją grodową w Polsce wczesnofeudalnej: Problem terytorialności grodów kasztelańskich', *Kwartalnik Historyczny*, 77 (1970), 3–29; id., 'Gospodarcze funkcje organizacji grodowej w Polsce wczesnofeudalnej (wiek X–XIII)', *Kwartalnik Historyczny*, 86 (1979), 363–84; and Karol Modzelewski, *Organizacja gospodarcza państwa piastowskiego: X–XIII wiek* (Wrocław, 1975). See also the treatment of this process in Łowmiański, *Początki Polski*, vols. iv–v. Modzelewski's views on the character and significance of the *ius ducale* have been challenged by Oskar Kossmann, *Polen im Mittelalter*, ii: *Staat, Gesellschaft, Wirtschaft im Bannkreis des Westens* (Marburg/Lahn, 1985), 303–89, 430–51, 484–536, *passim*. (Kossmann is also implictly polemicizing with Buczek in much of what he writes.) For a convenient guide in English to this problem, compare Karol Modzelewski, 'The System of the *Ius Ducale* and the Idea of Feudalism', *Quaestiones Medii Aevi*, 1 (1977), 71–99; and Tadeusz Wasilewski, 'Poland's Administrative Structure in Early Piast Times', *Acta Poloniae historica*, 44 (1981), 5–31.

[8] The Christianization of Poland and the relationship between the Church and the Piast rulers in the early Middle Ages is treated by Zygmunt Sułowski, 'Początki Kościoła polskiego', in Jerzy Kłoczowski (ed.), *Kościół w Polsce*, i:

needs of the *ius ducale*, obligations were defined and particular groups were given specialized duties, rights, and privileges. Vestiges of this phenomenon can be seen to this day in the place-names of localities which date to the early Piast period. These have come to be called service villages and reflect a degree of specialization associated with their inhabitants. The population would have continued to be involved in farming. But, in addition, they functioned as cooks or bakers (thus we have settlements named Kuchary and Piekary, i.e., cooks and bakers); as beaver keepers or mare breeders (hence Bobrowniki and Kobylniki); as armament manufacturers such as shield, arrow, or helmet makers (thus Szczytniki, Grotniki, and Szłomniki); and even as church servants (hence place-names like Świątniki).[9]

The *ius ducale* was a system which, though it may have analogues elsewhere, was derived from the native, local traditions, and it owed little or nothing in its structure to influences from the west. But other aspects of the early Piast state reflect greater contact with the world to the west of the frontier.

From its very beginnings Poland welcomed foreigners. The earliest bishops of the Polish Church came from abroad, chiefly from the German lands. The first, Jordan (though there continues to be controversy over his origins), probably came from within the Empire when he arrived in Poland in the 960s, shortly after Mieszko's conversion, to establish a missionary see subject directly to the papacy. His successor Unger, and later figures such as Poppo and Reinbern, also came from the German lands. But the most important representative of Christian piety in early Piast Poland was the German Bruno of Querfurt, who found a martyr's death—probably among the Jaćwings—in 1009. Other important priests and monks came from Italy, while the marriage of Mieszko II to the niece of Emperor Otto III established firm Polish ties with the Rhineland and with Lorraine. Thus during the tenth, eleventh, and twelfth centuries the Polish Church drew upon the contribution

Średniowiecze (Cracow, 1966), 17–123, and, more briefly, id., 'L'Église polonaise à ses origines', in Jerzy Kłoczowski (ed.), *Histoire religieuse de la Pologne* (Paris, 1987), 17–51.

[9] Occupational and service settlements, and the names associated with them, are discussed in detail by Zofia Podwińska, *Zmiany form osadnictwa wiejskiego na ziemiach polskich we wcześniejszym średniowieczu: Źreb, wieś, opole* (Wrocław, 1971), who identifies more than 400 such places. See also Wasilewski, 'Poland's Administrative Structure', 17–21.

of these foreigners to establish both an organizational structure and enduring traditions of spirituality.[10]

Another important category of foreigners in Poland, particularly from Germany, was knights. Bolesław Chrobry, and after him his successors, utilized foreign troops, especially in expeditions to the east against the Kievan state. The old historiographical fiction about the 'Norman' or 'Varangian' influence in the formation and development of the early Polish state can no longer be upheld, and with the demise of this theory goes much ambiguous evidence about the use which Poland's early rulers made of foreign troops.[11] But enough concrete information remains to enable us to speak with confidence about foreign participation in Polish military activity.[12] Two examples, among many, may be chosen to illustrate this point. Gallus Anonymous tells us in his *Chronicle* about Bolesław Chrobry's utilization of such troops by commenting that he (Bolesław) would invite foreign knights to his court and 'if any honourable man won recognition from him in knightly service, he was no longer called a knight but a royal son. And if he learned—as it sometimes happens—that one of them had had bad luck with his horses or anything else, then he would lavish on him endless gifts.'[13] Another example comes from Thietmar of

[10] The standard treatment on ecclesiastical organization remains Władysław Abraham, *Organizacja Kościoła w Polsce do połowy wieku XII* (3rd edn., Poznań, 1962). More briefly, see Sułowski, 'L'Eglise polonaise', 41–51, and Urszula Borkowska, 'La Reconstruction et le développement: Fin du xie et xiie siècle', in Jerzy Kłoczowski (ed.), *Histoire religieuse de la Pologne* (Paris, 1987), 56–67. For secular contacts, see the details in Herbert Ludat, *An Elbe und Oder um das Jahr 1000: Skizzen zur Politik des Ottonenreiches und der slavischen Mächte in Mitteleuropa* (Cologne and Vienna, 1971).

[11] The 'Norman Theory' on the origins of Poland is discussed and its repudiation traced by Gerard Labuda, 'Początki państwa polskiego w historiografii polskiej i niemieckiej', in *Stosunki polsko-niemieckie w historiografii* (Poznań, 1974), 150–217. The unsoundness of this theory was demonstrated in Western scholarship by Herbert Ludat, *Die Anfänge des polnischen Staates* (Cracow, 1942).

[12] Compare the older treatment by Karl Bartels, *Deutsche Krieger in polnischen Diensten von Misika I. bis Kasimir dem Großen, c.963–1370* (Berlin, 1922), with Kossmann, *Polen im Mittelalter*, ii. 171–87, and Benedykt Zientara, 'Foreigners in Poland in the 10th–15th Centuries: Their Role in the Opinion of Polish Medieval Community', *Acta Poloniae historica*, 29 (1974), 5–28, at 5–11.

[13] 'Et quicumque probus hospes apud eum in militia probabatur, non miles ille sed regis filius vocabatur; et si quandoque, ut assolet, eorum aliquem infelicem in equis vel in aliis audiebat, infinita dando ei circumstantibus alludebat', *Galli chronicon*, ed. August Bielowski, *MPH* i (Lwów, 1864, repr. Warsaw, 1966), 379–484, at 410. There is a newer edition of this chronicle by Karol Maleczyński, *MPH*, NS 2 (Cracow, 1952), which I have not been able to consult.

Merseburg's *Chronicle*, when he records the story of the German knight Erik the Proud who fought on Bolesław's side against his own countrymen, was taken prisoner, and languished some years in prison. He eventually returned to Poland to fight under Bolesław in one of the Kiev campaigns, on which he died in 1018.[14]

It is not surprising that foreigners should be invited to Poland. The land was underpopulated in comparison with lands to the west, and rulers often recruited settlers. Such individuals were granted the special status of free guest (*hospes*), were guaranteed personal freedom, and were given special protection.[15] By the end of the twelfth century the number of these *hospites* was beginning to grow, but their arrival was part of a series of developments which must be introduced below.

Before doing so, however, it is appropriate to note here that other foreigners came to reside in Poland in the early centuries of the Piast period, though not in a voluntary way. These were individuals captured during wartime, either by Poles raiding into other lands or in expeditions by others into Poland. These prisoners were often resettled in Poland. A number of place-names suggest they were founded by prisoners of war who had been settled by ethnic grouping. Thus we have in the vicinity of Cracow alone the following villages: one Czechy (Czechs), three Sarbias (Serbs or Sorbs), a Ruszca (Ruthenians), a Prusy (Prussians), two Węgrzce and a Węgrzynowice (Hungarians), a Pieczeniegi (Pechenegs), and a Pomorzany (Pomeranians). A little further from Cracow are Prusy, Prusinowice, Morawiany (Moravians), and more. Such place-names, with the same origin, can be replicated throughout other regions of Poland.[16] Whatever the origins of the populace in such places and their originally

---

[14] Thietmar of Merseburg, *Chronicon*, ed. Robert Holtzmann (SRG, Berlin, 1935), 418, 528–9.

[15] On the status and the origins of the free guests, compare Stanisław Trawkowski, 'Die Rolle der deutschen Dorfkolonisation und des deutschen Rechts in Polen im 13. Jahrhundert', in Walter Schlesinger (ed.), *Die deutsche Ostsiedlung des Mittelalters als Problem der europäischen Geschichte* (Vorträge und Forschungen 18, Sigmaringen, 1975), 349–68, at 351–4; and Kossmann, *Polen im Mittelalter*, ii. 187–205. See also the brief comments of Modzelewski, *Organizacja gospodarcza*, 184, 258.

[16] Halina Modrzewska, 'Osadnictwo jenieckie we wcześniejszym średniowieczu polskim', *Kwartalnik Historii Kultury Materialnej*, 17 (1969), 345–83. This preliminary work was further developed in her Ph.D. dissertation, *Jeńcy i ich osady w Polsce wcześniejszego średniowiecza* (Warsaw, 1977).

unfree condition, by the beginning of the thirteenth century all traces of any pejorative status had been lost, and the settlements were totally assimilated into the local scene.

By the middle of the twelfth century certain fundamental aspects of the political and economic institutions of Poland were undergoing rapid change. In the first place, the power of the monarchy was rapidly collapsing. In the second place, the system of the *ius ducale* was being undermined. In the midst of these changes, Poland's position on an ethnic and linguistic frontier was to have important ramifications for the new political and economic order that emerged in the thirteenth and early fourteenth centuries.

Ironically, it was some of the achievements of the early Piast rulers which laid the foundation for the problems of the monarchy in the twelfth century. The new state structure of Mieszko I and Bolesław Chrobry and the introduction of Christianity created an aggressive élite within society anxious to challenge the monarch in order to extend their own rights, privileges, and prerogatives. The royal title was lost after the nobility drove Bolesław II the Bold into exile in 1079. The former king's younger brother Władysław Hermann was little more than a puppet of the noble interests. Efforts by his son Bolesław III, the Wrymouth, to undo these developments were only partially successful. He relied chiefly upon the lesser knights to counterbalance the greater nobles, and, through a vigorous foreign policy—directed in part against the Empire over the district of Lubusz (Lebus)—he provided these knights with some opportunities for the aggrandizement they sought. At his death in 1138, Bolesław attempted to regularize the decentralizing tendencies by dividing the kingdom into duchies, based roughly upon the historic provinces, and by establishing the territories of Little Poland and Pomerania as the possessions of a grand duke (or *senior*), with succession to the grand duchy to be through the line of the oldest living member of subsequent generations. His effort to stabilize Poland failed within two generations, however, and for the next century and a half Poland was riven by petty particularism and political fragmentation. The *regnum Poloniae* continued to exist as an abstraction, but the political reality was what contemporary Polish scholarship calls feudal disintegration.[17]

[17] The outlines of this political process may be traced in Jerzy Wyrozumski,

This political collapse came at the same time as the economic limitations of the system of *ius ducale* were becoming evident. Indeed it may be possible to argue that one of the inherent weaknesses of the early Piast state was the constraints which this system placed upon the ability of the ruler to extend and develop the economic resources of the state. For example, the particular functions which both free and unfree peasants performed were in addition to their role as part of the agrarian economy. As a result, a true division of labour did not occur, and—with some exceptions—specialized services and production were thwarted. At any rate, it is clear that, in the absence of any central order, the system of *ius ducale* could not be maintained. The door was opened to those who sought to preserve and extend their local authority through encouraging foreign settlement and the development of a market economy.[18] Let us turn to each of these elements in order to lay the foundation for the eventual restoration of the Polish monarchy. As we shall see, the frontier position of Poland is a dimension which will loom large in this process.

Throughout the twelfth and thirteenth centuries, especially in Silesia, a familiar pattern developed. Local dukes (and in Silesia the Piast line descending from Bolesław III the Wrymouth was soon further subdivided) sought to preserve their own authority by making land grants to nobles and to the Church and by inviting settlers from abroad to their lands. It was possible to do this in part because western views on land tenure and lordship had become increasingly prevalent in Poland.[19] In particular, the idea that a territory belonged to the duke or prince as one of his attributes of

Historia Polski do roku 1505 (Warsaw, 1982), 80–111; and, more briefly, in my article in *The Dictionary of the Middle Ages*, ix. 719–21. There are two excellent co-operative works on this period by Polish scholars: Henryk Lowmiański (ed.), *Polska w okresie rozdrobnienia feudalnego* (Wrocław, etc., 1973); and Aleksander Gieysztor (ed.), *Polska dzeilnicowa i zjednoczona: Państwo—społeczeństwo—kultura* (Warsaw, 1972). On the historiographical implications of the use of the phrase 'feudal disintegration', see my comments in 'Feudal Poland: Division and Reunion', *Polish Review*, 23/2 (1978), 40–52, at 50–2.

[18] See the insightful comments of Benedykt Zientara, '*Melioratio terrae*: The Thirteenth-Century Breakthrough in Polish History', in J. K. Fedorowciz (ed.), *A Republic of Nobles: Studies in Polish History to 1864* (Cambridge, 1982), 28–48, at 34–5.

[19] This point is more fully developed in the context of Silesia and with reference to the older literature and the controversies associated with the problem by Benedykt Zientara, *Henryk Brodaty i jego czasy* (Warsaw, 1975).

power was a powerful tool. For this meant that land could be distributed to others or organized by colonists who would apply new methods adopted from the West. These included the introduction of the three-field system, new crops, and new agrarian technology.[20] These were, of course, also utilized on the lands which had been granted to others, for all saw the economic benefits which accrued from the transformation. The Church and local nobles were also quick to invite settlers to their lands.[21]

In the thirteenth century much new land was brought under cultivation by thousands of newcomers. In a region as relatively sparsely populated as Poland, it was not surprising that new rural settlers could be attracted. Many came from the German lands and their arrival in the Polish territories created scores of rural villages with German populations.[22] They came in part because they were

[20] There is considerable controversy as to the degree to which these 'new methods' were really innovations in the Polish lands or whether they represented simply an intensification and an extension of what had already obtained before the arrival of new colonists. The complexities—and the passions—of German and Polish views on these matters may be traced in the literature cited by Trawkowski, 'Die Rolle der deutschen Dorfkolonisation', 349 n. 2. In general, recent Polish historical writing has tended toward a sociological approach which traces how new economic and legal forms, transmitted by colonists from the German lands, were taken up by Polish society. An example of this attitude is found in Jerzy Topolski, *An Outline History of Poland* (Warsaw, 1986), 45: 'The process [of the development of a market economy and of large landed properties] was favoured by technological advances in agriculture. The regular three-field system . . . became common . . . [This system] was gradually followed by the advent of the [heavy compound wheeled] plough, which . . . not only loosened the soil but turned it as well.' On the question of the introduction of this plough to the Slavonic world, see the comments by H. W. Dewey, 'Agriculture and Nutrition iv: The Slavic World', in Joseph R. Strayer (ed.), *The Dictionary of the Middle Ages*, i (New York, 1982), 96–103, at 97, basing his observations on the work of Witold Hensel. For a more detailed analysis of technological change in this period, see the treatments of Zofia Podwińska, *Technika uprawy roli w Polsce średniowiecznej* (Wrocław, 1962), and Henryk Dąbrowski, *Rozwój gospodarki rolnej w Polsce od XII do połowy XIV wieku* (*Studia z dziejów gospodarstwa wiejskiego* 5/1; *Studia i Materiały z Historii Kultury Materialnej* 11, Warsaw, 1962).
[21] Cistercian settlements were, for example, quick to utilize this technique. See Stanisław Trawkowski, *Gospodarka wielkiej własności cysterskiej na Dolnym Śląsku w XIII wieku* (Warsaw, 1959). For a careful analysis of the way in which such churchmen enhanced their control of the local economy—and, by extension, of the local population—see Piotr Górecki, '*Viator* to *Ascriptitius*: Rural Economy, Lordship, and the Origins of Serfdom in Medieval Poland', *Slavic Review*, 42 (1983), 14–35, which focuses upon specific developments at Henryków, Tyniec, and Trzebnica.
[22] These early settlements had relatively little impact upon the native population, for they were separate from older villages. On this point, which has important

given certain grants which effectively exempted them from the older traditions of the *ius ducale*. They were, in a sense, much like the 'free guests' of earlier periods, in that they were guaranteed personal freedom, protection, and immunities. The obligations of the *ius ducale* were replaced for them by a system of fixed rents in grain or money. But they came also to seek a better life and conditions than they had known in the lands between the Rhine and the Elbe. There, conditions of overpopulation and repression had made prospects to the east appealing.[23] It is worth noting that similar motives drove others to Poland and the east, for Flemish and Walloon settlers may also be found in good number in this period. Indeed, one of the most eloquent testimonies to the motivation of these settlers, whether Germanic or Romance, is the famous Flemish song first published more than a century ago, describing the desire to move to the east in order to live better.[24] The overall effect of this process of colonization was to accomplish what had often been stated explicitly in the land grants and invitations, that is, that they were being issued *pro melioratione terrae*. Indeed the most felicitous description of this stage of the development of the Polish lands is that given by the late Benedykt Zientara, who called this period '*melioratio terrae*: the thirteenth-century breakthrough'.[25]

It was not only in the countryside that this 'breakthrough' occurred. The urban life of Poland was also transformed. Before the end of the twelfth century most urban centres in Poland were characterized by the presence of a stronghold and fortified service *suburbium* (this was especially true in the places which served as centres of provinces and territorial administration), by a number of ecclesiastical foundations, and by a suburban market settlement

implications for the history of German–Polish relations on the frontier, see Benedykt Zientara, 'Die deutschen Einwanderer in Polen vom 12. bis zum 14. Jahrhundert', in Walter Schlesinger (ed.), *Die deutsche Ostsiedlung des Mittelalters als Problem der europäischen Geschichte* (Vorträge und Forschungen 18, Sigmaringen, 1975), 333–48, at 339.

[23] See, for fuller details, Siegfried Epperlein, *Bauernbedrückung und Bauernwiderstand im hohen Mittelalter: Zur Erforschung der Ursachen bäuerlichen Abwanderung nach Osten im 12. und. 13 Jahrhundert* (Berlin, 1960).

[24] *Oude vlaemsche lideren*, ed. J. F. Willems (Ghent, 1848), 35–40. The Walloons in the region have most recently been studied by Benedykt Zientara, 'Walloons in Silesia in the 12th and 13th Centuries', *Quaestiones Medii Aevi*, 2 (1981), 127–50.

which handled small-scale commerce.[26] There were perhaps 250 urban centres in Poland (though not all had a fortified *castrum*), but none of these settlements had a very substantial population—a town of over 3,000 was a large settlement—and few extended over more than five hectares.[27] During the thirteenth and fourteenth centuries, however, the impact of what is sometimes called 'the period of location' was fully felt.

The word 'location' has a number of meanings. It may mean simply 'foundation' (*fundatio*), and indeed there are many instances where the establishment *de novo* of a settlement where there had been none before is clearly intended. For example, when the bishop of Wrocław issued a grant to Peter of Nysa in 1237 to 'locate' new villages in the Nysa region, it was necessary for a colonial population to immigrate to these villages, either from elsewhere in the locality or from abroad.[28] The pool from which such a migration could be drawn was constituted by the approximately 2,000 persons a year who came from the German lands west of the Elbe in the twelfth and thirteenth centuries to resettle east of the Oder. It has been estimated that, in the thirteenth and fourteenth centuries, some 250,000 Germans settled in a Poland whose indigenous population probably did not exceed 1,500,000.[29]

Although this settlement was uneven, it was more densely

[26] See Paul Knoll, 'The Urban Development of Medieval Poland, with Particular Reference to Kraków', in Bariša Krekić (ed.), *Urban Society of Eastern Europe in Pre-Modern Times* (Berkeley, Los Angeles, and London, 1987), 63–136, at 69.

[27] Irena Gieysztorowa, 'Badania nad historią zaludnienia Polski', *Kwartalnik Historii Kultury Materialnej*, 11 (1963), 523–62, at 543–4, and, more briefly, by the same author, 'Research into the Demographic History of Poland: A Provisional Summing-up', *Acta Poloniae historica*, 18 (1968), 5–17, at 10. The number 250 is taken from the estimate given by J. K. Fedorowicz (ed.), *A Republic of Nobles: Studies in Polish History to 1864* (Cambridge, 1982), 135.

[28] For this example, see the extremely rich collection of documents, Herbert Helbig and Lorenz Weinrich (eds.), *Urkunden und erzählende Quellen zur deutschen Ostsiedlung im Mittelalter* (2 vols., Darmstadt, 1968–70), here ii, no. 24, pp. 150–3.

[29] See Walter Kuhn, 'Die Siedlerzahlen der deutschen Ostsiedlung', in Karl Gustav Specht *et al.* (eds.), *Studium sociale: Karl Valentin Müller dargebracht* (Cologne and Opladen, 1963), 131–154, at 132–6. Kuhn also points out, and this observation is emphasized by Benedykt Zientara, 'Nationality Conflicts in the German–Slavic Borderland in the 13th–14th Centuries and Their Social Scope', *Acta Poloniae historica*, 22 (1970), 207–25, at 212, that compact settlement, traditionalism, and high fertility (these may, of course, be related) tended to double the population in a period of 23–26 years, i.e. every quarter century.

concentrated in parts of Silesia, in the lands of western Great Poland (*Polonia Maior*), along the Baltic littoral, and in the major towns. Over time, the effect of this kind of 'location' changed the ethnic composition of the countryside. That this was not, however, a simple process by which Germans crossed a linguistic frontier and settled among Poles will be clear below. Before turning to that question, it is necessary briefly to take up two other meanings of the word location.

A second understanding is the process by which the physical, or spatial, organization of an existing settlement was changed. The new form regularized the pattern of settlement and communications routes within the town. Where necessary, existing structures were destroyed and an effort was made to employ a town plan—roughly grid-like—based on models from towns in the lands between the Elbe and the Oder.[30] This category of location, given for example to Cracow in 1257, established the central market square as the focus of urban life and provided for residences on the square for the merchant strata, with the best locations held—not surprisingly— by the wealthiest. In this meaning of location there were often specific rights and exemptions granted to the inhabitants of the located site which might make it an attractive place to settle and do business in. The third meaning of location referred to the legal process by which a settlement—whether one created *de novo* or an existing one to be spatially transformed—was separated from the administration of the grantor (usually the local duke) and placed under the jurisdiction of some other law, typically German law of some kind. This grant of location was given to the headman of the settlement (Latin *scultetus*, German *Schultheiss* or *Schulze*, and Polish *sołtys*; or Latin *advocatus*, German *Vogt*, and Polish *wójt*).[31]

---

[30] Tadeusz Zagrodzki, 'Regularny plan miasta średniowiecznego a limitacja miernicza', *Studia Wczesnośredniowieczne*, 5 (1962), 1–101, is now the standard work on this subject. See also the comments of Benedykt Zientara, 'Zur Geschichte der planmäßigen Organisierung des Marktes im Mittelalter', in *Wirtschaftliche und soziale Strukturen im säkularen Wandel: Festschrift für Wilhelm Abel zum 70. Geburtstag* (3 vols., Hanover, 1974), ii. 345–65.

[31] All three meanings of *locatio* are discussed by Richard Koebner, 'Locatio: Zur Begriffssprache und Geschichte der deutschen Kolonisation', *Zeitschrift des Vereins für Geschichte Schlesiens*, 63 (1929), 1–32; and developed with more precision by Benedykt Zientara, 'Socio-Economic and Spatial Transformation of Polish Towns During the Period of Location', *Acta Poloniae historica*, 34 (1976), 57–83, at 63–6. This article is a translation of his important presentation in a symposium on the

During the thirteenth and fourteenth centuries grants of autonomy were made to foreign merchants, many of whom were German, so that they would practise their trade in the Polish lands and in the Polish cities. When these merchants were present in sufficient numbers in individual towns, they tended to unite to defend their common interests against all outsiders, whether the duke, the *scultetus/advocatus*, or even the local population. These merchant groups bought up most of the municipal properties they did not control, they transformed the right of the duke to income from the town either by buying him out or by negotiating a fixed tax, and they obtained control of or effected the abolition of the position of *scultetus/advocatus*. All of this involved the creation of an urban outlook and a municipal mentality.[32]

The period of location thus had a twofold impact upon the territories lying on the German–Polish frontier. It established a colonial population in the countryside and created an urban population, both of which were in significant degree different from the rural population that had existed before and the city society of the early Middle Ages.

In the middle of the thirteenth century the *Vita major* of St Stanisław presented a parable. Its author described the way the dismembered body of the martyred eleventh-century bishop of Cracow had miraculously grown together. This was taken as a portent of political unity which could be the destiny of a divided Poland.[33] Such a hope might have seemed vain if one had looked

sociotopography of 'feudal' towns in central Europe in conjunction with the XIth General Congress of Polish Historians in Toruń in Sept. 1974. The Polish version, 'Przemiany społeczno-gospodarcze i przestrzenne miast w dobie lokacji', was published in Aleksander Gieysztor and Tadeusz Rosłanowski (eds.), *Miasta doby feudalnej w Europie środkowo-wschodniej* (Warsaw, 1976), 67–97; this volume also includes the text of the important discussions that followed the papers.

[32] The most convenient synthesis of current scholarship on this process is Maria Bogucka and Henryk Samsonowicz, *Dzieje miast i mieszczaństwa w Polsce przedrozbiorowej* (Wrocław, 1986), 45–88 ('Lockacje, ich znaczenie, przebieg, skutki prawne') and 89–104 ('Układ przestrzenny miast'). I have treated some of the issues in the foregoing paragraphs in my 'Urban Development', 71–6.

[33] 'Et sicut ipse corpus martiris in multas partes secuit et in omnem ventum dispersit, sic Dominus regnum eius scidit et plures principes in eo dominari permisit et, ut peccatis nostris exigentibus in presenciarum cernimus, hoc regnum in se ipsum divisum in conculcacionem et direpcionem vastantibus per circuitum dedit. Sed sicut divina potencia idem beatissimum presulis et martiris corpus sine cicatricum notamine redintegravit et ipsius sanctitatem signis et prodigiis declaravit, sic

ıt the welter of events in which petty Piast princelings vied
nconclusively with one another in a series of efforts at self-
ıggrandizement. But beneath the surface there were factors which
nade reunification possible. Indeed, one major thrust in this
lirection had been taken earlier in the century when Duke Henry
he Bearded of Wrocław and, after him, his son Henry the
ᵖious had briefly united Silesia and Little Poland.[34] But there had
ᵖeen no one to follow this example for half a century. By the 1270s
ınd 1280s this was beginning to change.

Many factors created sentiment for reunification. One of these
vas based in the economic linkages that bound various Polish
ands together. These caused many to feel that political frag-
nentation was no longer tenable. The merchants of the cities and
he middle and upper strata of the urban population regarded the
ᵖolitical difficulties of Poland as inimical to their interests.[35] They
hus became influential elements which favoured unity. Many
owns, especially in Little Poland and Silesia, saw in a Piast from
ᵖilesia the best hope for reunification. The newly dynamic Polish
economy thus created the foundation upon which unity could
ʳest.

Another factor making for unity was the Piast dynasty itself.
Though the country was politically disunited and the actions of
nany Piast dukes were narrowly self-serving, the traditions of the
Piast dynasty helped maintain a sense of the royal heritage. The
family was associated with the memorable accomplishments of
Poland, and the chroniclers of the thirteenth century (the most
ımportant of whom was Bishop Vincent Kadłubek of Cracow)

ᶠuturum est, ut per eius merita regnum divisum in pristinum statum restauret,
ᴉusticia et iudicio roboret, gloria et honore coronet', *Vita (major) sancti Stanislai
Cracoviensis episcopi*, ed. Wojciech Kętrzyński, *MPH* 4 (Lwów, 1884, repr.
Warsaw, 1961), 319–438, at 391–2.

[34] These efforts are treated by Zientara, *Henryk Brodaty*; Jan Baszkiewicz,
Powstanie zjednoczonego państwa polskiego (na przełomie XIII i XIV wieku)
Warsaw, 1954), 41–89; and, more briefly, in Aleksander Gieysztor *et al.*, *History
ᵒf Poland* (Warsaw, 1968), 105–6.
[35] The political interests of the cities have been studied against the backdrop of
economic developments by Bogucka and Samsonowicz, *Dzieje miast i mieszczaństwa*,
284–91. Some important comments about this period are made in the article
ᵇy Aleksandra Popioł-Szymańska, 'Poglądy szlachty i mieszczan na handel
wewnętrzny w Polsce od końca XV wieku do połowy XVII wieku', *Roczniki
Historyczne*, 37 (1971), 39–83. The views of Baszkiewicz, *Powstanie zjednoczonego
państwa*, 347–66, regarding the cities must be used with caution.

helped celebrate these.[36] Moreover, with the exception of part of the region of Pomerania, members of the dynasty still ruled in each of the regions which were traditionally regarded as parts of the Polish kingdom. This unique status meant that it was possible for someone from the Piast family to put himself forward as the representative of Poland's interests and traditions and have that candidacy seem reasonable to important segments of the population.

Yet another factor which tended to promote unity was the Polish Church. Under a single archbishop, this institution had not been divided during the twelfth and thirteenth centuries. This ecclesiastical unit was visible to all, and it represented a focus which could, in the hands of a forceful personality, be used to foster Polish unity. Such an individual was Archbishop Jakub Świnka, who served in that capacity from 1283 to 1314.[37] His vigorous activities within the Church to enforce archiepiscopal control over the bishops and his vision of political unity gave actuality to the potential role which his undivided institution could play in divided Poland.

A fourth factor which tended to promote unity was the growing threat to Poland from some of its neighbours. The margraves of Brandenburg and the knights of the Teutonic Order in particular constituted aggressive challenges to the territorial integrity of the *regnum Poloniae*. The Ascanian family in Brandenburg sought to expand at Polish expense and were successful in establishing the New March, a territorial wedge driven up the Warta, separating Great Poland and western Pomerania.[38] The establishment of the Teutonic Order in Prussia had given rise to an equally great threat.

---

[36] Zientara, '*Melioratio terrae*', 43–4. For Polish historical writing in the Middle Ages, especially as it bears on the question of national union and identity, see—among many possible variant versions of his presentation of this theme—Roman Heck, 'Historiography and Polish Medieval National Consciousness', *Quaestiones Medii Aevi*, 3 (1986), 93–110. A more general treatment of medieval Polish historiography is provided in the standard work by Jan Dąbrowski, *Dawne Dziejopisarstwo polskie (do roku 1480)* (Wrocław, 1964); Kadłubek is treated on 70–82.

[37] In addition to Władysław Karasiewicz, *Jakub II Świnka arcybiskup gnieźnieński 1283–1314* (Poznań, 1948), and Tadeusz Silnicki and Kazimierz Gołąb, *Arcybiskup Jakub Świnka i jego epoka* (Warsaw, 1956), there is, in English, the useful study by Daniel Buczek, 'Archbishop Jakub Świnka, 1283–1314', in Damian S. Wandycz (ed.), *Studies in Polish Civilization* (New York, n.d. (1971?)), 54–65.

[38] Wiktor Fenrych, *Nowa Marchia w dziejach politycznych Polski w XIII i XIV wieku* (Zielona Góra and Poznań, 1959).

These knights had in 1226 accepted a vague invitation from Duke Conrad of Mazovia to assist him in the pacification and conversion of the pagan tribes to Poland's north and north-east. In the half-century after their arrival, the Order completed the conquest of Prussia and established there an *Ordensstaat*, whose territorial ambitions had a direct impact upon Poland.[39]

All of the above factors were compounded by an element which was the direct by-product of the thirteenth-century breakthrough. This was the growing antagonism between Poles and Germans. This period, for example, is almost surely when the prototype of a famous Polish proverb is to be found: *Jak świat światem, nie będzie Niemiec Polakowi bratem* ('As long as the world is the world, the German will never be brother to the Pole').[40] It is true that in the beginning, the arrival of German farmers, artisans, and merchants had not created severe tensions. Indeed, many Germans had quickly adapted to life in a new region and had made no effort to surbordinate their new home to the Empire or any of its individual states. Many had contracted marriages with ethnic Poles, and the taking of Polish names by Germans and German names by Poles often makes it impossible for the historian to distinguish between the two groups after two or three generations.[41] In addition, the evidence suggests that Polish dukes and others distinguished between *Theutonici* who lived in German states and 'in Germany'

[39] Karol Górski, *Zakon Krzyżacki a powstanie państwa pruskiego* (Wrocław, 1977), 7–55; and more briefly Paul Knoll, *The Rise of the Polish Monarchy: Piast Poland in East Central Europe 1320–1370* (Chicago, 1972), 31–2.

[40] Gerard Labuda, 'Geneza przysłowia "Jak świat światem, nie będzie Niemiec Polakowi bratem"', *Zeszyty Naukowe Uniwersytetu im. A. Mickiewicza (Poznań): Historia*, 8 (1968), 17–32, esp. 18–19.

[41] Materials touching personal names are discussed briefly by Zientara, 'Die deutschen Einwanderer', 341; see also his n. 30, which criticizes some of the conclusions regarding the German or Polish character of cities drawn by Walter Kuhn, 'Die deutschrechtlichen Städte in Schlesien und Polen in der ersten Hälfte des 13. Jahrhunderts', *Zeitschrift für Ostforschung*, 15 (1966), 278–337, 457–510, 704–43, at 710–23. The point Zientara makes is that the evidence clearly indicates a mixing by marriage of the linguistic/ethnic communities and increasingly thorough assimilation of the newer arrivals—together with their location privileges—despite the explicit prohibition of such developments in the original document of location, for example, of Cracow: 'Hoc eciam nobis iidem advocati promiserunt, quod nullum ascripticium nostrum vel ecclesie seu cuiuscumque alterius vel eciam Polonum liberum, qui in rure hactenus habitavit, faciant suum concivem, ne hac occasione nostra vel episcopalia aut canonicorum vel aliorum predia ruralia desolentur', Helbig and Weinrich (eds.), *Urkunden und erzählende Quellen*, ii, no. 77, pp. 290–7, at p. 294.

on the one hand and those in their own lands who were of German background on the other. That is, the latter were not *Theutonici* in any narrow sense.[42] But over time, this generally flexible attitude began to change, especially among the ruling élite, the clergy, and the knights. Some of the hostility may simply have been against the foreigner, the *alienigena*, in a general sense, but more of it takes on a specifically anti-German character with the passage of time.

For example, the resentment of German clergy and knights in Poland was by the end of the thirteenth century becoming sharp. Archbishop Świnka found that he could not always obtain submission from the German clergy in Poland for ordinances which were binding upon Polish priests. As early as 1285 he had written to the Roman curia to complain about the whole *gens Theutonica*. His immediate concern was with Franciscans of German descent in Silesia who wished to separate their province from Poland and have it admitted into the Saxon province. But, because these Franciscans had supported the duke of Wrocław against the bishop in trying to oppose regulations of the Polish Church, Świnka's argument was elevated into an attack upon all Germans.[43] An even more inflammatory instance was the quarrel with Bishop John Muskata of Cracow, against whom Świnka eventually took action. Muskata was accused of supporting Germans in the Polish Church, and the witnesses against him were nearly unanimous that he did not promote Poles, but foreigners and Germans; that he did not even promote worthy Poles; and that he actually regarded Poles as being incapable of holding responsible positions in the Church. Another witness reported that Muskata had said he would rather die than give up his plan to eliminate the whole Polish people.[44] Similar anti-German feelings

---

[42] See e.g. the references made by Henry the Bearded about an expedition *contra Teutonicos* which was directed against the archbishop of Magdeburg, even though Henry's troops included many of his own German subjects from Wrocław, *Schlesisches Urkundenbuch*, i, ed. Heinrich Appelt (Vienna, Cologne, and Graz, 1963–71), no. 305, pp. 225–6.

[43] *Codex diplomaticus Maioris Poloniae*, ed. Ignacy Zakrzewski and Franciszek Piekosiński (5 vols., Poznań, 1877–1908), i, no. 616, pp. 574–5. See also František Graus, *Die Nationenbildung der Westslawen im Mittelalter* (Nationes 3, Sigmaringen, 1980), 121.

[44] *Monumenta Poloniae Vaticana*, iii: Analecta Vaticana, ed. Jan Ptaśnik (Cracow, 1914), 80, 82, 90 (no. 121). The full controversy over Muskata is recorded on pp. 78–95 and 100–36 (the latter pages are documents nos. 126–31). On the

:ould be found among the laity. The lesser knights (who were to 0ecome a special source of support for Władysław Lokietek) resented the preferment given to Germans. The duke of Cujavia, for example, was often challenged by his knights for his promotion of Germans, and in 1273 they forced him to promise not to maintain at his court and in his land German knights or sons of German knights.[45] The fear of German influence is reflected also in accusations that the advisors to the dukes of Głogów who were ruling in Great Poland had counselled the rulers to exterminate the entire Polish nation, both clergymen and laypeople, and especially the knights.[46]

This anti-German hostility helped fuel the beginnings of a Polish national or ethnic consciousness. It was, to a significant degree, related to matters of language. For example, when the knights of Little Poland repressed a revolt against Władysław Lokietek in 1311, it was reported that all who could not pronounce the Polish words *soczewica* (lentil), *koło* (wheel), *miele* (grinds), and *młyn* (mill) were assumed to be Germans and were executed.[47] One of the charges levelled against the Teutonic Knights falls into this category too, for they were accused of wanting to exterminate the Polish language.[48] There was not yet a fully developed Polish

dispute, see Władysław Abraham, 'Sprawa Muskaty', *Rozprawy Akademii Umiejętności: Wydział historyczno-filozoficzny*, 30 (1894), 122–80.

[45] 'Anno denique predicto primates terre Cuyauie cernentes, quod Semomisl dux eorum ipsis spretis Fratrum Barbatorum interim conciliis eorum utebatur in omnibus sequens favores, adheserunt Boleslao duci Polonie. Semomisl vero se tam confuse derelictum prospiciens Boleslao duci Polonie nobile castrum Cruszuiciense dono assignavit, ut ipsius industrioso favore milicie Cuyauie reconciliatus ipsos ad sue obediencie gremium revocaret', *Chronica Poloniae Maioris*, ed. Kürbis, 124. See also *Codex diplomaticus Maioris Poloniae*, i, no. 482, p. 422: 'sub talibus ordinationibus . . . quod prelios militum Teuthonicalium in terra et curia sua servare denegaret'. These developments are discussed by Janusz Bieniak, 'Rola Kujaw w Polsce piastowskiej', *Ziemia Kujawska*, 1 (1963), 27–71, esp. 45–6.
[46] 'Et dederunt eis consilium, ut totam gentem Polonicam exterminarent, tam ecclesiasticas personas quam seculares milites', *Annales capituli Posnaniensis*, ed. Brygida Kürbis, *MPH*, NS 6 (Warsaw, 1962), 21–78, at 55.
[47] 'Albertus advocatus Cracoviensis cum concivibus suis civitatem Cracoviensem tradiderunt, et privati sunt advocacia, et qui nescibant dicere *soczovycza, koło, myelye młyn* decolati sunt omnes', *Annales Krasinsciani (Rocznik Krasińskich)*, ed. August Bielowski, *MPH* 3 (Lwów, 1878, repr. Warsaw, 1961), 127–33, at 133.
[48] 'rex Wladizlaus . . . dominus Cracovie et tocius Polonie regni per temerarios fratres et rabidos, fratres Thorunenses cruciferos, invasus, temere contra Deum et iusticiam terram suam occupare volentes . . . conantes exterminare ydyoma Polonicum . . .', *Annales capituli Cracoviensis (Rocznik Kapitulny Krakowski)*, ed. August Bielowski, *MPH* 2 (Lwów, 1872, repr. Warsaw, 1961), 779–816, at 815.

national consciousness, for there was as yet no ethnically consciou‹
urban population to support an ideology of national consciousnes‹
which would be articulated by the clergy or other segments o›
society. As František Graus has so effectively shown in his recen›
comparative study of the western Slavs, this was a fundamenta»
element of fully developed national consciousness that was not ye›
in place.[49] But the Polish attitude had gone far beyond a simple
Heimatgefühl or even a more sophisticated *Landespatriotismus*.[50]
There was an emerging sense of the Polish people as a distinc›
group. It was rooted in the concept of the *gens Poloniae*, expressec
in the *lingua Polonica*, and focused upon the tradition of the
regnum Poloniae and, after the reunification of the kingdom
increasingly upon the *corona regni*.[51] And these attitudes, es›
pecially when combined with the growing territorial threat from
German neighbours, became yet another powerful force makin‹
for Polish unity.

The crucial question was, who would accomplish it? Duke
Henry IV Probus of Wrocław attempted it, and in general hac
the support of the townspeople; but he died prematurely in 1290
Duke Przemysł of Great Poland was crowned king by Archbishop
Świnka in 1295, and he had the support of the knights of his
territory, the German upper classes of the cities, and—of course—
the Church; but he was murdered in 1296. Thereafter the
Přemyslid ruler of Bohemia, Wenceslas II, who also held much of
Silesia, was successful in a brief reunion beginning in 1300, for he
had the support of the townspeople and of the Polish Church,

---

[49] Graus, *Die Nationenbildung*, 87–9 and 110.

[50] Ibid. 123–9. While I find much in the arguments by Roman Heck about the
development of national consciousness in medieval Poland to be quite helpful ir
understanding the Polish scene (see most recently his article, above n. 36), it seems
to me he pushes his interpretation too far and sees a more fully developed 'national
consciousness than the sources will support. There is a substantial Polish literature
on this subject, which is briefly reviewed by Zientara, 'Nationality Conflicts in the
German–Slavic Borderland', 219 n. 25.

[51] Oswald Balzer, 'Polonia, Poloni, gens Polonica w świetle źródeł drugiej
połowy wieku XIII', in *Księga pamiątkowa ku czci Bolesława Orzechowiczc*
(2 vols., Lwów, 1916), i. 71–93; Graus, *Die Nationenbildung*, 182–90 (Appendix VI
'Polonia—Poloni—Polonica lingua'); Jan Dąbrowski, *Korona królestwa polskiego
w XIV wieku: Studium z dziejów rozwoju polskiej monarchii stanowej* (Wrocław
1956), translated as 'Die Krone des polnischen Königtums im 14. Jh.: Eine Studie
aus der Geschichte der Entwicklung der polnischen ständischen Monarchie', ir
Manfred Hellmann (ed.), *Corona regni: Studien über die Krone als Symbol des
Staates im späteren Mittelalter* (Darmstadt, 1961), 399–548.

which saw him as a check upon German influences. Archbishop winka crowned him king of the *regnum Poloniae* at Gniezno in 300, but this effort, too, failed. Wenceslas died unexpectedly in 305, and his young son was murdered the next year without ver coming to Poland. The field was left open to Władysław okietek of Cujavia, who had the support of the lesser nobility, esser knights, and even the peasantry, for all of whom Bohemian ule had been devastating.[52]

Lokietek (as he is called in Polish historiography) had more lifficulty in winning over the towns. Indeed many of them, ncluding Cracow, supported the candidacy of the new ruler of 3ohemia, John of Luxemburg, who claimed the Polish title as heir o the Přemyslids. These towns saw in the Bohemian ruler a better ;uarantor of their interests than Lokietek, who had in previous *ffforts to gain and hold Little Poland and Cracow demonstrated iis hostility to burgher interests.[53] The revolt of Cracow against okietek in 1310–11 was in large measure in reaction to this oolicy, though its suppression was eventually joined to some of the ostility to the ethnic background of the German leaders, ncluding the *advocatus* of Cracow, Albert, about whom a famous Polish *chanson* eventually was written.[54] Only gradually and with consider diplomatic difficulty was Lokietek able to overcome opposition. He never recovered control of Silesia for Poland—

[52] Janusz Bieniak, *Wielkopolska, Kujawy, Ziemie Łęczycka i Sieradzka wobec problemu zjednoczenia państwowego w latach 1300–1306* (*Roczniki Towarzystwa Naukowego w Toruniu*, 74/2, Toruń, 1969), and—more briefly—id., 'Zjednoczenie państwa polskiego', in Gieysztor (ed.), *Polska dzielnicowa i zjednoczona*, 202–78. See also Paul Knoll, 'Władysław Lokietek and the Restoration of the *Regnum Poloniae*', *Medievalia et humanistica*, 17 (1966), 51–78.

[53] See the analyses by Bogucka and Samsonowicz, *Dzieje miast i mieszczaństwa*, 291, and the older—but still useful—study by Stanisław Piekarczyk, *Studia z dziejów miast polskich w XIII–XIV wieku* (Warsaw, 1955), 134–49. Despite its rather rigid Marxism, this latter work effectively studies municipal policies and outlooks, with careful reference to the sources.

[54] The older literature on this event is best represented by Edmund Długopolski, 'Bunt wójta Alberta', *Rocznik Krakowski*, 7 (1905), 135–86, and his later, but largely unchanged, treatment in *Władysław Lokietek na tle swoich czasów* (Wrocław, 1951), 138–64. These and other, similar, presentations should be read cautiously, however, in the light of the interpretation in the text above, which is, in part, derived from Zientara, 'Die deutschen Einwanderer', 343–4, and Jerzy Dowiat, *Polska—państwem średniowiecznej Europy* (Warsaw, 1968), 281–307, esp. 299. I have accordingly modified my own treatment of these events as found in *Rise of the Polish Monarchy*, 33.

indeed, his hostility to burgher interests undoubtedly played an important role in this. And territory which had traditionally been regarded as Polish—the region of Gdańsk Pomerania—was lost to Lokietek and to Poland when the knights of the Teutonic Order captured Gdańsk in 1308 and conquered the rest of the region by 1311.[55] Finally, however, Lokietek gained sufficient strength among the several strata of Polish society and, of considerable importance, with the Church, to be able to petition the papacy for a crown in 1319. The following year, in a solemn ceremony in the cathedral on Wawel hill in Cracow, he was crowned king. With this act, Poland's long generations of division had come to an end.

And so we come to a moment of a new departure for Poland in the Middle Ages. The rule of the last two Piasts, Władysław Lokietek and Casimir the Great, was—to be sure—rooted in the traditions of the past and deeply influenced by the political and economic institutions of the previous centuries. But the fifty years when these two monarchs, father and son, presided over a *regnum Poloniae* restored to a significant and influential role within the region were a half-century that looked as much to the future as to the past. During the lifetimes of these two the western frontier was stabilized. In their lifetimes, Poland took the fateful steps into the steppe-lands of Ruthenia and off the edge of Latin civilization (Indeed, the etymological roots of the word for the region of the Ukraine mean literally 'at the edge', i.e. on the frontier.) And these Piasts prepared the way for the opening to Lithuania which in the agreements of Krewo in 1385, in the treaty of Horodło in 1413, and—ultimately—in the Union of Lublin in 1569 were so profoundly to change Poland's orientation and character. It was not that the kingdom and the people ceased to be a part of the Western, Latin tradition. Rather, it was that this continuo in the concert of Polish civilization was enhanced by the obbligato of eastern interests that were to engage old Poland until its demise in the partitions of the eighteenth century.

Thus it is appropriate for us to draw this picture of Poland's medieval political and economic institutions on the frontier between Germanic and Slavonic civilization to a close. Let us do so by returning to reflect upon the matrix with which we began and the dichotomy which was posed at the outset.

[55] Knoll, *Rise of the Polish Monarchy*, 28–32.

How was it that some could see a natural hostility between the Poles and the Germans, while at the same time others could assert that the two cultures lived in partnership together? Precisely because the relations between Pole and German on this cultural, linguistic, and ethnic frontier were neither simple nor static. The early Polish polity and economy evolved out of the needs and conditions of the early Piast period. But these institutions were not phenomena that grew within a vacuum. Contacts with the German lands to the west shaped some of the developments of this period. The political structure of Poland was closely involved—in geopolitical terms and terms of personnel—with the lands to the west. And as the limitations of the early Piast state and the economy of the *ius ducale* become only too evident, the impact of the lands to the west of the frontier upon the territories to the east was substantial. The Polish economy was transformed. The Polish polity, which had shattered on the particularism of dynastic self-interest and on the ambitions of social strata that had emancipated themselves from dependence upon the Piast state, was also transformed. By a process of economic interaction and political response, the new institutions of the fourteenth century were forged from the seeming confusion of the thirteenth century.

We cannot apply too rigidly the tripartite schema which Thomson used to explicate Czech–German relations. Nevertheless, we can see that the history of Polish political and economic institutions on the frontier which is our focus was not a simple one. Hostility alone—i.e. reaction—will not fully explain it. Dominance of one over the other alone—i.e. action—will not fully explain it. Active engagement and involvement—i.e. interaction—must be included as elements in our vision.

It should not be surprising to the historian that an understanding of the political and economic institutions on the Polish–German frontier is not simple. After all, we are used to ambiguity and contradiction. It seems somehow appropriate that *odium naturale* as well as courtesy and friendship were all part of a larger whole that included much interaction.[56]

---

[56] In many ways the Polish–German frontier, at least in the High Middle Ages, was an orderly frontier. There was little of the indiscriminate cross-border raiding by bands and sub-tribal units that characterized other European frontiers. In the later Middle Ages, this tradition was, in significant degree, altered. Tensions between ethnic groups in the cities and even in the country, and the hostility of the Polish upper clergy and knights, made relations on the frontier far less stable.

Part III
CULTURE AND RELIGION

8

Bards and Barons: The Anglo-Irish Aristocracy and the Native Culture

KATHARINE SIMMS

The controversy that is currently raging on whether the colonial aristocracy of later medieval Ireland saw themselves primarily as members of the wider English nation, defined in a political rather than a territorial sense,[1] or as a separate 'middle nation', as Anglo-Irishmen, has been conducted without reference hitherto to a large body of literature of a political, propagandist nature, commissioned during the later Middle Ages and throughout the Tudor and Early Stuart period by the nobles themselves.

This material consists of bardic poetry, chiefly in the form of eulogies and elegies, together with prose genealogies, family histories, and statements of traditional rights, composed by the hereditary secular learned class of Gaelic Ireland, the professional praise-poets and historians. The language is Early Modern Irish, and these works are identical in conventions and format with a parallel body of compositions addressed to the Gaelic Irish chieftains, though there are some interesting variations in content and emphasis. A rough estimate suggests that well over half the bardic poems addressed to Anglo-Irish patrons have either never been published at all, or have been published without a translation, but none the less a worthwhile number have long been available in editions that include an English translation.[2]

---

[1] Steven G. Ellis, 'Nationalist Historiography and the English and Gaelic Worlds in the Late Middle Ages', *Irish Historical Studies*, 25 (1986), 1–18, has abundant bibliographical references to earlier writings on the subject.

[2] e.g. *Aithdioghluim Dána: A Miscellany of Irish Bardic Poetry*, ed. Lambert McKenna (2 vols., ITS 37 and 40, Dublin, 1939–40), nos. 35–41, i. 138–71 (text), ii. 83–102 (trans.); Tadhg Dall Ó hUiginn, *Bardic Poems*, ed. Eleanor Knott (2 vols., ITS 22–3, London, 1922–6), nos. 17–23, i. 120–72 (text), ii. 80–114 (trans.); Osborn Bergin, *Irish Bardic Poetry*, ed. David Greene and Fergus Kelly (Dublin, 1970), nos. 11, 17, 20, 35, 36, pp. 52–60, 73–81, 88–92, 139–45 (texts), pp. 233–7, 244–8, 252–4, 276–9 (trans.); and, most recently, *Poems on Marcher Lords*, ed. Anne O'Sullivan and Pádraig Ó Riain (ITS 53, London, 1987). Major untranslated editions include *Poems on the Butlers*, ed. James Carney (Dublin,

Historians may have been induced to neglect these works not so much because of an actual language barrier, as because of the obscure diction and unfamiliar conventions of bardic composition. More importantly, they may have felt that poems, in particular, voice the attitudes and aspirations of the poets themselves rather than their audience, and that, since the bards were all Gaelic Irishmen, their works are not a reliable indicator of the cultural outlook and prejudices of their Anglo-Irish patrons.

I have recently argued, in relation to praise-poems addressed to Gaelic chieftains, that the weight of evidence suggests strongly that bardic poems were tailor-made to reflect the individual patron's preoccupations.[3] They were, after all, expensive items to purchase. A first-class bardic ode was a complex metrical structure, and its composition was an art confined to trained professionals, who charged heavily for their services. The single annual eulogy with which a court poet discharged his obligation to his permanent employer was traditionally paid for with a gift of twenty milch cows every May Day, and a tax-free farm of land.[4] At other times the expected fee for a first-class poem was a riding-horse with saddle and harness, or a suit of clothes, or a gold ring or jewelled goblet. Poems were offered or commissioned for a particular occasion, a banquet, a wedding, a funeral, or a house-warming, and payment followed on satisfactory performance. It was very rare for a patron to pay in advance, sight unseen. When we find therefore that a number of poets from varying backgrounds tend to address the same message to a particular patron at some crucial stage in his career, it seems legitimate to conclude that their message reflects the patron's wishes rather than any personal emotions felt by the poets.

Ostensibly the earliest extant bardic poem in praise of a colonist

1945) and, for poems *by* an Anglo-Irish author rather than *to* a patron, Gearóid Iarla (i.e. Gerald Fitz Maurice FitzGerald, earl of Desmond), 'Duanaire Ghearóid Iarla', ed. Gearóid MacNiocaill, *Studia Hibernica*, 3 (1963), 7–59. Major unpublished collections are the Roche poems in the Book of Fermoy, Dublin, RIA MS 23 E 29 (1134), and the Dillon poems in Dublin, RIA MS A v 2 (744).

[3] Katharine Simms, 'Bardic Poetry as a Historical Source', in Tom Dunne (ed.) *The Writer as Witness* (Historical Studies 16, Cork, 1987), 60–7.

[4] Giolla Brighde Mac Con Midhe, *Poems*, ed. N. J. A. Williams (ITS 51 London, 1980), no. XIII, verses 8–9, pp. 138–9; *Aithdioghluim Dána* no. 6, verses 25–6, i. 19 (text), ii. 11 (trans.); Pádraig A. Breatnach, 'The Chief's Poet', *PRIA* 83 C (1983), 3–79, at 60–4.

was addressed to Richard Mór de Burgh, in or soon after the year 1213,[5] at a time when he held lands in the modern counties of Limerick and Tipperary, together with an as yet unrealized claim to lordship over the province of Connacht. Since Richard was apparently the fruit of a marriage between William de Burgh and a daughter of Domhnall Mór Ó Briain, king of Limerick, there is nothing inherently improbable in his understanding and appreciating an Irish bardic poem. However, this particular composition forms part of a cycle illustrating the adventurous career of the semi-legendary poet Muireadhach Leasa-an-Doill Ó Dálaigh, and may well be a literary reconstruction rather than a contemporary ode.[6] The verses are none the less undoubtedly the work of a professional practioner of the medieval period, and in some ways are almost equally interesting as a pastiche, based on the themes a fourteenth- or early fifteenth-century bard considered suitable when addressing a member of the conquering élite. The poem emphasizes the mingling of foreign and Gaelic ways at the young noble's court: *a dhream ghaoidhealta ghallda*, 'o ye who are become Gaelic, yet foreign'. Significantly, it affirms Richard's position of leadership within his own 'surname' (extended kin) as due both to his personal merit and his right of inheritance, a very live issue among aristocratic kindreds from the late thirteenth century onwards, but surely premature *c.*1213–14, when Clan William had not yet developed into the numerous tribe it was later to become:

Not equal in length are the tops of the fingers; all men are not equally strong; there is no chessboard without a king; there is no brood without a leader.

Thou art head of thine own race, O FitzWilliam of the golden sheen, he that is best in each stock is head of the family . . .

O young Richard of the bright land, since thy father William lives not, all Clanwilliam has obeyed thy round curling saffron-yellow locks.[7]

The poem continues with praise for the magnificence of the lord's residence, and a version of the *Teagasca Ríogh*, the bardic in-structions to a young king about to take up the reins of power,

---

[5] Bergin, *Irish Bardic Poetry*, no. 20, pp. 88–92 (text), 252–4 (trans.).
[6] Simms, 'Bardic Poetry', 59; Brian Ó Cuív, 'Eachtra Muireadhaigh Í Dhálaigh', *Studia Hibernica*, 1 (1961), 56–69.
[7] Bergin, *Irish Bardic Poetry*, no. 20, verses 15–16, 18, pp. 90–1 (text), 253 (trans.).

urging him to rule justly but firmly, to reverence the Church, and so forth. Since such poetic instructions may have formed an integral part of the inauguration ceremony for kings in pre-Norman Ireland,[8] this passage returns to the earlier theme of Richard's accession to his father's inheritance, an event that took place historically in 1214, with his coming-of-age.[9] If this poem is indeed a pastiche, its author was remarkably well informed.

From the early fourteenth century onwards we are on much firmer ground. Not only do we have poems, tracts, and manuscript compilations unquestionably produced at the behest of Anglo-Irish patrons, but the Irish annals record the names of various learned Irishmen who were employed by the 'foreigners' as musicians, judges, poets, and historians.[10] We even have members of the colonial aristocracy producing their own poetry, using the Gaelic language and the recognized bardic metres. On the basis of all this material some general points can be made. Steven Ellis has referred to cultural Gaelicization as taking place chiefly in marginal areas around the outer edge of the colony's administrative effectiveness, and as being a by-product of economic decline and the withdrawal of English influence in the wake of military and political failure during the fourteenth century.[11] However there is nothing marginal or isolated about such patrons as Richard de Burgh, the 'Red Earl' of Ulster (d. 1326), the first, second, and third earls of Desmond, James Butler, the 'White Earl' of Ormond (d. 1452), and his protégé Richard Nugent, Baron Delvin. Apart from the second earl of Desmond, who died young, every one of these men at some point in his career held office as chief governor of the colony.

Another argument would explain the employment of native

---

[8] *Audacht Morainn*, ed. Fergus Kelly (Dublin, 1976), p. xiv.

[9] Goddard H. Orpen, *Ireland under the Normans 1169–1333*, (4 vols., Oxford 1911–20), ii. 148.

[10] *Annals of Connacht (Annála Connacht)*, ed. A. Martin Freeman (Dublin, 1944), 264–5, 480–1, 488–9, 556–7, 636–7, *s.a.* 1328: 12, 1438: 3, 1446: 5, 1471: 16a, 1519: 9; *Annals of Loch Cé*, ed. William M. Hennessy (2 vols., RS, 1871), ii. 450–1, 462–3, *s.a.* 1582, 1584; *Annals of Ireland . . . Translated . . . by . . . Duald MacFirbis*, ed. John O'Donovan, in *Miscellany of the Irish Archaeological Society*, (Dublin, 1846), 198–302, at 225; *Annals of the Kingdom of Ireland by the Four Masters*, ed. John O'Donovan (7 vols., Dublin, 1848–51), iv. 908–9, *s.a.* 1436; *Annals of Ulster (Annála Uladh)*, ed. William M. Hennessy and Bartholomew MacCarthy (4 vols., Dublin, 1887–1901), iii. 324–5, *s.a.* 1487.

[11] Ellis, 'Nationalist Historiography', 4–5.

Irish praise-poets, particularly by men who like the Red Earl of
Ulster had been reared in England, or like the White Earl had an
English mother, as a somewhat cynical exercise in public relations,
designed to make the lord's authority more acceptable in the eyes
of his native Irish subjects. This is comparable to the view that the
brehons, the hereditary judges of native Irish law, were retained
by the earls purely to mediate in quarrels between their Gaelic
tenants and vassals.[12] It is, of course, perfectly true to say the poet
was employed as an image-maker. His function in Gaelic lordships
had always been to confer an aura of legitimacy on the authority of
the reigning chief. On the other hand, it would be a mistake to
assume that bards could only exercise their influence over a native
Irish audience. When the fourteenth-century Gofraidh Fionn
Ó Dálaigh explained apologetically to the first earl of Desmond

In the foreigners' poems we promise that the Irish shall be driven from
Ireland; in the Irishmen's poems we promise that the foreigners shall be
routed across the sea.[13]

the former category must refer to compositions designed to please
the conquerors, not the conquered.

If we confine our attention to poems antedating the sixteenth
century, when novel concepts were introduced by the turmoil of
the Tudor reconquest, the northern European Renaissance, the
Reformation, and the Counter-Reformation, we are dealing with a
much smaller number of surviving texts, but, none the less, certain
themes emerge in their subject-matter, some of which distinguish
the poems addressed to Anglo-Irish nobles from those intended
for Irish chiefs, and some of which are common to both groups.

Like their Gaelic counterparts, the colonial aristocracy enjoyed
praise of their personal appearance, their mental qualities, the
nobility of their ancestry, and their liberality to poets. Equally

[12] However the presentments of jurors in the southern and eastern counties
of Ireland in the first half of the 16th century, when complaining that the nobility
were undermining the rule of law by taking 'canes' for thefts and 'ericks' for
bloodshed, using Irish law and Irish brehons, sometimes explicitly state that the
'gentry' or the 'King's subjects' are living under this regime: Herbert Hore and
James Graves (eds.), *The Social State of the Southern and Eastern Counties of
Ireland in the Sixteenth Century* (Dublin, 1870), 109, 162–3, 182, 186–7, 189, 192,
199, 204, 233–4.
[13] David Greene, 'The Professional Poets', in Brian Ó Cuív (ed.), *Seven
Centuries of Irish Learning* (Dublin, 1961), 45–57, at 47; *Dioghluim Dána*,
ed. Lambert McKenna (MacCionaith) (Dublin, 1938), no. 67, verse 46, p. 206.

acceptable was the archaic convention which represented the lord's territory as his spouse, fertile and blossoming in the presence of its true ruler, withering and drooping if he was absent or dead. Literary allusions assume the audience to be familiar with the heroic tales of Cúchulainn and the Warriors of the Red Branch, and Fionn MacCumhaill and the Fianna. This assumption receives some confirmation from the fact that the amateur verse of Gerald the Rhymer, third earl of Desmond, does indeed show an encyclopaedic knowledge of both these saga-cycles.

On the other hand, motifs adapted to 'foreign' tastes include boasting about the patron's influence at the court of the king of England;[14] recalling the repeated invasions by which, according to tradition, Ireland became populated—a device that set the Normans' land-rights on the same legal footing as those of the Milesian Celts; and adverting to the possibility of political co-operation between Gaelic and Anglo-Irish, envisaged as taking place under Anglo-Irish leadership.[15] The apologue, or illustrative tale often inserted in a bardic eulogy as a vehicle for some complimentary moral or comparison, could be drawn from Arthurian rather than native Irish literature,[16] and while the *caithréim*, or record of triumphs and victories in a patron's military career, was a very old-established native tradition, the Anglo-Irish seem to have been particularly keen on this.[17] An early panegyric to Sir William de Bermingham by Murchadh *gan crios* MacCraith, no longer entirely legible, is also full of allusions to weapons, armour, and battle-standards, with praise for the courage and prowess of his household.[18]

The master-poets, like the native historians and judges, enjoyed a very high, quasi-clerical status in Gaelic society. Like the heralds of medieval Europe such men had a privileged immunity, so that killing or wounding one was an outrage to social custom, if not a kind of sacrilege. Moreover the official court poet of any chief was traditionally held, by his very appointment to office, to have

---

[14] Bergin, *Irish Bardic Poetry*, no. 17, verses 8–13, pp. 74–5 (text), 244–5 (trans.); *Aithdioghluim Dána*, no. 36, verses 15–16, i. 141 (text), ii. 85 (trans.).

[15] *Poems on Marcher Lords*, 24–5.

[16] Ibid. 28–33.

[17] *Aithdioghluim Dána*, nos. 37–40, i. 145–68 (text), ii. 86–100 (trans.); *Poems on Marcher Lords*, nos. I, II, IV, pp. 1–43, 67–83; *Poems on the Butlers*, no. XVIII, pp. 88–93; *Dioghluim Dána*, no. 101, pp. 338–44.

[18] London, BL Add. MS 19995, fo. 9.

entered into a kind of mystic marriage with his master, which entitled him to sit by his side at formal banquets, share the same plate and cup, and sleep in the same bed.[19]

It may well be that Anglo-Irish etiquette baulked at the practice of cup-sharing with the poets. Certainly the chronicler Froissart reports an Anglo-Irish squire as remonstrating with four Irish kings over this 'unseemly' and 'unreasonable' custom.[20] However the colonial nobility did have their personal poets. The anonymous author of the lament for the Red Earl of Ulster states that as the earl's poet it was a great tragedy for him not to have shared in his death, the late earl was his friend, instead of the bed he occupied in past times, he now lies on the hero's grave.[21] Similar themes occur in elegies for James Purcell and Philip Hacket in late fifteenth-century Tipperary.[22]

The annals indicate that some, at any rate, of the Anglo-Irish shared the Gaelic respect for the privileged immunity of the learned classes and took steps to enforce it, whereas administrators from England showed a hostility almost as marked as that of Elizabethan governors. During the fifteenth century this polarization of attitudes coincided with the deep rift in administrative personnel and policies caused by the struggle for control between the factions of James Butler, the White Earl of Ormond, and John Talbot, Lord Furnival, later earl of Shrewsbury. Already in 1394, in the early stages of Richard II's first expedition to Ireland, we are told in a contemporary annal that a master-poet and historian from East Galway, Cam Cluana Ó Dubhagáin, was killed in captivity by 'stuttering Galls', that is, foreigners who spoke little or no Irish.[23] The later annalistic compilation by the Four Masters has it that he was slain in Dublin by the 'people of the king of England'.[24] Nowhere is it expressly stated that Ó Dubhagáin was killed *because* he was a poet, but twenty years later a curious sequence of

---

[19] Breatnach, 'The Chief's Poet', 39–48.

[20] Jean Froissart, *Chronicles*, selected and trans. Geoffrey Brereton (Harmondsworth, 1968), 414.

[21] Library of the O'Conor Don, Clonalis, Co. Roscommon: Book of O'Conor Don, fo. 337 (Do gabh Éire a húain cumhadh'). Also in BL Add. MS 19995, fo. 8b (aceph.).

[22] *Poems on Marcher Lords*, 22–3, 70–7.

[23] *Miscellaneous Irish Annals*, ed. and trans. Séamus Ó hInnse (Dublin, 1947), 152–3, no. 31.

[24] *Annals . . . by the Four Masters*, iv. 732–3, *s.a.* 1394.

events cumulatively indicates intentional harassment of the bardic orders.

According to an entry for 1414 in the *Annals of Connacht* the king's lieutenant in Ireland, Sir John Stanley, disregarded all claims to sanctuary by the Church and the various learned professions, plundering and exposing to cold and beggary every cleric and sage he came across, in particular plundering the formidable poet Niall Ó hUiginn at the hill of Usnagh in Westmeath. Usnagh was situated in 'Dalton's Country', the modern barony of Rathconrath,[25] and Henry Dalton responded to the raid by plundering his neighbour James Tuite and the 'people of the king, and took from them a cow for each cow, and a horse for each horse, and a sheep for each sheep, and a pig for each pig which Niall had lost and gave them to the Uí Uicinn' and afterwards escorted the poet, his followers, and livestock across the River Shannon into Connacht. Niall Ó hUiginn was already credited with causing the death of some enemies by a 'poetic miracle' earlier in his career, and now he joined other members of the Ó hUiginn family in composing such poisonously powerful satires against Sir John Stanley that he died in five weeks.[26]

His successor John Talbot, Lord Furnival, was made of sterner stuff and in 1415 plundered some of the most eminent poets in Ireland, including Ó Dálaigh of Meath, head of his sept, Aodh Óg MacCraith in Munster, Dubhthach MacEochadha in Leinster, Muirghius Ó Dálaigh and Ó Dálaigh of Corcumroe in modern County Clare.[27] Such a roll-call of bards suggests more than a failure to exempt their lands from the ordinary ravages of war. Either Talbot believed the tale of Sir John Stanley's assassination by satire and wished to wreak vengeance on the poets of Ireland, or, as seems more likely, he feared the story lent them a spurious credibility and hoped to undermine their pernicious influence by demonstrably surviving unscathed after a series of outrages against their order.

A petition of the 'commons' to the king's Council in England against Talbot's government, made by Ormond's sympathizers about the year 1416, naturally said nothing about the grievances of

[25] Paul Walsh, *Mide magen Chloinne Cuinn* (Leaves of History series 1, Drogheda, 1930), 34.
[26] *Annals of Connacht*, 422–3, *s.a.* 1414: 16.
[27] Ibid. 424–5, *s.a.* 1415: 2.

wild Irish poets, but echoed the accusations of the *Annals of Connacht* in complaining that 'several people of the Holy Church' besides lords and commoners among the king's lieges were being held in prison, fined, and evicted without indictment or trial. A curious appendix to this document enumerates the historical grounds for the English kings' right to the lordship of all Ireland, including the Gaelic chieftaincies, but hints that the papal grant by Adrian IV and Alexander III may hold good only as long as the king preserves the liberties of Ireland's Holy Church unblemished.[28] The point was apparently taken. In a meeting of the king's Council 26 February 1417, purveyance of corn and livestock from churchmen by the officials and soldiers of the lieutenant against the liberties of Holy Church was picked out as one of the three main complaints of the king's lieges in Ireland.[29] In a further petition compiled under Ormond's auspices in 1422 Sir John Stanley was named together with Talbot as guilty of extortions and oppressions, though again Talbot was particularly charged with oppressing 'religious orders and others of Holy Church'.[30] The Talbot faction counter-attacked and in 1429 accused certain unnamed magnates and nobles of Ireland who instigated the Irish enemies and English rebels to burnings and other enormities during the lieutenancies of their political opponents,[31] and in 1441 also alleged the earl of Ormond made Irishmen and grooms and pages of his household knights of the shire in several parliaments,[32] accusations which were flatly contradicted at the time, but are curiously echoed in a bardic eulogy for Ormond to be cited below.

Eventually in 1444 Ormond was summoned to London to explain the continuing strife and scandal. He appointed Richard Nugent, Baron Delvin, as his deputy,[33] but within months the government of Ireland passed to Richard Talbot, archbishop of Dublin, and then in 1446 to his brother John Talbot, earl of Shrewsbury. During this period there were renewed assaults on

---

[28] *Proceedings and Ordinances of the Privy Council of England*, ed. Harris Nicolas (7 vols., London, 1834–7), ii. 47, 51–2.

[29] Ibid. 219.

[30] *Statutes . . . of the Parliament of Ireland: King John to Henry V*, ed. Henry F. Berry (Dublin, 1907), 568–71.

[31] *Rotulorum patentium et clausorum cancellariae Hiberniae calendarium*, i (Dublin, 1828), p. 248, no. 13.

[32] *Proceedings . . . of the Privy Council*, v. 318–19.

[33] *Calendar of Ormond Deeds*, ed. Edmund Curtis (6 vols., IMC, Dublin, 1932–43), iii, no. 161, pp. 157–9.

poets in the province of Meath. According to the MacFirbhisigh annals, the treasurer Barnwall (whose claim to the title of Treasurer of Ireland had been rejected by Ormond in 1444[34]), in alliance with the Tyrell family of Westmeath, plundered the Meath Ó Dálaigh and killed a young trainee poet, Fearghal Ó Dálaigh, in 1445. The following year the head of the Petit family and some Tyrells plundered another Ó Dálaigh and sent him prisoner to the earl of Shrewsbury.[35] Also in 1446, the head of another poetic family of Meath, Ó Cobhthaigh, and his two sons were put to death by their aristocratic neighbours, the grandsons of Art Ó Maoilsheachlainn, probably in pursuance of some unconnected feud, but not inconceivably as a result of an understanding with Talbot supporters among the Anglo-Irish gentry of Meath. Richard Nugent, Baron Delvin, was also a Meathman, but far from encouraging or condoning the assaults on poets we hear that in 1447 he imprisoned a grandson of Art Ó Maoilsheachlainn 'in revenge for the killing of . . . Ó Cobhthaigh, and the Irish and English of Meath marched together . . . so that they chased the sons of Art's son to Connacht and they were not suffered to stay in Connacht, and that for the Irish tongue's sake'.[36]

Delvin's patron, the earl of Ormond, apparently shared his regard for poets. The prolonged struggle for control of the Anglo-Irish administration culminated in an absurd and mercifully aborted duel near London in 1447, and the White Earl's vindication and triumphant return to Ireland was celebrated with an ode by the most skilled and eminent bard of his day, Tadhg Óg Ó hUiginn. The contents of this poem, 'Aoidhe i nÉirinn an t-Iarla', are intensely political and at first sight might seem to lend support to the view apparently held by the Talbots that Irish poets were a bad influence:

By the wickedness of the Goill [i.e. 'foreigners'—English or Anglo-Irish] he was out of office for a time, and Éire was, as it were, given over to the rule of the nobles of the Gaoidhil [native Irish] . . .

I shall not cease to reproach Séamus Buitilléar until he resolve, when leaving Éire for a time, to leave her in charge of her native princes.

---

[34] *Calendar of Ormond Deeds*, ed. Edmund Curtis (6 vols., IMC, Dublin, 1932–43), iii, no. 159, pp. 141–2, 147–8.
[35] *Annals . . . Translated . . . by Duald MacFirbis*, 210–11, 216.
[36] Ibid. 216–17.

Let every Gall in this land understand clearly, before Séamus embarks, that he must have either Séamus or someone like him to stay here so that he (the Gall) may not behave in insolent and unruly fashion . . .

Let the Greek Goill be told that, if thou ceasest to protect them, and goest oversea, Éire will run that very night to her armoury . . .

Unless the Goill of Éire are going to acknowledge thee as king's Vice-regent I will not ask thee to remain here.

The Goill who do not agree to the Earl being arbiter over them, would, if they had not him with them, be lucky to get time to leave the country![37]

Elsewhere Tadhg Óg can be shown to have tailored his message to his patron's needs,[38] and if he was not actually commissioned to address this precise line of argument to Ormond, we must assume he anticipated a favourable reception for such sentiments. The message the poem contains is, on the face of it, directed at the colonists ('Greek Goill') and the fact that it contains no disrespect towards the English king, no ranting about Tara and the highkingship of Ireland, reinforces the probability that it corresponded closely to Ormond's own views. Bards did not influence their patrons' culture and politics, they reflected them.

The puzzle for historians reviewing the Talbot–Ormond struggle has been to identify what principles, if any, divided the two parties, aside from mere personal dislike. Both factions professed their aim was to strengthen and defend the four counties of the Dublin Pale, to control or abolish coign and livery, and to reconquer as much of Ireland as possible from the Gaelic chiefs. The White Earl of Ormond claimed the whole island could be conquered in a single year if the campaign was financed on the scale of Hundred Years War expeditions to France.[39] It has to be borne in mind, however, that every single petition, accusation, and counter-accusation generated by this controversy was directed at one audience only, the king and his Council in England, so that, as in the case of bardic praise-poems, the uniformity of sentiments prompted by the desire to win a favourable hearing tells us more about the orthodox policies of the English court towards Ireland than the aims of either Talbot or Ormond.

---

[37] *Aithdioghluim Dána*, no. 36, verses 11, 22–3, 28, 32–3, i. 140–3 (text), ii. 84–6 (trans.).

[38] Simms, 'Bardic Poetry', 62.

[39] *Libelle of Englyshe Polycye*, ed. George Warner (Oxford, 1926), 36.

   The incidents involving bardic poets suggest a natural difference
of approach as between a party headed by a newcomer from
England, and that of a long-established Anglo-Irish aristocrat,
straws to show which way the wind was blowing. More fundamentally, the coincidence between the Talbot accusations and the
message in Ó hUiginn's eulogy anticipates the blackmailing
policies of the Great Earl of Kildare and his son, whose periods
out of supreme office tended to coincide with military uprisings
among their Irish allies.[40] In neither period is there a suggestion
that the earls identified their interests with those of the wild Irish,
but rather that they found them useful tools for maintaining their
personal supremacy. This attitude is neatly summarized in a
speech that tradition, as recorded by Edmund Campion, puts into
the mouth of Cardinal Wolsey, haranguing the ninth earl of
Kildare: 'the earle, nay, the kinge of Kildare. For when yow are
disposed yow reigne more like then rule in the lande; where yow
are malycious the truest subjectes stande for Irish enimyes; where
yowe are pleased the Irish enimy standes for a duetifull subject.'[41]
It may well be, as the poem implies, that such magnates sincerely
felt the best interests of the colony itself lay in the protection
afforded by their network of territorial and military lordship over
Gaelic chiefs and marcher lords when combined with the authority
they could wield as king's representative in Ireland. It may also be,
as repeated accusations maintained, that they took active steps at
times to ensure that the most militarily efficient and determined
governors from England, such as Talbot, would be unable to take
their place successfully.

   Bardic poetry of its nature deals with current events. For a more
long-term view of the colonists' perception of the worth of the
native culture and their own place in Irish society, the work of the
seanchaidh or Irish historian is more revealing. It is probably no
coincidence that the second half of the fourteenth century, which
witnessed a recovery of political power by the Gaelic chiefs, also
saw a sudden flowering of patronage for the exponents of Irish
literature and history which resulted in the compilation of great

---

[40] G. O. Sayles, 'The Vindication of the Earl of Kildare from Treason, 1496',
Irish Historical Studies, 7 (1950), 39–47; Richard Bagwell, *Ireland under the Tudors*
(3 vols., London, 1885–90), i. 114–15, 132, 140, 151–5, 158.
   [41] Edmund Campion, *Two Bokes of the Histories of Ireland*, ed. Alphonsus F.
Vossen (Assen, 1963), 122.

manuscript anthologies, the Book of Uí Mhaine, the Book of Ballymote, the Yellow Book of Lecan, and the Great Book of Lecan being among the earliest.[42] The contents of these volumes testify to a desire to revive and emulate the learning of the great monastic schools of pre-Norman Ireland. Indeed, in 1345 Ó Conchobhair of Sligo commissioned the retracing of the faded lettering of a famous Clonmacnoise manuscript of the eleventh century, *Lebor na hUidre* 'the Book of the Dun Cow', after he had acquired it as ransom for the son of Ó Domhnaill's master-historian.[43] *Lebor na hUidre*'s contents were purely literary, but like the twelfth-century *Book of Leinster* and Rawlinson B 502, the anthologies newly compiled in the fourteenth century betray an additional preoccupation with tracing the genealogical lines of contemporary chieftains back to the pre-Norman kings, with certifying the traditional extent of their territories and the wealth their ancestors could claim as tribute.

These were not topics likely to appeal to the colonists, and there is no evidence for Anglo-Irish involvement in the first stage of the revival. However, poems like 'Triallam timcheall na Fodla',[44] which listed the traditional kingdoms of Ireland with no acknowledgement of the more recently established Anglo-Irish lordships, challenged their very right to exist, gave expression to what might be termed in a Spanish context 'an ideology of reconquest', and demanded an answer in kind.

Munster in the fifteenth century held a fairly flourishing Anglo-Irish community both rural and urban under the leadership of the FitzGerald earls of Desmond, but relationships with the Dublin government and the English king were repeatedly strained, first by the unauthorized succession of the sixth earl of Desmond, James the Usurper (*c.*1414–62), who was opposed by Talbot but supported by the White Earl of Ormond. The rift was to become

---

[42] Dublin, RIA MSS 23 P 2 (535), 23 P 12 (536), D ii 1 (1225); NLI MS G 4; TCD MS 1318 (H. 2. 16). See H. P. A. Oskamp, 'The Yellow Book of Lecan Proper', *Ériu*, 26 (1975), 102–21; William O'Sullivan, 'Ciothruadh's Yellow Book of Lecan', *Éigse*, 18 (1981), 177–81; Thomás Ó Concheanainn, 'The Book of Ballymote', *Celtica*, 14 (1981), 15–25; R. A. Breatnach, 'The Book of Uí Mhaine', in *Great Books of Ireland* (Thomas Davis Lectures 1964, Dublin, 1967), 77–89.

[43] *Lebor na Huidre*, ed. R. I. Best and Osborn Bergin (Dublin, 1929), pp. x–xi.

[44] Seaán Mór Ó Dubhagáin and Giolla-na-naomh Ó Huidhrín, *The Topographical Poems of John O'Dubhagain and Giolla na naomh O'Huidhrin*, ed. John O'Donovan (Dublin, 1862), ed. James Carney (Dublin, 1943); see Katharine Simms, *From Kings to Warlords* (Woodbridge, 1987), 17.

wider with the execution of James's son the Great Earl of
Desmond by Tiptoft, earl of Worcester, in 1468 'for horrible
treasons and felonies as well in alliance fosterage and alterage with
the Irish enemies of the king as in giving to them horses harness
and arms, and supporting them against the king's faithful
subjects'.[45]

During the lifetime of James the Usurper, Anglo-Irishmen in
Munster commissioned at least two great manuscript compilations
from native Irish historians. About 1457–61 David Mór Roche,
lord of Fermoy, ordered the Book of Fermoy, containing, besides
a miscellany of tales, hagiography, apocrypha, and poems in the
Irish language, a series of bardic eulogies for David himself and
members of his family, a list of the Roche lands, certain of their
rights and prerogatives, and an anthology of the delightful
amateur verse in Irish by Gerald the Rhymer, third earl of
Desmond.[46] The whole was bound in with a copy of the *Lebor
Gabála*, 'the Book of the Taking of Ireland', a pseudo-historical
account of the origins of the Irish race, whose significance for the
Anglo-Irish is made clear elsewhere in a number of bardic poems,
for example 'Ní deiredh d'anbhuain Éirionn', addressed to Walter
mac Philip Burke,[47] where the invasions of the 'Greeks', the
Nemedians, the Fir Bolg, Fir Ghailian, Fir Dhomhnann, Tuatha
Dé Danann, Milesian Celts, and 'Franks', or Anglo-Normans, are
listed without distinction as conquests by successive suitors for the
hand of the irresistibly attractive Ireland.

Still more remarkable was the Psalter of MacRichard Butler,
commissioned by a nephew of the White Earl of Ormond, and
largely compiled 1453–4, at various locations in Counties Tipperary
and Kilkenny. It is a miscellany of historical, hagiographical, and
saga material with no specifically Anglo-Irish items at all. Much or
all of the contents of folios 73–122 are allegedly extracted from a
famous lost manuscript of about the eleventh century, the Psalter
of Cashel, frequently alluded to elsewhere as an authentic source
for early tracts on Munster kings and saints.[48] The full and
informative marginalia tell us that Edmund MacRichard Butler

[45] Edmund Curtis, *A History of Medieval Ireland* (Dublin, 1923), 335–7, 350–3,
378; *Statute Rolls of the Parliament of Ireland: I–XII Edward IV*, ed. Henry F.
Berry (Dublin, 1914), 465.
[46] Dublin, RIA MS 23 E 29 (1134).
[47] Book of O'Conor Don, fo. 345b.
[48] Myles Dillon, 'Laud Misc. 610', *Celtica*, 5 (1960), 64–76, at 66.

had been fostered by the native Irish archbishop of Cashel, Richard Ó hEidigáin, and that his relationship with the scribes themselves was close. They included members of the hereditarily learned families of MacAodhagáin and Ó Cléirigh, and at least one shared MacRichard's bed on occasion.[49]

At the battle of Pilltown in 1462, where the Great Earl of Desmond defeated the Lancastrian Butlers, Edmund MacRichard was captured, and Desmond exacted the 'Psalter' from him as ransom. For the next hundred years this manuscript was treasured by the earls of Desmond, who employed their own historians, the Ó Maolchonaire family, to restore its lettering in the early sixteenth century.[50] We know even more about the library of Gerald Mór FitzGerald, eighth earl of Kildare, because a list of his books survives, seemingly compiled some time before his acquisition of an important medical manuscript in 1500, since this volume, which cost him twenty head of cattle, is not mentioned. However, twenty books in Irish are named, along with seven in English, eleven in French, and twenty-one in Latin. Hagiography and apocrypha predominate among the Irish titles, but there is also a translation of Giraldus Cambrensis, the Boyhood Deeds and Death of Cúchulainn, with a couple of other sagas, what seems to have been the *Lebor Gabála*, and a book described as the 'Psalter of Cashel', in other words a manuscript similar in content to, or even transcribed from, MacRichard's Psalter.[51]

This growing interest shown by Anglo-Irish magnates in Gaelic pseudo-history and genealogy is signposted for us by the gradual migration of the Uí Mhaolchonaire, the most eminent of the native Irish historians, beyond the borders of their native Roscommon, where they had practised their profession since pre-Norman times, and where their *ollamh*, or master-scholar, traditionally in-augurated the kings of Connacht. In 1419 David Ó Maolchonaire, *ollamh* of the Roscommon area, died 'in his own house' in the parish of Rathmolyon, County Meath, and was buried in the priory of St John the Baptist at Newtown Trim. In 1446 Tanaidhe Ó Maolchonaire died while visiting the Bermingham's country,

---

[49] Myles Dillon, 'Laud Misc. 610 (cont.)', *Celtica*, 6 (1963), 135–55, at 135, 144–5, 150–1.
[50] Dillon, 'Laud Misc 610', 67.
[51] Standish H. O'Grady, *Catalogue of Irish Manuscripts in the British Museum*, i (London, 1926), 154–5.

barony of Carbury, County Kildare, and was buried in the priory of Holy Trinity, Ballyboggan, County Meath. Maoilín mac Torna Uí Mhaolchonaire, who died in the priory of Abbeyderg, County Longford in 1519, was described as *ollamh* of the Roscommon area, 'a man full of good fortune and wisdom; who had been chosen by the FitzGeralds and the Galls from all the ollavs of Ireland; who used to get jewels and treasure from all of whom he sought them'.[52] This man's brother, Torna Óg mac Torna Uí Mhaolchonaire, was employed in restoring the Psalter of MacRichard while residing in the Curragh of Kildare.[53] Earlier he addressed a genealogical poem to James, earl of Desmond (d. 1487), 'Cá mhéid ngabháil fuair Éire?', which goes far to explain why Geraldines should squander their wealth on such men.

According to Torna, the successive invasions of Ireland enumerated in the *Lebor Gabála* culminate with the arrival of the Anglo-Normans, described as the conquest of Ireland by Maurice FitzGerald. As a piece of historical research his work leaves something to be desired, since he confuses the thirteenth-century ancestors of the Kildare and Desmond Geraldines, but the effect is to credit the earl of Desmond with more than his fair share of illustrious forebears. Throughout the poem the terms 'kingship', 'viceroyalty', and 'earldom' are deliberately juggled to imply that the justiciarship of Ireland was a hereditary right of the FitzGerald family.[54] Once again the bardic poem commissioned by an Anglo-Irish noble echoes the accusations of enemies.

With a similar mixture of flattery and shaky history Torna mac Maoilín, presumably a nephew of Torna Óg, traced the genealogy of the Butler earls of Ormond in a *crosántacht*, or eulogistic mixture of verse and prose, addressed to Richard Butler, Viscount Mountgarrett (d. 1571), asserting his fame and that of his ancestors outshone the blood of Ó Néill or Ó Briain.[55] The defensive purpose underlying such compositions was made even clearer when John son of Oliver Burke (d. 1580), whose claim to the title of MacWilliam Burke was in dispute, commissioned a list of the Burke lands and rights, an illustrated history of his family,

[52] *Annals of Connacht*, 444-5, 488-9, 636-7, *s.a.* 1419: 12; 1446: 5, 1519: 9.
[53] Dillon, 'Laud Misc. 610 (cont.)', 138-9.
[54] *O'Clery Book of Genealogies*, ed. Séamus Pender (*Analecta Hibernica*, 18, Dublin, 1951), 169-72. What appears to be an autograph copy is to be found in London, BL Add. MS 30 512, fo. 12.
[55] *Poems on the Butlers*, no. 1, pp. 1-8.

and a genealogy tracing them back to Charlemagne. This compilation was summarized in a poem by Tadhg Dall Ó hUiginn, which again begins with the invasions in the *Lebor Gabála*:

The land of Banbha is but swordland: . . . Neither the sons of Míl of Spain nor any who have conquered her have any claim to the land of Fál save that of taking her by force . . .

Should any say that the Burkes of lion-like prowess are strangers—let one of the blood of Gael or Gall be found who is not a sojourner among us.

Should any say they deserve not to receive their share of Ireland—who in the sweet, dew-glistening field are more than visitors to the land?

Though the descendants of Gaedheal Glas used to speak of the race of Charles, set stones of Banbha's hills, as foreigners—foreigners were they who spoke thus.

Ireland cannot escape from them, for four centuries and ten years has the warm, ancient, humid land been under the fair warriors of the seed of Charles.[56]

The sixteenth-century *seanchaidhe* made no attempt to conceal the foreign origins of their patrons, though the fact was obviously becoming an embarrassment when Tadhg Dall wrote in 1579. In 1616, the year Aodh Mór Ó Néill, earl of Tyrone, died in exile, a poetic contention broke out as to whether the highkingship of Ireland belonged historically to the north or the south of the country. Tadhg mac Dáire Mhic Bhruaideadha, poet-historian to Donnchadh Ó Briain, fourth earl of Thomond, championed the cause of the south, and invited the nobles of Munster as descendants of Heber son of Milesius, the first Celt in Ireland, to reward him. Among the 'sons of Heber' he includes not only the Gaelic chieftains of Munster, but the Anglo-Irish nobility because of their frequent intermarriage with the chiefs:

There sprang other lofty trees from the root of our fragrant tree. That their names are not like those of the Gaoidheal keeps me not from mentioning them.

Count owing to their female ancestors as worthy brethren of Eibhear's stock, the Burkes, Butlers, Barrys, Roches, though all of foreign stock.

[56] Tadhg Dall Ó hUiginn, *Bardic Poems*, no. 17, verses 1, 4, 17–20, i. 120, 122–3 (text), ii. 80–1 (trans.). See T. Ó Raghallaigh (ed.), 'Senchus na mBúrcach', *Journal of the Galway Archaeological and Historical Society*, 13 (1924–7), 50–60, 101–38; 14 (1928–9), 30–51, 142–67.

On the female side from our race comes Thomas Earl of Ormond . . .
from our stock also sprang the race of the bold Fitzgeralds descended
from our womenfolk.

If the powerful prince Richard [fourth Earl of Clanrickard] were present
now in bright-yewed Éire, would any branches of the wood seem fairer,
though you look all round the fair plain of Éire?[57]

By the mid-seventeenth century many Anglo-Irish families had
gone one step further, and procured for themselves ludicrous
pedigrees which traced their ancestry in the male line from some
Gaelic king, or, in the case of the Barnwalls, from a thirteenth-
century official of the king of Connacht, Íomhar Ó Beirn.[58] At this
date the relationship between the ideological framework set forth
in bardic poems and genealogical tracts and the political reality of
the Catholic Confederation of Kilkenny is crystal clear. On the
other hand, the exact purpose served by this eminently functional
literature in the fourteenth and fifteenth centuries is more open to
discussion.

Gofraidh Fionn Ó Dálaigh spoke in the mid-fourteenth century
of poems which promised 'that the Irish shall be driven from
Ireland', and he himself urged that the second earl of Desmond
should conquer MacCarthaigh's territory in south-west Munster:

Avelina's son, slayer of the Gael, soon will he come to our aid across the
wild surge of the sea, he the counterpart of Lugh . . .

Till he turn the face of the hosts to the south-west, let not the son of the
Geraldine, of the noble shapely hands, love banqueting or pleasure . . .

Let not the soft-eyed Guaire leave Munster, land of Lugaidh's descendant,
for any other, until the fresh green land is his own.[59]

Politically, therefore, the fourteenth-century magnates still identified their interests with those of the English court, and hoped for a
final conquest of the island, but culturally they were acquiring
distinctive tastes.

The thirteenth-century pattern of great landowners taking an

---

[57] *Iomarbhágh na bhFileadh: The Contention of the Bards*, ed. Lambert
McKenna (2 vols., ITS 20–1, London, 1920 for 1918–19), no. XXIX, verses 31–5,
ii. 246–7.

[58] Brian Ó Cuív, 'Bunús Mhuintir Dhíolún', *Éigse*, 11 (1964), 65–6; *O'Clery
Book of Genealogies*, 190; see *Annals of Connacht*, 152–3, 158–9, *s.a.* 1269: 2,
1271: 4.

[59] Bergin, *Irish Bardic Poetry*, no. 17, verses 51, 57, 59, pp. 80–1 (text), 248
(trans.).

active interest in their estates on both sides of the Irish Sea had given way to a division between those more or less permanently resident in Ireland and the constant absentees.[60] For the resident nobility there was no royal court to act as a centre of chivalric culture and no university to provide a focus for Latin learning. Consequently the bardic classes met with little competition. Even Giraldus Cambrensis had waxed lyrical about the skill of Irish musicians.[61] In 1329 'the king of Music-Making', Maolruanaidh MacCearbhaill, a famous tympanist, was employed by John de Bermingham, earl of Louth, at the time of the Braganstown massacre.[62] Three years earlier the elegy on the Red Earl of Ulster spoke of his being lamented with music by professional keening women.[63] The bardic praise-poems and the lays of Fionn Mac-Cumhaill and the Fianna were also accompanied by music,[64] and were designed to entertain guests during banquets. In this context the Irish elegies or commemorations of martial deeds can be seen as provincial successors to the *sirventes* or *chansons de geste* that had been more readily obtainable in the cosmopolitan thirteenth century.

Equally the schools of native Irish learning provided a pale substitute for the non-existent university, since the larger centres might attract several branches of study, as did the MacAodhagáin law-school in Ormond, where history, poetry, divinity, and perhaps music were also cultivated.[65] Much of the contents and practice of their teaching was inherited from the twelfth-century

[60] Robin Frame, *English Lordship in Ireland, 1318–1361* (Oxford, 1982), 52–74.
[61] Gerald of Wales (Giraldus Cambrensis), *Topography of Ireland*, trans. J. J. O'Meara, *Gerald of Wales: The History and Topography of Ireland* (Harmondsworth, 1982), 103–4.
[62] *Annals of Connacht*, 264–5, *s.a.* 1328: 12; James F. Lydon, 'The Braganstown Massacre, 1329', *Journal of the County Louth Archaeological and Historical Society*, 19 (1977), 5–16, at 5.
[63] 'Do gabh Éire a húain cumhadh' as above, n. 21. See Katharine Simms, 'The Poet as Chieftain's Widow: Bardic Elegies', in L. Breatnach, K. McCone, and D. Ó Corráin (eds.), *Sages, Saints and Storytellers: Celtic Studies in Honour of Professor James Carney* (forthcoming).
[64] Eleanor Knott, *Irish Classical Poetry* (Dublin, 1957), 57–8; Giolla Brighde Mac Con Midhe, *Poems*, no. XVIII, verse 30, pp. 212–13; *Book of Magauran*, ed. Lambert McKenna (Dublin, 1947), no. III, verse 23, no. VI, verse 7, pp. 26–7, 54–5 (text), 299, 310 (trans.).
[65] *Annals . . . by the Four Masters*, iii. 648–9, iv. 766–7, 930–1, *s.a.* 1369, 1399, 1443; *Annals of Ulster*, iii. 124–5, *s.a.* 1432; *Annals of Loch Cé*, ii. 268–9, *s.a.* 1529; Robin Flower, *Catalogue of Irish Manuscripts in the British Museum*, ii (London, 1926), 519; *Leabhar Breac* (facsimile, Dublin, 1872–6), pp. ix–x, xiv–xix.

monastic schools: for instance in 1482 we find the historian Urard
Ó Maolchonaire described as 'ollav of Sil Murray in learning and
poetry, the chief chronicler of the western world, specially learned
in the phases of the moon, translator of part of the scriptures from
Latin into Irish'.[66] Clerical kinsmen of the bardic classes, or
practitioners of medicine, might even obtain university degrees
abroad.[67]

It was this intellectual respectability that caused the Anglo-Irish
to turn to the study of pseudo-history when they felt a need to
validate their titles in the fifteenth century. As the area of royal
control contracted to the four counties round Dublin, it was not
enough for the earls and barons ruling beyond the Pale to appeal
to feudal tenure or a charter from the king as the basis of their
authority. They were anxious to be proclaimed as heirs, by right of
conquest, to the dues and boundaries of specific pre-Norman
kingdoms, and as mystical husbands of the territories they now
ruled by virtue of their strength and justice. There was no
rejection of the English king's authority, it was simply becoming
irrelevant. Emotional commitment to the continuance of the
Anglo-Irish colony itself, the solidarity of the Goill, lasted longer,
but in a poem to Edmund Butler, Lord Dunboyne (*fl.* 1445),
'Cúich do leannán, a Lámh Óir?',[68] the common theme of a love-
match with the land is already reinforced by allusion to his
descent from Irish kings on the mother's side as grounds for
sovereignty, and, as we have seen, by the late sixteenth and early
seventeenth centuries this desire to be accepted as fully Irish had
accelerated. The word *Éireannach* or 'Irelandman' was coined,
and as early as 1419 was used in the Irish annals to boast of the
exploits of a mixed force of Gaelic and Anglo-Irish soldiers
fighting in France under Butler leadership.[69] By the late sixteenth
century the monoglot English speaker, Richard Stanihurst of
Dublin, dismissed this compromise term as absurd and preferred

---

[66] *Annals of Connacht*, 584–5, *s.a.* 1482: 3.

[67] Ibid. 264, 416, 428, *s.a.* 1328: 13, 1413: 2, 1416: 8; *Annals of Ulster*, iii. 256,
548, 564–6, *s.a.* 1475, 1522, 1527; *Annals . . . by the Four Masters*, v. 1870, *s.a.*
1588; Augustin Theiner (ed.), *Vetera monumenta Hibernorum et Scotorum
historiam illustrantia* (Rome, 1864), 349; Donald Mackinnon, *A Descriptive
Catalogue of Gaelic Manuscripts* (Edinburgh, 1912), 21–2; Raphael Holinshead,
Holinshed's Irish Chronicle, ed. Liam Miller and Eileen Power (Dublin, 1979),
110.

[68] *Poems on the Butlers*, no. XVIII, pp. 88–93.

[69] *Annals of Connacht*, 442–3, *s.a.* 1419: 5.

to be known as an 'Irishman' plain and simple: 'Who so will grate upon such nice diuersities in respect that he is ashamed of his country, truly in mine opinion, his country may be ashamed of him.'[70] Consistently with this approach his list of 'the names or surnames of the learned men and authours of Ireland' draws no distinction between pre-Norman saints and scholars, bards of his own day, and colonial writers, though he names far more of the latter. He is scrupulous to point out he has included St Patrick 'notwithstanding he be no Irish man borne', whereas the others are all viewed as 'countrymen'. Stanihurst's loyalty to his 'countrymen' is magnified a thousandfold in the Irish verse of his contemporary William Nugent, son of the baron of Delvin:

Land of warriors and of poets, Banbha of the gold-tressed women, land of blue bird-haunted clear streams, and of bold deedful men . . .

Her masses, her religious orders, her musicians who were my companions, and the poets of that land where Goill and Gaoidhil dwell; all should be included in our enumeration.

My dwelling-house here [in England] is cold and false; bitter is the wind of these regions. My soul's love goes to the dear race who live in Conn the Battler's Banbha.[71]

The Renaissance and the Counter-Reformation have here given rise to new concepts of patriotism that were to find their fullest expression in the literature and politics of the seventeenth century. But the roots of this change go back to the fifteenth century, and each stage in its development has been articulated for us through the services of the native poets and historians, who from time immemorial were trained and paid to clothe aspirations in words.

[70] *Holinshed's Irish Chronicle*, 12.
[71] 'Poems of Exile by Uilliam Nuinseann mac Barúin Dealbhna', ed. Gerard Murphy, *Éigse*, 6 (1948), 8–15, at 12 and 15.

9

Czech–German Relations as Reflected in Old Czech Literature

ALFRED THOMAS

Since the Slavs entered central Europe in the fifth and sixth centuries they have faced a German majority along their southern and western borders.[1] The Slavs' response to the German hegemony was to adopt a policy of appeasement and resistance, whichever was required by the situation. The Slav–German relationship became most complex and paradoxical in Bohemia and Moravia, where the two races lived in close proximity from the twelfth century until the end of the Second World War, when 3.5 million Bohemian Germans were forced to leave their homeland. It is the aim of this essay to explore this relationship as reflected in Old Czech literature from the end of the thirteenth to the beginning of the fifteenth century. From the outset, the Czechs entertained ambivalent feelings toward their more powerful neighbours. In political and cultural matters they often sought to emulate the foreigners, yet at the same time felt resentful of their prosperity and accomplishments, especially when the Germans began to receive special favours from the Czech kings.[2]

To understand the reasons for this ambivalence we should examine more closely the political and economic situation in the Czech lands at the close of the twelfth century. At this period the Czech kings decided to invite German immigrants to colonize their undercultivated territory. In the tenth century Bohemia and Moravia had just one quarter of a million inhabitants. Only the Elbe and Moravian plains had proper settlements; elsewhere the country was sparsely inhabited. Thick forests extended as far as thirty miles from Prague. The first wave of German immigrants were farmers who were required to pay for the borderland which

[1] For the early history of the Slavs see A. P. Vlasto, *The Entry of the Slavs into Christendom* (Cambridge, 1970).
[2] For a general study of Czech–German relations from the earliest times to the present century see Emanuel Rádl, *Válka Čechů s Němci* (Prague, 1928).

they occupied, but, in return, received considerable privileges from the Crown, for example, exemption from taxation in the first ten years and from compulsory work. Furthermore, they were not required to submit to Bohemian law, only to their own Nuremberg legal code. The agricultural colonization amounted to a series of fortified villages along the border traditionally known as the Sudetenland. With the development of technology the kings wished to exploit the country's rich mineral reserves of silver and gold, and miners and skilled artisans were invited from Germany. Royal towns arose as centres of silver mining, such as Kutná hora (a calque from the German name Kuttenberg), Stříbro (meaning literally 'silver'), Příbram, Jihlava, Kremnica, even as far afield as Levoča and Košice in Slovakia.[3]

These two waves of immigration were the deliberate policy of the three most powerful sovereigns of the Přemyslid dynasty: Přemysl Otakar I (1198–1230), Wenceslas I (1230–53), and Přemysl Otakar II (1253–78). The kings had considerable economic power, which they wished to use against the feudal lords in order to reduce their political influence. In response to this threat the nobles identified themselves with the cause of the 'people'; in reality, they were simply concerned to further their own interests. To aid them in their struggle against the Crown, the nobles sought allies in the clerics employed in their service. In their capacity as *literati* (that is, men trained to write in Latin)[4] this class of clerics created a vernacular literature which would serve the double purpose of religious edification and political propaganda. In spite of their serious moral content these early Czech texts, dating from the end of the thirteenth century, were written in a direct vigorous style, coloured by folk idioms and proverbs drawn from the every day language. Consequently the early literature appealed not only to the nobility but, eventually, to the common people as well. It is an interesting irony that Czech literature arose and flourished as an ideological reaction to German influence in the affairs of state.

To coincide with this immigration policy, German poets were also invited to Bohemia as guests of the Czech kings. The late Přemyslid rulers wished to transform their provincial court at Prague into a major centre of German culture to enhance their

---

[3] Rádl, *Válka*, 35–8.
[4] For early Czech religious poetry in Latin see Francis Dvornik, *The Slavs in European History and Civilization* (New Brunswick, 1962), 152–4.

prestige among the German princes in the Empire. Slav by race, these kings saw themselves as Germans by language and culture. Wenceslas I invited several *Minnesinger* to his court, the most notable of whom was Reinmar von Zweter. These poets compared their patrons to biblical, classical, and chivalric heroes. Meister Sigeher and the knight Friedrich von Sonnenburg eulogized Wenceslas, likening him to Solomon and King Arthur.[5] In addition to lyric verse, the courtly romance also found favour with the royal patrons. The most prolific writer of romance at the court during the reigns of Přemysl Otakar II and Wenceslas II was Ulrich von Eschenbach, author of a voluminous life of Alexander the Great (1287).[6] Ulrich portrayed his patron, Přemysl Otakar, as Alexander conquering the pagan Persians. In the Middle Ages Alexander was seen as a precursor of the crusader-knight, the model warrior-prince who brought Western civilization to the pagans of Asia.[7]

Middle High German prosody had a fundamental influence on the formation of the Czech literary language. The three-line form of the lyric (*leich*) and the octosyllabic line of the epic and romance were the models for Czech narrative verse. The early Czech vernacular was intended primarily as a religious literature, making Latin sacred and liturgical texts available to a wide lay audience. These texts were based on two principal Latin models, the passionals and the apocrypha. The earliest surviving narrative verse in Czech consists of apocryphal lives of the saints and biblical figures such as the Virgin Mary, Judas, and Pontius Pilate. Based on the popular *Legenda aurea* by Jacobus de Voragine, these early fragments are of such a high literary standard that they must have been preceded by an accomplished tradition which is now lost. It is not certain whether these fragments are by one or by several hands. From the historical point of view the most important fragment is the *Apokryfa o Jidášovi (Apocryphal Legend of*

---

[5] Konrad Bittner, *Deutsche und Tschechen: Zur Geistesgeschichte des böhmischen Raumes*, i (Brno, 1936), 52.

[6] For information on Ulrich's life and work see Hans Friedrich Rosenfeld, 'Ulrich von Eschenbach', in Wolfgang Stammler and Karl Langosch (eds.), *Die deutsche Literatur des Mittelalters: Verfasserlexikon* (5 vols., Berlin and Leipzig, 1933–55), iv, cols. 572–9; for background on his *Alexander*, see Herwig Buntz, *Die deutsche Alexanderdichtung des Mittelalters* (Stuttgart, 1973), 26–30. The *Alexander* was edited by Wendelin Toischler (Tübingen, 1888).

[7] For the image of Alexander in medieval literature see George Cary, *The Medieval Alexander* (Cambridge, 1956).

Judas), which has only 281 lines.[8] The anonymous author or a later redactor, as is more likely, refers to the assassination of the last Přemyslid king, Wenceslas III, on 4 August 1306. In a strongly phrased apostrophe addressed to treachery the writer accuses the Germans of the king's murder, referring to them, in biblical language, as the 'cursed tribe' (*proradné plémě*) and equating them with the traitor Judas:

All because of you, treacherous tribe, many a land has been laid waste! I know that you let nothing past but one day you too will perish! (Muzeum Fragment, 23–6)

Pontius Pilate was another figure with whom the hated Germans were compared.[9] Religious and temporal issues were virtually indistinguishable: the foreigners' presence was regarded as a manifestation of evil in the world. Czech literature at the close of the Přemyslid era was pervaded by this sense of menace and foreboding.

The first extensive work of art in Old Czech literature is the *Alexandreida* (1290–1300), a life of Alexander the Great based on the twelfth-century Latin source by Walter of Châtillon (*c.*1180).[10] The Czech version survives in seven fragments, the largest, the St Vitus Fragment, consisting of 2,460 lines. The hero of the Czech poem is a thirteenth-century feudal lord, a model of chivalric virtue as outlined by contemporary tracts and manuals of knighthood. The author attempts to make his narrative as vivid as possible by introducing local elements familiar to his audience: Alexander's knights are given recognizably Czech names and the descriptions of sieges and battle include military tactics typical of the time. The Czech poem is in a style completely different from that of the Latin source: the cumbersome classical apparatus so integral a feature of Walter's poem is replaced by a bare narrative style. The Czech poem is structured as a series of self-contained

---

[8] Ed. Jiří Cejnar, *Nejstarší české veršované legendy* (Prague, 1964), 155–80.

[9] Later Latin verses composed by Prague students in the 14th century announce that the Germans originate in Pontius Pilate's anus; see Roman Jakobson, *Moudrost starých Čechů: Odvěké základy národního odboje* (New York, 1943), 118–19.

[10] For background on and dating of the *Alexandreida* see Albert Pražák, *Staročeská báseň o Alexandru Velikém* (Prague, 1946). The edition of the *Alexandreida* used here is *Die alttschechische Alexandreis*, ed. Reinhold Trautmann (Heidelberg, 1916). The spelling of the quotations is modernized.

exempla on a particular theme such as treachery or pride, each concluding with an authorial reflection often in the form of a gnomic triplet. The homiletic tone of the *Alexandreida* suggests that the poet did not belong to the royal court but was attached to a baronial household or even to a monastery.

The old-fashioned ideal of knighthood outlined in the poem and the long passages of homiletic reflection suggest that the author was a cleric rather than a member of the lower nobility (*zemané*) as was traditionally claimed by scholars.[11] From the internal evidence provided by the text we can reconstruct something of the author's status and character. He was most likely a priest of considerable learning, perhaps a confessor or tutor in the household of a petty nobleman in the provinces. The powerful detailed descriptions of battle indicate, however, that he was at home in the real world and that he even experienced warfare at first hand. As the poem is unfinished it is impossible to assess the poet's overall intention, especially his view of Alexander. This problem is further complicated by the presence in the text of later interpolations which were probably added either during the reigns of Wenceslas II or Wenceslas III, or after the death of this last member of the dynasty, when the country was plunged into a constitutional crisis. The Budějovický Fragment, for example, includes passages of a later date than the composition of the original poem. Similar in tone and content to the apostrophes in *Judas*, these additions are of a political and topical nature suggesting that the redactor wished to make the story fit his own political message. At one point he makes an unusual reference to the situation in Bohemia, claiming that the Czech king should emulate Alexander's crusading fervour:

May God deign to listen and reveal to his Christian people a Czech king such as he (Alexander); I hope that before long, the Latvians, Tartars, Turks, Prussians and the schismatic Russians will experience such terror that they will adopt the Christian faith and relinquish their idols. (B 226–36)

---

[11] For the problem of authorship see A. V. Šembera, 'Kdy a od koho jest sepsán Alexander český?', *Sitzungsberichte der königlichen böhmischen Gesellschaft der Wissenschaften* (1859), 30–6; K. W. Titz, 'Ulrich von Eschenbach und der Alexander boëmicalis', *Jahresbericht der Lese- und Redehalle der deutschen Studenten in Prag* (1880–1), 13–22.

The writer adds that this would be possible if there were no
Germans present in the realm to deflect the king from such a
worthy enterprise:

This could happen if it were not for the Germans who are guests here and
who desire that no Czechs should be visible on the bridge (which God
forbid); and all this could happen if they were not visible. (B 237–44)

The reference to the bridge is probably a paraphrase of an alleged
statement made by Přemysl Otakar II as he left his castle at
Hradčany and crossed the Prague bridge on his way to a campaign
in the north-east.[12] This king was constantly embroiled in disputes
and conflicts with his nobles who distrusted and resented his pro-
German policies. So strong was their antagonism that they allied
themselves with Rudolph of Habsburg, Přemysl's main rival for
the title of Holy Roman Emperor. The bitter comment attributed
to Přemysl that there should be no Czechs on the bridge upon his
return to Prague certainly has an authentic ring.

The original poet is much more subtle in his allusions to the
political situation than the somewhat crude redactors. A favourite
device is to introduce folk proverbs which serve as coded
comments on a particular topical theme. In the prologue the poet
defends his work against the criticism of ill-wishers, a rhetorical
formula which originated in the judicial practices of the classical
age. He introduces a folk proverb in the form of a couplet (52–3)
the vigour of which contrasts with the formality of the preceding
topoi: 'you sing the best way you know how.' This remark has
been interpreted as an allusion to the *Minnesinger* at the court of
Wenceslas II; the king was himself a gifted lyric poet and in the
famous *Manesse Codex* is depicted on his throne surrounded by
Minnesinger and *joculatores*.[13] Miloslav Šváb maintains that the
subject of the sentence is the poet, justifying himself for writing in
Czech; but it is also possible that the subject is the ill-wishers (that
is, the German poets) who sing the best they can, by implication
not very successfully. When one considers the tone of the poem as
a whole, one must conclude that the poet is not being apologetic

[12] The so-called Dalimil chronicler attributes these words to Přemysl: 'The king
said, "When I return from the war,/I will make problems for the Czechs"' (ch. 92
49–50). See the edition *Nejstarší česká rýmovaná kronika tak řečeného Dalimila*
ed. Jiří Daňhelka *et al.* (Prague, 1958).
[13] See Jan Šusta, 'Skládal Václav II milostné písně?', *Časopis české historie*
21 (1915), 217–46.

here but vigorously asserting the dignity, indeed superiority, of the Czech language as a valid literary medium.[14]

The position of Czech writers at this period was complicated by their double allegiance to the nobility and to their sovereign. Although they were spokesmen for the nobility's cause, they also admired a strong enterprising king despite his pro-German policies. This explains the writers' ambivalence toward Přemysl Otakar II, who as a crusading knight won their approval but whose favouritism toward the Germans incurred their wrath. The so-called Dalimil chronicler, writing a few years later than the author of the *Alexandreida*, praises Přemysl in high-style courtly terms while criticizing his severity toward the nobility and his excessive generosity toward the Germans.[15] This ambivalence is reflected in a more oblique form in the *Alexandreida*. The poet clearly admires Alexander (the prototype for Přemysl) but as a Christian is forced to see the sin of pride (*superbia*) behind the hero's exploits, a sin to which Přemysl himself fell prey in his struggle for political domination of central Europe. About the time the poem was composed Bohemia suffered invasion by Brandenburg troops in the aftermath of Přemysl's disastrous defeat by Rudolph of Habsburg at the battle of the Marchfeld in 1278.[16] Darius's prayer before the final battle against Alexander's army echoes the plight of Přemysl as he faced ruin and death against a superior foe. The Persian king's speech to his troops is a curious affirmation of the Christian virtue of *humilitas* and honour (*čest*) in the higher spiritual sense of the word. The Greeks are referred to as 'unworthy guests' (1321), a clear allusion to the German invaders during the times of trouble: 'Remember that you are free and these guests unworthy who are now subject to your will.' In such passages the Czech author transcends narrow national concerns and expresses an universal Christian rejection of worldly power.

We can assume that the *Alexandreida* was written for a conservative-minded lower nobility; it addresses a feudal élite anxious to preserve its rights and privileges against the encroach-ments of a new growing class of burghers, both German and

[14] Miloslav Šváb, *Prology a epilogy v české předhusitské literatuře* (Prague, 1966), 169, 245.
[15] Ch. 89. 3–4: 'Just as God placed the rose in the meadow,/so too did he glorify the Czech land with Přemysl' and ch. 92. 5–6: 'Then the king began to neglect his own [people]/and began to give towns and villages to the Germans.'
[16] See Pražák, *Staročeská báseň*, 199–200.

Czech.[17] The poet, or later redactor, occasionally reveals his contempt for the wealth of the new urban patriciate, as in the Babylon episode, where the ostentatious gifts presented to the victorious Alexander by the leading burghers and officials (*l'udí úřědních*) are a source of distaste (B 182–91). It is not difficult to discern in this passage an allusion to the German minority. The power of money is anathema to a class which bases its own *raison d'être* on the prestige of high birth. Later in the same fragment we find a description of a tournament held in honour of Alexander. The details of the joust reveal the writer's ironic reservations about this sport. The knights are unhorsed with such vigour that their feet catch in the stirrup, dragging the saddle from the horse's back (B 172–7). The Czech word for pastime—*kratochvíle*—is probably a calque from Middle High German *kurzwîl* (literally 'short time'), a pun on the tedious length of the proceedings, which are finally curtailed with a gesture from Alexander (B 178–81).

The so-called *Dalimil Chronicle* (*c.*1314) was probably written by a member of the lower nobility. Its artistic realization is completely different from that of the *Alexandreida*; the language is communicative, the verse lacks a metrical pattern, and the rhymes are mostly grammatical. The chronicle is unusual for its time in that it omits the favourite features of the genre, such as legends, fables, and stories of chivalric exploit. Individual figures are not described with concern for their physical characteristics but become the personification of ideas; the author's own political views are not couched in complicated allegorical language but are expressed quite bluntly. Speaking from the standpoint of the lower nobility, the author considers this class to be the decisive political factor in the state. He elaborates his own philosophy of Czech history, which has two principal aspects—disinterested allegiance to the community (*obec*) and the belief that Bohemia should belong to the Czechs alone. The idea is sustained throughout the whole work, presented from different angles, and summarized at the end with a practical programme for the state. At the conclusion of his chronicle, Dalimil warns the new incumbent of the Czech throne, the Frenchman John of Luxemburg (1314–46), to follow the counsel of his nobles or leave the kingdom (106. 13–14).

[17] See Josef Hrabák, *Studie ze starší české literatury* (Prague, 1956), 228–9.

Unlike the *Alexandreida*, the *Dalimil Chronicle* is a direct political tract, a *tour de force* whose patriotism and anti-German virulence anticipates the Hussites in the early fifteenth century. The chronicle is well constructed, each episode a self-contained story with a particular point or theme, usually contrasting the heroic ideal of remote Czech history with the degeneracy and corruption of the present. The author makes the topos *laudatio temporis acti* serve as an organizing principle for his whole work. Taking stories from the mythical past of the Czechs, Dalimil reinterprets them to fit his political message. In chapter 41, he relates the legend of Prince Oldřich and the peasant girl Božena, adapted from the first chronicle of the Czechs, the *Chronica Bohemorum* (c.1110), by Cosmas, dean of the Prague chapter: while out hunting in the forest Oldřich comes across a beautiful Czech maiden named Božena. He is so captivated by her beauty that he decides to marry the girl despite his betrothal to a German princess. The prince's speech to his nobles in which he explains the reason for his morganatic marriage is in fact an extension of Dalimil's campaign against the Germans' interference in the state. Oldřich argues that we all come from one father—Adam—and that nobility can stem from humble origin (41. 13–16); a German wife would pose a threat as she would have a German entourage and would bring up her children to speak German, thus placing the future of the Czech dynasty in serious jeopardy.

Dalimil is outspoken on the subject of German courtly mores and customs. Using a well-known ineptitude topos established by Peter of Blois in the twelfth century he claims that the introduction of the joust to Bohemia is a symptom of decadence and of a decline in military standards.[18] He further criticizes the court's love of sumptuous attire, elaborate horse trappings, and covers (84. 7–8). For Dalimil a jouster rarely makes a good warrior (74. 19–22). In chapter 102, pointedly entitled 'On the evil ways of the Czech lords', Dalimil condemns the practices of the court, especially the pernicious influence of the ladies who distract the knights with trivial customs such as sending valiant knights love tokens (*chrústy*, 102, 20). He also castigates gambling such as the playing of cards as a futile pastime (102. 17–18).

Another work which presents historical events in politically

---

[18] See R. L. Kilgour, *The Decline of Chivalry as Shown in the French Literature of the Late Middle Ages* (Cambridge, Mass., 1937), 418.

loaded terms is the *Life of St Procopius* (*c*.1350). A true heir to *Dalimil* in its xenophobia, the legend is based on a Latin life of the saint who founded the monastery of Sázava, the centre of the Slavonic rite until 1096–7, when the pro-Catholic Břetislav II expelled the monks and installed a German abbot.[19] The anonymous Czech author reshapes the original story for his own nationalistic purpose. The language of the work is reminiscent of *Dalimil* in its directness and its proximity to everyday speech. Procopius is depicted as a simple monk of peasant origin, the ascetic ideal of Czechness as understood by these writers. Even as a young man he shuns all trivial pleasures, devoted to his chosen life and to his brothers. After his death the monks are ousted by Germans, for the author an allegory of the general political situation in Bohemia. The story reaches its climax when Procopius returns in person to force the German monks from the monastery, finally resorting to beating them over the heads with his crozier, a fine example of Czech medial-style realism.

Another important literary medium for political comment was the mystery plays, which, as performed texts, had direct access to a large heterogeneous audience. Unlike the works we have considered hitherto the mystery plays were not written by the spokesmen of the lower nobility but probably by members of the student populace, which had grown into a large minority of impoverished intellectuals. This new group of *literati*—the authors of such forms as the courtly love lyric, satires, and perhaps even the romances—had their own political and economic axe to grind. Their object of resentment and ridicule was primarily the burghers. The most important example of Czech medieval drama is the so-called *Mastičkář (Unguentarius)* (*c.* 1320), a Czech version of the spice merchant episode which forms part of the Resurrection plays written in several European languages.[20] The principal butt of the satire is the burgher class represented by the spice merchant himself, Pustrpalk, a parody of a dull-witted German. His servant is the anarchic figure Rubín who subverts all the social values held by the burghers. Language plays a vital part in the play's humour: Pustrpalk asks in German where Rubín is

---

[19] Vlasto, *Entry*, 107.

[20] See Václav Černý, *Staročeský Mastičkář* (*Rozpravy Československé akademie věd*, 65, řada SV, 7, 1955); Jarmila F. Veltruský, *A Sacred Farce from Medieval Bohemia* (Ann Arbor, 1985).

('Rubíne, vo bistu?') to which the anarchic assistant answers with a rhyming line: 'Here master, holding this hairy bitch by the arse.' The play is also interesting as anti-courtly satire, for example, Rubín's comic question addressed to the Three Marys as they approach to buy unguents for the anointing of the dead Christ, with its insinuation of indolence: 'Good morning, beautiful ladies/ have you just got up/holding your heads as heavy as hinds?' (Schlägel MS, 239–40).[21]

Another mystery play pointing to a similar *vagranti* authorship is the so-called *Play of the Merry Magdalene*, a fragment of about one hundred verses. The author introduces satirical elements in a low register reminiscent of *Mastičkář*. The play has a special interest as it contains two fragments of courtly love lyric, the earliest attestation of the genre in Czech apart from certain lyric elements in the verse romance *Duke Ernest* (*Vévoda Arnošt*) (*c.*1350). The close association of the courtly and the popular in Czech literature at this time suggests that, unlike German and French medieval literature, Czech courtliness was not synonymous with the royal court and the highest levels of society; courtliness in Czech literature grew out of the religious lyrics of the twelfth and thirteenth centuries and, as the middle classes gained greater power and influence in the social order, became their preserve, a case of *gesunkenes Kulturgut* whereby an aristocratic fashion loses its exclusiveness and is gradually taken over by the lower classes.

The largest fragment of a Czech medieval mystery play is *Resurrectione domini* which contains over nine hundred lines. In contrast to *Mastičkář* the humour and satire are subtle. Like the authors of the satires, the writer castigates the members of various trades, millers, cobblers, publicans, and bakers. He takes the standpoint of a cynical burgher mocking the knights who stand guard at the Sepulchre. They boast of their bravery but flee in terror when the Angel appears. Once again the new-style German chivalry is the butt of the joke: the speech of the second knight is a pastiche of the topoi of conventional romance, such as the *infirmitas* formula where the character is unable to express adequately the splendour of their knightly attire.

The satires (*c.*1360) draw on a tradition established by *Dalimil*. The *Satires of the Artisans* depict the vices and failings of the

---

[21] The mystery plays are edited in *Staročeské skladby dramatické původu liturgického*, ed. Jan Máchal (Prague, 1908).

burgher class. They take the form of exempla with a particular
artisan as the central figure who commits the sin in question, such
as bribery, corruption, and theft. The *Decalogue* (*The Ten
Commandments*) has a similar exemplary structure. The authors
are probably the members of the rootless student class. The most
original satire from this period is the mock dispute of *The Groom
and the Scholar*. An impoverished groom and student are drinking
in a tavern and as they succumb to the effect of beer start telling
tall tales about their respective lifestyles. The student depicts
himself as a high cleric, the groom as a courtier (*dvořák*). As
the dispute degenerates into direct abuse there is no attempt at
consistency or versimilitude. The humour is directed at members
of medieval society from the *vagranti* class to the burghers, as the
mock pious conclusion reveals.[22]

From the second half of the fourteenth century come the
chivalric romances adapted from German sources, *Duke Ernest
Laurin*, *Tandariáš and Floribella*, and *Tristram and Izalda*.[23] They
reflect the public taste for exoticism which coincided with the reign
of Charles IV (1346–78), when the Czech vernacular literature
blossomed, boasting all the genres current in the West—the epic
romance, satire, lyric, drama, and theological prose. The new
romances mark a significant departure from the austere knightly
ethos of the *Alexandreida*. Written with the affluent burgher
audience in mind, they present the remote world of chivalric
adventure in an accessible form, shorn of the courtly ethic. The
emphasis is placed on a dynamic narrative frequently punctuated by
dialogue, unlike the models, which consist of long reflections and
monologues addressed to Lady Love. The authors of the romances
understood that the courtly aristocratic ethos of the German
sources was not suitable to the needs of their own audience. An
interesting example of the popularizing tendency in the romances
is *Tristram and Izalda*, a conflation of three sources, Eilhart von
Oberge's twelfth-century *Tristrant*, Gottfried von Strassburg's
courtly version, and Heinrich von Freiberg's continuation of

[22] For the background on the Czech satires see the introduction to the edition
Staročeské satiry Hradeckého rukopisu a Smilovy školy, ed. Josef Hrabák (Prague
1962).
[23] For a study of the romances see Josef Hrabák, 'Česká středověká rytířská
epika', in *Československé přednášky pro VII. mezinárodní sjezd slavistů ve Varšavě*
(2 vols., Prague, 1973), i. 159–67; also Eduard Petrů, 'Specifičnost rytířské epiky ve
slovanských literaturách', *Slavia*, 52 (1983), 250–8.

Gottfried's masterpiece. Toward the end of the work in an episode based on Heinrich, the hero undergoes various adventures with his companion Kaedín to gain access to the queen. In the German version he remains a courtly figure throughout, but in the Czech reworking he ceases to be a knight altogether and is more reminiscent of the anarchic *joculatores* in the mystery plays or the trickster figure of the early versions of the story. In one scene Tristram the Fool smears himself from head to foot with goat's cheese, and bites into it so that it oozes into his beard; he then throws it at King Mark, shouting the insult 'peasant'. The cheese misses Mark and hits a lady of the court instead so that it splatters across her face (7437–52). (In the source Tristan simply throws the cheese to the queen for her to bite into.) Similar in style to the verse romances are the prose works *Bruncvík* and *Štilfríd*, also dated around the second half of the fourteenth century. Their prose belies an older verse form, revealed by the frequent rhymes at the close of certain phrases. These works also present an outsize world of adventure with the emphasis on hyperbolic action and brave deeds rather than a strict observance of courtly etiquette.[24]

Not all Czech texts in the second half of the fourteenth century were written by *vagranti* for the benefit of a burgher audience. One writer whose name is known to us is the high nobleman (*pán*) Smil Flaška of Pardubice. Smil is the author of two principal works, *The Father's Counsel to his Son*, in which an elderly nobleman instructs his son on the courtly precepts of knighthood, and *The New Council of Animals* (*c.*1385), a didactic-allegorical work in which the Lion King is advised by his subjects on how to rule his kingdom. The Council is entitled 'New' because the extant version is probably a second redaction of a lost original. The earlier version was written for the benefit of the new King Wenceslas IV, the son of Charles IV. It was a positive, benevolent guide to the young king reminiscent of Aristotle's counsel to Alexander in the *Alexandreida*; indeed certain verses seem to paraphrase the older poem. The writer insists on the king's dependence on his nobility, a defence of the aristocracy's rights and privileges. The second version, written around 1385, was composed as a response to a crisis in the kingdom when the king's unpopular policies provoked armed resistance from the nobility.

[24] For the background to the prose romances see Winfried Baumann, *Die Sage von Heinrich dem Löwen bei den Slaven* (Slavistische Beiträge 83, Munich, 1975).

Smil took an active part in the nobles' council known as the Lords' Union (*Panská jednota*). The new version reflects the author's ambivalence toward the figure of the king and his German court; some of the animals seem to be in favour of extravagant kingship, others are firmly opposed to the courtly way of life. The text signals a certain schizophrenia in the Czech author's view of kingship and the courtly ethic. It is probable that Smil began life as a conservative (as the earlier *Father's Counsel to his Son* indicates) but became increasingly suspicious of the Crown and its antagonism toward the nobility. Certain elements in the *New Council* hint at a radical conception of the state not dissimilar to the Hussites' position in the early fifteenth century. One of the most interesting counsels in the work is the speech of the Horse, an example of the anti-chivalric satire so common in the fourteenth century. The pastime of the joust is mercilessly mocked as a cruel and futile sport: the knights strike each other full in the face with their lances; when they are unhorsed they cry out 'reta! reta!' ('help!') from the sandpits into which they are cast.[25]

This sceptical attitude to German-style courtliness is shared by the other writer of the period whose name is known to us. Tomáš of Štítný (*c*.1333–1401/9) was a member of the gentry who wrote edifying religious and secular works for the education of his daughters but who later addressed a wide audience consisting mainly of his own class. In his tract on the estates of society he complains of the pride of those knights whose sole desire is to outshine each other in the splendour of their attire. He disapproves of the scandalous *risqué* fashions of court society in the manner of contemporaneous sermons, castigating those who wear long hoods and pointed shoes with straps which are so elaborate that the wearer has difficulty in moving about. He reminds his audience that the joust is not a suitable pastime for knights; those fatally wounded may receive the sacrament but may not be buried in hallowed ground for having contravened the laws of the Church.[26]

Throughout the thirteenth and fourteenth centuries a major source of conflict was the antagonism between the king and the

---

[25] For background information on Smil Flaška and the dating of the *Nová rada*, see the edition by Jiří Daňhelka (Prague, 1950); also Jan B. Čapek, 'Vznik a funkce Nové rady', *Věstník*, 1 (1938), 1–100.

[26] For editions of Tomáš of Štítný's major works see *Knížky šestery*, ed. Karel Jaromír Erben (Prague, 1852).

nobility which in literary texts is expressed as hostility to the
courtly ethic. A sensitive barometer of this tension is the debate
Tkadleček (*The Little Weaver*) (*c.*1409).[27] This masterpiece of
Czech medieval prose, a debate between the Lover and Misfortune, can be interpreted in a number of ways: as a theological
treatise on scholasticism; as a meditation on the courtly way of life
with Misfortune opposed to courtliness and Ludvík the jilted lover
its advocate; or a Freudian opposition between the ego and the
superego. Seen in the context of Czech literature the work
presents us with the conventional opposition between the court
and the nobility. Misfortune emerges as the traditional hostile
critic of courtliness, Ludvík its defender. In chapter 4 Misfortune
tells us that Ludvík's girlfriend Adlička had been at court in
Königgratz; here she introduces a whole series of unflattering
epithets revealing Misfortune's unchivalrous attitude to the heroine
and to womankind in general. In chapter 12 we have a long portrayal
of Ludvík as a courtly writer, in part a manifestation of
Misfortune's dislike of the courtly, in part a didactic passage aimed
at the courtly ethic itself. A central theme of the debate is the
problematic role of the writer in society; the very title 'weaver' is
an allegorical appellation for writer or textor. The theme of the
writer's crisis of identity is linked with the recurrent motif of the
orphan; Ludvík refers to himself as an orphan on more than one
occasion. This is traditionally interpreted as the jilted lover's sense
of loss and despair; but it can also be seen in purely political
material terms as the writer's alienated position in late medieval
society. At the beginning of the fifteenth century the feudal system
began to develop deep fissures, a crisis reflected in *The Little
Weaver*. As a consequence of this growing split in the national
psyche, Czech literature in the Hussite period lost its rich
diversity, degenerating into a polarized conflict between social and
religious groups. The Hussite tracts of the period are little more
than anti-Catholic satires while the Catholic satires were more
inventive and original, drawing on the illustrious tradition of the
previous century.

[27] Ed. Hynek Hrubý and František Šimek (Prague, 1923). For the relation of
Tkadleček to *Der Ackermann aus Böhmen* see Antonín Hrubý, *Der Ackermann
und seine Vorlage* (Munich, 1971). For a recent article on the Czech text see
Helmut Rosenfeld, 'Der alttschechische *Tkadleček* in neuer Sicht: Ackermann-
Vorlage, Walldenserallegorie oder höfische Dichtung?' *Welt der Slaven*, 26/2
(1981), 357–78.

The Hussites' attitude to the Germans was also paradoxical. As nationalists they were of course suspicious of the encroachment of the German language and the growing importance of Germans in political affairs. In his homilies Jan Hus expresses concern for the purity of the Czech language, insisting that a Czech who has a German wife should educate his children to speak Czech and not mix the two languages together. He cites the example of the Emperor Charles IV, who decreed that the citizens of Prague should bring up their children to speak Czech and use their native tongue during legal business in the town hall. He proceeds to list certain German household terms which threaten to oust the native Slavic words, such as *haustuch* (napkin), *šorc* (apron), *knedlík* (dumpling), *trepky* (stairs), *mantlík* (coat), *hauzschnecht* (house boy), and so on.[28] Elsewhere Hussite tracts affirm that the Germans are the political, but not necessarily the ideological, enemies. If they embrace the new reformed faith they are to be loved like Czechs. But political events did not always bear out such religious tolerance. In response to mounting pressure, Wenceslas IV passed the notorious *Decree of Kutná hora* (1409) whereby the German vote at the Charles University in Prague, the oldest seat of learning in central Europe (1347), was reduced from three to one, the Czech vote increasing from one to three. As a result the German students left Bohemia to found a new university in Leipzig. In this way the Charles University lost its pre-eminence as an international centre of learning and scholarship.[29]

During the period of economic stability and growth which coincided with the reign of Charles IV the political and religious conflicts fermenting in Czech society remained concealed. It is not within the scope of this essay to trace the events of the following reign which led to the breakdown of the feudal system and the struggle between the reformers and the Roman Catholic Church. The crisis of the early fifteenth century is accurately reflected in the polarized function of the literature of the time. This crisis is anticipated in *The Little Weaver*, an exploration of the increasing schizophrenia in the national psyche. In the conflict between reason and emotion, soul and body, puritanism and courtliness, two distinct literary traditions clash head on—the didactic tradition

---

[28] *Výbor z české literatury doby husitské*, i, ed. Bohuslav Havránek *et al.* (Prague, 1963), 147.

[29] Rádl, *Válka*, 38–42.

from the apocryphal legends to the Hussite tracts and the courtly tradition from the early religious lyrics of the twelfth century to the Catholic satires of the Hussite period. The Czech–German relationship can only be properly understood when it is seen as part of a larger political and ideological struggle between the estates of medieval society. Hostility toward the Germans was one important part of a more extensive political-religious upheaval which culminated in the Hussite Wars of the fifteenth century.

10

Religion, Culture, and Ideology on the Late Medieval Castilian–Granadan Frontier

ANGUS MACKAY

Professor López de Coca has provided an excellent discussion of the frontier institutions and peace-keeping mechanisms of the late medieval frontier between Christian Castile and Muslim Granada.[1] This paper deals with the same frontier and covers much the same chronological period, but concentrates on religious, cultural, and ideological aspects. However, the same political background is common to both our concerns and, given its importance, some salient aspects should be briefly re-emphasized at the outset.

If, for the moment, we exclude the reign of the Catholic Kings, the abiding impression we have of the history of late medieval Castile is one of internal political anarchy and a related decline in the impulse of the Reconquest against the Moors. Plagued by civil wars and the military intervention of foreign powers, it is hardly surprising that Castilian kings tried to avoid involvement on yet another military front. During the period 1350–1460, for example, the frontier enjoyed some eighty-five years of 'official' truce and only twenty-five years of 'official' war.[2] Such a situation, it might be thought, implied a degree of ordered relationships between the Castilian Christians and the Granadan Muslims, and this in turn prompted collaboration, respect, and even admiration, and a marked degree of acculturation. Indeed at times it would almost seem as if the frontier had in some ways ceased to exist.

For a start, internal dissensions in both kingdoms helped to promote trans-frontier alliances at the highest levels. Thus Muḥammad VI (*el rey Bermejo*), who was suspected of having assassinated Ismail II and was opposed by Muḥammad V, was butchered to death by Peter I in Seville because he had supported Aragón against Castile; and Muḥammad V, for his part, was Peter

---

[1] See ch. 6.
[2] Angus MacKay, 'The Ballad and the Frontier in Late Medieval Spain', *Bulletin of Hispanic Studies*, 52 (1976), 15–33, at 19.

I's ally in the civil war against Henry of Trastámara.[3] Then, too, there were the 'puppet' kings, such as Yūsuf IV, who briefly gained the throne with the help of John II, or Muḥammad XII (Boabdil), who collaborated with the Catholic Kings in the final conquest of Granada.[4] Bearing in mind such alliances, as well as the fact that a ruler like Yūsuf V lived for a time as a refugee at the Castilian court or that a king like Henry IV actually had Moorish knights attached to his household, it is small wonder that chroniclers found themselves describing frontier incidents in which, so to speak, the Castilian king's Moors engaged Moorish Moors.[5]

Moreover, if kings and sultans indulged in such alliances, these were commonplace on the frontier itself. The chronicles and the documents are replete with complaints and accusations relating to 'treacherous' alliances. The example of Alfonso Fajardo (Fajardo el Bravo) during the 1450s was notorious. Based on Lorca, on the eastern frontier, Fajardo's Christian and Moorish allies devastated and terrified frontier towns and settlements.[6] As Fajardo himself put it in a famous letter addressed to Henry IV:

And I say to you, Your Highness, that I am the person in your realms who has done the greatest number of both good and evil deeds, making myself known in foreign kingdoms and lordships . . . And, Sire, you should not complain about me so much, because you know that I could hand over the castles which I hold to the Moors and become a vassal of the king of Granada, and yet still live as a Christian, as others are doing . . .[7]

Similarly in the early 1470s repeated indignation was expressed about the way in which the frontier plans of the Constable and the lord of Aguilar were constantly divulged to the Moors by the count of Cabra, his sons, and his son-in-law Martín Alonso de

[3] On the assassination of Muḥammad VI, see Pero López de Ayala, *Corónica del rey don Pedro*, ed. Constance L. and Heanon M. Wilkins (Madison, 1985), 128. For diplomatic relations during the second half of the fourteenth century, see Miguel Ángel Ladero Quesada, *Granada: Historia de un país islámico (1232–1571)* (2nd edn., Madrid, 1979), 124–30.

[4] Ladero Quesada, *Granada*, 139, 185–96.

[5] On Yūsuf V at the Castilian court, see ibid. 143–4. For an example of Henry IV's Moors engaging Moors from Granada, see Diego de Valera, *Memorial de diversas hazañas*, ed. Juan de Mata Carriazo (Madrid, 1941), 22.

[6] Angus MacKay, *Anatomía de una revuelta urbana: Alcaraz en 1458* (Albacete, 1985), 38–9.

[7] For the complete text of the letter, see Juan Torres Fontes, *Fajardo el Bravo* (Murcia, 1944), 176–8.

Montemayor, who had allied themselves with the king of Granada 'in a very great and close friendship, *amigos de amigos y enemigos de enemigos*', had developed an extensive pro-Moorish spy system on the Christian side of the frontier, and were actively helping the Moors to attack the lands of their Christian enemies. Yet such indignation seems less convincing in the light of the fact that the lord of Aguilar's plans involved military support for the powerful lineage of the Abencerrajes against the sultan of Granada, who of course was allied to the count of Cabra.[8]

Such alliances meant that contact between Moors and Christians could be frequent and intense. The same was true of the frontier peace mechanisms. Muslim and Christian *alfaqueques* criss-crossed the frontier, the *rastreros* on both sides co-operated extensively in their crime-detection tasks, and both Muslims and Christians carefully negotiated the parameters of the semi-official system of 'controlled reprisals'. The 'minutes' of the town-council deliberations of Jaén demonstrate just how varied and sophisticated such trans-frontier collaboration could be. In dealing with practical problems, for example, the Moors appealed for Christian co-operation in dealing with people who accidentally strayed across the frontier by invoking the concept of 'good neighbourliness'; and faced with the problem of a runaway Christian youth, they invited his mother and his relatives to cross the frontier and persuade him to return home. Similarly Christian frontier authorities could see beyond mere hostility, and could agree, for example, that the Moors were justified in murdering a Christian in retaliation for a previous murder because no reparation had been made.[9]

It is fortunate that such municipal documentation is paralleled by chronicles—in the case of Jaén by the richly detailed chronicle of the deeds of the Constable of Castile, Miguel Lucas de Iranzo, who settled himself and his court in the town for a period of some thirteen years.[10] In effect this chronicle provides us with the narrative descriptions which bring frontier relationships vividly to life. As far as 'contact' or 'neighbourliness' is concerned, for

[8] See e.g. *Hechos del condestable don Miguel Lucas de Iranzo*, ed. Juan de Mata Carriazo (Madrid, 1940), 434, 441–3, 464–7.

[9] See Juan de Mata Carriazo, 'Los moros de Granada en las actas del concejo de Jaén de 1479', *Miscelánea de estudios árabes y hebraicos*, 4 (1955), 81–125, repr. in *Homenaje al profesor Carriazo* (3 vols., Seville, 1971–3), i. 265–310; MacKay, 'The Ballad and the Frontier', 23–7.

[10] *Hechos del condestable*, passim.

example, there is the long account of the events which accompanied
the diplomatic visit of the Moorish castellan of Cambil and some
Moorish knights from Granada to Jaén during the period of
Carnival in 1463. On the Sunday, the Moorish guests were treated
to the spectacle of a *juego de cañas*—that is, jousting with canes
instead of lances. This was followed at night by what can only be
described as a *son et lumière* procession through the town, which
was ablaze with light, drowned with the noise of drums, trumpets,
and other wind-instruments, and filled with 'masquers' (*momos*)
and 'characters' (*personajes*) who danced and performed revels or
theatrical 'happenings' (*invenciones*) in all the available squares
and open places. The Moors were to witness more *fiestas* on the
following Tuesday. In the evening a huge bonfire was lit in the
square in front of the Constable's palace and a burlesque variation
of the chivalrous game or exercise of tilting at the ring was acted
out. In front of an audience consisting of all the dignitaries and
plebs (*gente plebea*) of the town, a richly attired 'fool' called 'the
Master of Santiago' presided at the tilting. But this was attempted
by another 'fool' who, after succeeding in carrying off the ring
three times, so enraged 'the Master of Santiago' that he summoned
his pages to attack the successful 'fool'—which they duly did with
clubs of leather filled with wool, giving him so many blows that he
eventually fled. This was followed by an open-air dinner nearby in
a space littered with rich carpets, brocades, and French cloth
drapings. Then, after dinner, two companies of masqued *momos*,
dressed in contrasting liveries, danced genteelly for a long time,
with the Constable and his relations joining in towards the end.
Finally, after the dancing, some 150 men arrived, each wearing a
round helmet and armed with three or four long and dried out
gourds or calabashes, and to the sound of trumpets and drums a
carnivalesque fight broke out with some 600 gourds rebounding
and resounding off the helmets of the participants. The Moors
were particularly delighted with this last spectacle, and exclaimed
their pleasure and amazemenet by saying '*axudy*' to each other.[11]
Clearly, the frontier could be fun!

Frequent contacts and negotiations also meant that both sides
were well informed about each other. The chronicle of Miguel
Lucas, for example, gives a long and detailed account of the

---

[11] *Hechos del condestable*, 109–12.

circumstances surrounding the infamous massacre of the Abencerrajes which took place inside the Alhambra palace in 1462.[12] It is not difficult to imagine how such information was acquired. For, quite apart from trans-frontier alliances and the activities of spies, *alfaqueques* were entrusted with gathering intelligence information, and someone like Fray Diego de la Guardia, in charge of collecting tribute money, could spend over four months in Granada itself negotiating his mission.[13] Moreover, although this is a matter which cannot be properly quantified, there was probably a not inconsiderable number of Moors who could speak Castilian fluently (sometimes referred to as *moros ladinos*) and Christians who could speak *algarabía* (the local Arabic dialect), quite apart from those *alfaqueques*, *trujumanes*, and dragomen who dealt with the more formal tasks of interpreting both the written and spoken word.[14]

Men and women also crossed the frontier and converted to the other religion, and the laconic remarks made by chroniclers suggest that such a transition could be fairly simple. When ʿAlī el Curro of Gibraltar became a Christian, for example, he simply changed his name to Diego el Curro.[15] Moreover although it is difficult to believe that anyone could have changed religion eight times, as was alleged in the ballad of *Bovalías el Pagano*,[16] there certainly were cases of reconversions. Luis de Jaén started off life as a Christian, became an *elche* (that is, an apostate or convert to Islam), served as a page to the sultan of Granada, and then subsequently reconverted to Christianity.[17] Similarly another Muslim knight and ex-Christian for long served in the household of the Moorish castellan of Moclín, el Cabçaní, before reconverting to the religion of his youth.[18] Small wonder, therefore, that there is even evidence of religious confusion. St Ginés de la Jara, for example, performed miracles for both Christians and Moors, and some of the latter are recorded as crossing the frontier to visit his

[12] Ibid. 83–4.
[13] Ibid. 90.
[14] See e.g the incident involving an *alfaqueque*, Christian prisoners in Montefrío, Moors, and *moros ladinos*, ibid. 103–9.
[15] Diego de Valera, *Memorial de diversas hazañas*, 75.
[16] For the text of this ballad, see *Cancionero de romances (Anvers, 1550)*, ed. Antonio Rodríguez-Moñino (Madrid, 1967), 249.
[17] Diego de Valera, *Memorial de diversas hazañas*, 13.
[18] *Hechos del condestable*, 145.

sanctuary.[19] More spectacularly, perhaps, the Franciscan heretic Fray Alonso de Mella, who sought refuge in Granada, wrote to John II to tell him that he and his followers had discovered that the Muslims were in fact Christians who worshipped the same and only true God.[20]

All this evidence suggests the possibility of such a degree of cultural confusion, in the broadest sense of the term, that it is almost as if a frontier, as it is normally envisaged, hardly existed. The point is perhaps best made by appealing to the visual senses. Imagine the following typical scene in Jaén with the mind's eye. Knights on horseback appear, practising their skills of speed and mobility using cane spears, but doing so in a manner which is virtually indistinguishable from that of Moorish knights: they carry heart-shaped Moorish shields known as *adargas*, are lightly armoured and ride in the Moorish manner, *a la gineta* (that is, with short stirrups and a low saddle). Those who are judged to be the most skilled will be given prizes from a collection of Moorish shirts, Tunisian head-dresses, Moorish veils, Moorish hoods, and fine Moroccan leather boots. They are of course Christian knights.[21] Their lord is the Constable of Castile, and he too likes to ride *a la gineta*, dressed *a lo morisco*, carrying an azagay in one hand, bearing an *adarga* with the other, and accompanied by young pages of a very Moorish appearance (*muy moriscos*). Indeed, when the bishop of Salamanca comes on a visit, the Constable will give him the best present he can think of—four Moorish horses *de la gineta*, with the relevant saddles, stirrups, bits, and spurs, and of course an azagay.[22]

These Moorish-like Christian scenes can be compared to the Christian-like Moorish scenes, dating from the fourteenth century, which cover three domes in the Hall of Justice in the Alhambra of Granada.[23] Precisely because Islam was hostile to the representation

[19] See Juan Torres Fontes, *El monasterio de San Ginés de la Jara en la Edad Media* (Murcia, 1965), 5–21.

[20] For the text of Mella's letter, see Darío Cabanelas, 'Un franciscano heterodoxo en la Granada nasrí: Fray Alonso de Mella', *Al Andalus*, 15 (1950), 233–50.

[21] See *Hechos del condestable*, 116–17.

[22] Ibid. 59, 138.

[23] On these paintings and for what follows, see the excellent study by Jerrilynn D. Dodds, 'The Paintings in the *Sala de Justicia* of the Alhambra: Iconography and Iconology', *Art Bulletin*, 61 (1979), 186–97, which summarizes previous researches and opinions, and provides new and important arguments.

of living beings, these scenes, which are 'northern-style' depictions of elements of Christian chivalric legends, are particularly intriguing. In fact the confusion in style and content is so extreme that the most diverse opinions have been expressed about the identity of the artist (or artists) involved. Was he a Muslim artist who 'borrowed' from the northern Gothic style? Or was he 'undoubtedly a Western Gothic painter, probably an Italian'?[24] Or was he a French war captive? The latest explanation, which sees the paintings as being the indirect result of a trans-frontier alliance, is the most convincing. According to this, Muḥammad V, who was Peter the Cruel's ally against Henry of Trastámara, borrowed the Castilian king's *mudéjar* artists to execute the scenes. These *mudéjares*, who were Muslims living in Christian Castile and accustomed to producing works which had a 'Christian' content but were executed with 'Islamic' techniques, were precisely the kind of 'middlemen' who were capable of introducing elements of northern legends into the very heart of the Alhambra—'The Tryst Beneath the Tree' from the legend of Tristan and Isolde; the theme of 'The Fountain of Youth'; the episode of 'Lancelot's Crossing of the Bridge of Swords' from the Arthurian Cycle; and the theme of the wodehouse or Wild Man.[25] This last episode, in which a damsel holding a chained and sleepy lion is saved from a Wild Man by a Christian knight, who is in turn killed by a Moorish knight, is the most puzzling episode. It may be a variation of the tale of Enyas, which was known in fourteenth-century France and England but which has not survived in a literary form, and its closest surviving analogies are to be found in scenes depicted on French ivory caskets of the first half of the fourteenth century and in entries in a detailed inventory made for Louis, duke of Anjou, in the 1360s.[26] For example, one of these is as follows:

A covered drinking bowl . . . [and] inside the said bowl [there is] a blue enamel, and the said enamel has a man on horseback who is coming out of a castle, and in his right hand he has a naked sword in order to attack a Wild Man who is carrying off a damsel, and inside the cover of the bowl

[24] Ibid. 188.   [25] Ibid. 190–5.
[26] On the story of Enyas and the scenes on the ivory caskets, see Roger S. Loomis, 'A Phantom Tale of Female Ingratitude', *Modern Philology*, 14 (1916–17), 175–9. I owe this reference to a final-year undergraduate dissertation submitted in the History Department of the University of Edinburgh by Mr Martin O'Donnell in 1981.

there is another blue enamel on which there is a damsel who has a chain in her hand to which a lion is attached, and on this lion there is a Wild Man.[27]

The Alhambra version of this tale has of course an important variation: a Muslim knight kills the Christian rescuer of the damsel. But such 'twists' were to be expected, and are in fact paralleled in *aljamiado* literature—that is, literature written by *moriscos* in romance dialects but using Arabic characters. Here 'Alī, Muḥammad's son-in-law, is the Islamic equivalent of the Christian Santiago, and the other heroes of the *aljamiado* legends are cast in the mould of Roland, the Twelve Peers of France, Tirant lo Blanc, and Amadis of Gaul.[28]

Having established himself in the Alhambra, the Wild Man could of course recross the frontier. In fact we can, so to speak, catch him in the act. In Diego de San Pedro's famous and archetypal *Prison of Love* the story begins with the narrator returning from the war against Granada. In the Sierra Morena he meets a Wild Man, who, carrying the sculptured figure of a beatiful woman, drags after him a groaning captive who is subsequently imprisoned in a highly complex and metaphorical 'Prison of Love'.[29] Both the Alhambra paintings and San Pedro's novel, of course, can be classified as 'high art', but the same elements can be detected at other levels of frontier life. Just after his wedding celebrations in Jaén, for example, the Constable rode out to chivalric encounters with knightly adventurers with a 'prison' on his saddle, and inside the prison there was an effigy of himself with a sword through its heart and its hands tied with a chain.[30] On both sides of the frontier men could indulge their fantasies with chains, Wild Men, and prisons of love.

The same points can be made by appealing to the oral senses, taking as an example the frontier ballads of the period.[31] At times

---

[27] Loomis, 'A Phantom Tale', 176.

[28] See Louis Cardaillac, *Morisques et chrétiens: Un affrontement polémique (1492–1640)* (Paris, 1977), 33. See also the astonishing case of the *morisco* story-teller of chivalrous tales) Román Ramírez, who was tried by the Inquisition because of his 'diabolic' skills, in Leonard P. Harvey, 'Oral Composition and the Performance of Novels of Chivalry in Spain', *Forum for Modern Language Studies*, 10 (1974), 270–86.

[29] Diego de San Pedro, *Cárcel de Amor*, ed. Keith Whinnom (Madrid, 1971).

[30] *Hechos del condestable*, 58–9.

[31] In order to avoid needless and repetitive citing it should be noted that the texts of the ballads which are discussed here are to be found among the following

these demonstrate a striking ability to see matters from the other's point of view. Such is the case of the story narrated by the beautiful Moorish girl Moraima, who is fooled into opening her door to a Christian rapist precisely because he speaks *algarabía* fluently and can pass himself off as a Moor.[32] The ballads also reveal examples of intense friendship, even of love, between Moors and Christians. In a spirit of mutual affection and chivalric respect Alonso Fajardo, whom we have already encountered, plays at chess with the sultan of Granada (echoing, perhaps, another scene in the Alhambra paintings where a Christian youth plays chess with a maiden). Even more telling is the ballad of Abenámar, in which John II of Castile woos a personified and beautiful Granada, asks her hand in marriage, offers her a reverse dowry consisting of Córdoba and Seville, and receives a wistful and nostalgic refusal because Granada points out that she is already married and has a very possessive Moorish husband.[33]

Even the so-called 'formulaic diction' of the ballads can convey precisely customs which were common to both sides of the frontier.[34] One of the ballads on the loss of Antequera, for example, begins with a typical evocation, 'La mañana de San Juan', and then proceeds to describe the great festivities or *gran fiesta* of the Moors of Granada on St John's day. The description is a miracle of precision. The festivities begin at the crack of dawn ('al punto que alboreaua'), the action takes place on the plain outside the city, and the participants are richly attired knights who

works: Marcelino Menéndez Pelayo, *Antología de poetas líricos castellanos*, viii–ix (rev. edn., Madrid, 1945); Ramón Menéndez Pidal, *Flor nueva de romances viejos* (22nd edn., Madrid, 1968); Colin C. Smith, *Spanish Ballads* (London, 1964); Roger Wright, *Spanish Ballads (with English Verse Translations)* (Warminster, 1987).

[32] For a dissenting opinion on this traditional view of this particular ballad, see Louise Mirrer-Singer, 'Revaluating the *Fronterizo* Ballad: The *Romance de la morilla burlada* as a Pro-Christian Text', *La corónica*, 12 (1985), 157–67.

[33] On these two ballads, see MacKay, 'The Ballad and the Frontier', 22–3; Juan Torres Fontes, 'El Fajardo del "Romance del juego de ajedrez"', *Revista bibliográfica y documental*, 2 (1948), 305–14; id., 'La historicidad del romance "Abenámar, Abenámar"', *Anuario de estudios medievales*, 8 (1972–3), 225–56.

[34] By referring to 'so-called "formulaic diction"', I do not mean to deny its existence or its supposed importance as a technique for ballad-singers. But in the example which follows, the formulaic 'La mañana de San Juan' opens the ballad and serves another purpose. See Angus MacKay, 'Los romances fronterizos como fuente histórica', in *Actas del IV Coloquio de Historia Medieval Andaluza* (Almería, in press).

deftly whirl their horses ('revolbiendo sus caballos'), 'play at lances' ('jugando de las lanças'), and engage in skirmishes or *escaramuzas*. But this was a festival celebrated by Christians and Moors alike—the midsummer solstice, which was St John's day for the Christians and '*anṣara* for the Moors—and the ballad accurately summarizes some of the elements of the *fiesta*.[35] As far as the Muslim side of the frontier is concerned, this Christian ballad contains definite echoes of a late eleventh- or early twelfth-century *kharja*—that is, the stanza, in Vulgar Arabic, or in Spanish, or in a mixture of both, which comes at the end of the Hispano–Arabic form of poem known as the *muwassaha*, which was in classical Arabic. In this *kharja* a Muslim invokes the 'albo día' of '*anṣara*, proclaims his intention of donning his richly brocaded doublet, and looks forward to participating at playing at lances.[36] The evidence is even better for the Christian side of the frontier. On St John's morning in Jaén, for example, drummers and musicians carefully marked off the countdown to the crack of dawn. By that point everybody of note was already up, richly attired, and mounted. In fact half an hour *before* sunrise the Constable and some of his knights, dressed as Moors and riding *a la gineta*, left the town and headed for the river where they covered themselves with many branches and flowers. Meanwhile those knights who had remained in the town sallied forth as Christians, and they and the Constable's party of 'Moors' engaged in a fine skirmish (*vna fermosa escaramuça*)—'at times some attacking and others fleeing, at other times those who were fleeing whirling round [*boluiendo*] against those who were following them' (cf. the ballad's 'revolbiendo sus caballos'). And, of course, this was subsequently followed by 'playing at lances'.[37] What exactly did this entail? The Christian ballad simply refers to 'playing at lances'. The Muslim of the *kharja* refers to a 'breaking' of lances. The chronicle of Miguel Lucas provides the solution. The 'play' element was due to the fact that real lances were not used. Instead canes or *cañas* were provided, and the 'breaking' of

---

[35] See Samuel G. Armistead and Joseph H. Silverman, '*La Sanjuanada*: ¿Huellas de una harǧa en la tradición actual?' in their *En torno al romancero sefardí (Hispanismo y bálcanismo de la tradición judeo-española)* (Madrid, 1982), 13–22.

[36] For the text of this *kharja*, see ibid. 13.

[37] See the detailed description of all this in *Hechos del condestable*, 170–6.

these demonstrated the dexterity of the participants in hitting their intended targets.[38]

In this particular example of the St John's day or 'anṣara festivities it is virtually impossible to disentangle the movement and play of influences across the frontier. Indeed it may well be that a common and ancient Mediterranean tradition can be invoked as an explanation. To this day Muslims in Morocco observe similar rituals at 'anṣara, bathing themselves and their animals in the sea and rivers, in some cases before sunrise and in all cases in the early morning. For on this particular morning water is endowed with *baraka*, the mysterious wonder-working force which brings blessing from God and which remove sickness and misfortune. In many cases, too, communities split up into opposing groups and hold ritual skirmishes or fights.[39] Similarly in the Abbruzzi region of Italy villagers until recent times used to take themselves and their animals to the river and immerse themselves at daybreak on St John's morning.[40] The explanation for doing this was of course Christianized, reference being made to St John's baptism of Christ, but undoubtedly the animals were thought to benefit from something akin to *baraka*. And in the case of Spain once the Moors were forced to convert to Christianity, becoming *moriscos*, their favourite *fiesta* was to be that of St John, which they continued to associate with an early morning ritual wash.[41]

Referring to customs and incidents on both sides of the frontier, it may also be possible that some ballads derived their inspiration from a trans-frontier Christian-Muslim basis. It has been argued, for example, that the ballad of Abenámar was composed by a 'latinized Moor' (*moro latinado*) and that the ballad of Moraima was simply a Christian version of an Arabic song.[42] Such views

---

[38] On all the various chivalrous 'games' or 'physical exercises' at the Constable's court, see the excellent study by Lucien Clare, 'Fêtes, jeux et divertissements à la cour du connétable de Castille, Miguel Lucas de Iranzo (1460–1470): Les Exercices physiques', in *La Fête et l'écriture: Théâtre de cour, cour-théâtre en Espagne et en Italie, 1450–1530 (Colloque international: France–Espagne–Italie, 1985)* (Aix-en-Provence, 1987), 5–32.

[39] See Edward Westermarck, *Ritual and Belief in Morocco* (2 vols., London, 1926), ii. 188–99.

[40] My wife, who comes from this region, remembers this custom from her childhood.

[41] Cardaillac, *Morisques et chrétiens*, 26, 32–3.

[42] With respect to the ballad of Abenámar, see the summary of such opinions

now seem less implausible following the recent discovery of a
ballad in the walls of a convent in Albacete, because this text,
which concerns a love-story between a Christian and a Mooress,
contains a remarkably large amount of Arabic speech within the
Castilian 'frame'.[43]

Nevertheless, despite all the evidence which has been examined
so far with respect to trans-frontier influences, collaboration, and
mutual respect and admiration, the underlying long-term trend
was quite different. Although truces were frequent, a definitive
peace was unacceptable to both sides. The number of those who
crossed the frontier and converted to the other religion may at first
sight seem striking, but in fact they were exceptions. Examples of
respect and friendship contrast starkly with patterns of savage
cruelty. It was common practice, for example, for frontier
Christians to return from their forays with the severed heads or the
sliced-off ears of their defeated Moorish opponents. Indeed
rewards were paid for the heads or 'scalps' of Moorish *almogávares*
(frontier 'commandos' or raiders).[44] At times the barbarity was
sickening. In a minor incident on 18 February 1470 four Moorish
almogávares stumbled into a group of Christian soldiers, with two
being killed and two captured. Two severed heads and two
captives were dispatched to Jaén, but since the Constable was in
Andújar, the two heads were forwarded on to him there:

given by Paul Bénichou, *Creación poética en el romancero tradicional* (Madrid,
1968), 71 n. 12. On the ballad of Moraima, see Josep M. Solà-Solé, 'En torno al
romance de la morilla burlada', *Hispanic Review*, 33 (1965), 135–46.

[43] For the text of this ballad, see Francisco Mendoza Díaz-Maroto, 'Un nuevo
manuscrito emparedado de fines del siglo XVI', *Al-Basit*, 9 (1983), 27–45. A
detailed analysis of the Arabic of the text is given by Samuel G. Armistead and
James T. Monroe, 'A New Version of *La Morica de Antequera*', *La corónica*,
12 (1984), 228–40.

[44] Archivo Municipal Murcia, Actas Capitulares 1435, fo. 49ᵛ, meeting of the
council on Saturday 29 Jan., contains a typical example: 'There appeared Pero
Çurana and Bartolomé Canovas and Matheo Serrana, *vecinos* of Aledo, and they
said . . . that they [the council] well knew . . . how they had brought the heads of
three Moorish *almogávares* to this city, who they had killed in the incident of Aledo
and who had crossed over to do evil and damage in this region. Therefore, and also
so that they and the others who had been present at the killing of these Moors
should be more willing to follow the trails (*rastros*) of such Moors in the future, . . .
they [the council] should be pleased to give them something . . . And, having seen
and heard about this, and inasmuch as the city has an old ordinance whereby 100
maravedíes are payable for the head of each Moorish *almogávar*, they ordered . . .
that 300 *maravedíes* be granted and paid . . .'

And when he saw them and heard the news, he was pleased; and he ordered the heads to be spiked on lances, and thus they were taken into Andújar. And there the children of the town dragged the heads through the streets, and afterwards they let the dogs eat them.[45]

Out on campaign in 1487, the troops of Rodrigo Ponce de León, marquis of Cádiz, operated on a grander and more systematic scale—they defeated and killed 320 Moors, put another 80 who had been captured to the sword, and made a triumphal entry into the royal camp with the 400 severed heads spiked on their lances.[46]

Religious beliefs underlay and justified such acts of savagery. The task of reconquest was a 'holy undertaking' (*santa empresa*) and a 'most holy pilgrimage' (*tan santa romería*).[47] The chronicles provide evidence of a sense of 'manifest destiny' and of the inevitable unfolding of a divine plan to which popes lent their religious authority and financial help.[48] Small wonder, then, that when the Catholic Kings took up the task in earnest, they were regarded as being sent, elected, and illumined by God.[49] Transfrontier alliances did exist but, unless they were opportunistically exploited in the interests of the greater ultimate objective of final victory, they were regarded as a form of sacrilege and as being *contra naturam*. And as each place fell to the Christians, so it was ritually cleansed of 'the filth' of Muḥammad. Thus on 29 June 1236 the bishop of Osma, accompanied by other bishops, purified the great mosque of Córdoba, 'throwing out the filth of Muḥammad and spraying holy water throughout it'.[50] Similarly over two centuries later the marquis of Cádiz, after taking Alhama, had the chief mosque of the town consecrated, built altars inside it, provided it with vestments, books, crosses, and chalices, placed a statue of the Virgin on the main altar, and dedicated the mosque-church to Santa María de la Encarnación.[51] Even in small places,

---

[45] *Hechos del condestable*, 417–18.
[46] See the chronicle of the *Historia de los hechos del Marqués de Cádiz (1443–1488)* in *Colección de documentos inéditos para la historia de España*, cvi (Madrid, 1893), 143–317, at 270–1.   [47] Ibid. 267, 294.
[48] For a typical example of such a passage, see *Hechos del condestable*, 84.
[49] See e.g. *Historia de los hechos del Marqués*, 145, 159–60, 267, and, more generally, Jocelyn N. Hillgarth, *The Spanish Kingdoms, 1250–1516* (2 vols., Oxford, 1976–8), ii. 363, 372–4, 392–3.
[50] See the *Primera crónica general de España*, ed. Ramón Menéndez Pidal (2 vols., Madrid, 1955), ii. 733–4; Angus MacKay, *Spain in the Middle Ages: From Frontier to Empire, 1000–1500* (London, 1977), 60.
[51] *Historia de los hechos del Marqués*, 207.

the priest moved in after the knights, as at the castle of Montecorto where a priest with all the necessary ornaments was sent in along with the first Christian castellan in order to administer the sacraments of Holy Mother Church.[52] This, after all, was what the Reconquest was about.

This religious factor, however, was not a constant, and it changed through time and space. The late medieval frontier was a Mariological one. In town after town the Virgin took pride of place in the way that cathedrals and churches were dedicated.[53] The mosque-cathedral of Córdoba was named in honour of the Virgin, and the marquis of Cádiz dedicated the chief mosque-church of Alhama to her because she had appeared to him and ordered him to do so.[54] In all frontier towns the major churches belonged to the Virgin, with other parish churches being shared out among other saints. Her supremacy, as Ángela Muñoz has recently shown, was overwhelming.[55]

But in this process the frontier did not simply follow a general European trend. The Virgin was there on the frontier herself, helping out in battles and providing a new sense of continuity of purpose. Frequently statues or images of the Virgin played a crucial role. It was the effigy of Our Lady of Linares, for example, which enabled Ferdinand III to take Córdoba. And in many such cases these statues were believed to have been venerated by the Visigoths: at the time of the Muslim invasion the Christians had hidden them but now, as areas were being reconquered hundreds of years later, these same statues would miraculously reappear or be discovered.[56]

Although it might be thought that such legends were elaborated long after the events in question, there is enough evidence to demonstrate that this was not the case. A good example is Argote de Molina's sixteenth-century account of the miraculous victory of the Christians at the battle of Las Navas de Tolosa in 1212. He literally attributes this victory to the representations, or manifes-

---

[52] *Historia de los hechos del Marqués*, 193–4.

[53] See the excellent study by Ángela Muñoz Fernández, 'Cultos, devociones y advocaciones religiosas en los orígenes de la organización eclesiástica cordobesa (siglos XIII–XIV)', in *Actas del V Coloquio de Historia Medieval Andaluza* (Córdoba, in press).

[54] *Historia de los hechos del Marqués*, 200.

[55] Muñoz, 'Cultos, devociones y advocaciones', *passim*.

[56] Ibid.

tations, of the Cross carried into, or evident at, the battle. But the Virgin also played her part:

The fourth and final reason [for the victory] was the glorious banner with its picture of the most sacred Virgin Mary . . . with the baby Jesus in her arms, and holding the world in her hand with the insignia of the Cross . . .[57]

Yet Argote de Molina was by no means 'inventing' such legends three hundred years after the event. Already in the poems of the *Cántigas de Santa María*, which date from 1255–84, the efficacious use of such a banner against the infidel is confirmed, and indeed the actual banner, exactly as described by Argote, can be seen in the corresponding miniatures.[58] And just as she saved Carlisle from the besieging Scots in 1385, so too in the miniatures of the *Cántigas* a statue of the Virgin can be seen on the ramparts of a Christian castle, saving its inhabitants from the perfidious attack of the Moors.[59] Throughout the whole of the late medieval period she appeared at crucial points, her banner continued to be used, and the great frontier lords displayed an inordinate and fervent attachment to her.[60] St James—Santiago 'matamoros'—could still be invoked in battle, but his great age now lay well in the past.

But in addition to the Virgin there were 'sacred frontier objects', wonder-working relics from past history. A good example is the sword of Ferdinand III, St Ferdinand, which was kept appropriately in the cathedral of Santa María la Mayor in Seville. Ferdinand III had taken Seville in 1248—or, to be more accurate, the Virgin had personally appeared to him, given him the keys of the city, and put him inside.[61] In 1407 another Ferdinand—and

[57] See Gonzalo Argote de Molina, *Nobleza del Andalucía* (Seville, 1588), 96–7.

[58] See José Guerrero Lovillo, *Las Cántigas: Estudio arqueológico de sus miniaturas* (Madrid, 1949), lámina 198 (*Cántiga* CLXXXI). This work reproduces the miniatures and their captions, and the references are to the number of the reproduction (*lámina*) and to the number of the 'song' to which the minautres refer (*Cántiga*).

[59] Ibid. láminas 204–5 (*Cántiga* CLXXXV). For the incident at Carlisle see below, ch. 11, at n. 45.

[60] In the case of the marquis of Cádiz the Virgin in person appeared and conversed with him, and in more general terms frontier society seemed to be particularly devoted to Our Lady of Guadalupe. See *Historia de los hechos del Marqués*, 152, 162, 184–5, 187, 199–200, 204–5, 212, 227, 262, 311; *Hechos del condestable*, 31–2, 63, 162.

[61] *Historia de los hechos del Marqués*, 148.

names had also acquired their own wonder-working qualities—turned up in Seville to mount his own campaigns. This was Ferdinand 'of Antequera', and the efficacy of the sword was not lost on those who were present. As one count remarked to Ferdinand: 'Sire, it would seem that this sword is virtue (*virtud*), and you should process it round the church, and then take it on horseback throughout the city.' The advice was accepted, and of course Ferdinand also took the sword with him, only returning to press it into the hand of Ferdinand III's corpse once his campaign was over.[62]

As this episode illustrates, there was an intense awareness of some aspects of past history. How sophisticated was this awareness, how meaningful was it, and how was it achieved in the face of a marked absence of formal schools and universities?[63] As far as the all-important nobles and knights were concerned, an awareness of the past, as well as the present, was mainly acquired by means of two social institutions. The first of these was what may be termed the lineage-*bando*—that is, the socio-political grouping which was not unlike a Florentine *consorteria* or a Genoese *albergo*, for example. The lineage-*bando* usually had a dominating lineage, from which the *bando* derived its name and to which other lineages associated themselves, a *pariente mayor* or leader, and a wide variety of associated members who were variously described as *parientes* (relatives), *deudos* (kin, both real and artificial), *vasallos*, *abogados* (supporters), and *criados* (servants; officials). The lineage-*bando* usually also controlled well-defined areas, such as a region, a town, or a carefully delimited zone within a town. Important lineages tended to have their own lineage-churches, chapels, and even convents, while at the level of the more extensive *bando* it is easy to detect the use of livery and maintenance. The second institution was the community in which people lived, which as far as the surviving evidence is concerned was almost always the town and its lordship. Of course these social institutions overlapped, with urban oligarchs becoming attached to

[62] *Crónica de Juan II de Castilla*, ed. Juan de Mata Carriazo (Madrid, 1982), 129–31, 189–91.

[63] In what follows I am not of course denying the existence of highly literate individuals, such as the *letrados*, or a humanist noble like Nuño de Guzmán. Rather, I am concerned with the predominant way in which frontier knights and nobles acquired an 'education'.

lineage-*bandos*, and members of the latter holding important
urban and ecclesiastical offices.[64]

Frontier ideology was largely shaped by what may be termed
lineage culture and by the communities within which the lineage-
bandos operated.[65] What did lineage 'education' consist of? In the
first place it implied attachment at an early age to a household
related to a lineage-*bando*. For example Fernando de Narváez,
who became castellan of Antequera and *alcalde mayor* of
Córdoba, was brought up from his early years in the household of
the great Alvaro de Luna.[66] More typically, perhaps, Alonso de
Monroy was sent at the age of 13 to the household of a relation,
Don Gutierre de Sotomayor, Master of the Order of Alcántara,
'so that he should be brought up there (*para que se criase allá*)'.[67]
Hence the ambiguous and subtle nuances in the meaning of such
words as *criar*, *criado*, and *crianza*, which do not simply imply
qualities associated with a mere 'servant' but refer to processes of
education, formation, and 'bringing up'.

What did the young *parientes*, *deudos*, and *criados* actually
learn? Above all, of course, they were taught how to fight with all
the relevant knightly weapons and to fight on horseback. Indeed,
as Lucien Clare has strikingly demonstrated with respect to the
Constable's court in Jaén, even the wide variety of leisure
activities seems to have been principally designed to promote and
maintain a constant level of physical fitness.[68] But such men also
learned about the heroes and heroic deeds of the past in stories
which served as exempla and provided models of behaviour.
Naturally epic heroes tended to dominate. The Roland legend, for
example, followed in the wake of the Reconquest, and the tales
which circulated about him in Andalusia and Portugal were

[64] See Jacques Heers, *Le Clan familial au Moyen Âge* (Paris, 1974); María C.
Quintanilla Raso, 'Estructuras sociales y familiares y papel político de la nobleza
cordobesa (siglos XIV–XV)', *En la España medieval*, 3 (1982), 331–52; Lucien
Clare and Jacques Heers (eds.), *Colloque sur les 'bandos' et querelles dynastiques
en Espagne à la fin du Moyen Âge* (Paris, in press).
[65] See Angus MacKay, 'Los bandos: Aspectos culturales' in Clare and Heers,
Colloque sur les 'bandos'.
[66] *Crónica de don Alvaro de Luna*, ed. Juan de Mata Carriazo (Madrid, 1940),
444.
[67] Alonso de Maldonado, *Hechos de don Alonso de Monroy, Memorial histórico
español*, vi (Madrid, 1853), 1–110, at 25.
[68] Clare, 'Fêtes, jeux et divertissements', 27.

subsequently carried to the New World and to Goa.[69] But Castile's own heroes were far more prominent in the tales, ballads, and myths—above all, the Cid and Count Fernán González. The general historical framework, as well as the starting-point for all thinking about the past and the present, revolved around the concepts of 'the destruction of Spain', 'the rise of Castile', and the ongoing Reconquest. In his castle-palace at Segovia Henry IV set aside a special area which contained statues of all the kings of Castile and León from the time of 'the destruction of Spain'—that is, from Pelayo down to himself. But, although they were not kings, he also included the Cid and Count Fernán González 'because they were such noble knights and did such great deeds'.[70] In fact Henry IV and the Constable even went to the monastery of Arlanza and had Fernán González's tomb opened up so that they could have a look at him.[71] What these heroes stood for or signified could be used to praise or condemn frontier actions and behaviour. Hence the marquis of Cádiz was not only held up as 'the second and good Count Fernán González' but also as 'the second and most saintly knight Cid Ruy Díaz'.[72] In contrast, when Henry IV merely played at frontier warfare, inviting his queen to fire a few arrows at the Moors, the reaction of knights was swift, sarcastic, and to the point: 'Absolutely! This war is just like those which the Cid used to wage in his time!'[73]

In addition to these indigenous epic heroes and to more specific lineage myths and stories,[74] there was also a vague knowledge of the classical past and an awareness that the frontier formed part of a larger undertaking or *empresa*. Writing to the pope and

---

[69] See Jacques Horrent, 'L'Histoire légendaire de Charlemagne en Espagne', *Actes du VIIe Congrès International de la Société Rencesvals* (2 vols., Paris, 1978), i. 125–56; Charity C. Willard, 'Un écho de Roncevaux au nouveau monde', *Actes du IXe Congrès International de la Société Rencesvals* (2 vols., Modena, 1984), i. 203–10; Zacharias P. Thundyil, 'La Tradition de Charlemagne chez les chrétiens de Kerala (Inde)', *Actes du VIe Congrès International de la Société Rencesvals* (Aix-en-Provence, 1974), 389–98. I am grateful to Mr Philip E. Bennett for these references.

[70] Diego de Valera, *Memorial de diversas hazañas*, 294.

[71] *Hechos del condestable*, 23.

[72] *Historia de los hechos del Marqués*, 151, 231.

[73] Diego de Valera, *Memorial de diversas hazañas*, 45.

[74] See e.g. the astonishing mastery of the details of the stories and history of a specific case revealed in a letter of privileges granted by Henry II to Rodrigo Zepero, in *Colección diplomática del Archivo Histórico Municipal de Jaén*, ed. José Rodríguez Molina (Jaén, 1985), 3–7.

amenting the dangers which the civil wars posed on the frontier itself, Miguel Lucas de Iranzo put it this way:

So to whom can we Christians, your most faithful sons, appeal, most blessed Father, except to your Holiness? To whom shall we go now that my lord the king cannot help because of his labours and necessities; and his knights are even less willing, with some of them being more hostile to us than Christ's own enemies? Now Charlemagne who used to [fight against the Moors?], Godfrey de Bouillon who dared to [go on Crusade?], and our most holy kings who won this land [of Andalusia] are detained by Death and cannot come to our aid.[75]

Lineage 'education' also helped to stimulate a sense of affinity, a sense of identity, a spirit of bravery and endeavour, and above all a concept of *vergüenza* or shame. Strength lay not in numbers but in *vergüenza* and courage, which would prevent knights from besmirching their ancestral glory by acts of cowardice.[76] Hence the succinct words of wisdom imparted by Count Juan Ponce de León to his son: 'Act as the person you are, and consider the lineage from which you are descended.'[77] Lineage culture also promoted a highly prized rhetorical ability to be deployed at times of crisis. At such times *parientes mayores* and other leading members of a lineage-*bando* were expected to summon up the courage of their men to the sticking-point by means of *prólogos*, *oraciones*, and *hablas*. Thus when Don Rodrigo Ponce de León, who 'could not go against the blood of the lineage to which he belonged', found himself surrounded by thousands of Moors, he delivered such an effective *oración* to his men that Luis de Pernia replied:

My lord Don Rodrigo Ponce de León, I am very pleased with what you have so cogently presented to us, displaying such a remarkable courage and giving such a noble account of the lineage from which you are descended . . . So let us, with God's blessing, attack them.[78]

Ballads, myths, and stories depended very heavily on oral and visual communication, but they were also consciously exploited to protect the future memory of events. The point is best illustrated by digressing slightly away from lineage culture, in order to note how a boundary dispute betwen the frontier towns of Andújar and Jaén was settled in 1470. On Monday 7 May the Constable

---

[75] *Hechos del condestable*, 474.
[76] See e.g. Maldonado, *Hechos de don Alonso*, 17, 51.
[77] *Historia de los hechos del Marqués*, 164.　　　　　[78] Ibid. 166, 173.

assembled as many people as possible from both these towns, as
well as their associated villages, concentrating particularly on
securing a large number of youths and children. His objective was
to beat the agreed bounds in order to establish a collective
memoria of them, and to this end he 'inserted' each crucial
landmark into this collective memory by organizing an unforgettable
'happening'. At the first landmark, which was a well, the Constable
threw a lance inside it, then ordered a young aspiring knight to
jump in fully dressed, and finally let the youths and children
indulge in a water fight. At the next landmark the youths and
children played a game called 'Mares in the Field' and then had a
fist-fight until the Constable stepped in and parted them. At the
third earthen landmark the youths and children, joined by others
from nearby villages, killed a ram, cut off its head, and buried the
head in the middle of the landmark. At the fourth and final
landmark the Constable organized a bullfight and, after the animal
had been killed, he ordered the meat to be shared out among the
poor of the neighbouring villages. The express purpose of all these
events was 'to establish a memory so that in future times there
would not be any doubt or debate about the said boundaries'.[79]

Songs and ballads—*coplas*, *cantares*, and *romances*—served a
similar purpose within the context of lineage culture. The
minstrels not only sang about military deeds and frontier events,
but they also sang in the service of the lineage-*bandos*. Frontier
ballads related the deeds of the *parientes mayores* or the other
leading figures of the lineages: the ballad of Río Verde told of the
martyr's death of Juan Arias de Saavedra in Granada; the ballad
of Álora described how the *adelantado* Diego de Ribera was
treacherously shot through the neck and killed by a Moorish
archer; the ballad of the duke of Niebla related the death of the
pariente mayor of the Guzmanes at Gibraltar; and the ballad about
the battle of Los Alporchones celebrated the victory of the frontier
bandos, particularly that of Alonso Fajardo, over a large Muslim
army. But the point of such ballads was not simply to celebrate or
mourn a particular frontier incident, but deliberately to establish
its 'memory' in oral history. On this point the evidence is very
clear. For example, after a particularly glorious frontier campaign
by the Constable in 1462, the king, who happened to be on the

[79] *Hechos del condestable*, 425–31.

frontier, ordered that a ballad should be composed 'so that a stronger *memoria* should be established [about it]':

And this was thought to be such a great feat that our lord the king ordered that a ballad should be composed about the constable so that a stronger memory should be established [about it], and he ordered the singers of his chapel to give it assonance.[80]

How effective was this oral history? In fact in its own way it was sometimes more effective than written history. Once again Argote de Molina, writing in the late sixteenth century, provides us with useful evidence. His massive treatise on the Andalusian nobility is both lineage- and frontier-orientated. When dealing with Pero Díaz de Quesada, lord of Garcíez, for example, he highlights his successful defence of Baeza against the king of Granada in 1407, 'a defence the *memoria* of which has come down to us in *cantares*, especially the ancient ballad "Moricos, los mis moricos", which Argote then cites in its entirety.[81] In another chapter, entitled 'The Victory of the Moors against Don Gonzalo de Zúñiga, bishop of Jaén, and an account of his lineage and of the death of Ruy Pérez de Torres', he comments that the chronicles do not give an account of this victory but that its *memoria* remains in sung form, and he quotes the ballad 'Día es de San Antón'.[82] In fact Argote cites a whole succession of ballads which are directly linked to the appropriate lineages and frontier events: the ballad of the siege of Álora, the ballad of Fadrique of Aragón, the ballad of the knights of Moclín, another ballad about a different siege of Baeza by the Moors, and of course the ballad in which Alonso Fajardo plays chess with the king of Granada.[83]

Of course we know about these operations of the collective oral memory precisely because they are described in *written* accounts. But quite apart from the emphasis which such accounts place on the oral and visual communication which they report, it is also a remarkable fact that much of this written evidence was itself the product of lineage-*bando* culture. Both the *Chronicle of Miguel Lucas de Iranzo* and the *History of the Deeds of the Marquis of Cádiz*, for example, promote the fame and glory of the *pariente mayor* and his *bando*.

Fomented by associated clan-like groupings and affinities,

---

[80] Ibid. 90.   [81] Argote de Molina, *Nobleza del Andalucia*, 587–8.
[82] Ibid. 648–51.   [83] Ibid. 153, 477–9, 544, 667.

lineage culture was nevertheless also attached to the geographical
areas of towns with which the *bandos* were identified. Hence
proverbs, stories and ballads also celebrated the collective nature
of urban communities. Frontier townspeople were accustomed to
witnessing, and participating in, the endless rehearsals of military
skills, such as the *alardes* or musters of cavalry and footsoldiers,
the 'games' of the *sortija* and *cañas*, and of course archery. In
addition each town had its own particular relic or saint. Jaén, for
example, had 'the Verónica', which, like the Turin shroud, had the
face of Christ impressed on it.[84] Despite her universality, even the
Virgin was multiplied into different Virgin Marys with distinct
characteristics and 'localized'. In Jerez de la Frontera, for
example, a Marian cult developed on the morrow of its reconquest,
having as its focus a statue in the *alcázar* or fortress. But
subsequently the images and statues proliferated, and it was the
Black Madonna in the convent of the Mercedarians that was
particularly associated with frontier victories over the Moors, the
townspeople organizing prayers and processions in her honour 'so
that Our Lord God and the Holy Virgin Mary, and all the
heavenly court, may grant victory against the Moors, enemies of
the Holy Catholic Faith'.[85]

The religious beliefs and ideology of frontier communities were
even sustained by theatrical representations or paradramatic
'happenings'.[86] Each year at Epiphany, for example, the townspeople of Jaén were treated to 'The Three Kings', which was
organized by the Constable and took place either in the open air or
in the great hall of his palace:

And when they had dined and the tables had been cleared away, a lady
entered the hall, riding on a small ass and with a little boy in her arms, and
she was playing the part of Our Lady the Virgin Mary, with her blessed
and glorious son, and accompanied by Joseph. And the lord Constable
received her in a very devoted manner and took her up to the chair where
he was, and he sat her down between his lady Countess and the lady *doña*
Guiomar Carrillo, her mother, and the lady *doña* Juana, her sister, and
the other ladies and damsels who were there.

And the lord Constable withdrew to a room which is at the other end of

[84] See the photograph of this 'Holy Face' and the editor's notes in *Hechos del
condestable*, facing p. 272.

[85] Hipólito Sancho de Sopranis, *Historia social de Jerez de la Frontera al fin de la
Edad Media* (2 vols., Jerez, 1959), ii. 105–6.

[86] See Clare, 'Fêtes, jeux et divertissements', *passim*.

he hall, and shortly after he came out of the room accompanied by two
very well-dressed pages, all wearing masks and with crowns on their
heads, in the manner of the three wise kings, and bearing presents. And
thus he moved down the hall very slowly and gracefully, looking at the
star which was guiding them and which was being pulled by a string in the
hall. And so he reached the end of the hall, where the Virgin and her child
were, and he offered up their presents amidst a great noise of trumpets,
drums, and other musical instruments.[87]

Such theatrical representations could easily move into the realm of
'frontier fantasy'. During the Christmas festivites of 1463, for
example, the king of Morocco visited Jaén, accompanied by a
large number of Moors and by the prophet Muḥammad carrying
the Koran. The purpose of the visit was explained in a *carta
bermeja* (that is, a Muslim chancery letter) which was formally
handed to the Constable. In effect the king of Morocco had heard
of the great defeats which the Constable had inflicted on the
Moors of Granada, and he was now challenging the Christians to
fight his Moors at *cañas*, offering, should he lose, to convert to
Christianity. The fighting took place in the main square of the
town, predictably named the *plaza de Santa María*, and some three
hours later 'the game was up', in both senses of the expression,
and the Moors had lost. The king of Morocco, therefore, publicly
rejected his religion, the Koran, and Muḥammad and was baptized
into the Christian faith along with his followers—apart of course
from Muḥammad, who was thrown into a public fountain.[88]

Cultivated within the contexts of the lineage-*bandos* and the
local communities, processes of frontier 'education' could nevertheless transcend these particular contexts and, as in the theatrical
examples just cited, deal with the much more universal problems
of religion and politics. In concluding this chapter, therefore, it
will be argued that frontier ideology also had all-important
repercussions on the perceptions of kingship in Castile, and that
the success or failure of individual kings often depended on how
they lived up to the frontier role ascribed to them.

The Cid once again served as a basic exemplum here.[89] Probably

[87] *Hechos del condestable*, 70–2. Elsewhere mention is made of the participation
of Herod and the play is actually given a title: ibid. 101–2, 162.

[88] Ibid. 98–100.

[89] In what follows I have drawn inspiration from the seminal study by Lucien
Clare and Michel García, 'La crónica de Miguel Lucas de Iranzo' in *Colloque sur*

the most famous line from the epic poem is: 'God, what a good vassal! If only he had a good lord!' (!*Dios, que buen vassalo! ¡S oviesse buen señor!*). The lord referred to in the epic is of course King Alfonso VI, and although he almost fails the test, he does redeem himself by the end of the poem. And in this context it is surely of great significance that both the lives and the chronicles of Miguel Lucas de Iranzo and the marquis of Cádiz seem to have been consciously modelled on the Cid epic, with all the important implications for the kings in question that such a strategy entailed. Like the Cid, the Constable goes into exile because of the activities of intriguers at court—the theme of 'malos mestureros' being one that his chronicle constantly harps on. On the frontier, the Constable finds to his sorrow that his exploits against the Moors are curtailed by royal truces with Granada and by civil wars within Castile. On the few occasions when the king and the Constable meet up again, the emotional scenes parallel the epic poem closely. But above all the Constable, like the Cid, remains absolutely loyal to his natural lord Henry IV, despite the latter's defects and despite the treachery of courtiers.[90] The case of the marquis of Cádiz is more direct and less subtle. Here we are told that the marquis *is* a second Cid and his exploits are described accordingly. And if the original Cid's triumphs, valour, and fame are measured in the poem by the increasing number of horses which he sends as presents to the king, the marquis does the same—sending his nephew to the Catholic Kings with twenty richly apparelled horses after his capture of Zahara, and increasing this to thirty horses after a later frontier triumph.[91] Implicit in the cases of both these frontier nobles is the acting-out of Cid-like triumphs which will provoke kings to live up to their predestined roles on the frontier, and to 'pass' the tests posed by their almost perfect vassals.

How did kings live up to such assumptions? Ferdinand of Antequera, the Castilian prince who became king of Aragón, played the game for all it was worth. Even before becoming king he founded a chivalric order, that of 'the Jar' and 'the Griffin', which was dedicated to the purity of the Virgin at the Annunciation

les '*bandos*' and have extended the argument to include the *Historia de los hechos del Marqués*.

[90] See e.g. *Hechos del condestable*, 95–6, 150, 192, 328–9, 396.
[91] *Historia de los hechos del Marqués*, 151, 231, 234, 271.

and to the final defeat of the Moors with the help of the Virgin's intercession.[92] Henry IV, on the other hand, was a disaster. A king who ate and dressed like a Moor, who was accused of all kinds of perversions which were also 'projected' on to the Moors, and who was perceived as failing his frontier obligations was bound to be regarded as a total failure. When the Castilian nobility presented him with a long list of reforms during the great crisis of 1465, these were headed by demands for an immediate resumption of the Holy War against the Muslims at all points on the frontier.[93] Rejecting the reforms, the king quickly acquired the demonic characteristics of an Antichrist in the eyes of his enemies.

Mention of the Antichrist leads to my final point and to the greatest 'success story'. The late medieval frontier was an eschatological one.[94] It was thought or believed by many that the Antichrist would make his appearance in Seville, that the forces of a Spanish Messianic king or 'Last World Emperor' would disembark at Cádiz, that a titanic battle would take place, and that the Messianic forces would then clear out the filth of Islam and conquer Granada. Subsequently, too, the Messianic king would of course conquer Jerusalem and the rest of the world. This Spanish Messianic king was known variously as the *encubierto* or 'the hidden one', the *murciélago* or 'bat', and 'the New David'. The beginning of each new reign, therefore, aroused eschatological expectations. Was the new king the *encubierto* and 'bat' who would defeat the Antichrist in Andalusia, conquer Granada, cross the sea, defeat all Islam, take the holy city of Jerusalem, and become the last world emperor? Suddenly between 1480 and 1513 there was an explosion of exuberance as events matched eschatological expectations. As the successes of Ferdinand and Isabella

[92] Juan Torres Fontes, 'Don Fernando de Antequera y la romántica caballeresca', *Miscelánea medieval murciana*, 5 (1980), 83–120.

[93] MacKay, 'The Ballad and the Frontier', 29–30.

[94] For what follows, see the excellent study by Alain Milhou, *Colón y su mentalidad mesiánica en el ambiente franciscanista español* (Valladolid, 1983), *passim*; id., 'La Chauve-souris, le Nouveau David et le roi caché: Trois Images de l'empereur des derniers temps dans le monde ibérique: XIIᵉ–XVIIᵉ siècles', *Mélanges de la Casa de Velázquez*, 18 (1982), 61–78; Angus MacKay, 'Andalucía como factor dinámico de la historia entre Oriente y Occidente', in *Actas del V. Coloquio de Historia Medieval Andaluza* (Córdoba, in press); and the apocalyptic treatise of Fray Alemán, reproduced in Ramón Alba, *Acerca de algunas particularidades de las Comunidades de Castilla tal vez relacionadas con el supuesto acaecer terreno del Milenio Igualitario* (Madrid, 1975), 180–97.

multiplied, so too did the prophetic texts, commentaries, and even
ballads which identified Ferdinand as 'the hidden one' and 'the
bat' who would conquer Jerusalem and the whole world. When the
marquis of Cádiz, 'the second Cid', had tested his lord Ferdinand,
he could hardly have expected such triumphs. Ferdinand was not
simply a good lord or a good king—he was in fact 'the hidden one'.
And so the marquis circulated a letter to the great nobles of Castile
in 1486 informing them of what had been revealed to him about
Ferdinand:

> . . . there will be nothing in this world capable of resisting him . . . because
> all this glory and victory is promised by God to the rod, that is to say, the
> Bat, because he is the Hidden One . . . and he will subdue all the nations
> from sea to sea, and he will destroy all the Moors of Spain . . . and not
> only will his Highness soon gain the kingdom of Granada, but he will
> subdue all Africa . . . and he will take the Holy House of Jerusalem . . .
> and with his hands he will put the banner of Aragón on Mount Calvary, in
> the same place where the holy and true cross was placed on which Our
> Lord Jesus Christ was crucified; and he will be Emperor of Rome, and of
> the Turks, and of Spain . . . and he will keep the see of Rome vacant for
> three years; and afterwards, by the will of God, he will install a Holy
> Father of very saintly life . . . and he will not only be Emperor, but he will
> be monarch of all the world . . .[95]

Love and hate are perhaps inherent to all intense relationships,
and both emotions are to be found along the late medieval frontier
between Castile and Granada. In the ballad of Abenámar, John II
of Castile courted the personification of the beautiful lady
Granada. Ferdinand the Catholic, however, intended to take the
lady by force. Courtly love had given way to Messianic lust. When
Ferdinand finally entered the Alhambra palace, he would find that
a Wild Man from the north had beaten him to it by over a hundred
years. That Wild Man, however, had been killed. Ferdinand the
Catholic could still cherish the dream of fulfilling the prophecies by
going on to conquer the Holy House of Jerusalem. But what was
this 'Holy House'? Ironically, the very phrasing of this Christian
and Messianic notion reflected the Muslim concept of Jerusalem as
Bayt al-Maqdis (the Holy House).[96] Even on his deathbed in 1516

---

[95] *Historia de los hechos del Marqués*, 247–51.
[96] See F. E. Peters, *Jerusalem: The Holy City in the Eyes of Chroniclers, Visitors,
Pilgrims, and Prophets from the Days of Abraham to the Beginnings of Modern*

Ferdinand the Catholic would be reassured by a prophecy from the famous visionary Sor María de Santo Domingo that he would not die until he had conquered Jerusalem.[97]

Times (Princeton, 1985), 176–8, 181, 194, 236, 339–40. I am very grateful to Dr Gary Dickson for his help in solving the puzzle of the 'Holy House'.

[97] I owe thanks to Dr Geraldine McKendrick for drawing my attention to this incident. See also Hillgarth, *Spanish Kingdoms*, ii. 570–1, 605–6.

II

Religion and Warfare in the Anglo-Scottish Marches

ANTHONY GOODMAN

Much of the medieval frontier line between Scotland and England, as constituted by treaty in 1237, corresponds to the modern line. It is now about 110 miles in length from the Solway Firth to just north of Berwick upon Tweed. The medieval frontier lacked the defensive qualities of what may be loosely described as its predecessor, Hadrian's Wall: much of the medieval line was, indeed, an obstacle for armies, but no insuperable barrier to small-scale communications. The Solway Firth, wrote William Camden, was 'a fordable arm of the sea at low waters, through which they [the Scots] made many times out-rodes into England for to fetch in booties'.[1] Sir Robert Bowes had declared in his survey of 1550 that all along the Tweed—the frontier for over twenty miles west of Berwick—'there be . . . sundry fords or passages for horsemen'.[2] James IV, invading England in 1496, was able to have his artillery hauled over the Tweed with the help of local fishermen.[3] But most of the frontier line bisects the central highland masses, often along valley burns and across higher ground as determined by the processes of settlement and land exploitation in individual lordships.[4] Lateral communications were in many places difficult: this hampered co-operation in frontier defences between adjacent regions. Consequently, when in the fourteenth century the Borders were divided in both England and Scotland into military commands, these were constituted as separate East and West Marches under their own Wardens.

Frontier defences were hampered too by the frequent separation

---

[1] 1586; cited in James L. Mack, *The Border Line* (rev. edn., Edinburgh and London, 1926), 74.

[2] Between Tweedmouth and Reddenburn; cited ibid. 36.

[3] *Accounts of the Lord High Treasurer of Scotland*, i: *1473–1498*, ed. Thomas Dickson (Edinburgh, 1877), 299.

[4] For a recent study of settlement in a Border region, A. J. L. Winchester, *Landscape and Society in Medieval Cumbria* (Edinburgh, 1987).

of the national frontier from the divisions between areas where
tillage played an important part in mixed farming and areas where
pastoralism predominated. Indeed, these two types of interrelated
economies and their characteristic societies cannot always be
differentiated in a clear-cut way in the Borders. The physical
boundaries between them were often gradual and underwent shifts
in our period. But we can distinguish a spectrum of settlement
types, from nucleated agrarian vills to scattered pastoral communities. Tensions and hostility sometimes predominated in the
complex social relationships between lowland agriculturalists and
upland pastoralists. Such hostilities weakened defences: some
communities felt an affinity with those who had similar habits and
interests on the other side of the frontier and made alliances with
them directed against neighbours of their own nationality. Such
were 'our lawless people', who, wrote Thomas Musgrave, 'will be
Scottish when they will, and English at their pleasure'.[5]

How were ecclesiastical institutions and religious habits affected
in the Borders by the problems of defending the frontier, in the
context of the Anglo-Scottish hostilities of the later Middle Ages?
What parts did they play in economic and social life there? In the
pre-medieval period, the patterns of monastic foundation and
missionary endeavour reflected the existence of the Anglian
kingdom of Northumbria, stretching across the Tweed, and the
British kingdom of Strathclyde, stretching at times across the
Solway. Christian culture made links between the kingdoms and
provided social binding within them. Missionary activities radiating
from lowland settlements brought the mores of upland farmers into
line with theirs. St Cuthbert set out on travels to instruct villagers
who 'neglecting the sacrament of their creed, had recourse to
idolatrous remedies . . . He was mostly accustomed to travel to
those villages which lay in out of the way places among the
mountains, which by their poverty and natural horrors deterred
other visitors' (the Cheviots or Lammermuirs).[6] Jocelyn of
Furness, the twelfth-century biographer of St Kentigern (d. 612),
when describing his missionary labours south of the Solway, may
have incorporated memories of more recent Cumbrian activities.

---

[5] Cited in George M. Fraser, *The Steel Bonnets* (London, 1971), 65.
[6] Bede, *The Life and Miracles of St Cuthbert*, trans. John Stevenson and L. C.
Lane, in *Bede's Ecclesiastical History of the English Nation* (Everyman edn.,
London, 1910 and frequent repr.), 286–348, at 300 (ch. 9); cf. p 329 (ch. 32).

Kentigern, when he came to Carlisle, heard that there were many among the mountains given to idolatry or ignorant of the divine law. He 'converted to the Christian religion many from a strange belief, and others who were erroneous in the faith'.[7] In these incidents Bede and Jocelyn preserved memories of how missionaries bridged some of the social divisions in what were to be Border regions. This was a task which the Church needed to go on fulfilling in the medieval Borders, if it was to maintain a Christian society there.

After the medieval frontier hardened, the cults of Cuthbert and Kentigern helped to foster social links across the national divide as well as between disparate communities. There were churches and chapels in the Scottish Borders dedicated to Cuthbert and Cumbrian churches dedicated to Kentigern. In Scotland Cuthbert's cult was fostered by the grants to Coldingham Priory, refounded as a cell of Durham, of eighteen Border churches. This house, with its associations with the Anglian princess Aebba and its English monks, recalled the ancient political geography of Northumbria.[8] A variety of other cross-Border ecclesiastical links were prompted by the Norman settlements in Scotland and by Scottish kings' interests in English Border regions (such as their possession of Tynedale in the thirteenth century). In this socio-political environment, no problems were envisaged in the foundation of Holm Cultram Priory (Cumberland) as a cell of Melrose Abbey or its endowment with churches on the Scottish side of the Solway Firth: David I was then ruling Cumberland.[9]

The increase of religious foundations in the Borders in the twelfth and thirteenth centuries was facilitated by the economic development of these regions in an age of expansion, unhampered

---

[7] *Life of St Kentigern*, ed. A. P. Forbes, *Lives of St Ninian and St Kentigern* (The Historians of Scotland 5, Edinburgh, 1874), 74. For the significance of the church dedications in Cumberland to the saint, Kenneth H. Jackson, 'The Sources for the Life of St Kentigern', in Nora K. Chadwick *et al.* (eds.), *Studies in the Early British Church* (Cambridge, 1958), 273–357, at 316–17; E. G. Bowen, *Saints, Seaways and Settlements in the Celtic Lands* (Cardiff, 1969, repr. 1977), 83–9.

[8] James M. MacKinlay, *Ancient Church Dedications in Scotland* (2 vols., Edinburgh, 1910–14), ii. 250; Ian B. Cowan, *The Parishes of Medieval Scotland* (Scottish Record Society 93, Edinburgh, 1967), 215; *VCH Cumberland*, ii (1905), 14–15.

[9] For the geography of religious houses in the Borders, Anne A. Cardew, 'A Study of Society in the Anglo-Scottish Borders 1455–1502' (Ph.D. thesis, St Andrews University, 1974), 35–8.

by prolonged or endemic warfare across the national divide. Successful and prosperous monastic foundations stimulated the growth of settlements and markets and the improvement of communications. Pastoralism expanded: many of the chapelries which served outlying parts of parishes are first recorded in this period, and many of these chapelries emerge with full parochial rights.[10] Burghal growth stimulated the foundation of friaries, whose preaching circuits may have supplemented chapelries in integrating a spreading rural society into Christian worship. Certainly much later, in the sixteenth century, friars were familiar figures in some remote and lawless parts of the Borders. In 1525, when Tynedale was under excommunication, members of the Charlton kin-group brought in a Scottish friar to celebrate in Bellingham church.[11] It was alleged after the Reformation that in the upland parish of Ewes (Dumfriesshire), baptisms and marriages had been conducted by friars on their circuits.[12] The functioning in the early medieval Borders of the whole range of ecclesiastical institutions suggests that religious life there did not generally differ from that in neighbouring regions and that the defects in religious mentality attributed by sixteenth-century commentators to some parts of Border society were not then so apparent. Indeed, better-endowed parishes were concentrated in coastal regions, and uplands were probably more sketchily served in the early Middle Ages: some English parishes were very large. But upland communities were then integrated into a relatively flourishing society and therefore more susceptible to ecclesiastical disciplines and pious trends current there.

Border society was battered and transformed in the later Middle Ages. Causes of ruin and hardship frequently alluded to by contemporaries were destruction and levying in the Anglo-Scottish wars, truce-breaking, and theft. But epidemics here, as elsewhere, induced economic change and decline.[13] Comparisons of the

[10] Cowan, *Parishes*, 139: *Liber sancte Marie de Calchou*, ed. Cosmo Innes (2 vols., Bannatyne Club, Edinburgh, 1846), i, p. xxxiii; ii. 463. Other examples in the eastern Scottish Borders of chapelries which became parishes by the end of the 13th century are Nenthorn (originally dependent on Ednam), Smailholm (Earlston), and Stitchill (Ednam) (Cowan, *Parishes*, 155, 184, 188).

[11] *Letters and Papers Foreign and Domestic of the Reign of Henry VIII*, iv, pt. I, ed. J. S. Brewer (London, 1870), no. 1429, p. 637.

[12] Robert B. Armstrong, *The History of Liddesdale . . .* (Edinburgh, 1883), 105.

[13] For the English Border economy in the later Middle Ages, J. A. Tuck, 'War and Society in the Medieval North', *Northern History*, 21 (1985), 33–52.

valuations of English parochial incomes in 1291 and 1535 show a general and often heavy fall, not only near the frontier, but in areas which had not been subject to Scottish raiding since the early fourteenth century.[14] Such falls in income are paralleled by the relatively few figures available for Scottish parishes over a comparable period.[15] Yet few Border parishes in England or Scotland permanently disappeared. The effects of warfare and raiding were often limited and temporary: though some expeditions systematically pillaged a region, many passed through quickly and in pursuit of limited or specific objectives. The 1535 valuations of parishes in the deanery of Carlisle are instructive. This was a region which had often been invaded by large Scottish forces in the fourteenth century. Since it bordered the Solway Firth and the Debatable Land, it was vulnerable at the time of the *Valor ecclesiasticus* to the predatory raids of some of the notorious surnames. The valuations suggest that the parishes close to the Debatable Land and on raiding routes from Liddesdale were reduced in value by the effects of warfare, whereas incomes in the more fertile Eden valley, where a greater density of settlement and the Carlisle garrison afforded better protection, were holding up relatively well. Some of the poor parishes near the frontier were, it was noted, of no value in time of war.[16] Contemporaries thus made careful distinctions about the effects of endemic warfare in an area within twenty miles of the frontier. The question of whether parochial worship could be sustained depended on the nature and resources of the community. Even proximity to the frontier was no bar to a continued measured of prosperity. In 1535 Rothbury, a large inland parish easily accessible to Scottish raiders, was valued at £56. 6s. 8d., the highest parochial valuation in Northumberland. This was a great decline from its late thirteenth-century valuation of £133. 6s. 8d., but a modest recovery from the 1357 figure of not more than £40.[17] Part of the

---

[14] *Taxatio ecclesiastica* (Record Commission, London, 1802), 316–20; *Valor ecclesiasticus* (6 vols., Record Commission, London, 1810–34), v. 273–92, 327–30.

[15] For allegations (1454) that the vicar of Ednam's cure was so devastated by English raids that he could not sustain himself from its income, and that the rector of Dornock could not lift his fruits during the frequent outbreaks of war, see Glasgow, Department of Scottish History, Glasgow University, Transcript of Register of Supplications in Vatican Archives, nos. 525, 547. I owe thanks to Professor Ian Cowan for arranging for me to see these transcripts.

[16] *Valor ecclesiasticus*, v. 274–81.

[17] *History of Northumberland* (15 vols., London and Newcastle upon Tyne,

explanation of Rothbury's relatively high valuation in 1535 can be found in a description of the parishioners' behaviour in the mid-century, as experienced by a visiting clergyman, Bernard Gilpin.[18] Their violent, feuding habits reflected an ability to defend their broad grazing lands—and to threaten those of their neighbours. In the later Middle Ages numbers of lowland Border cures had still been considered worth while as endowments for religious institutions in the form of appropriations—for new colleges as well as for Border abbeys desperate to augment their incomes. In 1357 Lord Greystoke founded a college of seven priests at Greystoke (Cumberland), on a main Scottish raiding route south of Carlisle. His provision for so many priests may have improved parochial services in this large parish, which had two outlying chapelries.[19] In the fifteenth century Scottish nobles appropriated Border parishes to colleges which they were founding, including colleges outside the Borders.[20] So, though there was a general decline of parochial revenues and services in the fourteenth and fifteenth centuries, there were few permanent collapses. In some parishes, indeed, as at Greystoke, there may have been an improvement of services.[21]

Long-established Border religious houses, generally heavily dependent on income from appropriated churches within the region, had their wealth diminished as a result of the decline of parochial incomes. In 1381 William earl of Douglas procured papal confirmation of the transference to the abbot and convent of Sweetheart (Dumfriesshire) of the advowson of Buittle (Galloway),

---

1893–1940), xv. 310–12; cf. the comments of Susan M. Keeling, 'Church and Religion in the Anglo-Scottish Border Counties, 1534–72' (Ph.D. thesis, Durham University, 1975), 63.

[18] George Carleton, *The Life of Bernard Gilpin* (London, 1636), 91–5.

[19] *VCH Cumberland*, ii. 55. In 1548 there were 3,000 communicants in the parish.

[20] Examples of such annexations were that of Chirnside as a prebend of Dunbar (1342), Hawick as a prebend of Bothwell (1447), Hutton in Merse (1451), and Edrom (1489) to the provostship of Dunglass, and Mordington as a prebend of Dalkeith (1477) (Cowan, *Parishes*, 31, 81, 84, 60, 151).

[21] Few Border parishes ceased to exist in the 14th and 15th centuries. Two that probably did were St James, Roxburgh, and Kirkandrews in the Debatable Land (ibid. 175, 117). The practice of farming parochial revenues to laymen was not unknown in the Borders. In 1436 Bishop Langley ordered the citation of the vicar of Eglingham (Northumberland) to answer for the illegal demise of his vicarage to laymen: *The Register of Thomas Langley, Bishop of Durham, 1406–1437*, iv, ed. Robin L. Storey (Surtees Society 170, 1961 for 1955), no. 1195, pp. 176–80.

'considering the great difficulty in collecting rents in those parts because of the depopulation along the Borders between England and Scotland'.[22] The siting of religious houses and their principal estates made them especially vulnerable. In 1517 the claustral buildings at Kelso Abbey bore the marks of violence: part of the cloister was unroofed, the lead having been removed by raiders. Tenements at Kelso had been let by the abbot without obligation to pay tithe or rent; the tenants received payment 'that they may be able to withstand and repel from the monastery the continual attacks of the enemies'.[23] English monasteries suffered worst in the decade after Bannockburn, from levying for English armies as well as from Scottish attacks.[24] But the only Border house dissolved before the Reformation seems to have been Lincluden Priory (Dumfriesshire).[25] Opposing army leaders and Wardens of the Marches were on occasion prepared to grant letters of protection to religious communities and their properties. The earl of Hertford reported that a huge amount of booty had been taken at Coldstream Priory (Berwickshire) in 1542: 'For by reason the prioresse toke hur self to be pattisid, all they of the countrey had conveide theire corn, and goodes unto hir'.[26] Similar protections

[22] *Calendar of Papal Letters to Scotland of Clement VII of Avignon 1378–1394*, ed. Charles Burns (Scottish History Society, 4th ser., 12, Edinburgh, 1976), 67–8; Cowan, *Parishes*, 23. For an English example of appropriation as a remedy for war damages, see the mandate for the appropriation of Alwinton (Northumberland) to Holystone Priory, *Calendar of Entries in the Papal Registers Relating to Great Britain and Ireland: Petitions to the Pope*, i: *1342–1419*, ed. W. H. Bliss (London, 1986), 214.

[23] John Duncan's account of Kelso Abbey; text in Alistair Moffat, *Kelsae* (Edinburgh, 1985), 90–2.

[24] There are petitions concerning losses and impoverishment dating from the 1310s to the 1330s from the houses at Hexham, Holystone, Blanchland, Tynemouth, and Newminster in *Ancient Petitions Relating to Northumberland*, ed. Constance M. Fraser (Surtees Society 176, 1966 for 1961), nos. 159–60, 162, 169–70, 172–4, 180, 202, pp. 184–5, 187, 192–3, 194–7, 201–2, 225–6. For some 15th-century examples of reduced English monastic incomes, including hardships resulting from the fighting in the Borders between Lancastrians and Yorkists in the 1460s, Cardew, 'A Study of Society', 39–41.

[25] See below, n. 33. In the 1310s the canons of Hexham and monks of Newminster had to leave their houses for several years as a consequence of war (*Ancient Petitions . . . Northumberland*, nos. 159, 180, pp. 184–5, 201–2). It is remarkable that regular life apparently continued in Canonbie Priory, so near the frontier, especially when the problem of the Debatable Land became acute in the later fifteenth century. For an international settlement of the prior's complaint of thefts in 1494, Armstrong, *History of Liddesdale*, pp. xv–xvi.

[26] *The Hamilton Papers*, ed. Joseph Bain (2 vols., Edinburgh, 1890–2), i, no. 245, p. 313. The episode is discussed in Keeling, 'Church and Religion', 159.

may have been customarily sought from English officials by the abbots of Kelso: among the abbey buildings in 1517 were 'granaries and other places where merchants and neighbours store their corn, wares and goods and keep them safe from enemies'.[27] It is likely that tenants and neighbours contributed to the cost of such letters of protection. For the enemy leader, then, the system had the advantage that the head of the religious house acted as his agent for the collection of tribute. But such arrangements did not provide booty for the soldiery or for raiding bands. The concentration of goods under protection provided them with a tempting target: immunity too had its hazards.

Religious houses depended heavily for defence and for reconstruction on their local nobility. The surviving later medieval building works at Border abbeys, most notably at Melrose, were probably funded in part by lay benefactors.[28] Such patronage, besides procuring spiritual benefits, advertised the commitment of nobles to the defence of the region, and therefore encouraged their dependants and neighbours to rally to their service. Similar political benefits flowed from the foundation of collegiate churches in vulnerable places, such as the church founded by the ambitious Homes at Dunglass (Lothian), just outside the East March, within

In view of the proximity of the Coldstream nuns to the frontier, it is likely that they had customarily sought English protections: one was granted to them and their tenants at Lennel in 1381 by John of Gaunt as royal lieutenant (*John of Gaunt's Register 1379–83*, ii, ed. Eleanor C. Lodge and Robert Somerville (Camden 3rd ser., 57, London, 1937), no. 1177, p. 371).

[27] Moffat, *Kelsae*, 91. In an undated petition the prior and monks of Holm Cultram petitioned the Crown for sanction for their payment of £200 as ransom to the Scots for a year's immunity, under threat of having their church and abbey burnt by the earl of Douglas (*Calendar of Documents Relating to Scotland*, ed. Joseph Bain (4 vols., Edinburgh, 1881–8), iv, no. 343, p. 78). In 1405 Henry IV granted letters of protection to the abbot and convent of Melrose and their possessions, on condition of their victualling the English garrison at Roxburgh when necessary: *Liber sancte Marie de Melros*, ed. Cosmo Innes (2 vols., Bannatyne Club, Edinburgh, 1837), ii, no. 498, p. 473.

[28] Ian B. Cowan, *The Scottish Reformation* (London, 1982), 27–8. For relationships between Border monasteries and secular society, Cardew, 'A Study of Society', 44–9. An example of how monastic financial need led to lay exploitation is the lease by the abbot and convent of Jedburgh of teind sheaves to Philip Pyle for life, in return for sums amounting to 500 merks, a transaction referred to in 1455 (Glasgow, Transcript of Register of Supplications in Vatican Archives, no. 553). For Pyle, burgess of Jedburgh and Edinburgh and an international trader, see Anthony Goodman, 'The Anglo-Scottish Marches in the Fifteenth Century: A Frontier Society?', in Roger A. Mason (ed.), *Scotland and England 1286–1815* (Edinburgh, 1987), 18–33, at 26 and n. 67.

easy range for the English garrison at Berwick. The Homes thus committed themselves to the defence of the region around their dynastic cult centre. Religious houses were sometimes of strategic importance in time of war as bases which could provide hospitality and a concentration of supplies, as Archbishop Lee asserted in his plea to Cromwell in 1536 for the retention of Hexham Priory.[29] English Border houses, helping to service the king's armies, had learnt this to their cost during the Scottish Wars of Independence.[30] Reliance on close secular associations may have helped to preserve religious life in the borders during conflict, but sometimes threatened it with a reduction of quality as well as of scale. In 1379 the prior of Coldingham was accused of maintaining a military company which terrorized the neighbourhood,[31] and in 1443 the prior was accused of having delivered the priory church to Sir Alexander Home, 'to hald as hous of weer'; there Home had installed a 'garyson of refars'.[32] Archibald Douglas, seeking papal support for the dissolution of Lincluden Priory in 1389 in order to replace it with a collegiate church, accused the nuns of dressing their daughters sumptuously and spending their time producing cloth: 'the local neighbours, who are very evil men, repair to the monastery in order to defend themselves from the enemies of Scotland, the monastery being situated on the borders'.[33] Dr Keeling has noted that, in some petitions for the provision of abbots to Scottish Border abbacies in the early sixteenth century, the candidate's ability to defend the house from attack is listed among qualifications for office.[34] At Hexham the dissolution commissioners were confronted by 'five or six canons of the house, with divers other persons, like men of war, in harness with swords girt about them, having bows and arrows and other weapons, and stood upon the steeple head and leads in defence of their house'.[35]

[29] *The Priory of Hexham*, i (Surtees Society 44, 1864 for 1863), p. cxxvi.
[30] See above, n. 24.
[31] R. B. Dobson, 'The Last English Monks on Scottish Soil', *Scottish Historical Review*, 46 (1967), 1–25, at 5.
[32] *Correspondence . . . of the Priory of Coldingham* (Surtees Society 12, 1841), 149. For several years Edward II had maintained the abbot and monks of Newminster in a castle (*Ancient Petitions . . . Northumberland*, no. 180, pp. 201–2). There are remains of the impressive castle which the monks of Tynemouth built around their priory.
[33] *Cal. of Papal Letters . . . Clement VII*, 145.
[34] Keeling, 'Church and Religion', 170–1.
[35] *Priory of Hexham*, i, pp. cxxvii–cxxx.

Insecurity increased the interdependence of the laity with the secular as well as the religious clergy. As we have seen, Border communities were often poorly endowed and structured for defence. Families often lived in scattered and isolated farmsteads, precariously dependent on the willingness of neighbours over a wide radius to respond to the signs of emergency. Bellingham (Tynedale) was such a community: 800 communicants were expected to gather at its church at Easter 1524.[36] Professor Bossy has explored the harmonizing and reconciliatory roles played by parochial institutions in medieval communities.[37] These roles were crucial to defence in Border communities liable to be split by feud, like the feud at Rothbury which Gilpin encountered. Also, in a 'society organized for war', the parish clergy were probably valued for their physical as well as their spiritual contributions to defence. Arrays of the clergy for the defence of the realm were not uncommon in the later fourteenth and early fifteenth centuries in England.[38] English bishops with Border dioceses were at least expected to help to organize the defence of the Marches and on occasion took a personal part in warfare. In 1388 Bishop Skirlaw of Durham was in the field with the bishopric's forces at the time of the battle of Otterburn: he refused to approach the place of combat and withdrew to Newcastle. A contemporary chronicler asserted that if he had stayed there till morning, 'he would certainly have been overwhelmed by the stones flung by women avenging the slaughter suffered by their husbands in battle'.[39] The frontier bishopric *par excellence* was Carlisle: its bishops were frequently appointed among the Wardens of the West March and as keepers of Carlisle Castle for much of the fourteenth century. Bishop Appleby, after his third appointment to a Wardenship

---

[36] *Letters and Papers . . . Henry VIII*, iv, pt. I, no. 1429, p. 637.

[37] John Bossy, 'Blood and Baptism: Kinship, Community and Christianity in Western Europe from the Fourteenth to the Seventeenth Centuries', in Derek Baker (ed.), *Studies in Church History*, 10 (Oxford, 1973), 129–43.

[38] Bruce McNab, 'Obligations of the Church in English Society: Military Arrays of the Clergy, 1369–1418', in William C. Jordan, Bruce McNab, and Teófilo F. Ruiz (eds.), *Order and Innovation in the Middle Ages: Essays in Honor of Joseph R. Strayer* (Princeton, 1976), 293–314.

[39] *The Westminster Chronicle 1381–1394*, ed. and trans. L. C. Hector and Barbara Harvey (Oxford, 1982), 348–9. For a royal letter of 1323 rebuking the bishop of Durham for failing to defend his bishopric from the Scots and ordering him to go there with an armed force, *Foedera*, 2, pt. 1 (Record Commission, London, 1818), 506.

(1369) protested to Edward III that he was unable to execute some of the duties of office without grave blemishment to his conscience and great prejudice to his episcopal dignity. Edward sensibly excused him from performing such duties, but expected him to discharge the office faithfully.[40] Qualms such as Appleby's do not seem to have troubled an earlier bishop, John Kirkby. Dr Rose has traced the military adventures of this Augustinian canon, who, when bishop, made contracts with the Crown to lead military retinues, and was heavily involved in person in Border fights between 1335 and 1345.[41] Dr Keeling has identified a kindred spirit to Kirkby's in the sixteenth century—Cuthbert Ogle, member of a leading Northumberland family and a clerical pluralist there, who was ordered by the Crown to join raiding parties into Teviotdale in 1523 and 1538, the latter with a military retinue of ten.[42] Examples for the patriotic involvement of the clergy in warfare with the Scots were set by saints, whose cults helped to cement regional (and, presumably, parochial) ties when danger threatened. A widely diffused and long-remembered anecdote related how Cuthbert had appeared to David II in a vision in 1346, warning him of the dire consequences which he would suffer if he dared to invade the saint's lands.[43] James IV was to be as heedless

[40] Carlisle, Cumbria Record Office, Register of Bishop Appleby, fo. 210[r]. Copied into the register are his commissions as Warden and documents relating to his discharge of the office (e.g. fos. 155[r]–156[v], 164[v]–165[r], 173[r], 214[r], 218[r], 219[r]). His protest has been commented on by Richard K. Rose, 'The Bishops and Diocese of Carlisle: Church and Society in the Anglo-Scottish Borders, 1292–1395' (Ph.D thesis., Edinburgh University, 1984), 98–9.

[41] Rose, 'Bishops and Diocese of Carlisle', 64–5, 67–88.

[42] Keeling, 'Church and Religion', 135–8. The bishops of St Andrews and Glasgow, whose dioceses covered most of the Scottish Marches, do not seem to have been so regularly involved in Border affairs as their English counterparts. In 1419 the distance of St Andrews from the Borders and the difficulties of communicating between it and Kelso Abbey were among the justifications for the grant to the abbots of the right to discharge certain episcopal functions in the abbey's dependencies, including the rededication of churches, said to be frequently polluted as a result of Anglo-Scottish wars (*Calendar of Scottish Supplications to Rome 1418–22*, ed. E. R. Lindsay and A. I. Cameron (Scottish History Society, 3rd ser., 23, 1934), 73–4). For a reference to a visitation in the eastern Borders by the bishop of St Andrews in 1330, *Correspondence . . . of the Priory of Coldingham*, Appendix, p. vii.

[43] *Liber Pluscardensis*, ii, ed. Felix J. H. Skene (The Historians of Scotland 10, Edinburgh, 1880), 224; *A Description . . . of . . . the . . . Rites . . . of Durham* (Surtees Society 15, 1842), 22; Mervyn James, *Family, Lineage and Civil Society* (Oxford, 1974), 56. The prior and monks of Durham were on the fringes of the battle with a relic of St Cuthbert (*Description . . . of . . . the . . . Rites . . . of Durham*, 20–1).

as David; after Flodden, Bishop Ruthal of Durham wrote that 'all believe it [the victory] has been wrought by the intercession of St Cuthbert'.[44] In the eyes of many Englishmen, this Anglo-Scottish saint was displaying distinctly nationalist tendencies, involving himself in the ruin and destruction of Scottish kings. In Carlisle it was believed that the Virgin Mary was performing a similar protective function. In 1385 she had appeared in a vision to confound a Scottish besieging force.[45]

The fervour which inspired and broadcast this cult miracle may have been intensified by the fact that the besieging Scots were regarded as schismatics—which provided an excuse for the burning by the English royal army that year of abbeys in the Borders and Lothian. The involvement of the Scottish clergy in the expression of national hostilities is evident in the charges made against the English monks of Coldingham by Robert II and the estates in 1378, and by the consistory court of St Andrews in 1379. Professor A. L. Brown has argued that Robert's expulsion of the monks and annexation of the priory to Dunfermline Abbey had nothing to do with the Great Schism. The outbreak of the Schism is likely to have hampered Durham Priory's efforts to recover its cell, but, remarkably, it succeeded in doing so in the 1390s, long before the end of the Schism.[46] Nevertheless, the Schism produced difficulties and conflict for some of the Border clergy. A conflict of jurisdiction arose between the sees of St Andrews and Durham, when in 1390 Boniface IX granted Bishop Skirlaw diocesan powers in Berwick, Roxburgh, and whatever other parts of the diocese of St Andrews the English might occupy.[47] The following year the bishop of St Andrews united the convent at Berwick and its possessions to Dryburgh Abbey, which had been 'devastated by hostile fire', on the grounds that the nuns no longer maintained proper conventual life—presumably, too, because they were in the Roman allegiance. The Schism and the conflict of diocesan

---

[44] Cited in MacKinlay, *Ancient Church Dedications*, ii. 249–50.

[45] R. B. Dobson, 'Cathedral Chapters and Cathedral Cities: York, Durham and Carlisle in the Fifteenth Century', *Northern History*, 19 (1983), 15–44, at 41–2.

[46] A. L. Brown, 'The Priory of Coldingham in the Late Fourteenth Century', *Innes Review*, 23 (1972), 91–101. In 1316 two canons of Dryburgh were said to have been expelled by the Scots because they were English (*Cal. of Docs. Relating to Scotland*, iii, no. 509, p. 97).

[47] R. L. Storey, *Thomas Langley and the Bishopric of Durham 1406–1437* (London, 1961), 146.

jurisdictions probably presented delicate problems for the Scottish religious in or near English spheres of influence, like the monks of Kelso.[48]

When the Scots abandoned the schismatic allegiance in 1419, former ecclesiastical links were restored, though Durham maintained its control of Coldingham with difficulty and finally lost it in 1462.[49] The cross-Border links between houses and their cells and advowsons were once more among the factors which fostered social contacts: so were common allegiances to cults. The saints had roles to play as conciliators. In a petition to the papal curia dated *c*.1420, the monks of Kelso claimed that both English and Scots flocked to the abbey on its patronal feast of St John the Baptist and on that of the Assumption of the Blessed Virgin. They sought the right to grant an indulgence, in part in order to help make good war damage and to soften the hearts of potential raiders—'that malefactors of both kingdoms may be more favourable . . . in times of war'.[50] The names of Kentigern and Mungo appear as Christian names in Carlisle in the sixteenth century; among the series of late medieval panel paintings in the cathedral illustrating the life of St Cuthbert is one showing his sojourn at Melrose and instruction by Boisil, with an explanatory inscription in English.[51]

[48] *Cal. of Scottish Supplications to Rome 1418–22*, 196–7; cf. Glasgow, Transcript of Register of Supplications in Vatican Archives, no. 97 (23 July 1466). It is probable that there were some rival presentations to Scottish benefices in English occupation, such as Old Roxburgh, a prebend in Glasgow cathedral (*Cal. of Papal Letters . . . Clement VII*, 30; *Calendar of the Patent Rolls (1377–81)* (London, 1895), 445; *Calendar of the Patent Rolls (1385–89)* (London, 1900), 445).

[49] Dobson, 'The Last English Monks'.

[50] *Cal. of Scottish Supplications to Rome 1418–22*, 73–4. In 1472 the abbot of Melrose made reforming ordinances for Melrose's cell of Holm Cultram when present there for the election of a prior (*Liber . . . de Melros*, ii, no. 577, pp. 596–9). In 1318 Edward II had granted a safe conduct for the abbot of Melrose to go to Holm Cultram for such an election (*Foedera*, 2, pt. I, p. 370); in 1327 the prior and monks of Holm Cultram were granted permission to survey his grange in Galloway and treat with the abbot of Melrose regarding the rule of the house, during the truce (*Cal. of Docs. Relating to Scotland*, iii, no. 906, p. 165).

[51] Kentigern Hodchon in 1549 (Carlisle, Cumbria Record Office, Ca 3/1/51, fo. 10ᵛ); Mungo Smythe in 1577 (PRO E 310/40/5, no. 568). I owe thanks to Dr Henry Summerson for these references. He also drew my attention to the links of commemorative prayer made between the canons of Holyrood (Edinburgh) and Carlisle in the 1490s (*The Holyrood Ordinale* (The Book of the Old Edinburgh Club 7, 1914), pp. xlviii–xlix, 19–20) and to the evidence for the late medieval flourishing of the cult of St Ninian in northern England (David Palliser, 'Richard III and York', in Rosemary Horrox (ed.), *Richard III and the North* (Hull, 1986),

Abbeys which were famous cult centres might gain some protection as a result from attack, and so might churches and chapels: Edrom church (Roxburghshire) was being promoted as a cult centre in the 1390s.[52] But parish churches were the type of ecclesiastical structure most likely to be attacked in the Borders. Since they were the only buildings in which parishioners could customarily claim to have common obligations and rights, and were likely to be among the sturdiest structures in parishes, they were often important for communal defence. In 1429 Bishop Langley ordered the parishioners of Carham to cease using the parish church as a stable—a prudent habit as Carham was situated on the Tweed frontier.[53] The towers of some churches were rebuilt in the fourteenth century in defensive form, such as that at Newton Arlosh (Cumberland), which the appropriator, Holm Cultram Priory, had been licensed to fortify in 1304. In 1573 it was reported that this tower 'hath been ever a notable safeguard and defence . . . as well for all the tenants on the east side of the river Waver, as well also of the east stock and goods'.[54] The defensive usage of churches gave patrons as well as parishioners an additional incentive to ensure that the parish functioned as a religious community, so that the fabric was adequately maintained. George Clarkson, in his 1561 survey of the Percy estates, is explicit about the defensive imperative for the maintenance of both churches and vicarages—a number of the latter built as tower-houses in the fourteenth century remain in England. Clarkson's remarks suggest that fortified vicarages were regarded as part of the village's communal defences, not just as a shelter for the vicar and his household.[55]

The use of churches as depositories and strong points threatened

---

51–81, at 60–1; *State Papers: Henry VIII*, iv (Record Commission, London, 1836), 503–4).

[52] In 1393 an indulgence was granted to all who visited the parish church of St Mary of Edrom, 'which is noted for the miracles performed there, that in the past have attracted countless pilgrims' (*Cal. of Papal Letters . . . Clement VII*, 196–7).

[53] *The Register of Thomas Langley, Bishop of Durham, 1406–1437*, iii, ed. Robin L. Storey (Surtees Society 169, 1959 for 1954), no. 811, pp. 153–4.

[54] Keeling, 'Church and Religion', 176.

[55] Cited ibid. 71–2. For a financial account for Coldingham Priory's repairs to the chancel at Ednam in the 1330s, *Correspondence . . . of the Priory of Coldingham*, Appendix, pp. x–xi. This expenditure may have been partly in anticipation of a visitation by the bishop of St Andrews (ibid. p. ix).

them with at least pollution and at worst destruction, such as that visited on Annan kirk (Dumfriesshire), when it was destroyed by an English army in 1542.[56] According to a letter written by the earl of Northumberland in 1528, the Scottish surname chief Sym Armstrong had boasted to him that he had 'laid down' thirty parish churches in Scotland.[57] Armstrong was behaving in a manner perhaps excusable to pious Borderers: he and his like were drawn to attack churches as a means of sustaining their estate. Such attacks, though they inconvenienced parochial worship, did not necessarily undermine it. In 1436 Bishop Langley licensed the vicar of Newton in Glendale (Northumberland) to administer divine offices and parochial services away from the church, at whatever place in the parish was secure, during the war with Scotland.[58] Archbishop Hamilton, on his visitation of Berwickshire churches in 1555, found the parochial masses being celebrated in the unroofed kirk or in the kirkyard at Ayton.[59] Presumably the kirk had been attacked in the recent Anglo-Scottish wars, and the rector and parishioners were reluctant to undertake repairs, in view of the proximity of Berwick. Yet they struggled to maintain worship in these inclement conditions. The vulnerability of churches to attack made many rectors and parishoners reluctant to invest in elaborate building works, instruments of worship, and furnishings. Nevertheless, parts of the surviving fabric of some English churches, particularly in coastal Northumberland, have a stylishness characteristic of richer regions. Evidence of poor liturgical facilities in many later medieval Border churches cannot be taken as proof of the poverty of a parish or of the moribundity of parochial life. But the qualifications of curates prepared to reside in insecure, upcountry parishes are doubtful. There the curate is less likely to have been distinguished by adherence to the canonical requirements of behaviour and education than by ties of kinship and service with the chief families and by a high degree of identification with their habits and interests. Upland chaplains first come as a distinctive group into documentary light in Bishop Fox's strictures on their way of life in Tynedale and Redesdale in

[56] Keeling, 'Church and Religion', 66.
[57] Armstrong, *History of Liddesdale*, pp. xxx–xxxi.
[58] *Depositions and Other Ecclesiastical Proceedings from the Courts of Durham* (Surtees Society 21, 1845), 25.
[59] Cited in Keeling, 'Church and Religion', 64–5.

1498.[60] Yet the curates there were not unaware of their duty of obedience to ecclesiastical superiors. In 1524 Lord Dacre, Warden of the East March, claimed that Fox's excommunication of recalcitrant thieves had been an effective means of asserting secular authority. He successfully urged the application of similar measures, though these were not to prove entirely effective. In Tynedale Charlton chiefs were defiant in 1525, having the temerity to take the sacrament out of Bellingham church to their house, together with the wine and a stock of bread, intending to have the parish communion celebrated there.[61] Early Tudor officials found that even ill-disciplined Border clergy were useful as an instrument for controlling society.

Fox's identification of inhabitants of certain regions in the Borders as having a distinctive and in important respects unchristian way of life is frequently paralleled in sixteenth-century official reports and literary works. In 1554 the Merchant Venturers of Newcastle first banned the taking of apprentices from Tynedale, Redesdale, 'or any other such like place'.[62] In the mid-century Bernard Gilpin was shocked because some of the Rothbury parishioners failed to attend church because of feuds and, when they did come, congregated in two armed groups, one in the chancel facing the other in the nave.[63] Privy councillors in both realms came to regard this way of life as associated particularly with the warlike and thieving 'riding' surnames and as a threat to the peace and prosperity of the more 'civil' parts of the Borders and neighbouring regions. The problem had not been analysed so fully and so precisely in fifteenth-century denunciations of thieving

[60] *The Register of Richard Fox . . . 1494–1501*, ed. Marjorie Peers Howden (Surtees Society 147, 1932), 80–4, 110–12.

[61] Ibid.; *Letters and Papers . . . Henry VIII*, iv, pt. I, nos. 1289, 1429, pp. 564–5, 637: James, *Family, Lineage and Civil Society*, 54. Cf. the archbishop of Glasgow's excommunication of Scottish Border thieves (text in Fraser, *Steel Bonnets*, 382–5).

[62] *Extracts from the Records of the Merchant Adventurers of Newcastle-upon-Tyne*, i (Surtees Society 93, 1895 for 1894), 27. A revision of this ordinance added the explanation 'wheras the parties there brought upp ar knowen either by educatyon or nature, not to be of honest conversatyon'. In 1676 the court referred to the repeal of this act, 'in regard those parts are more civilized than formerly' (ibid. 27 n., 28–9). It is likely that the rapid expansion of the coal industry and trade along the Tyne in the period after the Merchant Adventurers' ban provided unprecedented work and immigration outlets for the inhabitants of the upland lordships which significantly affected their culture.

[63] Carleton, *Life of Bernard Gilpin*, 91–5.

habits and activities.[64] It is likely to have become more acute in the sixteenth century through a combination of factors—international and (particularly in Scotland) national political instabilities, population growth, spreading into the more barren uplands, and the price rises (following different progressions in England and Scotland) which made it more difficult for some surname chiefs and their dependants to maintain living standards. Consequently tensions increased between the more prosperous and more precariously placed parts of Border society, which ecclesiastical institutions had become ill conditioned to alleviate.

Some of these tensions are evident in the small corpus of 'riding' ballads which were collected from singers in the Borders between the late seventeenth and early nineteenth centuries.[65] A frequent theme in them is hostility to the sort of order represented by the Wardens and associated officials and by the urban environment where their power and support was concentrated. Most of these ballads are concerned with situations, and in some cases with documented events, occurring in the later sixteeth century, and they are mostly related from the viewpoint of riding surnames. The surviving texts are clearly based on, and in many cases substantially close to, contemporary compositions, though in some cases they have been 'improved' by the collectors. The compositions rely heavily on common material; they tend to be precisely particularized and highly localized; they have, for the most part a consistency of archaic form, outlook and subject-matter. They adhere to a code of loyalty to the bonds of kinship and alliance and extol valorous and cunning conduct. In this sense they are as pedagogic in intent as a Renaissance educational treatise. But they conspicuously lack Christian invocations, or sentiments of pity for victims or of repentance for evil done to them. The absence of

---

[64] In 1414 the commons of Northumberland petitioned against the outrages committed by the inhabitants of the franchises of Tynedale, Redesdale, and Hexhamshire (*Rotuli Parliamentorum* (6 vols., London, 1767–77), iv. 21–2). For complaints by priors of Durham of their cattle thefts later in the century, Durham, Dean and Chapter of Durham Archives, Prior's Kitchen, Reg. Parv. III, fos. 13d–14r, 117r. Charges brought before the Scottish justices at Jedburgh in 1493 and 1495 suggest some local thieves habitually colluded with English ones, who are often said to be of Tynedale (Edinburgh, Scottish Record Office, RH 2/1/5, Cur. Itin. Just., transcripts, vol. i, 1493–1504, fos. 36, 39, 49–50, 56–7, 70, 82, 182).

[65] Most of the texts are in Francis J. Child, *The English and Scottish Popular Ballads* (5 vols., Boston and New York, 1882–98, repr. New York, 1965). The best account of the ballads is in James Reed, *The Border Ballads* (London, 1973).

such invocations and retractions puts them in a different category from the one genuine surviving medieval Border ballad of action, *Adam Bel*, which combines a taste for bloodshed and cruelty with expressions of conventional piety. This ballad reflects pious attitudes among Cumberland villagers.[66] Sir Walter Scott's judgement on the society which produced the riding ballads highlighted the problem of the significance of the attitudes to religion found in them:

Upon the religion of the Borderers there can very little be said. We have already noticed that they remained attached to the Roman Catholic faith rather longer than the rest of Scotland. This probably arose from a total indifference upon the subject; for we nowhere find in their character the respect for the church which is a marked feature of that religion.[67]

The progress of the Reformation in the Scottish Borders provides a significant background to the religious indifference found in the riding ballads. The planting of the reformed ministry was carried out most successfully in Berwickshire: there the majority of parishes had ministers or readers either in 1567 or the years immediately following. In Tweeddale and Teviotdale there was a well-established ministry by the late 1560s, but for many parishes the first evidence of a reader dates from 1574; though in 1585 ministers had replaced readers in a number of parishes, there was difficulty in getting some adequately served. Further to the west, in Nithsdale and Annandale, there had been a vigorous planting of the ministry in the 1560s; in northern Nithsdale and the region around Dumfries continuity of service was maintained in the 1570s and 1580s, but in some coastal parishes this seems to have been broken.[68] In Ettrick, Ewesdale, Eskdale, and Liddesdale there is no evidence for continuity of reformed service in most parishes until the second and third decades of the seventeenth century. In

[66] Child, *English and Scottish Popular Ballads*, iii. 14–39, no. 116. For a discussion of the ballad and a reference to its heroes dating from 1432, James C. Holt, *Robin Hood* (London, 1982), 66–71.
[67] *Minstrelsy of the Scottish Border* (5th edn., 3 vols., Edinburgh, 1821), i, p. xc.
[68] This and the following analysis is based principally on Edinburgh, Scottish Record Office, Assignation and Modification of Stipends, E.47, 3 (1585–1586), 6 (1593–1594, 1595), 7 (1596, 1597), 8 (1599, 1601), 9 (1607, 1608), C. H. Haws, *Scottish Parish Clergy at the Reformation 1540–1574* (Scottish Record Society, NS 3, Edinburgh, 1972); *Register of Ministers and Readers in the Kirk of Scotland, from the Book of Assignation of Stipends, 1574*, in *The Miscellany of the Wodrow Society*, i, ed. David Laing (Edinburgh 1844), 319–96.

1604 the Liddesdale parishes of Castleton, Ettleton, Wheelkirk, and Belkirk were united under Castleton by royal authority, as they were said to be destitute of all instruction and 'bringing up in the fear of God, be lack of pastoris to preach the word sen the Reformation of religion and letteris'.[69] Moreover, in the last decades of the sixteenth century there was a centre of Roman Catholic activity at New Abbey in coastal Dumfriesshire, a small-scale affair, to which, however, significant missionary activity in the western dales was attributed by its opponents.[70] The success of this venture depended on the protection of surname chiefs sympathetic to the old religion (particularly the Maxwells). But this was not always to be relied on, as they sometimes found it expedient to adhere to the Reformed Kirk in order to avoid the wrath of the General Assembly or the Privy Council. The absence of religious sentiment in the riding ballads may in part reflect atmospheres of doubt and division over religion in parts where the Reformed Kirk established itself fitfully and where Catholicism lingered and sometimes flared up—parts which coincide largely with the territories occupied by the Scottish surnames who figure in the ballads. Instruction in both the old and new ways was erratic, and the anonymous ballad singers, whose aim was to please (and whose livelihood sometimes depended on doing so), found it expedient to eschew confessional partisanship. Adapting a common stock of material, they preferred a repertoire which was neutral in religion, and which could be transmitted among surnames where religion varied. This neutrality helps to explain why riding ballads practically from this period alone continued to be widely sung by the Presbyterian Border peasantry of the seventeenth and eighteenth centuries in a remarkably unchanged form—whereas earlier heroic ballads, which, like *Adam Bel*, presumably had the trappings of later medieval piety, disappeared

---

[69] Cited in Armstrong, *History of Liddesdale*, 69.

[70] The leading spirit in this enterprise for a number of decades was a local laird, the incorrigible priest Gilbert Brown, commendator of New Abbey (Sweetheart); see e.g. *Calendar of Border Papers*, ed. Joseph Bain (2 vols., Edinburgh, 1894–6), i, nos. 404–6, 411–12, pp. 216–18; *Register of the Privy Council of Scotland*, iv: *1585–1592*, ed. David Masson (Edinburgh, 1881), 773–4; ibid. vii: *1604–7*, ed. David Masson (Edinburgh, 1885), 87–8. This mission has been neglected and would well be worth examining. Catholicism persisted in the Scottish West March well into the 17th century, not just as a 'country house sect' among the nobles or as a hotchpotch of traditional beliefs among uplanders: it is found among the townsfolk of Dumfries.

from the stock of oral culture, or survived, like the ballads about the medieval conflict of the Percys and Douglases, in a much altered form.

The riding ballads which the Borderers continued to cherish were based on a set of secular values which their ancestors had either abhorred when they were composed or had rejected soon afterwards. They cherished these ballads because they gave a heroic tinge to their environment and society, a special significance which these lacked in the eyes of the wider world until the ballads were published by the antiquarian ballad collectors and romanticized by Scott. As we have seen, the secular morality of the ballads was a positive one: it was not just ballast for a religious void. It was propagandist in exalting and systematizing traditional values and habits which underpinned the surname society. The ballads' silence about religion sprung only partly from confusion and prudence: it also reflected an awareness of the threat posed by the Reformation. The ecclesiastical disciplines which reformers such as Gilpin stood for—and, even more, the disciplines of the Reformed Kirk—threatened the social basis of the surname society. Dr Keith Brown has recently analysed the attacks by ministers of the Kirk and by James VI and his bureaucratic circles on the related aristocratic concepts of honour and kindness, and the violence which they engendered.[71] They recognized these problems as acute in parts of the Borders. As the provision in the Anglo-Scottish treaty of 1597 for the plantation of churches there shows, the connection between reformed discipline and pacification had become axiomatic in governing circles.[72] Moreover, it is unlikely that the occasional agents of the Counter-Reformation in the Borders had sympathy with traditional values: one of the most stinging denunciations of Border barbarity had been penned by a Catholic bishop, John Leslie.[73] The ideal Border cleric, in the eyes of society generally, was no longer one whose office was in part validated by his role in sustaining social cohesion in the face of chronic threats of violence and occasional ones of invasion, but one who helped to solve the internal crisis gripping Border society, by helping to make the riding surnames conformable to the social

[71] *Bloodfeud in Scotland 1573–1625* (Edinburgh, 1986).
[72] D. L. W. Tough, *The Last Years of a Frontier* (Oxford, 1928), 129–30.
[73] *The Historie of Scotland*, i, trans. James Dalrymple, ed. E. G. Cody (Scottish Text Society 5, 14, Edinburgh, 1888), 97–103.

norms found in the Border burghs and their hinterlands. Missionary Cuthberts and Kentigerns were once more required. The fact that the old violent way of life had crumbled away by the end of James VI's and I's reign was in part a testimony to the success of the reformed churches in accomplishing this task. Perhaps the most impressive architectural monument to this achievement is the church at Arthuret, in the deanery of Carlisle, within a few miles of the frontier. Here, within the territory of the notorious Graham surname, conventional parochial life seems to have long been at a low ebb. In the early seventeenth century a large new church was built in what must have been among the last ecclesiastical designs before the Gothic revival in a basically Perpendicular style.[74]

To conclude: in the fourteenth century there developed on both sides of the frontier 'societies organized for war', which, as well as having distinctive secular institutions, had distinctive customs and values, first described by sixteenth-century commentators and later analysed by Sir Walter Scott. His view that this Border society was one in which secular values were especially predominant has remained influential. But conventional religious values and the ecclesiastical institutions which embodied and promoted them were well established in the Borders by the end of the thirteenth century. During the subsequent era of conflicts Border society never lost this underlying ecclesiastical structure. But it was exploited in order to provide a fragile society with the material and spiritual cement necessary to organize its defences. The military commands exercised in person by some English bishops exemplify the involvement of the clergy in war and the importance of this involvement to Border society. Despite royal pressure to align them on national lines (reinforced by the Great Schism), the clergy continued to foster some cross-Border institutional and cult links. The Church had roles in maintaining social connections between embattled communities and also in trying to limit the destruction of war.

The effects of the development of a society at war on

---

[74] Nikolaus Pevsner, *Cumberland and Westmorland* (The Buildings of England, Harmondsworth, 1967), 61–2. The church of Arthuret was valued in 1291 at £80, its vicarage at £30 (*Taxatio ecclesiastica*, 319). In 1535 the church was valued at 40s. in time of peace, nothing in time of war (*Valor ecclesiasticus*, vi. 279). The rebuilt church can be compared with the contemporary ones of classical design found in remoter parts of southern Europe, symbols and centres of the proselytizing missions of the Counter-Reformation.

12

The Crusading Idea and the Conquest of the Region East of the Elbe

FRIEDRICH LOTTER

THE TENTH- AND ELEVENTH-CENTURY BACKGROUND

The process by which the Baltic and Elbe Slavs, the so-called Wends, were incorporated into the German nation was very complicated.[1] In the middle decades of the tenth century, King Otto I, the future emperor, subdued all the Slav tribes in the area between the Elbe-Saale in the west, the Erzgebirge in the south, and the Oder-Bober line in the east. In this region there existed three large tribal units, which were more or less coherent: the Abodrites in the north-west, the Wilzes in the north-east and midlands up to the lowlands of the Havel and lower Spree, and the Sorbs in the south. In order to further the integration of the western Slavs, Otto started a policy of Christianization, which he supported by creating an ecclesiastical organization. Thus in 948 he founded two bishoprics, Brandenburg and Havelberg, for the Wilzes; in 968 one, Oldenburg in Wagria (east Holstein), for the Abodrites and three, Merseburg, Zeitz (later Naumburg), and Meissen, for the Sorbs. Oldenburg was incorporated into the ecclesiastical province of Hamburg-Bremen,[2] and the other five were allocated to the new archbishopric of Magdeburg which was also founded in 968.[3] But although the Slav nobility in general was

[1] Francis Dvornik, *The Making of Central and Eastern Europe* (London, 1949); A. P. Vlasto, *The Entry of the Slavs into Christendom* (Cambridge, 1970); Charles Higounet, *Die deutsche Ostsiedlung im Mittelalter* (Berlin, 1986); Joachim Herrmann (ed.), *Die Slawen in Deutschland: Ein Handbuch* (Berlin, 1972; rev. edn. 1985).
[2] Helmut Beumann, 'Die Gründung des Bistums Oldenburg und die Missionspolitik Ottos des Großen', in his *Ausgewählte Aufsätze 1966–1986* (Sigmaringen, 1987), 177–92.
[3] Theodor Schieder (ed.), *Handbuch der europäischen Geschichte*, i (Stuttgart, 1976), 694–5 (K. Reindel), 857–68 (M. Hellmann) with literature; James Westfall Thompson, 'The German Church and the Conversion of the Baltic Slavs', *American Journal of Theology*, 20 (1916), 205–30, 372–89.

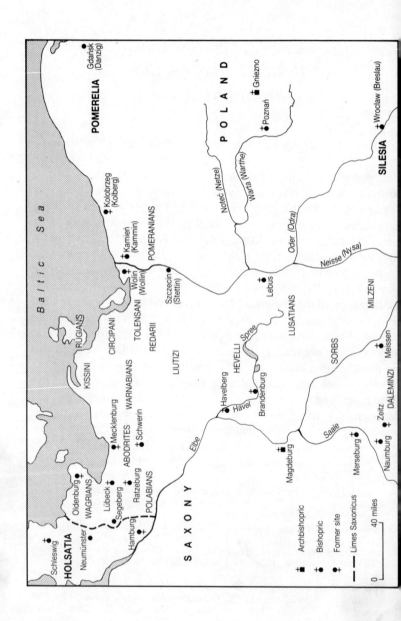

not disinclined to be baptized, the local ecclesiastical organization was far from complete by the end of the century.

To consolidate German overlordship, Otto I, as early as 937, installed two margraves in the area: Hermann Billung in the territory of the Abodrites and Gero in the region between the middle Elbe and the Oder. Possibly there was another march in the southern region of the Sorbian tribes. Later Hermann's descendants, the Billungs, became dukes of Saxony, the last of them, Magnus, dying in 1106; thus the dukes of Saxony were always also margraves of the March of the Billungs in the land of the Abodrites. The margraviate of Gero, however, was subdivided after his death in 965; afterwards there were six marches between the Elbe-Saale and Oder-Bober, out of which, at a later date, three larger margraviates emerged: the Nordmark in the region of the Wilzes (later, the Liutizi), the Ostmark, subsequently called the March of Lusatia (Lausitz), and the March of Meissen in the territory of the southern Sorbian tribes.[4]

In the tenth century the political system of the Sorbs south of the land of Teltow dissolved and their ruling classes disappeared, possibly through German acts of violence; we know of the murder of thirty Slav princes who had been invited to a banquet by margrave Gero. Nevertheless the local Slav nobility mainly co-operated with the German overlords and even accepted Christianization and Germanization. Thus the Ottonian kings were able to establish direct German rule by adapting the Slav network of burgwards to their purposes. Those burgwards, fortified centres of districts containing between one and two dozen villages, had garrisons of mounted troops, most of whom were of Slav origin. One can hardly trace German rural settlement in this region before the end of the eleventh century.[5]

In the course of the ninth and tenth centuries, the political unit of the Wilzes had dissolved like that of the Sorbs. Despite their acceptance of German overlordship, however, all of the constituent tribes, especially the leading tribe of the Redarii, kept up their political and legal traditions in the face of Ottonian power. With the formation of a new union, that of the Liutizi, the tribes were

---

[4] Rudolf Kötzschke, 'Die deutschen Marken im Sorbenland', in his *Deutsche und Slawen im mitteldeutschen Osten: Ausgewählte Aufsätze* (Darmstadt, 1961), 62–88.

[5] Schieder, *Handbuch der europäischen Geschichte*, i. 865–6.

even able to set up a new political organization which made itself felt in the uprising of 983. This new tribal federation had a religious foundation in the pagan cult of the temple town of Rethra, the capital of the Redarii.[6]

The tribal community of the Abodrites was quite different from the other Wendish units, although it too was composed of several tribes: the Abodrites (in a narrower sense), the Wagrians, Polabians, and Warnabians. In the course of the process of their unification, which started in the mid-tenth century and continued till the beginning of the twelfth century, several adjacent tribes were annexed. In this way they approached a state-like organization similar to that of the Bohemians and Poles. There was a monarchic head above the tribal and local nobility which, from the mid-tenth century on, was represented by the dynasty of the Nakonids, who had been converted to Christianity early. The Nakonids recognized German overlordship but were able to employ these feudal ties to get the support of the Saxon duke and his followers for their own political ends.[7]

During the second half of the tenth century west Slav principalities emerged in Bohemia and Poland after having converted to Christianity and set up an ecclesiastical organization in co-operation with the Ottonian kings. The first beginnings of a Slav mission in Moravia in the ninth century may have stimulated the swift formation of a local clergy and native Church in the duchies of these west Slavs, which consolidated the national sovereign power and state system. Nevertheless the Polish rulers had to recognize their feudal dependence on the German king and the Bohemian duke was integrated within the German higher nobility.[8]

In the region between the lower Oder valley, the Warthe-Netze, and the lower Vistula, which was situated between the gradually consolidating and expanding Polish duchy on the one side and the various units of the Elbe Slavs on the other side, the principality of the Pomeranians emerged. Throughout the eleventh century, it strove successfully against Polish endeavours to annex and

---

[6] Schieder, *Handbuch der europäischen Geschichte*, i. 862–4.

[7] Ibid. 861–2.

[8] Ibid. 868–82, 902–13; Ferdinand Seibt (ed.), *Handbuch der europäischen Geschichte*, ii (Stuttgart, 1987), 1042–6 (F. Seibt) with literature about Poland; W. F. Reddaway *et al.* (eds.), *Cambridge History of Poland*, i (Cambridge, 1950), esp. 20–42 (S. Ketrzynski).

Christianize it.[9] Another powerful west Slav tribe was the Rugians or Rani, inhabitants of the island of Rügen (Rana) and fearsome pirates, who, in alliance with the coastal tribes, often raided the Danish coasts.[10]

The uprising of the northern Wends in 983, which followed the catastrophic defeat of Emperor Otto II in the battle of Cotrone against the Saracens in 982, was an important turning-point in the relations between Germans and western Slavs. The revolt broke out in the region of the Wilzes, where the four tribes of the Redarii, Kissini, Circipani, and Tolensani had formed the federation of the Liutizi. They endeavoured to wipe out German overlordship and Christendom altogether. The episcopal sees of Havelberg and Brandenburg were burnt down (and not restored for more than a century and a half), and the Christians who could not escape were slain. The revolt also touched the Sorbian marches, but they were defended successfully.[11]

Soon the Abodrites joined in the uprising, while apparently still adhering to Christianity. With the scarce and confused information we obtain from the sources, we cannot even attempt to disentangle the events of the various rebellions of the Abodrites in the 980s and 990s and in 1018. But when the Abodrite Prince Mistiwoj ravaged Holsatia (Nordalbingia or west Holstein) and Hamburg, an event which apparently did not take place before the early 990s, he was accompanied by his German chaplain Avico, and later on he died as a Christian. The episcopal see of Oldenburg was destroyed in that period too, but nevertheless we know that two bishops, one before 1013 and the other up to 1023, were working in Mecklenburg, that is, in the territory of the Abodrites, and were even baptizing large numbers of people there.[12] But a new uprising which started with an invasion of the Liutizi in 1018 resulted in the extermination of Christianity and the expulsion of the Nakonid prince.

[9] Seibt, *Handbuch der europäischen Geschichte*, ii. 327–8, 1051–2.

[10] Herrmann, *Die Slawen in Deutschland*, 121–2, 216–18, and *passim*.

[11] Wolfgang Brüske, *Untersuchungen zur Geschichte des Liutizenbundes* (MF 3, Münster and Cologne, 1955), 39–44; Wolfgang H. Fritze, 'Der slawische Aufstand von 983: Eine Schicksalswende', in Eckart Henning and Walter Vogel (eds.), *Festschrift der Landesgeschichtlichen Vereinigung für die Mark Brandenburg* (Berlin, 1984), 9–55; W. Coblenz, 'Das Sorbengebiet zur Zeit des Liutizenaufstandes', *Zeitschrift für Archäologie*, 18 (1984), 33–40.

[12] Friedrich Lotter, *Die Konzeption des Wendenkreuzzugs* (Vorträge und Forschungen, Sonderband 23, Sigmaringen, 1977), 50–1.

Subsequently the Saxon Duke Bernhard II (1011–59), in alliance with the Danish King Canute the Great (1014–35), succeeded in gradually re-establishing the rule of the Nakonids.[13] But it was not before the mid-eleventh century that the Abodrite King Gottschalk, in co-operation with the Saxon duke and the ambitious Archbishop Adalbert of Hamburg-Bremen, was strong enough not only to expand his domination over the Liutizian tribes along the Baltic Sea, the Kissini and Circipani, but also to make a new attempt to advance Christianization. After 1055, Adalbert, who intended to erect a northern patriarchate, founded three new bishoprics in the area of the old Oldenburg diocese: Oldenburg for the Wagrians, Mecklenburg for the Slav tribes on the Baltic coast, Ratzeburg for the Polabians. But Adalbert's policy in the Reich turned out a failure and, in 1066, provoked a new powerful insurrection of the Abodrites, who now turned against their own Christian dynasty.[14] Local Christianity was totally wiped out, the king was slain, and a new pagan prince, Cruto, elected. The pagan reaction soon reached beyond the frontier, and the whole of Holsatia up to the metropolis Hamburg was razed to the ground. As our chronicler Helmold of Bosau relates, all the Nordalbingians suffered the yoke of slavery for quite a time, paying tribute to the cruel Cruto, and hundreds of them left their homeland.[15]

In the mean time, however, the Liutizian federation was dissolving. The pagan alliance with the Abodrites in 1018 was only an interlude. Before that time the pagan Liutizi had been allies of the German King Henry II in his campaigns against the Christian duke of Poland, Bolesław Chrobry. Indeed, Henry was harshly criticized for that by ecclesiastical authorities.[16] And when Poland met with a long period of weakness, starting with the last years of Mieszko II (d. 1034), time and again disastrous invasions of the Saxon borderland by the Liutizi and punitive expeditions of German kings and Saxon dukes took place. But notwithstanding

[13] Wolfgang H. Fritze, 'Probleme der abodritischen Stammes- und Reichsverfassung und ihrer Entwicklung vom Stammesstaat zum Herrschaftsstaat', in Herbert Ludat (ed.), *Siedlung und Verfassung der Slawen zwischen Elbe, Saale und Oder* (Giessen, 1960), 141–219.

[14] Karl Jordan, *Die Bistumsgründungen Heinrichs des Löwen* (*MGH, Schriften* 3, Leipzig, 1939), 72–3; Thompson, 'German Church', 228–30.

[15] Helmold of Bosau, *Cronica Slavorum*, i. 26, ed. Bernhard Schmeidler (*SRG*, Hanover, 1937), 52–3.

[16] Schieder, *Handbuch der europäischen Geschichte*, i. 711 with n. 1; Brüske, *Untersuchungen*, 54–74.

this menace to their survival, in about 1056 a long fratricidal war broke out among the Liutizian tribes, which resulted in the submission of the northern tribes to the Abodrite king Gottschalk. In 1066, the last pagan reaction, starting from the pagan sanctuary of Rethra, led to the overthrow of King Gottschalk and Wendish Christianity. But as early as 1068 Bishop Burchard of Halberstadt inflicted a humiliating defeat upon the Liutizi. Afterwards the Liutizi even failed to take the opportunity to intervene in the conflict between the Saxons and King Henry IV, so that there was a period of peace in this sector of the Elbe frontier. At the same time Rethra lost its function as the religious centre of the Wends and was replaced by the sanctuary of the Rugians, Arkona, on the island of Rügen.[17]

About 1090, Henry, the last surviving son of Gottschalk, returned from Danish exile. He killed Cruto and, by defeating his Slav opponents in the battle of Schmielau in 1093, succeeded in re-establishing the Nakonid kingdom. With the support of the Danish king and the Saxon duke he consolidated his rule and in various campaigns subdued all the Slav tribes between the Elbe and the Oder up to the Havel lowlands.[18] It was the last time that a large Slav kingdom embracing all the Wendish tribes north of the Sorbs seemed about to come into being, assisted by active military support of the Christian neighbours. The Christian Abodrite King Henry, however, did not dare to Christianize his Slav subjects for fear of endangering his rule. Even in Havelberg and Brandenburg there were Slav counts or governors who were Christians, but ruled over a pagan population.[19]

THE TRANSITION PERIOD UP TO THE DEATH OF
EMPEROR LOTHAR III (1137)

At the beginning of the twelfth century the economic, political, and ideological situation on the Elbe frontier changed decisively. At this time, bishops, abbots, and local nobles in the region around the Elbe and Saale started to intensify rural settlement by

---

[17] Schieder, *Handbuch der europäischen Geschichte*, i. 864; Brüske, *Untersuchungen*, 81–103.

[18] Fritze, 'Probleme', 171–2.

[19] Lotter, *Konzeption*, 55–8; Hans-Dietrich Kahl, *Slawen und Deutsche in der brandenburgischen Geschichte des zwölften Jahrhunderts* (MF 30, 2 vols., Cologne and Graz, 1964), 26–76.

clearing woodlands and draining marshy grounds, founding new villages and allocating land to western settlers. At the same time new monasteries and churches were founded for the spiritual needs of the settlers as well as for the sake of Christianizing the pagan Slavs.[20] Moreover, the clergy got a fresh impetus from political changes.

In 1106 the Emperor Henry IV and the last Billung duke, Magnus, died, and the new King Henry V conferred the duchy of Saxony on Lothar of Supplinburg. In 1110 Duke Lothar invested Adolf (I) of Schauenburg with the county of Nordalbingia (Holsatia). Later on, when the conflict between the Saxon princes and the Salian king flared up anew, Duke Lothar, after the victory of the Welfesholz in 1115, consolidated Saxon autonomy. Therefore he was able to dispose of the appointment of the margraves in the Slav marches against the declared will of the emperor. Thus in 1123 he installed the Ascanian Albert of Ballenstedt, called the Bear, in the March of Lusatia, and Conrad, the ancestor of the house of Wettin, in the March of Meissen, and enforced these appointments against the emperor's candidates.[21] Later on Lothar, who in 1125 to everyone's surprise had been elected king in lieu of the Hohenstaufen candidate, gave his only daughter Gertrude in marriage to Duke Henry the Black of Bavaria and so established the Welfs in Saxony.[22] Now all the houses of German high nobility which decided the destiny of the region east of the Elbe in the twelfth century had made their appearance in the area.

In the mean time, however, the First Crusade, its impulses and consequences, had a heavy impact on the imagination and perspectives of the Christian world, especially with regard to attitudes to heathens. With their new self-confidence, Christians were less willing to tolerate the existence of pagans in the neighbourhood. Although the pagans had not raided the Saxon frontierland for quite a long time, Christian theology identified

---

[20] Seibt, *Handbuch der europäischen Geschichte*, ii. 244–5 with nn. 1–2 (H. Helbig).

[21] Ibid. 313, 317, 319 (H. Beumann); Walter Lammers, *Geschichte Schleswig-Holsteins*, iv/1: *Das Hochmittelalter bis zur Schlacht von Bornhöved* (Neumünster, 1981), 229–37; Eberhard Schmidt, *Die Mark Brandenburg unter den Askaniern (1134–1320)* (MF 71, Cologne and Vienna, 1973), 20; Johannes Schultze, *Die Mark Brandenburg*, i: *Entstehung und Entwicklung unter den askanischen Markgrafen (bis 1319)* (Berlin, 1961), 63–8.

[22] Seibt, *Handbuch der europäischen Geschichte*, ii. 322–3 with nn. 3–6.

paganism with peacelessness. Referring to the declared goal of Christianity of building a realm of peace, the Christian clergy kept emphasizing all the pagan invasions of the past by proclaiming that the whole region east of the Elbe had been Christianized long before and later lost to heathendom—and this was not to be tolerated any more.

This conception is first attested in 1108 by a document which purports to be an appeal by the bishops of the ecclesiastical province of Magdeburg and some princes of east Saxony.[23] It is addressed to all the Christians of the Western countries, clerical and lay, including several prelates and some princes, above all Duke Godfrey V of Lower Lorraine and the famous Count Robert of Flanders, who had distinguished himself by his feats during the First Crusade. The proclamation is no longer disputed as an authentic source of the time. However, we do not know whether it was an official note or just a draft—composed, as it seems, by a Flemish cleric. Although the appeal does not seem to have had any material effects, as an authentic description of the situation it at least highlights the change of mind which determined future politics on the Elbe border.[24]

Peter Knoch has convincingly pointed out the striking parallels in composition, contents, and even terms between the Magdeburg appeal and Pope Urban's preaching of the First Crusade in Clermont as it was rendered by Robert the Monk in his *Historia Iherosolimitana*.[25] However, we have five accounts of this speech by contemporaries, and all of them differ considerably from one another.[26] Thus there is no way to ascertain what Urban actually said. All the authors more or less mix up the crusading idea, as Urban preached it, with the further development of this idea after the First Crusade had been brought to a successful end. This is especially true of Robert the Monk, although he himself was an ear-witness of the preaching of the cross in Clermont.

[23] *Urkundenbuch des Erzstifts Magdeburg*, i, ed. Friedrich Israël and Walter Möllenberg (Magdeburg, 1937), no. 193, pp. 249–52; trans. in Louise and Jonathan Riley-Smith, *The Crusades: Idea and Reality 1095–1274* (London, 1981), 74–7.

[24] Peter Knoch, 'Kreuzzug und Siedlung: Studien zum Aufruf der Magdeburger Kirche vom 1108', *Jahrbuch für die Geschichte Mittel- und Ostdeutschlands*, 23 (1974), 1–33.

[25] *Recueil des historiens des croisades, Historiens occidentaux*, iii (Paris, 1866), 717–882, at 727–30.

[26] H. E. J. Cowdrey, 'Pope Urban II's Preaching of the First Crusade', *History*, 55 (1970), 177–88.

The parallels between the Magdeburg proclamation and Robert's account begin with the extensive description of pagan cruelties in torturing Christians to death and of the desecration of holy places. The Westerners are then exhorted to take up the gauntlet and to emulate former Christian heroes and princes by crushing pagan rule, as had been done by Charlemagne and his successors, in the former case, or the glorious crusaders in the latter. Then Robert describes the servitude of the holy city, that had to be liberated; the Anonymous refers to the eastern region as 'Our Jerusalem', that was free in former times and now had become a servant over which the heathens triumph.[27] Then the author of the Magdeburg appeal weaves in information about the organization of the campaign and the place and date of the army's rendezvous. Employing numerous biblical quotations, he exhorts the clergy to propagate the war of Christ everywhere.

Both appeals then close with promises. The pope proclaims an indulgence. Since this is something only the pope can decree, the Anonymous instead enters into general allusions concerning the crusaders' prospects of saving their souls. But this general promise is combined with another one he had also adopted from Robert: the promise of double reward, that is, an eternal and a temporal one. Robert more than the others had emphasized this promise of double reward by referring to the Bible: according to Matthew 19: 29, Christ himself said: 'Every one that has forsaken houses or lands . . . for my name's sake shall receive an hundredfold'; and according to Exodus 3: 8: 'Palestine is a land flowing with milk and honey'. Interpreting those references, Robert for the first time compares the crusaders with the children of Israel, to whom the Lord, after they have driven out the Canaanites, has given the land of Canaan as their inheritance (Leviticus 25: 38; Psalm 105: 11; Joshua 3: 10).[28]

---

[27] *Urkundenbuch . . . Magdeburg*, 251: 'Sicut Galli ad liberationem Hierusalem vos preparate: Hierusalem nostra ab initio libera, gentilium crudelitate facta est ancilla . . .'; cf. Knoch, 'Kreuzzug und Siedlung', 16.

[28] Of course, there is no evidence that Pope Urban actually included this temporal promise in his proclamation. Early testimonies of his crusading idea explicitly confine indulgence of penalty to those who do not wear the badge of the cross for greed after worldly profits. Not earlier than 1098, a new appeal by the patriarch of Jerusalem and several Greek and Latin bishops for the first time calls attention to the double reward: the Western knights are exhorted to go and take possession of the land that flows with milk and honey and abounds in all victuals; cf. Lotter, *Konzeption*, 60–1 with nn. 190–2; on indulgences, see James A. Brundage,

The Anonymous now applies this promise to the land of the pagan Wends, and even here he employs a number of biblical allusions: 'Prepare war, wake up the mighty men [Joel 3: 9], prepare like the French to liberate Jerusalem.' In some biblical quotations the Eastern crusaders are identified with the glorious Maccabees in their struggle to liberate the holy land, which is now enslaved.[29] Then he adds the temporal promise: 'The heathens are the worst men, but their land is the best of all with meat, honey, flour, when it is cultivated! Here, you Saxons, Franks, Lotharingians, Flemings, most famous conquerors of the world, you can save your souls and, if you want to, you will acquire the best land to live in!'[30] Again the allusions to the land of Canaan flowing with milk and honey are not to be ignored.[31]

But it has to be noticed that absolutely nothing is said about any intention of converting the pagans to Christianity, which had been the goal of the missionary wars waged by the Ottonian kings in the tenth century. But here, much more explicitly than in the papal speech as delivered by Robert the Monk, we see the combination of both rewards, the promise that all those who take part in crushing the heathens and liberating the Church from oppression will gain not only remission of all sins but also fertile land to settle in. It is this promise of both eternal and temporal rewards that made it possible to transfer the crusading idea to the Elbe frontier. For Christian settlement in the former pagan land, soon after it had begun about the turn of the twelfth century, had proved to be the only way to advance Christianization.

The Magdeburg appeal of 1108 is doubtless to be connected with a meeting of the king, Henry V, and a great number of ecclesiastical and secular princes of the Reich in east Saxony, which took place at the time set for departure. But we do not hear anything about a campaign in the Elbe region let alone a movement of western settlers.[32] Shortly afterwards, however, the Benedictine

---

Medieval Canon Law and the Crusader (Madison, 1969), 145–55; Hans Eberhard Mayer, *The Crusades* (Eng. trans., Oxford, 1972), 25–40.

[29] *Urkundenbuch . . . Magdeburg*, 250–1: 'accingimini, viri potentes' (1 Macc. 3: 58); 'facta est ancilla' (1 Macc. 2: 11).

[30] Ibid. 251: 'Gentiles isti pessimi sunt, sed terra eorum optima carne, melle, farina . . . hinc poteritis et animas vestras salvificare et, si ita placet, optimam terram ad inhabitandum acquirere . . .'; cf. Exod. 3: 8 and *passim*; Lev. 20: 24; Deut. 6: 3 and *passim*.

[31] Cf. Exod. 3: 8 and *passim*.   [32] Knoch, 'Kreuzzug und Siedlung', 21–31.

abbey of Berge in Magdeburg and the bishop of Brandenburg, Hartbert, regained a footing in the region beyond the Elbe east of Magdeburg. As Hartbert, in a charter of 1114, relates, he destroyed many pagan idols and built a church of stone in Leitzkau, which is about fifteen miles south-east of the centre of Magdeburg. In 1139 Bishop Wigger of Brandenburg, a former friend of Norbert of Xanten, the founder of the Premonstratensian Order and archbishop of Magdeburg from 1126 to 1134, installed a convent of those regular canons in Leitzkau. With that foundation which was later to be transformed into the cathedral chapter of Brandenburg, he opened one of the Premonstratensians' most meritorious fields of activity in the region east of the Elbe.[33]

First, however, the pagan regions between the Elbe and the Oder had to be subdued by force to direct Christian rule, since voluntary acceptance of the Christian faith could no longer be expected. This force was first exerted by Duke Bolesław III of Poland (1102–38). After having eliminated his rival and re-established Polish power, he started an extraordinarily bloody war against the Pomeranians, which lasted for nearly twenty years. First he annexed the land south of the Netze, then east Pomerania or Pomerelia between the Persante and the Vistula delta, and finally he took Stettin (Szczecin) on the Oder delta. The Pomeranian Duke Wartislaw submitted at last, recognized Polish supremacy, and promised to accept Christianity and to pay a heavy tribute.[34] Bolesław now crossed the Oder to the west and subdued the eastern Liutizian tribes too. In 1124 he consolidated his expansionary policy by founding the bishoprics of Leslau (Włocławek) on the Vistula for the east Pomeranians and Lebus on the Middle Oder for the Liutizi.[35] At the same time he wanted to Christianize the Pomeranians, but there was no Polish priest able or willing to do this work. Therefore Bolesław entrusted that delicate mission to Bishop Otto of Bamberg, whom he had come to know in his former function as chaplain of a Polish duchess.[36]

[33] Kahl, *Slawen*, 107–66.

[34] Reddaway *et al.*, *Cambridge History of Poland*, i. 46–7 (A. Bruce-Boswell); Jürgen Petersohn, *Der südliche Ostseeraum im kirchlich-politischen Kräftespiel des Reichs, Polens und Dänemarks vom 10. bis 13. Jahrhundert* (Cologne and Vienna, 1979), 214.

[35] Brüske, *Untersuchungen*, 94–6.

[36] Petersohn, *Ostseeraum*, 262–77.

With a large suite of clerics Otto travelled via Poland to Pomerania, where he was welcomed by the Pomeranian Duke Wartislaw, who agreed to support the work of evangelization.[37] Otto preached in several places in Pomerania, but at the beginning he was not very successful. Only when the duke of Poland threatened punitive measures, but at the same time, because of Otto's intervention, promised to mitigate the tribute in case of conversion, did Otto get his way with the Pomeranians.[38] So he was finally able to destroy some pagan sanctuaries, to found some churches, and to install Christian priests in nine places in Pomerania.

Soon after he had returned to Bamberg in the spring of 1125, however, a pagan reaction started in the towns of the Oder, Wollin, and Stettin. The pagan priests certainly did not dare to destroy the Christian sanctuaries, but they allowed the people to worship the 'German God' side by side with the heathen idols. This illustrates the character of this pagan religion as a tribal religion. Since every tribe or people had its own God, it seemed possible to gain the assistance of the powerful German God too by worshipping both the pagan and the Christian God side by side.[39] But the German priests and the Pomeranian duke could not agree to that. Therefore they urged Bishop Otto to come for a second time to resume and complete the work of evangelization.

In the mean time, the political situation had changed considerably. After 1125, Wartislaw of Pomerania, whose position had been consolidated by the war against Bolesław, had invaded and annexed the Liutizian land between the lower Oder and the Peene.[40] This territorial expansion of the Pomeranian duchy involved a shift in its political orientation toward the German Reich. Lothar of Supplinburg, who in 1125 had just been elected king, presumably agreed to, and maybe even assisted, Wartislaw's

---

[37] Ibid. 217–24; Robert Bartlett, 'The Conversion of a Pagan Society in the Middle Ages', *History*, 70 (1985), 185–201.

[38] *Vita Prieflingensis*, i.e. *Sancti Ottonis episcopi Babenbergensis vita Prieflingensis*, 2. 10, ed. Jan Wikarjak and Kazimierz Liman, *MPH*, NS 7/1 (Warsaw, 1966), 114; Herbord, *Dialogus de vita sancti Ottonis episcopi Babenbergensis*, 2. 30, ed. Jan Wikarjak and Kazimierz Liman, *MPH*, NS 7/3 (Warsaw, 1974), 118–21; cf. Ebo, *Vita sancti Ottonis episcopi Babenbergensis*, 2. 18, ed. Jan Wikarjak and Kazimierz Liman, *MPH*, NS 7/2 (Warsaw, 1969), 86–7; Petersohn, *Ostseeraum*, 218 with nn. 21–2; Bartlett, 'Conversion', 194–7.

[39] Petersohn, *Ostseeraum*, 219 with n. 31; cf. Bartlett, 'Conversion', 190–1.

[40] Petersohn, *Ostseeraum*, 219–20 with n. 32; Brüske, *Untersuchungen*, 94–100.

subjection of the northern Liutizi.[41] So we are not surprised to
hear that in 1128 it was not the Polish Duke Bolesław but the
German King Lothar and his representative, Albert the Bear, then
margrave of Lusatia, who safeguarded the second missionary
expedition of Bishop Otto to Pomerania. Thus at this time Otto
travelled not via Gnesen but via Magdeburg and Havelberg.[42] In
Magdeburg he learned that the archbishop was not willing to foster
his missionary activities in the church province Norbert looked
upon as his own. In Havelberg he was informed by the Wendish
Count Witikind that Norbert's endeavours to convert the Wends
around Havelberg had turned out a total failure and had only
provoked the hatred of the Slavs against the archbishop.[43]

Having arrived in Pomerania, Otto at first went to the island of
Usedom where Duke Wartislaw had assembled all the nobles and
representatives of the towns of west Pomerania. Meeting Otto's
demands, all those assembled there decided to adopt the Christian
faith and were promptly baptized.[44] At last the Christianization of
the Pomeranians proved successful. But just at this very moment,
Bolesław prepared for a new invasion; obviously he was disappointed at the Pomeranian duke's approach to the German
king. Otto now hurried to Bolesław and succeeded in bringing
about peace by offering the renewed recognition of Polish
overlordship by Duke Wartislaw. Otto's repeated contact with the
Polish prince, however, incurred the displeasure of King Lothar,
who ordered him to come back at once.[45]

But by this time the work was done in Pomerania: the power of
paganism had been broken, and the foundations for the Pomeranian
Church could be laid without provoking any new bloodshed. The
Polish chaplain Adalbert, who had been delegated by Duke
Bolesław to attend Bishop Otto and who was now provided by
the latter as bishop of the Pomeranian diocese, could not be
installed in his see in Wollin before 1140. The delay was due to
long quarrels, at first about the founding of an autonomous
Pomeranian Church, later about the submission of this Church to

[41] Petersohn, *Ostseeraum*, 220–1 with n. 34.   [42] Ibid. 221–2.
[43] Ebo, *Vita Ottonis*, 3. 3, pp. 99–100; Dietrich Claude, *Geschichte des
Erzbistums Magdeburg bis in das 12. Jahrhundert* (2 vols., MF 67, Cologne, 1972–
5), ii. 16–17.
[44] Herbord, *Dialogus*, 3. 3, pp. 152–5; Ebo, *Vita Ottonis*, 3. 6, pp. 104–6;
Petersohn, *Ostseeraum*, 222–3 with n. 40.
[45] Petersohn, *Ostseeraum*, 223 with nn. 41–5.

the Polish province of Gnesen or the German province of Magdeburg. The pope solved the problem by exempting the Pomeranian diocese, himself ordaining Adalbert the first bishop of Pomerania and attaching the bishopric to papal control. In 1175 the episcopal see of Pomerania was transferred to Kammin (Kamień).[46]

At this time, when Bishop Otto of Bamberg was successfully evangelizing the Pomeranians and when Archbishop Norbert of Magdeburg was making an unsuccessful new attempt to preach the Christian faith to the Wends in the Havel valley, a similar new effort was made with the Abodrites too. Archbishop Adalbero of Bremen (1123–48) once more endeavoured to set up the suffragan bishoprics and to establish his own ecclesiastical province in the Slav country. Thus in the autumn of 1126, he ordered the former master of the Bremen cathedral school, the priest Vicelin, to go to the seat of the Abodrite King Henry in Old Lübeck and to preach the gospel there. [47] But when King Henry died in the following spring, the attempt to make Old Lübeck a new missionary centre in the Abodrite lands proved a failure again. There are some indications suggesting that it may have been these very missionary efforts that cost Henry his life, that is, that he was murdered.[48] During the same year, the Wendish count of Brandenburg, Meinfrid, who may have been one of Henry's governors, was also murdered. Like Henry of Lübeck and Witikind of Havelberg, Meinfrid was a Christian with a German name, who ruled over pagan Slavs.[49]

With regard to Havelberg, however, we do not know of any heathen reaction before 1136, when the sons of Witikind, who were pagans or apostates, destroyed the church in the fortress.[50] After King Henry's death, his sons did not succeed in seizing their father's kingdom. In 1129, King Lothar III entrusted the Abodrite kingdom to Canute Laward, duke of Schleswig and nephew of the Danish King Nicholas (Niel).[51] With the active assistance of the Holsatian levies, Canute succeeded in securing the kingship over the Abodrites, but in 1131 was murdered by his Danish cousin

[46] Ibid. 262–300, 309–15.
[47] Lammers, *Geschichte Schleswig-Holsteins*, 263–70.
[48] Fritze, 'Probleme', 183 n.339.
[49] Lotter, *Konzeption*, 57 with nn. 174–5.
[50] Kahl, *Slawen*, 90–1; Lotter, *Konzeption*, 58 with n. 178.
[51] Kahl, *Slawen*, 90–1 with nn. 95 and 98.

Magnus.[52] After that two Slav princes took power, the Nakonid
Pribislaw in Wagria and Polabia and a certain Niclot in the eastern
regions of the Abodrites. Both of them may have been Christians
nominally, but they did not permit any further attempts to
Christianize the Abodrites.[53] Now there was no way left to
evangelize the Wends without bloodshed.

At that time, Vicelin had founded a convent of Augustinian
canons in Neumünster on the Holsatian–Wagrian frontier and
became its provost. After having unsuccessfully attempted to
convert the Slavs, he made Neumünster a centre of spiritual care
among the Holsatians, who, as Helmold relates, were considered
semi-pagans.[54] Vicelin did not content himself with that, but in
1134 induced King Lothar III and Count Adolf of Nordalbingia to
build a castle on the hill of Segeberg, which was just beyond the
Holsatian–Slavic frontier, as an outpost of a new policy of
Christianization in the Slav country. At the foot of the Segeberg
hill Vicelin built a new convent of canons, and land in the
surrounding area was assigned to settlers coming from Saxony.[55]
In the same year, 1134, King Lothar gave the Nordmark to Albert
the Bear, and in 1136 the March of Lusatia to Margrave Conrad,
who united it with his March of Meissen and thus laid the
foundations of the later Wettin electorate of Saxony.[56] In 1136 and
1137/8, Margrave Albert gained a first foothold in his march by
crossing the Elbe and descending on the Prignitz Slavs.[57]

In 1137 King Lothar died. Now the German princes, again
contrary to all expectations, did not elect his Welf son-in-law
Henry the Proud, the strong duke of Bavaria and Saxony, but the
Hohenstaufen candidate Conrad.[58] The result was a violent
struggle between the Welfs and the Hohenstaufen, which had the
most severe consequences for Saxony and the Saxon marches.
King Conrad III did not recognize the Welf's title to Saxony, but
invested Albert the Bear with the duchy of Saxony, and likewise
gave Nordalbingia to Henry of Badwide in lieu of Adolf II. The

---

[52] Lammers, *Geschichte Schleswig-Holsteins*, 237–49.
[53] Lotter, *Konzeption*, 57 n. 173.
[54] Lammers, *Geschichte Schleswig-Holsteins*, 270–5.
[55] Ibid. 277–80.
[56] Ibid. 282–3; Seibt, *Handbuch der europäischen Geschichte*, ii. 328 nn. 16 and
18; Schultze, *Mark Brandenburg*, 67–8.
[57] Schmidt, *Mark Brandenburg*, 27.
[58] Seibt, *Handbuch der europäischen Geschichte*, ii. 332–3.

following conflict between the Welf and the Hohenstaufen candidates lacerated Saxony and Nordalbingia. Now it was Pribislaw who took advantage of this situation by invading Holsatia and burning down the castle, church, and settlements of Segeberg and the convent of Neumünster.[59] It was the last raid into the Holsatian borderland by the Slavs.

THE CONQUEST OF WAGRIA AND POLABIA

The long period of peace on the Saxon–Slavic frontier, which was made possible by the consolidation both of the Slav kingdom of Henry of Lübeck and the duchy of Saxony under Lothar III, had stabilized the frontier region. But now the Saxons, and in particular the Holsatians, were unwilling to suffer any new afflictions or menaces to their existence. And the Holsatians, who had for quite a long time served King Henry of Lübeck as mercenaries, were not only skilled in arms but had also established their own militia, the leader of which, the so-called *overbode*, they appointed themselves.[60]

In the first winter following the Wendish raid, when all the swamps were frozen and could be crossed, Count Henry of Badwide assembled the Holsatian levies and ravaged the whole of Wagria, but failed to seize the fortified places. In the following summer, however, the controversy between the Hohenstaufen and Welf factions paralysed the frontier policy of the Saxon duchy. But now the Holsatians, as Helmold relates, seized the opportunity to take their revenge on the Slavs. Without their feudal lord, they marched off and devastated the entire Slav land; after having taken the strongest fortress, Plön, by storm, they slew all the inhabitants.

Helmold's comment upon this is even more remarkable than the occurrence itself: the Holsatians waged a very useful war, because nobody was there to hinder them. For the Saxon princes always used to spare the life of the Slavs for the sake of getting more tribute.[61] The argument Helmold here employs is a leitmotif of his

---

[59] Lammers, *Geschichte Schleswig-Holsteins*, 286–90.
[60] Ibid. 4–16, 288–9.
[61] Helmold, *Cronica Slavorum*, 1. 56, p. 110: 'Holzati . . . etiam *sine comite* castrum Plunem . . . obtinuerunt Slavis qui inibi erant occisioni traditis.

chronicle, which he had adopted from his predecessor Adam of Bremen. Adam, in the 1070s, wrote a history of the archbishops of Hamburg-Bremen, a work which Helmold copied and continued. Both clerics accused the Saxon princes of avarice, because they did not care about the evangelization of the Slavs, but only about their personal income. Unlike the glorious kings of former times such as Charlemagne, Henry I, and Otto I, the Saxon princes were not only neglectful of, if not positively disinclined towards, the conversion of the Slavs to Christianity, but even, by excessive suppression and exploitation, several times caused them to apostatize and return to heathendom.[62]

Those events and the chroniclers' comments upon them throw light upon the attitudes towards the Slavs of the various secular and ecclesiastical strata of German society on the eve of the conquest of the region east of the Elbe. The upper classes, the German and especially the Saxon nobility, did not seem to be very interested in Christianization, nor even in direct rule over the Slavs. They preferred to co-operate with Slav vassal kings and princes in order to raise tribute and to fight their personal opponents—no matter if they were Germans or Slavs, Christians or heathens. The free middle classes in the German frontierland entered the service of German and Slav princes and fought side by side with Slav allies like the Abodrites against other Slavs like the Liutizi, Rugians, or even Poles, no matter if they were heathens or Christians. But when the Slavs, after the collapse of this system of alliances, started to raid the frontierland again, the Saxons and above all the Holsatians were determined to beat back that new threat to their existence by all means, even by exterminating the Slav enemies. The lower clerics, who had abandoned the hope they formerly entertained of winning over the Slavs by preaching Christianity peacefully, now also pleaded for force. The higher clergy and the episcopate up to that time had not yet lost hope of converting the Slavs by missionary preaching; but whereas this

Gesseruntque eo anno *bellum perutile* . . . quod invenissent libertatem ulciscendi se de Slavis nemine scilicet obstante. Nam principes Slavos servare solent tributis suis augmentandis . . .'

[62] Friedrich Lotter, 'Bemerkungen zur Christianisierung der Abodriten', in Helmut Beumann (ed.), *Festschrift für Walter Schlesinger* (2 vols., MF 74, Cologne, 1973–4), ii. 395–442, at 396–7 n. 6, 407–15 with nn. 51–2 and 77. See Adam of Bremen, *History of the Archbishops of Hamburg-Bremen*, trans. F. J. Tschan (New York, 1959).

method had been successful to some extent in the more distant Pomerania, it had time and again failed in the neighbouring regions of the Elbe Slavs. So here resignation began to spread.

We do not know exactly what happened in the Slav borderland east of Holsatia during the years after the death of Duke Henry the Proud in 1139, but there are indications that all the land was laid waste by the Holsatians and most of its inhabitants slain or expelled. When in 1143 the controversies between the Hohenstaufen and Welf factions finally were settled, the duchy of Saxony was adjudged to the young Welf Henry the Lion, son of Henry the Proud. Adolf II of Schauenburg not only retained Nordalbingia, but gained Wagria too and so laid the first foundations for the later duchy of Holstein. Henry of Badwide, however, got Polabia, which was now named the county of Ratzeburg. Both counts now called in peasants not only from nearby Holsatia, but also from Flanders, Westphalia, Holland, and Frisia, who settled in the newly conquered territories and built new villages and churches. Only in the north of Wagria did a Slav reservation remain under the Nakonid Pribislaw, who, as a vassal of Adolf, had to pay tribute.[63] In the same year, 1143, Count Adolf founded the town of Lübeck on the island between the Trawe and the Wakenitz. These rivers formed a large harbour which was not far from the old seat of the Abodrite King Henry in Old Lübeck. Count Adolf eventually secured the work of colonization by making friends with the ruler of the neighbouring eastern Abodrites, Niclot, and his noble followers.[64]

THE WENDISH CRUSADE: THEORY, PRACTICE, AND CONSEQUENCES

The new conquests north of the lower Elbe were not yet consolidated when the news reached Europe that the county of Edessa, the most advanced Christian bulwark in Mesopotamia, had fallen into the hands of the infidels. Not only were the archbishop and thousands of Christians slain, but the very existence of the Christian principalities and the Holy Land itself

---

[63] Lammers, *Geschichte Schleswig-Holsteins*, 291–7, 301–7.
[64] Helmold, *Cronica Slavorum*, I. 57, pp. 56–7; Lammers, *Geschichte Schleswig-Holsteins*, 314–23.

was jeopardized.[65] In December of 1145 the urgent pleas for help by the eastern Christians induced Pope Eugenius III to call upon King Louis VII and the French nobility to undertake a new crusade in order to defend the Oriental churches and the holy places against the infidels: by fighting like their fathers and the valiant Maccabees, so the pope announced, the crusaders would triumph again over the enemy and gain remission and absolution of all their sins.[66] Louis VII agreed to undertake an armed pilgrimage to the Holy Land. But there was no wave of enthusiasm until the Cistercian abbot of Clairvaux, Bernard, the most famous ecclesiastical leader of the time, began to preach the cross. Just as in the First Crusade, the common people and the lower clergy soon seized upon eschatological and Sibylline ideas, and the populace was stirred up by a vulgar crusading misconception.[67] In the Rhenish towns a Cistercian colleague of Bernard, Radulf, preached the cross and called upon the populace to kill the Jews as enemies of Christ who are at hand. When Archbishop Henry of Mainz complained about Radulf's activities, Bernard hastened to the Rhineland to reprimand and banish Radulf. As a consequence, Bernard took upon himself the task of preaching the cross in Germany too.[68]

A new appeal of Bernard's proclaimed the crusade as an event in salvation history, a 'time of acceptance', for everyone who had committed mortal sins, even a murderer, robber, or adulterer, could gain indulgence and sempiternal glory. He should act like a shrewd merchant and seize the opportunity to gain plenty at a low price.[69] Then Bernard entered into details concerning the situation

[65] Seibt, *Handbuch der europäischen Geschichte*, ii. 174–98 (R. C. Schwinges); Lotter, *Konzeption*, 7 n. 1.

[66] Eugenius III, *epistola* 48, *Patrologia latina*, clxxx, ed. J. P. Migne (Paris, 1855), cols. 1064–6: '. . . in peccatorum remissionem iniungimus, ut . . . ecclesiam Orientalem . . . defendere . . . studeatis . . . Sit vobis etiam in exemplum, bonus ille Mathathias . . .'

[67] Hans-Dietrich Kahl, 'Fides cum Ydolatria', in *Festschrift für Berent Schwineköper* (Sigmaringen, 1982), 291–307; Paul Alphandéry and Alphonse Dupront, *La Chrétienté et l'idée de croisade* (2 vols., Paris, 1954–9), i. 166–86, 203–8, and *passim*.   [68] Lotter, *Konzeption*, 7–8, 31–4 with n. 78.

[69] Bernard of Clairvaux, *epistola* 363, in his *Opera*, viii, ed. Jean Leclercq and H. Rochais (Rome, 1977), 311–17; Giles Constable, 'The Second Crusade as Seen by Contemporaries', *Traditio*, 9 (1953), 213–79, esp. 247; cf. Étienne Delaruelle, 'L'idée de croisade chez S. Bernard', in *Mélanges Saint Bernard* (Dijon, 1954), 53–67; Pierre Dérumaux, 'S. Bernard et les infidèles', *Mélanges Saint Bernard* (Dijon, 1954), 68–79.

of the Jews. They are not to be killed, for, as St Paul has said, 'until the fulness of the gentiles be come in . . . all Israel shall be saved' (Romans 11: 25–6). Bernard argues that this message of salvation could not be fulfilled if the Jews were slain. Therefore they are to be spared, for they are submissive. And then he continues: even the infidels had to be tolerated, if they had not engaged in violence by taking up the sword against Christians.[70] Here he adopts a dictum of Pope Alexander II which his contemporary Gratian inserted in his *Decretum*: 'the cases of the Jews and the Saracens are obviously different. We fight righteously against the latter who persecute and expel the Christians from their cities and homes, the former, however, are everywhere willing to serve'.[71] Bernard continues in exactly this sense by borrowing from Virgil: 'Christian piety means to beat down the proud, but to spare the subjugated'.[72] According to this position fighting against the pagans is thought to be necessary so long as they are attacking and suppressing Christian people.

In December 1146 Bernard succeeded in persuading King Conrad III and many German princes and nobles to take the cross. An Imperial Diet was announced for March 1147 in Frankfurt. But there the Saxon princes refused to join the eastern crusade. The motive may have been the unwillingness of the Welf partisans to submit to the leadership of the Hohenstaufen king, but however that may be, they presumably employed the pretext of feeling endangered by the pagan Slavs. At all events, the consultations of Bernard, the king, the prelates, and the princes resulted in the decision that all the nobles who had not yet taken the cross for the eastern crusade were allowed to take it on equal terms against the northern heathens beyond the Elbe.[73] Pope Eugenius III

---

[70] Bernard, *epistola* 363, *Opera*, viii. 316–17, but cf. Lotter, *Konzeption*, 26 n. 62: 'Plane et gentiles, si essent similiter subiugati, *meo quidem iudicio* essent similiter expectandi quam gladiis appetendi . . .'

[71] *Decretum*, C. 23, q. 8, c. 11, *Corpus iuris canonici* i, ed. E. Friedberg (Leipzig, 1879), col. 955.

[72] Bernard, *epistola* 363, *Opera*, viii. 62–3: 'Est autem christianae pietatis, ut debellare superbos, sic parcere subiectis'; cf. Virgil, *Aeneid*, vi. 853.

[73] Eric Christiansen, *The Northern Crusades* (London, 1980), esp. 51–7; Lotter, *Konzeption*, 8–9; id., 'Die Vorstellungen von Heidenkrieg und Wendenmission bei Heinrich dem Löwen', in Wolf-Dieter Mohrmann (ed.), *Heinrich der Löwe* (Göttingen, 1980), 11–43; Hans-Dietrich Kahl, 'Wie kam es zum Wendenkreuzzug?', in Klaus-Detlev Grothusen and Klaus Zernack (eds.), *Europa Slavica–Europa Orientalis: Festschrift für Herbert Ludat* (Berlin, 1980), 286–96.

approved of this decision and likewise authorized King Alfonso VII of Castile and any other crusaders to fight against the Muslims in the Iberian peninsula. That was not unusual, since already on the occasion of the First Crusade Pope Urban II had ordered the Spanish Christians not to join the eastern crusade but to bestow all their efforts on the restoration of the archbishopric of Tarragona. But now all the European heathens were considered objects of the crusaders' concern; the crusade had become universal.[74]

Pope Eugenius soon promulgated a new appeal for the Wendish Crusade. He opens by hinting at the widespread willingness to defend the Christians in the Orient; then he promises those who will fight the northern Slavs an analogous remission of sins, but only on condition that nobody takes money or other benefits from the heathens in exchange for allowing them to remain infidels.[75] With this rule he introduced a new element into the goal of the crusade: the Wendish Crusade aimed at subjugating the pagan Slavs to the Christian faith. But Eugenius doubted that the Saxons were really willing to pursue this end. Therefore Bishop Anselm of Havelberg was appointed papal legate and ordered to ensure peace and unity among the crusaders and incessantly to remind them of this aim.

At the same time, Bernard published a similar appeal with some remarkable additions. First he likewise characterizes the general crusade as a war of God, who 'aroused the spirit of kings, princes and bishops to take vengeance on the pagan tribes and wipe out the enemies from Christian land'.[76] As he had done in his general appeal, he outlines a Satan who will pine away with grief as soon as he sees the most damned criminals doing good. But here he adds a new remarkable detail: the devil now is most terrified since he

[74] Saxo Grammaticus, *Gesta Danorum*, 14. 3, ed. J. Olrik and H. Raeder (2 vols., Copenhagen, 1931–57), i. 376: 'Singule autem Catholicorum provincie confinem sibi barbariem incessere iubebantur'; cf. Constable, 'Second Crusade', 213–44.

[75] Eugenius III, *epistola* 166, *Patrologia latina*, clxxx, cols. 1203–4: 'nullus de paganis ipsis . . . pecuniam vel aliam redemptionem accipiat, ut eos in sua perfidia remanere permittat . . .'; cf. Lotter, *Konzeption*, 17.

[76] Bernard, *epistola* 457, *Opera*, viii. 432: '. . . ad faciendam vindictam in nationibus et exstirpandos de terra christiani nominis inimicos'; cf. Hans-Dietrich Kahl, 'Christianisierungsvorstellungen im Kreuzzugsprogramm Bernhards von Clairvaux', *Przeglad Historyczny*, 75 (1984), 453–61, who deduces from this and the following phrases Bernard's intention of doing away now with all the heathen in the world; but cf. also below, n. 81, and Lotter, *Konzeption*, 13–19.

fears that the time of conversion of all pagans is approaching, which precedes the last events.[77] By imputing this anxiety to Satan, Bernard restrains himself from placing the crusade openly in an eschatological perspective. However that may be, Bernard too sets the Wendish Crusade the goal of propagating the Christian faith. But he also justifies the campaign as a defensive war, for the devil had set up the (Wendish) pagans against the Christians who for too long a time had tolerated their wickedness. Now, however, the heathen's pride is to be humiliated finally, and this must not infringe upon the Jerusalem expedition. Bernard therefore appeals to those who take the cross 'to extinguish totally or at least convert these pagan tribes'. But since he entertains the same suspicions as the pope, he prohibits them severely 'from making any agreements with the heathens for money or tribute before either the pagan rite as such or the people is extinguished'.[78] The appeal concludes with some further instruction about discipline, organization, and the gathering of the army.

The most striking statement of this proclamation is the notorious alternative of extinction: either the rite or the people is to be extinguished. For quite a long time most commentators apparently had no doubt about what Bernard called for: baptism or death. Of course, this cruel alternative is a topos in literature from Carolingian times on and even from earlier times; and, what is more, at times had also been translated into reality, for example, when Charlemagne subjugated the Saxons and when fanatical crusaders murdered the Jews during the First Crusade.[79] Also there can be no doubt that contemporaries of Bernard not only considered the Second Crusade as the fulfilment of long-cherished eschatological expectations, but also understood Bernard's appeal and preaching in this sense. Later on Helmold of Bosau as well as other authors even blamed Bernard for having falsely announced that the final day was coming, and maintained that the general

---

[77] Bernard, *epistola* 457, *Opera*, viii. 432: 'malignus . . . aliud damnum veretur . . . de conversione gentium, cum audivit plenitudinem eorum introituram, et omnem quoque Israel fore salvandum. Hoc ei nunc tempus imminere videtur'; cf. Rom. 11: 25–6.

[78] Bernard, *epistola* 457, *Opera*, viii. 433: '. . . denuntiamus armari christianorum robur adversus illos et ad delendas penitus aut certe convertendas nationes illas signum salutare suscipere . . . Illud . . . interdicimus, ne qua ratione ineant foedus cum eis . . . donec auxiliante Deo aut ritus ipse aut natio deleatur.'

[79] Lotter, *Konzeption*, 34–8.

crusade had aimed at the conversion of all infidels in the whole world.[80] But was that really Bernard's conception and, if so, could it justify the alternative in the sense mentioned-above, as is claimed by Hans-Dietrich Kahl?[81]

Of course, Bernard was always quite willing to see the events of his time in an eschatological light, and, moreover, he interpreted the issues of the Second Crusade in that sense. But if we look at his statements—of which there is no want—we do not find any evidence that he ever took it for certain that the last days were imminent. He was certainly always ready to face them, but he reckoned with their imminence as a possibility, not as a certainty.[82] When he, in his general appeal, declared that the Jews are not to be persecuted, he explicitly stressed the point that all of them might be converted before the final day, but this obviously was not yet in sight. Like the pope, he therefore announced the Wendish Crusade as a war which God wanted (*Deo volente*), as a just war, as it was defined by St Augustine,[83] as a defensive war against the felonious pagans who were set up against the Christians by the devil. Of course, as far as we know, by this time there had been peace on the Elbe frontier for several years, but even during those years the recurrent inroads by Wendish pirates on the Danish islands increased in frequency and caused havoc.[84] So Bernard had reason enough to accuse the pagans of hostility and aggression. Maybe for that reason the campaign was clearly aimed at the Baltic Slavs and spared the Wends in the Havel region.

But it was the goal of converting the pagan Slavs that, above all,

---

[80] Helmold, *Cronica Slavorum*, 1. 59, pp. 114–15: '. . . dicens appropiare tempora quo plenitudo gentium introire debeat . . .'; *Cronica sancti Petri Erfordensis moderna*, s.a. 1147, ed. Oswald Holder-Egger, *Monumenta Erphesfurtensia* (*SRG*, Hanover and Leipzig, 1899), 117–369, at 176: '. . . quorundam . . . hominum sermonibus territi . . . dicencium illud apostoli quod instaret dies Domini . . .'; cf. Lotter, *Konzeption*, 27–30.

[81] Hans-Dietrich Kahl, 'Die Ableitung des Missionskreuzzugs aus sibyllinischer Eschatologie', in Z. H. Nowak (ed.), *Die Rolle der Ritterorden in der Christianisierung und Kolonisierung des Ostseegebiets* (Colloquia Torunensia 1, Toruń, 1983), 129–39; id., 'Christianisierungsvorstellungen', *passim*.

[82] Bernard McGinn, 'St Bernard and Eschatology', in *Bernard of Clairvaux: Studies Presented to Dom Jean Leclercq* (Cistercian Studies Series 23, Washington, 1973), 161–85, esp. 170–1, 181–5.

[83] Cf. Gratian, *Decretum* C. 23, q. 4, c. 9, col. 933; Frederick H. Russell, *The Just War in the Middle Ages* (Cambridge, 1975), 16–85; Brundage, *Medieval Canon Law*, 3–45.

[84] Helmold, *Cronica Slavorum*, 1. 67, p. 124; Saxo, *Gesta Danorum*, 14. 2, i. 374.

distinguished this operation from other wars of this epoch against heathens and even from other crusades. And with regard to the alternative mentioned above, Bernard went even further than Pope Eugenius. But did he really call upon the crusaders to kill all the heathens who were not willing to be baptized? Against the background of canon law and the theological doctrine of the time, which were well known to a leading representative of the higher clergy like Bernard, this would have seemed a monstrosity. And there is no evidence that Bernard regarded the Elbian and Baltic Slavs as apostates; if this had been the case, the use of force for the sake of bringing them back to Church would have been sanctioned by the Church Fathers.[85]

But when we now enter into a more thorough analysis of the text of Bernard's appeal, we notice that he uses the verbe *delere* (destroy) only twice and then in connection with the collective term *natio(nes)*, and never relates it to Slav individuals, whom he nevertheless apostrophizes five times.[86] This can be no accident. Pagan individuals certainly form a *natio* or *nationes*, and they are united by tribal bonds. Even if the term *natio* is not always defined as precisely as the notion *populus* or *gens*, there can be no doubt what it means here: a nation is a human community united by origin, customs, language, law, etc.[87] To destroy such a community does not necessarily mean to kill the individuals, but it certainly means to destroy the communal bonds and traditions; and this can be done in various ways like subjugating, enslaving, or expelling the individuals or some of them from their homeland.

The actual meaning of Bernard's alternative 'ritus aut natio deleatur' can now be better understood: the Wends are to be allowed to continue to exist in national units under their own chiefs if they are willing to convert as the Poles and the Bohemians

---

[85] Lotter, *Konzeption*, 10–12, 34–8; cf. Hans-Dietrich Kahl, 'Compellere intrare: Die Wendenpolitik Bruns von Querfurt', in Helmut Beumann (ed.), *Heidenmission und Kreuzzugsgedanke in der deutschen Ostpolitik des Mittelalters* (Wege der Forschung 7, Darmstadt, 1963), 177–274.

[86] Lotter, *Konzeption*, 15–16 nn. 32–3.

[87] Cf. Regino of Prüm, *Epistula ad Hathonem archiepiscopum missa*, ed. Friedrich Kurze, *Reginonis . . . chronicon* (*SRG*, Hanover, 1890), pp. xix–xx: 'diversae nationes populorum inter se discrepant genere, moribus, lingua, legibus'; cf. Hans-Dietrich Kahl, 'Einige Beobachtungen zum Sprachgebrauch von *Natio*', in Helmut Beumann and Werner Schröder (eds.), *Aspekte der Nationenbildung im Mittelalter* (Nationes 1, Sigmaringen, 1978), 63–109, esp. 65–6, 77–87, but with different conclusions.

had done long ago or the Pomeranians shortly before. But if they refuse to do that, their political organization should be destroyed and they should be subjugated by Christian rulers, as had recently happened to the Wagrians and Polabians. In fact, in these words Bernard unconsciously defined the historical alternative the western Slavs in the region east of the Elbe had to face. Christianization now was inevitable, and it was only a question how it was to be carried out, by native or by alien rulers.

In any case Christianization by conquest was now justified by the connotation which was contained in the passage 'natio deleatur'. It is a term adopted from the Old Testament, above all from Deuteronomy, that relates the situation of the Wendish Crusade to the conquest of Canaan by the Israelites.[88] This comparison again seems to illustrate that the Wendish Crusade was not merely understood as a defensive or punitive war, but as a war of conquest: as the Israelites, on the order of God, destroyed the peoples of Canaan, so the crusader shall crush all Wendish tribes that will not agree to be baptized. Thus the biblical reference serves as a justification of the cruel alternative, as it was interpreted above: as in biblical Canaan the indigenous were to be killed only in so far as they would fight back and all those who would submit were to be spared. However, Bernard, just like the pope, is not sure that the crusaders would comply with his demands, and therefore forbids them severely to enter into agreements with the pagans before they are either baptized or wiped out as a nation. These suspicions soon turned out to be well founded.

The Saxon princes, as it seems, did not feel enthusiastic about waging war against the Slavs. When Niclot, after having learned about the preparations, asked the count of Holstein for a conference, Adolf refused, since he had to consider the other Saxon princes; but he implored his Slav friend to stick to their alliance.[89] And even when Niclot thereupon started a preventive raid and ravaged Lübeck and the borderland, Adolf of Holstein, as far as we know, did not join the crusaders. Two columns marched out of Saxony; the northern one was commanded by the Welf Duke Henry the Lion and Conrad of Zähringen, later his

---

[88] Cf. esp. Deut. 4: 38: 'ut deleret nationes maximas . . . daretque tibi terram eorum in possessionem'; cf. Lotter, *Konzeption*, 38–43.

[89] Helmold, *Cronica Slavorum*, 1. 62, pp. 62–3.

father-in-law, the southern one by Bishop Anselm of Havelberg, the Margraves Albert and Conrad, and the Count Palatine Hermann, all the latter partisans of the Hohenstaufen faction. The northern army aimed at Niclot's territory and laid siege to the fortress of Dobin, which was also attacked from the north by the Danes. The southern army marched against western Pomerania and the fortified towns of Demmin and Stettin. Another army of Poles and even orthodox Russians was to attack the pagan Prussians.[90]

Now the most important sources are unanimous that in both the German armies the ordinary soldiers accused the princes and their vassals of sparing the lives of the Slavs and stopping the army from attacking the enemies and taking the fortresses by storm. Helmold laments the lax conduct of the war by the vassals of Duke Henry and Margrave Albert, which he explains by their disinclination to waste their own future land and to curtail their own future income by fighting the Slavs.[91] The Annalist of Pöhlde reports that the knights were rebellious and had already begun to distribute the land which was not yet conquered.[92]

A third chronicler, Vincent of Prague, accuses the leaders of the southern army, Margrave Albert and Bishop Anselm, of taking advantage of the crusade for their own territorial interests.[93] Obviously both laid claim to the old Nordmark and the old diocese of Havelberg at the cost of the western part of Pomerania and the bishopric which had been installed there some years previously. So they fought against both pagan and Christian Pomeranians. But when they arrived in front of Stettin, the inhabitants put crosses on the walls. Eventually the Saxon bishops entered into a peace agreement with the Pomeranian Bishop Adalbert and the Duke Ratibor, and the army went home. Similarly the leaders of the northern army, after a crushing defeat of the Danes at Dobin, made an agreement with Niclot to retreat on condition that the Abodrites be baptized and all the Danish prisoners released. Helmold states sadly that the great expedition was only a modest

[90] *Annales Magdeburgenses, s.a.* 1147, ed. Georg Pertz, *MGH, SS* 16 (Hanover, 1859), 105–96, at 188; cf. Lotter, *Konzeption*, 70–2; id., 'Heidenkrieg', 21–4.
[91] Helmold, *Cronica Slavorum*, 1. 65, pp. 122–3.
[92] *Annales Palidenses, s.a.* 1147, ed. Georg Pertz, *MGH, SS* 16 (Hanover, 1859), 48–98, at 82.
[93] Vincent of Prague, *Annales, s.a.* 1147, ed. Wilhelm Wattenbach, *MGH, SS* 17 (Hanover, 1861), 658–83, at 663; cf. Lotter, *Konzeption*, 72–5.

success, for the Slavs did not take their baptism seriously and went on to ravage the Danish coasts.[94]

THE FINAL CONQUEST OF THE REGION EAST OF THE ELBE

Contrary to the opinions of contemporary authors, the Wendish Crusade did not prove fruitless in every respect. In the next year Saxon princes assisted Bishop Anselm in restoring his old see in Havelberg; and there even Duke Ratibor appeared and promised by oath that henceforth he would do his utmost to defend and propagate the Christian faith in Pomerania.[95] In the spring of 1149, Pope Eugenius instructed his legate Guido to negotiate with the Saxons about reinstating bishops in 'Leutizia'; he obviously meant the suffragans of the archbishop of Hamburg-Bremen in the land of the Abodrites. In the same year the newly elected archbishop of Bremen, Hartvig, a bitter enemy of Duke Henry, went to Rome to negotiate about the same business. Without so much as asking the duke, he thereupon, in 1149, ordained the provost Vicelin and a certain Emmehard bishops of two of the Abodrite dioceses; Vicelin went to Oldenburg, Emmehard to Mecklenburg.[96]

But now it turned out that Duke Henry did not care a damn for Christianizing the Slavs if his power politics were affected. He claimed not only overlordship over the Abodrites, but also the right to invest the bishops in their dioceses. Archbishop Hartvig, however, rejected this claim, which he considered a usurpation of royal rights. Whereas Hartvig forbade the bishops he had ordained to accept investiture from the duke, the duke stripped them of all means to carry out their functions for as long as they did not recognize his claim. But when in 1150 Vicelin eventually gave in, he was only poorly rewarded. For no less than ten years Henry paralysed missionary activity in order to compel the secular and ecclesiastical authorities to recognize his right to the investiture of bishops in the Slav land. In 1152 Frederick I of Hohenstaufen, a cousin and friend of Henry, was elected king. He was determined to re-establish the power of the Hohenstaufen kingdom by closely

---

[94] Helmold, *Cronica Slavorum*, i. 65, p. 123.
[95] Lotter, *Konzeption*, 76–7, 98; Jordan, *Bistumsgründungen*, 81–2.
[96] Jordan, *Bistumsgründungen*, 83–4.

co-operating with the mighty Welf duke. For that purpose he gave Henry a free hand in northern Germany and, in 1154, delegated the royal right of investiture to Henry the Lion. Henry promptly exercised the right and invested a bishop in Ratzeburg who had not been ordained before by the competent archbishop. It was not until 1158/9 that the king was able to induce Archbishop Hartvig and Pope Adrian IV to approve Henry's claim.[97] Now the new bishoprics could at last be adequately endowed. After Duke Henry, in 1158, had compelled Count Adolf of Holstein to surrender Lübeck to him, he reorganized it as a ducal town and bestowed upon it a very favourable municipal law. In 1160, he also translated the episcopal see from Oldenburg to Lübeck.[98]

Nevertheless up to this time not even the Christianization of the Wagrian Slavs had made much progress. Helmold relates a discussion between Gerold, the successor of Vicelin in his function as bishop of Oldenburg, and the Wagrian Prince Pribislaw in 1156. After having destroyed a pagan sanctuary in Wagria, Gerold preached the gospel to a Slav district assembly in Lübeck and requested them to be baptized and stop robbing and murdering the Christians. Pribislaw argued that the Saxon lords used to enslave and exploit the Slavs in such a ruthless way that death seemed better to them than life. He asked how the Slavs were expected to adopt the new faith, accept baptism and build churches, if at the same time they lived in permanent fear of being expelled. Under the circumstances they could hardly be blamed for securing their living by looting Danes and merchants. Gerold justified the Saxon princes by arguing that they did not believe maltreatment of idolaters and godless men to be sin. On the strength of their vested rights the Saxon and all the other Christian peoples were living in peace; the Slavs, however, were susceptible to pillage because of their being dissociated from the religion of all the neighbouring peoples. Pribislaw retorted that they would just love to become Christians, build churches, and pay their taxes, as soon as the duke would give them titles to property and incomes equal to those of the Saxons.[99]

This dispute highlights the situation. Gerold admits that the grievances of the Slavs were not exaggerated at all, but he makes

---

[97] Ibid. 84–91.
[98] Karl Jordan, *Henry the Lion* (Eng. trans., Oxford, 1986), 69–72, 75–7.
[99] Helmold, *Cronica Slavorum*, 1. 84, pp. 160–2.

an offer that contains a promise: the Slav nobles will enjoy the same privileges as the Saxon feudal lords, if they are willing to subdue themselves to the Christian faith and assist in leading their people the same way. Here Gerold does not speak the language of suppression but calls upon the Slavs to accommodate themselves to the customs and social laws of all neighbouring Christian peoples, the Saxons, Danes, and Poles. But Gerold conceals the fact that Duke Henry did not really care about the paganism of the Baltic Slavs, but about their resistance to his political power.

Gerold himself had to fight on two fronts: on the one hand he had to convince the duke in order to get the indispensable means he needed for his bishopric and missionary activities; on the other hand he had to persuade the pagans who were not yet ready to be converted.[100] And there were very few priests willing to preach the gospel to the Wagrians. Thus it happened that a certain priest Bruno, after having unsuccesfully attempted to Christianize the Wagrians in the environs of Oldenburg, asked Count Adolf to let some Saxons settle there. As Helmold relates, he did that because he knew their language and customs and thus was able to care for a familiar community. Only now could divine service be restored 'in the midst of the crooked and perverse nation', as Helmold quotes Philippians 2: 15.[101]

Soon afterwards Count Adolf II rebuilt the castle of Plön, where he founded a town and market too. At this time, Helmold continues, the Slavs withdrew and Saxons came to settle. Nevertheless, there remained some enclaves of Slavonic population in Wagria that made hard and unsuccessful mission work for the Saxon priests. Eventually, Count Adolf decided to make the Slavs adopt Christian customs and legal forms by force. He forbade them to practise their pagan customs such as swearing by holy trees, fountains, or stones, and ordered them to go to church on holidays and to bury their dead in the Christian cemetery. But it was not only Christian traditions that were established by force, but also the German legal order with fine and ordeal.[102] Thus Christianization virtually meant Germanization too, which was

---

[100] Lotter, 'Heidenkrieg', esp. 17–19, 26–32.

[101] Helmold, *Cronica Slavorum*, 1. 84, p. 164: 'obtinuit apud comitem, ut fieret illic Saxonum colonia et esset solacium sacerdoti de populo, cuius nosset linguam et consuetudinem.'

[102] Lotter, 'Heidenkrieg', 33. The parallels to the measures of Charlemagne in Christianizing the Saxons are obvious, cf. ibid. n. 83.

enforced because of the Slavs' refusal to become Christians under their own leaders. Of course, this refusal was due to the ill-treatment of the Slavs by the Saxon princes in virtue of which the Slavs had come to identify Christianity with exploitation by German overlords. But now the Slav nobles began to realize that even under German overlordship they could maintain their social position by supporting the process of Christianization. But this again was not yet possible without acknowledging the rule of the Saxon duke.

Some time after the Wendish Crusade, Prince Niclot re-established his alliance with Count Adolf of Holstein. In 1151 he asked Adolf to assist him in subduing the Kissini and Circipani again. During this campaign the Holsatians destroyed a pagan sanctuary with all the idols without being hindered by their Abodrite allies.[103] By the mid-1150s the Cistercian monk Berno began to preach the gospel in the region of Mecklenburg. Even though he succeeded in destroying heathen idols and baptizing some pagans, his situation was very precarious. The Abodrites were not yet willing to keep their promise of baptism, and Christianization did not make any progress before Duke Henry backed it up by military force.[104]

It was the Abodrites themselves, however, who furnished Henry the Lion with reason for taking action. In 1159, King Valdemar I of Denmark bought Duke Henry's pledge to prevent the Slavs from making further raids on Danish territory, and Henry exacted a promise to that effect from Niclot and his nobles. But as soon as he went to Italy with King Frederick I, the Slavs again started to raid the Danish islands. Presumably the control of the Abodrite prince and nobles over their subjects was not yet strong enough to restrain them from operating spontaneously. In the spring of 1160, however, Duke Henry, after having returned from Italy, outlawed the Abodrites and mobilized the Saxon levies against them.[105]

It is possible that the repeated violations of the peace settlement suited Duke Henry very well by giving him the welcome opportunity to subdue the Abodrites to Christian rule after all.

---

[103] Lotter, 'Heidenkrieg', 34.

[104] Ibid. 34–5; but cf. Petersohn, *Ostseeraum*, esp. 60–2, 72–5 with nn. 89–90 on the charters forged during the boundary dispute between the dioceses of Kammin and Schwerin.

[105] Lotter, 'Heidenkrieg', 35–9.

Therefore, in 1163, he defined the goal of the campaign in a charter for the cathedral chapter of Lübeck as if it was a crusade. He adopts here the vulgar alternative 'baptism or death' by asserting that he 'was triumphant over the Slavs by leading the obedience of the submissive to (eternal) life by baptism, but the obstinacy of the proud to death by bloodshed'. This remark, however, which is an isolated one among no less than 120 charters, should not be taken too seriously. Christian ideas and theological arguments were only important for Henry inasmuch as they could be employed as justifications of his otherwise undisguised power politics.[106] These power politics, however, had nothing to do with national expansionism. Henry regarded the Slav and Saxon nobility alike as being either his allies, vassals, and assistants or bitter enemies who had to be crushed if they did not unconditionally submit.

Thus in 1160, Duke Henry, in alliance with King Valdemar I of Denmark, devastated the whole Abodrite land with fire and sword. Niclot retreated to the fortified town of Werle in the extreme east, but was killed in a sally. His sons, Pribislaw and Wartislaw, eventually submitted. Henry, however, decided to keep the conquered Abodrite territory, subdivided it into new administrative districts, and established new counties in Schwerin and Mecklenburg. In Schwerin he founded a new town and shortly afterwards vested it with the city law of Lübeck. As early as 1160, he transferred the bishopric of Mecklenburg to Schwerin and appointed the monk Berno bishop. Like the bishoprics of Lübeck and Ratzeburg, Schwerin was then furnished with 300 *Hufen* (hides), a *Hufe* being the usual holding of a German peasant family.[107]

The sons of Niclot were allotted only the territories of the Kissini and Circipani. They became vassals of Duke Henry, were to pay the Slavonic tithe and to redeem the promise of Christianization. But in 1163/4, the Niclotid princes formed an alliance with the Pomeranian Princes Casimar and Bogislaw I to reconquer their lost territories. This war can by no means be considered a pagan reaction, since there is no evidence of any persecution of

[106] Lotter, 'Heidenkrieg', 11–12, 36–7; Käthe Sonnleitner, 'Die Slawenpolitik Heinrichs des Löwen im Spiegel einer Urkundenarenga', *Archiv für Diplomatik*, 26 (1980), 259–80.
[107] Petersohn, *Ostseeraum*, 62–4 nn. 28–32.

Christians, after the Slavs had taken some Saxon castles. Indeed, it was nothing other than a genuine dynastic conflict: the Slav princes just wanted their inheritance. Even Henry did not fail to realize the legitimacy of the Niclotid claims. Only after heavy losses and with the energetic assistance of Valdemar's fleet was Henry at last able to overcome the Slavs; and after Wartislaw was captured, he executed him. But later on he restored Pribislaw to his princedom.[108]

In the mean time the Danish kingdom under Valdemar I had strengthened remarkably and, because of the improvement of military technique and tactics, had succeeded in overcoming the Slav pirates. Brick towers and castles were built and, in combination with a newly installed system of coastal patrols, protected the islands; a new fleet of warships superior to the Slav boats was built and manned with excellent forces of archers.[109] When in 1168 the Rugians rebelled against Danish overlordship, Valdemar and his energetic Bishop Absalom of Roskilde at last decided to crush and Christianize the Rugians. Duke Henry, who at the time was engaged in suppressing a revolt of Saxon princes and nobles, ordered Pribislaw and the Pomeranian princes to assist Valdemar with their levies.[110] Presumably it was then that Henry realized that he depended on loyal supporters who would assist him against his internal enemies. Therefore he reinvested Pribislaw with his father's principality in the Abodrite territory, with the exception of the county of Schwerin. In this way Pribislaw, son of Niclot, became the ancestor of the dukes and later grand dukes of Mecklenburg.

With the assistance of his Slav allies, King Valdemar now invaded Rügen and fought a hard battle against the Rugians, after which they were forced to submit on condition that they abandoned paganism and were baptized. The sanctuary of Arkona with the huge idol of Svantevit was destroyed, and Danish and German priests began to preach the gospel and to build churches. Helmold relates that the Rugian Prince Jaromir when he came to know the true God and the Catholic faith, became a second Paul and, partly by preaching, partly by threatening, 'converted his

---

[108] Ibid. 64 nn. 35–6, cf. Lotter, 'Heidenkrieg', 39–40.
[109] Christiansen, *The Northern Crusades*, 64–5; on the development of archery in this period cf. Robert Bartlett, 'Technique militaire et pouvoir politique, 900–1300', *Annales: Économies, sociétés, civilisations*, 41 (1986), 1135–59, esp. 1138–9.
[110] Lotter, 'Heidenkrieg', 40–1 with n. 103.

crude people from its innate ferocity to the religion of the new way of life'.[111]

Pribislaw of Mecklenburg now became a loyal vassal of Duke Henry and a good Christian too. Thus during the next years, churches, abbeys, and houses of canons sprang into existence in the territories of the Baltic Slavs. In 1172 the Cistercian abbey of Doberan was founded by Pribislaw, that of Dargun by Casimar and other Slav nobles, and in 1173 another one was set up by Pomeranian nobles in Kolbatz east of the lower Oder. At the same time Premonstratensian convents were founded in Grobe on the island of Usedom and in Belbuk east of Kammin, where the Pomeranian bishopric was relocated about 1175.[112]

But there was no end to war. When King Valdemar refused to cede to Duke Henry half the tribute and territory of the island of Rügen, Henry ordered his Slav vassals, the Abodrites and Pomeranians, to attack the Danish coast with their navy. In order to compensate for the military inferiority of the Pomeranians, he sent to Casimar two archers, possibly foreign experts, who were to assist the Slavs in dealing with the Danish archers.[113] At last Valdemar gave in and made peace with Henry.[114] Some years later, in 1179, Henry ordered Casimar to invade the march of the Margrave Dietrich of Meissen with Pomeranian and Liutizian troops, who then devastated the land up to Lusatia.[115] But this was only a prelude to Henry's fall: in 1180 the Emperor Frederick I deposed Duke Henry and stripped him of all his fiefs.

By this time the territorial organization of the Baltic Slav lands had been settled finally. Most of the region was now incorporated in the territories of the Christian Slav dynasties in Pomerania and Mecklenburg. The one major problem that remained after the fall of Duke Henry the Lion was the question of sovereignty, which was now in dispute between the Reich and Denmark. But after the battle of Bornhöved in 1227 the issue was decided in favour of the

[111] Saxo, *Gesta Danorum*, 14. 39, i. 464–73; Helmold, *Cronica Slavorum*, 1. 108, pp. 211–12.

[112] Petersohn, *Ostseeraum*, 90–1, 326–8; Lotter, 'Heidenkrieg', 42; Christiansen, *The Northern Crusades*, 65.

[113] Saxo, *Gesta Danorum*, 14. 42, i. 484: 'Insignes ei sagittarii, Konon et Cirinus, fuere, ab Henrico in Sclavorum auxilium Danorum odio missi . . .'; cf. above, n. 109.

[114] Lotter, 'Heidenkrieg', 42 n. 108.

[115] Brüske, *Untersuchungen*, 116 n. 55; Schultze, *Mark Brandenburg*, 100 n. 17.

German emperor, although he had not taken an active part in the victory.[116] The princes of Slavonic origin, the dukes of Mecklenburg and Pomerania, like those of Silesia and Bohemia, were henceforth princes of the Reich, with rights and duties identical to the German princes. The offspring of Wartislaw I, soon called the 'Greifen', in Pomerania did not become extinct until 1637, and the Niclotids in Mecklenburg reigned up to 1918.

In the inland region between the middle Elbe and Oder, which, since 1134, was claimed by the Ascanian Albert the Bear as his march, political development took another course. In this region, the old territory of the Liutizian tribes, in contrast to the territories south of the Baltic coast, an extensive native sovereign power never could get a firm footing. Thus a political vacuum had grown up, which was invaded by the Abodrite kings and later the Pomeranian dukes from the north, by the Polish duke from the east, by the Wettin and Ascanian margraves and the archbishop of Magdeburg from the south and west. Only in the western part around the Havel valley before the mid-twelfth century did there exist a Slav princedom, under king Pribislaw-Henry of Brandenburg. The latter was a Christian like his predecessor Meinfrid and had both a Slavic and a German name. Margrave Albert after 1134 stabilized his position in the borderland by entering into friendship and alliance with King Pribislaw-Henry, analogous to the agreement between Count Adolf of Holstein and the Abodrite Prince Niclot. Before the Wendish Crusade Pribislaw-Henry, who was childless, had made Albert his heir as sovereign of the Brandenburg, and had destroyed the pagan idol of Triglav. In return, Albert presumably had promised to spare his territory during the crusade.[117]

After the crusade Albert succeeded in strengthening his grip on the land beyond the Elbe by taking possession of the castle of Havelberg in a joint action with Bishop Anselm. In 1150 King Pribislaw died, and Albert occupied the castle of Brandenburg. Soon afterwards, however, a Slav prince, Jacza of Köpenick, succeeded in capturing Brandenburg by way of treason. Jacza, who may have been a vassal of the duke of Poland, was Christian

---

[116] Seibt, *Handbuch der europäischen Geschichte*, ii. 896 with nn. 12–15 (A. v. Brandt); Lammers, *Geschichte Schleswig-Holsteins*, 393–401; Schultze, *Mark Brandenburg*, 137–8.

[117] Kahl, *Slawen*, *passim*, esp. 30–45, 55–65, 186–9.

too; but even if his attack was in no way a pagan reaction, the result was that the Hevelli of the region remained heathens It was not until 1157 that Albert, together with Archbishop Wichmann of Magdeburg, conquered Brandenburg finally.[118]

From that time the Ascanian margrave held the title of margrave of Brandenburg. Albert then succeeded in expanding his dominion over the whole Havel valley up to Potsdam. About this time Wichmann annexed the land of Jüterbog to the archdiocese of Magdeburg. In both the bishoprics of the new march, Premonstratensian convents were installed as cathedral chapters: in Havelberg this took place as early as 1150, in Brandenburg in 1161, when the convent was translated from Leitzkau.[119] When Albert had consolidated his new dominions, he made an appeal which he sent by emissaries to the lower Rhine region and the Low Countries. Helmold relates: 'He brought along a lot of people, Hollanders, Sealanders and Flemings, and let them dwell in the castles and villages of the Slavs. In virtue of the strangers the bishoprics of Brandenburg and Havelberg were improved, the churches multiplied and the tithes increased by far.'[120] As a matter of fact, the Frankish dialect of the immigrants has affected the dialect of the Brandenburgers far more strongly than the Saxon one has done. Many settlers from the Low Countries took possession of the river marshes or tablelands which up to that time had been sparsely populated, and most of the Slavs remained at the places they lived before.[121]

In 1171, Archbishop Wichmann founded the first Cistercian abbey in the Mark of Brandenburg at Zinna near Jüterbog, and in 1180 Margrave Otto I, son and successor of Albert (who had married a Polish princess), founded a second one at Lehnin south-east of Brandenburg.[122] In the 1190s the Ascanian margraves pressed forward against the tablelands of Barnim in the north and Teltow in the south. But it was not until 1230, after decades of struggling, above all against the Pomeranian dukes, that they were recognized as sovereigns of these territories.[123] By the mid-thirteenth century, however, they had already conquered the

---

[118] Kahl, *Slawen*, 327–36, 350–78, 384–94.
[119] Claude, *Magdeburg*, ii. 59–61, 94–100 with n. 169; Kahl, *Slawen*, 154–66.
[120] Helmold, *Cronica Slavorum*, 1. 89, pp. 174–5.
[121] Schultze, *Mark Brandenburg*, 87; Schmidt, *Mark Brandenburg*, 59–62.
[122] Schultze, *Mark Brandenburg*, 100–1.
[123] Wolfgang H. Fritze, 'Das Vordringen deutscher Herrschaft in Teltow und

Jckermark, the land of Lebus, and also some considerable tracts
of land east of the Oder. It was then that the Mark of Brandenburg
got its final shape.[124]

CONCLUSION

The reasons for the conquest, or rather the political and cultural
incorporation of the region east of the Elbe into the German Reich
of the Middle Ages, have nothing to do with any traditional racial
hostility, nor with any alleged 'Drang nach Osten' as was imputed
to the medieval Germans by modern Panslavistic and Pangermanistic
ideologies.[125] From the Carolingian to the Hohenstaufen epoch
the most constant impulse of this incorporation was Christianization,
but in the latest and most crucial period, the dynastic interests of
both German and Slav princes were also the main motives for
action. With regard to the conquests of the Ottonian kings in the
tenth century, only the Sorb marches remained under direct
German rule; but even in this case, that rule was exercised in co-
operation with Slav nobles and horsemen and did not encroach
upon the Slav village organization before the twelfth century,
when German immigration set in.

From the great Wendish rebellion of 983 up to the first decades
of the twelfth century all layers of German and Wendish societies,
Slavs and Saxons, mixed with one another on equal terms,
German and Slav princes and nobles co-operated, Christian and
pagan warriors fought side by side under Slav or German
command against other Slavs or Teutons (Poles, Liutizi, Danes),
both Christians and pagans. But after the First Crusade the
persisting paganism of the Wends interfered with these alliances,
and the question of faith became of more and more weight in their
mutual relations.

The Church, however, endeavoured in vain to raise armies of
knights and ordinary men against the pagans by promising both
the salvation of their souls and fertile land. During the Second
Crusade, it was mainly dynastic interests that caused Saxon princes

Barnim', in his *Frühzeit zwischen Ostsee und Donau*, ed. Ludolf Kuchenbuch and
Winfried Schich (Berlin, 1982), 297–374.

[124] Schultze, *Mark Brandenburg*, 136–59.
[125] Cf. Wolfgang Wippermann, *Der 'deutsche Drang nach Osten': Ideologie und
Wirklichkeit eines politischen Schlagworts* (Darmstadt, 1981).

and nobles to follow the appeal of Bernard of Clairvaux to
extinguish either paganism or the Wendish nations as such, as had
been done in the borderlands of Wagria and Polabia a short time
before. But even then the Saxon princes preferred the Wends to
be converted under their indigenous princes. Christianization
under Slav rule, however, had been successful in later time only in
Pomerania, since there the Slav lords themselves pressed it, after
Otto of Bamberg had preached the gospel. Yet Christianization
hindered the Abodrite princes in their prolonged efforts to
establish a strong Wendish commonwealth in the region, as had
been done in Poland or Bohemia; the result was a vacuum of
political weakness and unrest that caused intervention from all
sides. Only when the remaining territory of the Abodrite tribes
was Christianized was the Slav dynasty of the Niclotids able to
stabilize its rule under German overlordship. The western Abodrite
territories and the former Liutizian midlands, however, were
occupied by German lords directly. Thus the alternative of
Bernard of Clairvaux turned out to be the reflection of a historical
alternative: only by Christianization could the Slav nations retain
their state organization. But the belated Christianization in the
twelfth century east of the Elbe did not allow the Slavs to retain
their ethnic identity. At that time Christianization meant Germanization, after the Germans had won against the Poles and Danes
and occupied the political vacuum.

Only in some marginal western zones was the Slav population
eradicated or considerably diminished by bloody conquest. Even if
in some cases Slav peasants had to give way to German ones, the
Slav population not only survived as a massive ethnic substratum,
but also continued in existence, beside the Germans, in the higher
strata of society up to the ruling classes.[126] At the end of the
twelfth century, there was little difference between princes of
Slavonic or German origin with regard to politics, interests, and
cultural efforts. The settlement of German peasants was by no
means an invasion, since they were brought in by emissaries who
had been sent by both German and Slav (and prevailingly by Slav)
rulers. The motives of the latter were quite vulgar: to increase
wealth and revenues.

[126] Jan Brankačk, *Studien zur Wirtschaft und Sozialstruktur der Westslawen
zwischen Elbe–Saale und Oder aus der Zeit vom 9. bis zum 12. Jahrhundert*
(Bautzen, 1964), 184–203.

But we should not disregard the fact that there was another vacuum too, namely a lag behind technical civilization, particularly with regard to agricultural technique and economic efficiency. Without taking that into account, we could not explain the eagerness of even the Slav rulers to call in German peasants, burghers, and knights. After German peasants had started their settlement, which they first did on hitherto unpopulated marshy grounds and elevated plains, the superiority of German agriculture soon became known. This was not only due to the larger German land measure, the *Hufe*, but also, as it seems, to the German heavy plough with mould-board, which allowed deeper ploughing and the cultivation of heavy soil which had not been tilled before. The income from the German tithe, which came to a tenth of the actual product, was far more than that from the fixed tax on the Slavonic land measure, the 'hook', which had been named after the simpler Slavonic plough.[127] Soon both Slav and German lords realized that it meant considerably higher incomes than settlers under Slavonic law could ever furnish if they leased the soil under German law to Saxon or, in particular, Flemish peasants. Soon the Slavs had to adapt themselves to the new conditions and new way of life and let themselves also be settled under German law beside German settlers. But that meant Germanization too. The same effect was produced by the development of a new network of cultural centres through the foundation of abbeys and towns all over the land, by the introduction of new techniques and handicrafts, an advanced form of division of labour, and last but not least a more advanced market-controlled economy.[128] That does not mean that the Slavs had no culture or did not know town-life before. On the contrary, the relatively high standard of Slavonic civilization alleviated the rapid acculturation.[129]

Thus for most of the western Slavs, who were not Christianized before the twelfth century, the process of Christianization and acculturation meant Germanization too. First the Wendish dukes and nobles became Germans, and then the middle and lower

---

[127] Helmold, *Cronica Slavorum*, I. 12, 88, pp. 25, 174.
[128] M. M. Postan (ed.), *Cambridge Economic History of Europe*, i: *The Agrarian Life of the Middle Ages* (2nd edn., Cambridge, 1966), 452–9; but cf. Hermann, *Slawen*, 50–2; Brankačk, *Studien*, 144–6; F. L. Carsten, 'Slavs in North-eastern Germany', *Economic History Review*, 11 (1941), 61–76.
[129] Hermann, *Slawen*, esp. 73–122, 187–99, 219–20, 229–48; Brankačk, *Studien*, 93–146.

13

The Significance of the Frontier in the Middle Ages

ROBERT I. BURNS

The frontier is a heroic place to take one's stand. Who would not prefer to work on the frontiers of knowledge, the frontiers of art, the frontiers of outer space, or some New Frontier of politics? To any forward looking person, the frontier is a Good Thing. Sober academics must perforce don the coonskin cap, as improbable Clint Eastwoods of the lecture hall, venturing onto their own frontiers. The alternative is to be out of fashion, certainly not vital like the *Annales* crowd. On the other hand, the frontier in history, and its image in letters and film, is a concept umbilically attached to Frederick Jackson Turner, a historian half a century dead, whose theories have been savaged and repudiated. It is common to find Turner absurd, and by extension any multiplication of frontiers wherever descried. To be brave and forward-looking while simultaneously ridiculous and tied to a defunct tradition is an uncomfortable posture. In order to approach the significance of the frontier, then, one must first come to terms with the notion of frontier itself. This means confronting Turner and his Thesis. Turner has become a kind of vampire, killed on many a day with a stake through his Thesis, yet ever undead and stalking abroad. His paradigm for the history of the American West has currently transmogrified into separate varieties of neo-Turnerism. Their bibliography and historiography constitute, even today, a small industry.[1]

---

[1] Two recent introductions to and recastings of Turner are Donald Worster, 'New West, True West: Interpreting the Region's History', *Western Historical Quarterly*, 18 (1987), 141–56, and William Cronon, 'Revisiting the Vanishing Frontier: The Legacy of Frederick Jackson Turner', *Western Historical Quarterly*, 18 (1987), 157–76, with excellent bibliographical notes. See also Ray Allen Billington below in n. 5. On Turner himself (1861–1932) see Wilbur R. Jacobs (ed.), *The Historical World of Frederick Jackson Turner* (New Haven, 1968), and Ray Allen Billington, *Frederick Jackson Turner: Historian, Scholar, Teacher* (New York, 1973).

Though Turner pulled together many pre-existing themes, he took as his starting-point the conclusions confected under bizarre circumstances by an obscure Englishman, Robert Porter. Porter worked in the United States for three decades, as a journalist and in hack political jobs. Before returning to England, he supervised the haphazard and unreliable census of 1891, in which he deplored the passing of the 'frontier of settlement', since 'the unsettled area has been so broken into by isolated bodies of settlement that there can hardly be said to be a frontier line' with its 'westward movement'.[2] The frontier of settlement had not really disappeared, we now know; even in 1988 it covers '45 percent of the land area of the United States' where 'fewer than six people live per square mile', a region statistically more violent and dangerous than any urban ghetto.[3] Porter's incompetent census for his host country led to two lasting results—census reform and Turner's Thesis.

Turner's own West became a more slippery concept, not only a place, or at times a condition, but especially a 'process'—at once a physical movement of settlement into vacant land, an evolution through specific stages toward full civilization within each successive zone, and a psychological or imaginative transformation affecting the protagonists. This vision was chauvinist, unique to the United States; it was also pessimistic, after the nostalgic fashion of that day. As Donald Worster complains, Turner's process 'was a tangled web of many processes, all going on at once and including the whole development of American agriculture and industry, the history of population growth and movement, the creation of national institutions, and somewhere in the tangle, the making of an American personality type'. Worster turns shudderingly from this epic tangle to the more manageable if more provincial version of Walter Prescott Webb, whose West was simply geographic—the 'Arid Region' beyond the Mississippi into California.[4] Turner's own spin-off thesis about eight regions or 'sections' of the United States did little to clarify the confusion. When Turner's

---

[2] On Porter see Gerald D. Nash, 'Where's the West?', *Historian*, 49 (1986–7), 1–9, at 5–7; id., 'The Census of 1890 and the Closing of the Frontier', *Pacific Northwest Quarterly*, 71 (1980), 98–100.

[3] Peter Applebome, 'Some Say Frontier Is Still There', *New York Times* (12 Dec. 1987), 11, special report with map.

[4] Worster, 'New West', 144, detailing Turner's four processes and eight regions; 145–6 (Webb).

thinking did become clear, it was not very useful; when useful, it was not very clear.

Historians have salvaged elements from the Thesis, rearranged in novel forms. Some have broadened the definition of frontier. Some have repudiated the Thesis so strenuously as to become, by a kind of reactive acculturation or polarity, negative versions of Turner himself. Pragmatic scholars have retained his general vision or tone, without incorporating any of its specifics. Others have argued for one or other underlying specific. Defenders of the pure faith, exegetes of the master, are not lacking, with the prolific Ray Allen Billington a worthy standard-bearer through the decades. Wilbur R. Jacobs, reviewing 'the decade of controversy in the 1930s' over Turner, 'followed by searching criticism and reexamination in the years 1950 to 1970', hopefully concludes that at least 'the broad implications of his environmentalist view of the origins of the American nation are still generally accepted', that his work 'has encouraged a persistent debate about the nature of historical change', and that the Theory in that context 'remains one of the most important contributions to historical thought' ever made by an American. Margaret Walsh loyally presents Turner as a speculative point-of-departure, valuable for broad framework and not to be pursued rigorously, a jumping-off point to the wilderness interior. Jerome Steffen, an old hand on the comparative frontier, brings together four thematic frontiers in the American West (agriculture, fur trade, ranching, mining) to recast Turner in terms of more universal neo-Turnerian experience, where 'the demands of the environment and the mindset' of the intruders lead to both 'overt' and 'fundamental' (discontinuous) change.[5] In all the maze of bibliography, no one has come up with a truly competitive non-Turnerian approach by which to make sense of the American Western experience.

William Cronon has an appealing version of Turnerianism. He argues that Turner had no historiographical but rather a 'poetic' vision, which cannot be reduced to any logical thesis. It continues to hold us in thrall, and to pup variants of its original version:

[5] Ray Allen Billington, *Genesis of the Frontier Thesis: A Study in Historical Creativity* (San Marino, 1971); id., *The American Frontier Thesis: Attack and Defense* (American Historical Association pamphlet 101, Washington, 1971); id., *America's Frontier Heritage* (New York, 1966); Margaret Walsh, *The American Frontier Revisited* (Atlantic Highlands, NJ, 1981); Jerome Steffen, *Comparative Frontiers: A Proposal for Studying the American West* (Norman, Okla., 1980).

'However much we understand his analytical shortcomings, we still turn to him for our rhetorical structure.' Turner's vision supplies narrative structure and sense of movement, to fashion monographic themes into organic unity. It allows for comparative history from different spaces and eras. It encourages us to focus on the interaction between ordinary human beings and their landscape. It points up the dynamic between resources, as they wax or wane in the regional environment, and the settlers with their changing sets of constrictions and circumstances both local and international. Far from 'closing', this core of the frontier lets us 'trace his environmental dialectic as far backward or forward in time as we like'. Above all, the vision redefines and broadens frontiers, as contact-zones in which 'people of different cultures struggle with each other for control of resources and political power', so that 'environment' yields its centrality to 'contact zones of cultures'. Cronon believes Turner has bequeathed to us frontier questions which, when recast, 'remain very much alive'. He sees Turner as foreshadowing the *Annales* school, 'championing social history, quantification, *l'histoire problématique*, interdisciplinary studies, local case histories, "history from the bottom up", and the search for a relevant past'.

Turnerism thus becomes a call to study 'human beings working with changing tools to transform the resources' of an opened region (not just Turner's narrower idea of free land) 'and defining their notions of political and cultural community' within 'a context of shifting environmental and economic restraints'.[6] An important element in this broader approach is the substitution of zones of intercultural contact for Turner's winning of a wilderness, a substitution effected by a generation of historians, with contributions from anthropology and the social sciences. These human 'frontiers of exclusion' and 'frontiers of inclusion' or assimilation where invaders and invaded interact bid fair to replace the stricter neo-Turnerian systems which have 'gained sophistication but lost the elegant simplicity and force with which Turner's rhetorical excesses originally endowed it'.[7] With the frontier no longer

---

[6] Cronon, 'Revisiting the Frontier', esp. 161, 165, 170–3. On reactive anti-Turnerism dictating one's approach, see his confession on 160 n.

[7] David J. Weber, 'Turner, the Boltonians, and the Borderlands', *American Historical Review*, 91 (1986), 66–81, at 79–80. The exclusion/inclusion model comes from the geographer Marvin Mikesell (p. 72).

unique, frontiers were descried on all sides in modern history, notably in Australia, Brazil, Canada, Russia, South Africa, Latin America, and China (to which Owen Lattimore assiduously applied Turnerism).

One may select from among the neo-Turnerian adaptations, much as neo-Kantians or neo-Thomists variously innovate away from the system of the master. One may stubbornly avoid theoretical models and refuse to specify, merely using the vision as a hermeneutic or narrative device. One may do homage as a pro-Turnerian, anti-Turnerian, neo-Turnerian, or post-Turnerian. In this chameleon-like adaptation, the Turner Thesis resembles other great paradigms dominating historical thought. Burckhardt's Renaissance has been similarly both repudiated and variously co-opted. In founding the western regional branch of the Renaissance Society of America some decades ago, an agreement was made that no one define when the Renaissance began or ended, so fluid are its boundaries. As with chronology, so with content. Meanwhile other Renaissances have multiplied like Fibonacci's rabbits, from the High to the Early, Charles Homer Haskins's celebrated Renaissance of the Twelfth Century, W. T. Walsh's Thirteenth the Greatest of Centuries, Robert Lopez's Renaissance of the Tenth Century, the Carolingian Renaissance, Ottonian Renaissance, Anglo-Saxon Renaissance, the Revival of the Fourth Century, and even (*Iuppiter nos adiuvet!*) a Renaissance of the First Century. Like Turner too, Burckhardt lives on as incantation—in the textbooks, in television, and in the popular press. Like Turner, he pops up also in bizarre comparative or international contexts, such as the Renaissance of Islam. And like Turner, he has become an historiographical industry by himself and a hardy perennial on conference panels.

In the same fashion, to note only current offerings, neo-Turnerism has given us Stephen Dyson's *Roman Frontier*, in which frontier experiences on all sides during the Republic created behavioural patterns, policies, and institutions continuing alive even through the Empire period. The sociologist Murray Melbin has just published *Night as Frontier*, in which the familiar Turnerian patterns are resolutely translated from a geographic to a nocturnal realm, as the city's individualistic, opportunistic 'frontiers-man', in the 'new zone' created by electric light, goes off to work, lonely but gregarious, his destiny classless and decentralized, dangerous yet escapist. Bernard Bailyn's *Peopling of British North America* and its sequel volumes are examples of the new immigration history as a frontier/settlement phenomenon, where intra-Europe migrations led to transatlantic multiple migrations of many different populations into England's America. Comparative frontier studies at the University of Oklahoma led to the inauguration in 1976 of a series of symposia on comparative frontiers, with publication as *The Frontier: Comparative Studies*, ranging over the world and through the ages.[8]

Medievalists have always had a claim on Turner's vision. Though his Thesis involved turning away from European foundations toward a putatively unique modern experience, Turner also saw that experience as analogous at least to the creation of medieval society by its protagonists. Medieval history had an even more decided role in the genesis of his Thesis. Wilbur Jacobs notes that Turner's 'training [in American history] under William F. Allen, a Latin scholar and a medievalist', at Wisconsin before going to The Johns Hopkins, shielded him from the current orthodoxies about America's evolution, and freed him 'to interpret American history in the spirit of the medieval[ist] historians who had to deal with the growth of major institutions in their formative period'. Turner's current heir, dean of Turnerian studies and keeper of the flame, Ray Allen Billington, director of America's Library of Congress, stands firmly in the tradition of direct connection between the medieval and the American frontiers. He opened his very influential textbook on the American frontier: 'The settlement of the American continent was the last stage in a mighty movement of peoples that began in the twelfth century when feudal Europe began pushing back the barbarian hordes that had pressed in from east, north, and south to threaten the Holy

---

[8] Stephen Dyson, *The Creation of the Roman Frontier* (Princeton, 1985); Murray Melbin, *Night as Frontier: Colonizing the World after Dark* (New York, 1987); Bernard Bailyn, *Voyagers to the West: A Passage in the Peopling of America on the Eve of the Revolution* (New York, 1986); id., *The Peopling of British North America: An Introduction* (New York, 1986); David H. Miller and Jerome Steffen (eds.), *The Frontier: Comparative Studies*, i (Norman, Okla., 1977); William W. Savage jun. and Stephen I. Thompson (eds.), *The Frontier: Comparative Studies*, ii (Norman, Okla., 1979). See also W. Turrentine Jackson, 'A Brief Message for the Young and/or Ambitious: Comparative Frontiers as a Field for Investigation', *Western Historical Quarterly*, 9 (1978), 4–18; J. L. M. Gulley, 'The Turnerian Frontier: A Study in the Migration of Ideas', *Tijdschrift voor economische en sociale geographie*, 50 (1959), 65–72, 81–91.

City of Rome itself.' War with Islam triggered the rise of nation states, the quest for profits and souls to convert, and ultimately Columbus's landfall in the New World. Lynn White for North America and Luis Weckmann for South America have elaborately demonstrated the medieval patterns and inheritance on those modern frontiers.[9]

It has long been common to see the central Middle Ages, from 950 (or 1000) to 1300 (or 1350) as an essentially frontier experience, with both internal and external frontiers of expansion. In those years a suddenly urbanized, dangerously overpopulated, and (by the Gregorian Reformation) religiously energetic society overpoured its boundaries, transforming the world and the actors themselves, subjecting Byzantium and the Near Eastern trade, reaching out in India and the Mongol cosmos, and interacting with Islam at every level from theology to technology to the arts and to huge slave populations from the respective communities. The capture of the Mediterranean for European commerce and navies is part of that story: Sicily and South Italy, Sardinia and the Balearics, Palestine and the Byzantine Empire, and Islamic Spain. Societies in that era were more open to advance in classes, while forest clearance and agricultural yield increased, and great movements flourished in philosophy, the arts, and letters. The period 950–1350 even includes a Turnerian 'Closing of the Medieval Frontier' from 1250 on, a phrase consecrated by the 1958 *Speculum* article of that title, in which Archibald Lewis formally elaborated its details. Noting that Walter Prescott Webb had extended the frontier 'to include the entire Western European world' from 1500 to date, Lewis obligingly extended it backward by seven centuries more: 'Few periods can be better understood in the light of a frontier concept than western Europe between 800 and 1500.' When the American Historical Association honoured Lewis several years ago with a panel to commemorate his closure thesis, panelists and honouree revised his position; an open-ended

[9] Wilbur Jacobs, 'Frederick Jackson Turner: Master Teacher', *Pacific Historical Review*, 23 (1954), 49–58, at 52; Ray Allen Billington, *Westward Expansion: A History of the American Frontier* (New York, 1949; cf. 5th edn. 1982), 15; this is his first narrative chapter, after an essay on 'The Frontier Hypothesis'. Worster found the passage also a quarter-century later in the 1974 edition ('New West', 143); Lynn T. White, *Medieval Religion and Technology* (Berkeley, 1978), esp. ch. 7, his celebrated 'The Legacy of The Middle Ages in the American Wild West'; Luis Weckmann, *La herencia medieval de México* (Mexico City, 1984).

frontier or expansive situation persisted on sufficient fronts to bridge the century or so left until Columbus.[10]

In the same long tradition of a medieval frontier, the eminent Hispanist Julian Bishko conducted pioneering courses on comparative medieval frontiers; his article in 1963 on the 'Medieval Ranching Frontier' is still considered a classic.[11] The frontier modifier turns up regularly now in medieval publications. Robert Browning's *Byzantium and Bulgaria: A Comparative Study Across the Early Medieval Frontier* explores the interaction between those very different societies which divided the Balkan peninsula. Charles Halperin brings together three separated frontiers in west and far east, each already studied, for his comparative perspective 'The Ideology of Silence: Prejudice and Pragmatism on the Medieval Religious Frontier'. William Tebrake's *Medieval Frontier: Culture and Ecology in Rijnland* takes up the theme of reclamation and human geography in the Rhine delta. Angus MacKay's *Spain in the Middle Ages: From Frontier to Empire, 1000–1500* frames the narrative in explicitly frontier terms. Andrew Hess carries that same frontier into North Africa in his *Forgotten Frontier: A History of the Sixteenth-Century Ibero-African Frontier.*[12]

The most valuable recent assessment of medieval frontier theses is Lawrence J. McCrank's preliminaries to his study of 'The Cistercians of Poblet as Medieval Frontiersmen'. A student of Bishko's, he traces the projection of Turnerism until 'today frontier studies are part of every historical field', with the

---

[10] Archibald Lewis, 'The Closing of the Medieval Frontier, 1250–1350', *Speculum*, 33 (1958), 475–83 (quote 475), closing with a comparison between the American frontier of Walter Prescott Webb and Turner and the similarly 'frontierless existence' suddenly visited upon 14th-century Europe; James Muldoon, *The Expansion of Europe: The First Phase* (Philadelphia, 1977) tells the story of six frontiers in the central medieval period, through documents and interpretative comment; see too his book below in n. 16; and see Pierre Chaunu, *L'Expansion européenne du XIIIᵉ au XVᵉ siècle* (Paris, 1969).

[11] Charles J. Bishko, 'The Castilian as Plainsman: The Medieval Ranching Frontier in La Mancha and Extremadura', in Archibald R. Lewis and Thomas F. McGann (eds.), *The New World Looks at its History: Proceedings of the Second International Congress of Historians of the United States and Mexico* (Austin, 1963), 47–69. For the course, and more on Bishko, see his student L. J. McCrank below.

[12] Robert Browning (Berkeley, 1975); Charles Halperin in *Comparative Studies in Society and History*, 26 (1984), 442–66; William Tebrake (College Station, Tex., 1985); Angus MacKay (London, 1977); Andrew Hess (Chicago, 1978), an explicitly 'frontier history' (4, 10, and *passim*).

University of California's James Westfall Thompson as a pioneer early in this century in adapting the Thesis to medieval Germany 'with scarcely more than a change of dates and proper names'. McCrank stresses not only the many varieties of frontier at any given time, but also the individual historian's subjective sense of what the term means in a given case. Turnerism is not solely the product of Turner but what any of us wishes to redefine it to be, to suit his own needs. Every man becomes his own Turner. McCrank is particularly interested here in the frontier concept as framing the socio-economic aspects of Cistercian monastic expansion; previously he had thoroughly explored the conquest of Catalonia's Tarragona frontier. As a Hispanist he is sensitive to the prominent role the concept has for probing and relating the data of medieval Spanish history. If medieval Europe from the eleventh century constituted as a whole a frontier of optimistic expansion, adventure, and gain, the Iberian peninsula saw a notable concentration of the elements making up that experience; Iberia was indeed a packet of various allied frontiers, variously evolving, including Gabriel Jackson's 'miniature wild west' at the moving border with Islam. McCrank quotes Claudio Sánchez-Albornoz, arguably the most influential Spanish historian of the Reconquest, as concluding: 'The history of no other European people' has been 'so decisively modified by a frontier' as Castile, for 'century after century'.

For Bishko, McCrank's own mentor, the Reconquest was both frontier and a theatre of the wider crusade movement. In his recent *Studies in Medieval Spanish Frontier History*, Bishko unabashedly employs the frontier concept 'in the authentic North American sense' of Turner himself rather than in the more 'fashionable' sense of cultural interaction between ethnic groups. McCrank closes his own review and assessment by distinguishing two current orientations of the medieval Hispanists' frontier concept, both among New World historians and in Spain. There is the frontier as spatial transplantation of population and culture with resulting evolutionary modification, as favoured for example by Bishko and (with *Annales* overtones) by Lynn Nelson. A contrary approach is the more anthropological focus among those who are fascinated by the interaction of cultures, both by osmotic interchange and in the wake of violent conquest, an approach exemplified by Thomas Glick and myself. The two orientations are not necessarily exclusive, though they can be. To them must be

added the reservations about the whole frontier 'clutter' expressed
by Jocelyn Hillgarth and Peter Linehan, though these should be
read in the light of McCrank's critique, that the one position
represents a disinclination for comparative history and the other a
narrowly traditional understanding of the Turner Thesis rather
than its neo-Turnerian developments.[13]

My own view of those medieval centuries has been coloured by
personal experience. My early training had made me a fourth-
generation Turnerian through my mentor for several years, the
Jesuit William Lyle Davis, and through his mentor Herbert Bolton
at the University of California, who in turn had been formed in
Turner's seminars. My first doctorate was taken where Turner
himself did his frontier dissertation, The Johns Hopkins University,
on the same sacred grounds and Turnerian halls. My textbook for the
American West segment of my training, the resolutely Turnerian
Westward Expansion of Billington, is still heavily annotated over
most of its 800 pages. My second doctorate, under the director of
the Anthropos Institut then at the University of Fribourg in
Switzerland, brought me into the world of ethnohistory and
historical anthropology, the home air of neo-Turnerism. My first
books dealt with the clash of Indians and whites in the plateau
region of the Pacific Northwest of the United States during its
opening and settlement from 1840 to 1880. Like most historians of
my generation, I rejected the Turner Thesis itself but remained
affected by selected elements and particularly by the neo-
Turnerian focus on culture-clash and by its emphasis on social
history.

When I took up medieval history, with no intention of studying
frontiers, I found myself researching first the Catalan conquest and
settlement of Byzantine Athens in the fourteenth century, and
thereafter the thirteenth-century conquest and absorption of the
Islamic regions the crusaders called the kingdom of Valencia.
Numerous analogies between the American and Iberian situations
suggested themselves without effort; and it became obvious also
that actual roots of some Northwest frontier phenomena lay in the

---

[13] Lawrence J. McCrank, 'Cistercians as Frontiersmen', *Estudios en homenaje a
don Claudio Sánchez Albornoz en sus 90 años* (Cuadernos de Historia de España:
Anexos, 3 vols., Buenos Aires, 1983), ii. 313–60, esp. 313–32; quotations on 318–
19 (Thompson), 324 n. (Jackson), 325 (Sánchez Albornoz), 326 (Bishko; his
frontier course, 325), and 329 (Linehan).

distant medieval frontier experience. With all these Turnerian influences, though I have never followed the Turner Thesis, I have found the neo-Turnerian visions of the frontier stimulating and helpful. Last year, when invited by the National Park Service to deliver an address on the Pacific Northwest Indian frontier, I took the occasion to compare at length the medieval Valencian and the modern Northwestern experiences—as analogy, as roots, and as provocative entertainment. The study is published, appropriately enough, in the journal *Comparative Studies in Society and History*.[14]

The preceding pages have been historiographical, an approach the very title of this chapter invites. Two factors indeed make that approach necessary as a preliminary. First, one cannot take up the significance of the various frontiers themselves, without confronting at the outset the all-important epistemological problem. And secondly, the significance of hundreds of evolving frontiers in a dozen medieval countries cannot be generally assessed until their individual case-studies have been separately researched and presented. A symposium such as the present book marks only a beginning. The crusade frontier of Europe makes a formidable topic by itself, either in its impact upon the Europeans in their overseas lands (Outremer) or in its equally decisive if differently experienced impact on the wartime homelands. The Society for the Study of the Crusades and the Latin East reports steadily on the impressive cogitation and output in this single field.[15] In a more general way, the widest significance of medieval frontier as all the frontiers of Mediterranean Europe—from the commercial empires of Genoa and Venice, to the dynamic presence of a Jewish cosmos, to the constant interchange with Islam in technology, philosophy, letters, medicine, slavery, institutions, and mentalities—

---

[14] Robert I. Burns, 'The Missionary Syndrome: Crusader and Pacific Northwest Religious Expansionism', *Comparative Studies in Society and History*, 30 (1988), 271–85. My major work on the American frontier is *The Jesuits and the Indian Wars of the Northwest* (New Haven, 1966), now reissued in paperback by the University of Idaho (Moscow, Idaho, 1986). On Bolton and his neo-Turnerian school of some hundred historians he produced at my own University of California, where Turner had helped him win his appointment, see Weber, 'Turner, the Boltonians, and the Borderlands', 66–81.

[15] See their *Bulletin*, of which 7 (1987) has just appeared, with sections on publications, dissertations, papers read, work forthcoming, and work in progress. See e.g. its discussion of the school for studying crusader–Muslim relations at the University of Alexandria, Egypt.

has already become clearer in my own lifetime, and promises to yield a heavier harvest by the year. A chapter of synthesis might now be prepared on the significance of the various kinds of frontier in a given century for Germany, Catalonia, England, Sicily, Occitania, France, Hungary, Portugal, and so through each political entity. Christian thought as a frontier might need its chapter, and also the papacy, whose theology of international law and domestic arrangements came to be formed in many ways by Christendom's larger frontiers.[16]

The schema for this book, and the conference from which it originates, was conceived widely: the geographical or political frontier zone or boundary, moving or otherwise, but also the interaction in such places between societies or cultures. Organizing subthemes included settlement, institutions, religion and culture, each specifying the frontier dynamic. Understandably from the conference locale, the implications of a frontier approach for the medieval British Isles is prominent; but the Iberian peninsula and eastern Europe are also well represented. Each case-study reflects the subjective perception of the amorphous frontier concept and its modality as narrative, analysis, or mood. My own contribution to that set will be a brief case-study from the thirteenth-century Realms or Crown of Aragón.[17]

The multiple or variegated character discerned in any frontier is particularly notable in the Realms, even if attention is confined to the reign of James the Conqueror (1213–76). To begin with, the conquerors were a group of disparate peoples with different

[16] A topic brilliantly pioneered by James Muldoon, *Popes, Lawyers and Infidels: The Church and the Non-Christian World, 1250–1550* (Philadelphia, 1979).

[17] For background, see Thomas N. Bisson, *The Medieval Crown of Aragon: A Short History* (Oxford, 1986). The following section is drawn from my own works, where details and supporting bibliography can be found. See especially *The Crusader Kingdom of Valencia: Reconstruction on a Thirteenth-century Frontier* (2 vols., Cambridge, Mass., 1967), *Islam under the Crusaders: Colonial Survival in the Thirteenth-century Kingdom of Valencia* (Princeton, 1973), *Medieval Colonialism: Postcrusade Exploitation of Islamic Valencia* (Princeton, 1975), *Moors and Crusaders in Mediterranean Spain* (London, 1978), *Jaume I i els valencians del segle XIII* (Valencia, 1981), *Muslims, Christians and Jews in the Crusader Kingdom of Valencia* (Cambridge, 1984), (ed.) *The Worlds of Alfonso the Learned and James the Conqueror* (Princeton, 1985), and *Society and Documentation in Crusader Valencia* (Princeton, 1985). My first in the series, *Crusader Kingdom*, lists 'Frontier' in its index with fourteen lines of entries; see especially pp. viii, xiii, 8–9, 53, 301–3.

countries, languages, institutions, economies, and experiences. The Aragonese kingdom in this dynastic confederation at the start of James's reign was a rural-parochial, stock-raising, and feudal-warrior upland, with a centuries-long history of border warfare and advance against the Muslim neighbours. The Catalan regions were an urban-commune, commercial society akin to Italy's merchant communities, distributed along the international coastlines of the Mediterranean, orientated out to sea and the wider world, whose contact with Muslims had been far more mercantile than bellicose. Aragón proper, where James was a feudal king, enclosed in its heartlands a considerable population of subject Muslims, to whose agricultural labours it owed its basic prosperity. Catalonia, where James was a count somewhat like the doge of Venice or the count of Toulouse, held concentrations of subject Muslims only in two pockets—along its Aragonese border at the inland west and along its border with Islam at the extreme south. James was also the major presence in Occitania by a variety of claims, ranging from direct countship as at Montpellier, or cadet-branch relationship to a former appanage as in the lower Provence valley and Marseilles, to a pattern of feudal rights and privileges throughout the region. At that moment the warlike Franks were about to descend and begin their long colonial absorption of Occitania as their own frontier.

On the other side of James's long border, to the south, lay an Islamic situation of equal complexity. Under the appearance of monolithic control by the Berber Almohad empire, ruled from Marrakesh on the Saharan fringe, the eastern part of Spanish Islam or al-Andalus was a mosaic of regional communities with their own proud memories and interests. Islamic central control was always loose at this far eastern margin, and its collapse revealed component communities capable of independent life. The taifa states which had followed the collapse of the Spanish caliphate were now a memory a century old. The disastrous defeat of the Almohads at Las Navas de Tolosa in 1212 had precipitated another fragmentation, however, and an intricate pattern of civil wars amounting to near chaos. Each of the two great peoples—the Realms of Aragón with their papal-crusading support and the effectively independent Valencian waliate with its eventual support from the North African states and Granada—constituted a kaleidoscope of international and regional patterns.

The frontier zone for each bordered a home society in a turmoil of change and challenges. The movements of any actor in the frontier drama here must be assessed against the international pressures, limitations, and options affecting him. From 1228 to 1245 King James exploited his neighbours' chaos, first seizing the island emirate of Majorca and then the waliate of Valencia, setting up each as a kingdom. In the long Valencian conquest and the subsequent first decades of settlement, the role of each of James's three peoples was markedly different from that of the others; each related differently to the opportunities and to the subject Muslims themselves. The expectations and capacities of each Christian group differed seriously, as did the laws, organization, and institutions that each carried into the frontier zone. The accident that most settlers and the most powerful were Catalans soon made the conquered region an extension of Catalonia in language and culture, though with so many modifications from the Aragonese and Muslim presence as to breed a new frontier region, recognizably a variant of the Catalan homeland, with a populace recognizably a subculture. Conversely the Islamic society, shattered in defeat, reacted variously according to the several socio-economic strata each group occupied and according to their different environments.

First the people, now the land. Crusader Valencia was a region of great size and complexity, a kingdom more complicated and wealthy than England of that period. Valencia city had been the major entrepôt for the commerce of al-Andalus, and from the moment of conquest it became a balance or rival to the port of Barcelona, eventually surpassing it. The Valencia ports had been and remained a main component of the circle trade with North Africa, involving as well the larger Islamic cosmos. Pope Innocent IV, counselling a just division of the Realms between the heirs of James, assessed the new kingdom as wealthier in revenues than James's central realm Catalonia. As a prize and makeweight to the homeland, Archibald Lewis has compared Valencia to Britain's India frontier in the nineteenth century.[18] But crusader Valencia was more than a rich kingdom in the sea that would change the destiny of the Realms of Aragón. Its geography was peculiar and affected all activity by Muslim and Christian alike. Down its length, Valencia varies inland from lovely beaches through pine

[18] 'James the Conqueror: Montpellier and Southern France', in Burns, *Worlds of Alfonso*, ch. 6.

barrens and forested hills to bare and craggy mountains. Mountains also break the country into many fragments, and at places possess the land even down to the sea. Valleys and intensely cultivated plains are as lushly hospitable as the hills are bleak.

Much of Valencia is a hydraulic society, as water from the rivers or springs is captured and decanted into smaller and smaller channels to transform whole regions into green oases. These hydraulic areas, densely populated, gave Valencia the reputation of a Paradise throughout Islam, a reputation still echoing today. The hydraulic system also made it imperative to keep in place the highly skilled irrigation farmers, at least until those skills might be slowly absorbed by another generation of incoming settlers. The irrigated areas held a multitude of mini-farms, requiring not only individual initiative but an almost organic community co-operation, if the system were to survive. Stock-raising, from sheep and goats to cattle, was also prominent, better suited to other areas of Valencia; the kingdom's sheltering valleys received flocks from the international sheepwalks. Dry farming was as common as the irrigation type; grants of irrigated land usually included a balancing portion of the dry. There vineyards prospered and the olive. Above all, Valencia was an urban land, and the greatest opportunities lay in the port cities, with their cheap mill-power replicated on all horizons. Settlers there commonly received both an urban plot or shop and a suburban farm, the latter worked by a Muslim or a share-cropper. From fisheries and boat transport at the coast, with shipbuilding and such manufactures as ceramics or processed agricultural exports at the wharves, to the lumber-cutting in the highlands along the rivers, to the irrigation-network communities, to the upland stock industry, the land imposed its patterns. There were as many frontiers for the settler as there were contexts. The variables diversifying the incoming population combined with the variables of the land itself in a complex dance.

Patterns of settlement in Valencia, a resistant topic still under investigation, were conditioned by the overriding reality of Muslim demographic dominance. Despite the opportunities here and the numbers who streamed south to seize them, Christians remained a colonial minority in the land. Paradoxically, since Christians tended to group in certain areas such as the capital city, they could be at once a minority and a local majority. Our prime document for tracing urban and rural settlement patterns is the

Repartiment or book of land division, where royal notaries jotted thousands of contemplated concessions of houses, farms, public utilities, shops, mosques, and every form of property, at times on a street-by-street basis. Historians have approached these volumes statistically, toponymically, anthroponymically, and in other modes, sometimes with the naïve assumption that they present a reasonably complete catalogue, sometimes with the despairing sense that they essentially concern the king's favourites or select strata of society. In any case, we know that some of even this record is missing, and that it concerns only those lands in the king's own gift. Ambiguous and disconcerting though these codices are, they do provide data obviously useful for studying settlement in the early decades.

A dozen years after the close of James's crusade, his remarkable registers take up the story, touching on every aspect of the new kingdom's reconstruction. The register series was made possible by the Crown's taking control in the 1250s of the fabled paper industry of Játiva, still remaining in Muslim hands, and transforming it by power technology. With cheap paper, James now drafted a notarial original for each of thousands of charters, subsequently copying the parchment version which travelled to the addressee and from there in most cases into oblivion. For the twenty years of his reign now, some 14,000 of the more important charters leaving his chancery would begin and eventually survive in this notarial form. All his charters on the Valencian frontier are appearing in successive volumes of my *Diplomatarium*, a unique window on this world long gone.

In what sense was the region and process a 'frontier', or in what useful ways may the elements of that paradigm serve to clarify its story? First, of course, in the sense in which James himself uses it—his Latin *fronteria* was not merely a border but a region of warfare and peril to the realms, a permanent state perduring long after James's death. Secondly, Valencia was a cornucopia of resources which the king was anxious to distribute and maintain; at the end of his life he complained to the Barcelonans that only a third of the number of settlers necessary to retain the new kingdom had actually gone there. This land of free farms, shops, utilities, government and community offices, and business opportunities was a magnet for settlers coming from the surplus population of his older realms. Even the clergy prospered in spiritual opportunities, as missionaries plunged in to save the *massa damnata* and as a dozen religious orders hurried to set up shop in the captured capital. Thirdly, the various socio-economic frontiers constituting the larger region were themselves changing in character with each decade—Christian immigration increased, more Muslims were expelled, many Muslims moved to parts of the kingdom where their colleagues were numerically dominant and therefore supportive, and Christians of all classes imported more Muslims from abroad to work fresh lands as free share-croppers.

Fourthly, Valencia was a frontier experience for the home kingdoms as well, since the conquest had overbalanced the confederation with an enormous ballast of unassimilable Muslims. The conquered frontier brought to the Realms of Aragón new wealth and a strategic position, from which the subsequent conquest of Sicily and a Mediterranean empire became the inviting and almost inevitable course. The conquest conferred great-power status, so that first Italy's Guelphs and then the Ghibellines sought James as their champion, while the papacy and two ecumenical councils solicited his advice on the eastern crusades. All of Christendom rejoiced, as the pope announced, when James conquered Valencia—'Great Valencia' to the chronicler Matthew Paris in far-off England. It would be easy to trace this mutual impact of homeland and frontier colony, in domestic and international aspects, both for the Realms of Aragón and for the truncated al-Andalus. Fifth, the Valencian frontier created a new man, recognizably different from the Catalan or the Aragonese or the Occitan, in his speech, in his habits, in his laws, in his character, in his relation to his environment. And finally, Valencia was a frontier in the most modern focus of that term, a region of unremitting action between two cultures, at many levels from religion to domestic service, to medicine, to war, to reactive revulsion by both peoples.

General assessment leaves little room for particulars; but some sense of detail can be garnered from an overview of the charters during the reign. We see a frontier at once wild and coming under order. The Islamic world here had ended in a generation of debilitating political and economic confusion; its transfer into the hands of the infidel further demoralized and disorientated its essential institutions and self-image. Still, the application of traditional autonomy for the subjected Muslims, as well as a period of relative peace, restored basic order. Meanwhile the invaders brought down a flood of salaried functionaries to impose at least a governmental pattern. Notaries were appointed to every town; surveyors, land distributors, and auditors coursed the land, imposing the map of land grants; engineers took the irrigation systems in hand, expanding them to provide yet more land, while others threw up stone bridges and Gothic cathedrals. Roads were cut, rerouted, or improved; within the cities a European grid of streets began to emerge. Licences went out to cut windows or affix stairways on city walls as houses were incorporated in them, or to remodel a shop, or to restrain public nuisances.

A tax bureaucracy appeared, like mould on cheese, since revenues were a key both to progress here and to good relations with the homeland. Tax farmers and tax investors proliferated, their tax auctions and networks established. Their audits to the Crown are a very common item in the surviving records, a rich resource for examining crops, wages, prices, demography, and daily life. With Roman Law encouraged by the Crown to an extent not possible in the custom-ridden homelands, the graduates of Bologna headed south in great number, bringing along their professional courts, itinerant judges, obscure writs, and relentless barratry. Valencians would force the tide back, for a time outlawing Roman Law, but it soon returned with a vengeance. The first universally applicable code of Roman Law in Europe could be imposed here largely because the 'war of laws' among the customs of different immigrant groups required a code transcending divisive custom. In each large town a city hall administered its region through its executive board of jurates (elected by parish districts) and guarded its curial strongbox of major records. Regional peace officers, local superintendents of standards and public health, and castle garrisons went into place. A stream of privileges organized public behaviour, from the manner of cleaning the municipal sewers to the formation of police posses and firefighting crews at the sound of the cathedral bell. Mapping of local jurisdictions went vigorously forward, along with surveying of land grants on a systematic scale and much settling of local boundaries by lawsuits. From the very year in which the crusade ended, a university was chartered and preparatory education encouraged by law.

The degree of planning and the multiple emplacement of executive functionaries is impressive in the registered charters;

charter datelines show James constantly on the road, a vagabond king, to oversee this layered activity. Governments were embryonic in those days, however, very unlike the encompassing juggernauts they have become. Consequently the frontier zone remained in some ways wild—as other charters demonstrate with regard to crime, fraud, violence individual or communal, and even revolt or rioting. The result in these early years was a kind of channelled anarchy. In the economic sphere, banks were chartered, a detailed rate of exchange promulgated, and inflationary problems confronted. The Crown minted a coinage proper to this frontier alone, proclaimed or resited markets and butcheries, regulated trades (particularly the valuable paper industry), established depots for foreign Muslim and Christian merchants, offered tax exemptions and protection to encourage commerce, published tariff lists for all manner of imports, controlled the interest rates, introduced an office of standard weights and measures as well as saltworks and granaries, and reached trade agreements with neighbours and overseas.

The Crown ran its business on credit operations, by a kind of short-term proto-bond system, so that the frontier revenues funnelled north to affect the policies and options of the dynasty and its component realms. In Valencian administration, one curious phenomenon was the rapid turnover in castle management, as numerous fortifications and towers were handed over to creditors, who installed or maintained garrisons and castellans in the crown sectors and reported on expenses and achievements at the end of each short tenure. All these movements constitute a transfer and persistence of the homeland, a replication or mirroring of traditional patterns. This anti-Turnerian understanding of events is a strong element in the post-Turnerian frontier paradigm. The frontier can now be expressed as a dialectic of the old and new, or as a constricting and releasing and reshaping of the old by the new conditions and needs, or perhaps as a creation of the new with older materials. This in turn involved a violent derangement of the previous Islamic patterns, an explicitly expressed determination to 'reform paganism' into European modes of life and action. In the nature of things, the effort could be only partial during these early years, resulting in the frontier predicament of a Christian subculture constrained by the Islamic environment, with echoes of both cultures. Translated to a distant frontier, the old forms often underwent a change of scale as well; the expansion here of commercial and tax revenues, for example, even altered the activity and psychology of the realms at large.

As in all medieval unitary societies, religion played a paramount role on this frontier. The conquest itself was formally a papal crusade; even settlement of crusader lands had for contemporaries a sacral gloss. Many of the secular processes initiated to take control were offered as religious in their effects. Valencia city's major mosque was commandeered immediately as a cathedral, and a dozen mosques in the city neighbourhoods as churches. A network of parishes was thrown over the kingdom, and clergy installed, even where no Christians lived; the empty mosques-turned-churches stood as symbols in the remotest areas, to the supplanting of Islam's dominance. This diocesan Church deliberately ignored its overwhelming Muslim ambience—even though it used Muslim tenants and slaves, and legislated occasionally against Islamic influence. Instead it concentrated on planting on the frontier the Christian liturgy, institutions, and folkways. It expressed itself in European Gothic, virtually excluding even *mudéjar* art and architecture. As with the secular transfer, the Valencian bishops sought to recreate the spiritual world of Barcelona and Zaragoza.

How then was it a 'frontier' Church? In three ways. First it was consciously the custodian here of the Europe-wide crusade spirit, deliberately transforming its material surroundings to make little atolls in the sea of Muslims. Secondly, it was itself dominated by reactive acculturation. An environment can be acculturated as much by reacting as by conforming. A community in reactive acculturation hardens its cultural patterns until the effect is stressful and absurd; a 'golden ghetto' of an affluent society's citizens abroad, whether as invited garrison or colonial admin-istrators in a poor land, is a modern example. To stand in a sea of Muslims belonging to a high culture, in a territory still conformed to their socio-theological needs and purposes, and to refuse their presence or their products any notice as the Valencian Church did, is to bear intense silent witness. To refrain from action, where action is nearly unavoidable, is to act. Thirdly, the king used church personnel and institutions, as the most accessible of his major resources, for the transformation of his conquest.

This was not the whole story of the Valencian Church. Besides the dioceses, for whom evangelizing subject Muslims had never been the norm, there were the religious orders, especially the activist Mendicants. The orders made their several ways to this frontier, often coming in with the crusaders. Franciscans and Dominicans plunged into programmes of preaching-visits to the mosques, set up schools of Arabic for proselytizing, initiated metaphysical-theological discourse with the élites, lobbied for laws encouraging conversion, sent optimistic reports to Rome, composed linguistic and philosophical books as aids, set up convert groups around crusader Valencia, and appointed an official to visit those groups serially to give support. The Ransomer orders set up house here, travelling into Barbary to recover Christian slaves. Military orders functioned in these decades as an aggressive defence, as great landholders with Muslim tenants, and as advisory-supportive groups behind the throne. Among the Christians, the bizarre circumstances of the frontier confused the whole question of paying tithes and first-fruits. Laity and clergy lined up to fight the issue in the collecting fields and in the courts, raising a *brouhaha* throughout the new kingdom until the Crown imposed its arbitration.

What of the Muslims themselves? Valencia had been their land, and to many intents remained so. Most of the mosques were still in their hands, along with the religio-economic endowment foundations in rents and estates. The muezzins still called from the ubiquitous minarets, the cry penetrating Christian home and palace (as King James complained on being awakened). Islamic schools were protected by law as were the religious practices, internal taxes, farms, livelihoods, and lifestyles such as marriage customs or communal baths. Muslims formed a parallel and symbiotic society.

Though Christians at this period mixed with Muslims in many ways, most of Valencia's Muslims passed their lives in immemorial routine without entering a Christian court or house, and without meeting or dining with an infidel, or socializing or doing business with one. The harrying episodes by Mendicant friars were soon fended off. The Muslims here kept their arms, sent troops to the Christian wars, and were aware of the Granadan and North African solidarity they would several times summon to their assistance during revolts. Behind a rhetoric of 'expulsion' the Christian overlords valued Muslim services as a key to affluence, and systematically imported more Muslims from Castile and overseas.

But for Muslims too their conquered homeland had become a strange frontier. Though not a 'discontinuist' society, it was not a 'continuist' society either, to borrow the jargon of a current polemic over the fate of the Valencian Muslims. The very survival elements, the continuities themselves, were destructured until they constituted to some degree discontinuities. The destructively transforming embrace of an alien culture mutated the surviving elements into an Islamic subculture, a brave, withdrawn, adaptive community. When the Christian settlers' contempt for and harassment of this subject majority are factored in, with the progressive mistreatment and exploitation their situation invited, the tragedy of the Muslims on this frontier becomes clear.[19]

In 1893 at the American Historical Association's convention in Chicago, Frederick Jackson Turner delivered the address which launched his Frontier Thesis into full flight. Its title, 'The Significance of the Frontier in American History', is echoed by the title of the present study. Each term in our title, except one, has now been unpacked. We have wrestled with the concept of frontier, and have traced its application to medieval history, with attention to the complexities and contradictions lying under the surface of both terms. Finally, the word 'significance' demands some attention. The frontier has already been explored as a hermeneutic device—a post-Turnerian orientation or method or narrative-frame or attention-getter. This has an epistemological significance, and a value for historians as literary craftsmen. The quest for significance must also take up the substantive situations we choose to call frontiers. Here there seem to be at least four divisions: the significance of various kinds of frontiers, the kinds of significance possible, the chronology of significance, and the relational value of the concept for comparing frontiers. Obviously, if there are many categories of frontier, and various frontier stages

---

[19] A thorough discussion of the continuist/discontinuist debate with its allied problem of 'tolerance' is in my *Muslims, Christians, Jews*, 17–27. Kenneth Baxter Wolf has a provocative exploration of the mutual perception by Muslims and Christians in the reverse situation, when early Spanish Christians had come under Islam, in 'The Earliest Spanish Christian Views of Islam', *Church History*, 55 (1986), 281–93, and in his *Christian Martyrs in Muslim Spain* (Cambridge, 1988), ch. 7.

within each, there will be many significances. And significance itself may be economic, political, cultural-creative, religious or ecclesiastical or ideological, technological as in the work of Lynn White, or psychological.

Chronologically (for lack of a better term) a frontier may culminate or shape some previous evolution, or conversely it may produce patterns to replicate in future conquests—as in Spain's unique 'consistent policy to transplant its home institutions' (themselves influenced by frontiers) overseas to create 'other Spains'.[20] As a relational device, comparing experiences and places very different in time and/or character, the frontier makes a valuable tool. Just as Ira Lapidus was able to break through the barrier of dissimilarity inhibiting any comparison of Islamic cities and European commune-cities during the medieval centuries, by positing an analogy of functions, so the frontier becomes a functional basis for comparing such zones of interchange and conquest as the Islamic *thagr* and the Christian march, or the prayer-fortress *ribāṭ* and the military orders, or the shifting image of Christ in the pluri-ethnic mentality involved.[21]

What would Turner make of all this? He had declared the frontier unique, as well as closed and gone forever, with his Thesis to guide the autopsy, only to have us reverse the field and advance upon new frontiers ever multiplying as in a hall of mirrors. We now discern and pursue frontiers in the unlikeliest depths of medieval history. Given Turner's own ideas about his frontier, perhaps he would react as Claude Lévi-Strauss now reacts to the similarly unwieldy and mutated versions of structuralism. 'I practically

[20] Ernest J. Burrus, SJ, 'Alonso de la Vera Cruz (+ 1584), Pioneer Defender of the American Indians', *Catholic Historical Review*, 70 (1984), 531–46, at 531. He adds: 'nothing comparable was to be found among the other colonial powers at the time.'

[21] Ira M. Lapidus, *Muslim Cities in the Later Middle Ages* (Cambridge, Mass., 1967), pp. vii, 185–91. Américo Castro, following the lead of J. A. Conde and others, argued for a direct borrowing of the military order from Islamic precedent on the Spanish frontier, in *The Structure of Spanish History* (Eng. trans., Princeton, 1954), ch. 7. The intuitive arguments have now won more explicit support by the findings of Elena Lourie, 'The Confraternity of Belchite, the Ribāṭ, and the Temple', *Viator*, 13 (1982), 159–76. The Arabist Míkel de Epalza has traced the changing image of Jesus among the Muslim, Christian, and Jewish communities on the Spanish medieval frontier, as each community responded to the pressures of the other two, in *Jésus otage: Juifs, chrétiens et musulmans en Espagne (XIᵉ–XVIIᵉ siècle)* (Paris, 1987).

don't dare use the word "structuralist" any more, since it has been so badly deformed', he says; 'I am certainly not the father of structuralism.'[22] Turner *redivivus* might echo that repudiation with an indignant 'I am no Turnerian'. Still, great thinkers who survive as active agents into future generations do so at a Darwinian price in the academic Galápagos, evolving into less recognizable species. Turner enjoyed an enquiring and visionary mind, never committed much of its product to publication, and was constantly shifting the furniture in his Thesis. On balance, I think he would be stimulated by the contributions to the present book, and suitably grateful that his debate goes on.

[22] Interview with James M. Markham, 'Paris Journal: A French Thinker Who Declines a Guru Mantle', *New York Times* (21 Dec. 1987), 4.

BIBLIOGRAPHY

MANUSCRIPT SOURCES

Aberystwyth, NLW Kentchurch Court, no. 1027; Peniarth 280 D; Peniarth 404 D.

Cardiff, Free Library, Brecon Documents 2.

Carlisle, Cumbria Record Office, Ca 3/1/51; Register of Bishop Appleby.

Clonalis, Co. Roscommon, Library of the O'Conor Don, Book of the O'Conor Don.

Dublin, Genealogical Office, Dublin Castle 192.

Dublin, NLI 2; 3; 13; 761; D 8; G 4.

Dublin, PROI EX 1/1; EX 2/1; RC 7; RC 8.

Dublin, RIA 12 D 2; 12 D 10; 23 E 29 (1134); 23 P 12 (536); 23 P 2 (535); A v 2 (744); D ii 1 (1225).

Dublin, TCD 1318 (H. 2. 16).

Durham, Dean and Chapter of Durham Archives, Prior's Kitchen, Reg. Parv. III.

Edinburgh, Scottish Record Office, Assignation and Modification of Stipends, E.47; RH 2/1/5, Cur. Itin. Just., transcripts, vol. i.

Glasgow, Department of Scottish History, Glasgow University, Transcript of Register of Supplications in Vatican Archives.

London, BL Add. 4792; Add. 9924; Add. 19995; Add; 30512; Royal A xi.

London, PRO DL 29; E 101; E 310/40/5; JI 1; SC 2; SC 6.

Málaga, Archivo Catedral, file 62.

Murcia, Archivo Municipal, Actas Capitulares 1435.

Newcastle, Northumberland Record Office, Swinburne (Capheaton) Collection.

Oxford, Bodleian Library, Rawlinson B 495.

Seville, Archivo Ducal de Medinaceli, Sección Alcalá de los Gazules, file 59, no. 9; Archivo Municipal, Actas Capitulares 1450.

Shrewsbury, Shropshire Record Office 552 (Clun Court Rolls).

Simancas, Archivo General, Cámara-Pueblos, file 22.

PRINTED SOURCES

Accounts of the Lord High Treasurer of Scotland, I: *1473–1498*, ed. Thomas Dickson (Edinburgh, 1877).

Acts of Malcolm IV, King of Scots, 1153–65, ed. Geoffrey Barrow (*Regesta regum Scottorum* 1, Edinburgh, 1960).

Acts of William I, King of Scots, 1165–1214, ed. Geoffrey Barrow (*Regesta regum Scottorum* 2, Edinburgh, 1971).

ADAM OF BREMEN, *History of the Archbishops of Hamburg-Bremen*, trans. F. J. Tschan (New York, 1959).

Aithdioghluim Dána: A Miscellany of Irish Bardic Poetry, ed. Lambert McKenna (2 vols., ITS 37 and 40, Dublin, 1939–40).

Alexandreida, ed. Reinhold Trautmann, *Die alttschechische Alexandreis* (Heidelberg, 1916).

Ancient Petitions Relating to Northumberland, ed. Constance M. Fraser (Surtees Society 176, 1966 for 1961).

Annales capituli Cracoviensis (Rocznik Kapitulny Krakowski), ed. August Bielowski, *MPH* 2 (Lwów, 1872, repr. Warsaw, 1961), 779–816.

Annales capituli Posnaniensis, ed. Brygida Kürbis, *MPH*, NS 6 (Warsaw, 1962), 21–78.

Annales Cestrienses, ed. Richard C. Christie (Lancashire and Cheshire Record Society 14, 1887).

Annales Krasinsciani (Rocznik Krasińskich), ed. August Bielowski, *MPH* 3 (Lwów, 1878, repr. Warsaw, 1961), 127–33.

Annales Magdeburgenses, ed. Georg Pertz, *MGH*, *SS* 16 (Hanover, 1859), 105–96.

Annales Palidenses, ed. Georg Pertz, *MGH*, *SS* 16 (Hanover, 1859), 48–98.

Annals of Connacht (Annála Connacht), ed. A. Martin Freeman (Dublin, 1944).

Annals of Ireland . . . translated . . . by . . . Duald MacFirbis, ed. John O'Donovan, in *Miscellany of the Irish Archaeological Society*, i (Dublin, 1846), 198–302.

Annals of Loch Cé, ed. William M. Hennessy (2 vols., RS, 1871).

Annals of the Kingdom of Ireland by the Four Masters, ed. John O'Donovan (7 vols., Dublin, 1848–51).

Annals of Ulster (Annála Uladh), ed. William M. Hennessy and Bartholomew MacCarthy (4 vols., Dublin, 1887–1901).

Anonymi descriptio Europae orientalis, ed. Olgierd Górka (Cracow, 1916).

Apokryfa o Jidášovi, ed. Jiří Cejnar, *Nejstarší české veršované legendy* (Prague, 1964), 155–80.

Audacht Morainn, ed. Fergus Kelly (Dublin, 1976).

BEDE, *Ecclesiastical History of the English People*, ed. Bertram Colgrave and R. A. B. Mynors (Oxford, 1969).

—— *The Life and Miracles of St Cuthbert*, trans. John Stevenson and L. C. Lane, in *Bede's Ecclesiastical History of the English Nation* (Everyman edn., London, 1910 and frequent repr.), 286–348.

BERGIN, OSBORN, *Irish Bardic Poetry*, ed. David Greene and Fergus Kelly (Dublin, 1970).

Bernard of Clairvaux, *Epistolae*, in *Opera*, viii, ed. J. Leclercq and H. Rochais (Rome, 1977).

Boldon Book: Northumberland and Durham, ed. D. Austin (Chichester, 1982, supplementary vol. to *Domesday Book*, ed. John Morris).

Book of Fees (3 vols., London, 1920–31).

Book of Magauran, ed. Lambert McKenna (Dublin, 1947).

Bower, Walter, *Scotichronicon*, ed. Walter Goodall (2 vols., Edinburgh, 1759).

Brut y Tywysogyon: or, The Chronicle of the Princes, Red Book of Hergest Version, ed. Thomas Jones (Cardiff, 1955).

Caithréim Thoirdhealbaigh, ed. Standish H. O'Grady (2 vols., ITS 26–7, London, 1929).

Calendar of Ancient Correspondence Concerning Wales, ed. John Goronwy Edwards (Cardiff, 1935).

Calendar of Ancient Petitions Relating to Wales, ed. William Rees (Cardiff, 1975).

Calendar of Archbishop Alen's Register, ed. Charles McNeill (RSAI, Dublin, 1950).

Calendar of Border Papers, ed. Joseph Bain (2 vols., Edinburgh, 1894–6).

Calendar of Documents Relating to Ireland (1171–1307), ed. H. S. Sweetman (5 vols., London, 1875–86).

Calendar of Documents Relating to Scotland, ed. Joseph Bain (4 vols., Edinburgh, 1881–8); v, supplementary vol., ed. G. G. Simpson and J. D. Galbraith (Edinburgh, 1986).

Calendar of Entries in the Papal Register Relating to Great Britain and Ireland: Petitions to the Pope, i: *1342–1419*, ed. W. H. Bliss (London, 1896).

Calendar of Ormond Deeds, ed. Edmund Curtis (6 vols., IMC, Dublin, 1932–43).

Calendar of Papal Letters to Scotland of Clement VII of Avignon 1378–1394, ed. Charles Burns (Scottish History Society, 4th ser., 12, Edinburgh, 1976).

Calendar of Scottish Supplications to Rome 1418–22, ed. E. R. Lindsay and A. I. Cameron (Scottish History Society, 3rd Ser., 23, 1934).

Calendar of the Charter Rolls, 1226–1516 (6 vols., London, 1903–27).

Calendar of the Close Rolls (1296–1302) (London, 1906).

Calendar of the Gormanston Register, ed. James Mills and M. J. McEnery (for RSAI, Dublin, 1916).

Calendar of the Justiciary Rolls . . . of Ireland (1295–1303, etc.), ed. James Mills *et al.* (3 vols. to date, Dublin, 1905–).

Calendar of the Patent Rolls (1327–30); (1377–81); (1385–89) (London, 1891, 1895, 1900).

Calendar of Various Chancery Rolls 1277–1326 (London, 1912).

CAMPION, EDMUND, *Two Bokes of the Histories of Ireland*, ed. Alphonsus F. Vossen (Assen, 1963).

Cancionero de romances (Anvers, 1550), ed. Antonio Rodríguez-Moñino (Madrid, 1967).

CARLETON, GEORGE, *The Life of Bernard Gilpin* (London, 1636).

Cartae et alia munimenta . . . de Glamorgan, ed. George T. Clark (6 vols., Cardiff, 1910).

Chartularies of St Mary's Abbey, Dublin, ed. John T. Gilbert (2 vols., RS, 1884–6).

CHILD, FRANCIS J., *The English and Scottish Popular Ballads* (5 vols., Boston and New York, 1882–98, repr. New York, 1965).

Chronica Adefonsi imperatoris, ed. Luis Sánchez Belda (Madrid, 1950).

Chronica Poloniae Maioris, ed. Brygida Kürbis, *MPH*, NS 8 (Warsaw, 1970).

Close Rolls of the Reign of Henry III (1227–1272) (14 vols., London, 1902–38).

CLYN, JOHN, *Annals of Ireland by Friar John Clyn and Thady Dowling*, ed. Richard Butler (Dublin, 1849).

Codex diplomaticus Maioris Poloniae, ed. Ignacy Zakrzewski and Franciszek Piekosiński (5 vols., Poznań, 1877–1908).

Colección de fueros municipales y cartas pueblas de los reinos de Castilla, León, Corona de Aragón y Navarra, ed. Tomás Muñoz y Romero (Madrid, 1847).

Colección de privilegios, franquezas, exenciones y fueros, vi, ed. Tomás González (Madrid, 1833).

Colección diplomática de Baeza, ed. José Rodríguez Molina (Jaén, 1983).

Colección diplomática del Archivo Histórico Municipal de Jaén, ed. José Rodríguez Molina (Jaén, 1985).

Colección diplomática de Quesada, ed. Juan de Mata Carriazo Arroquia (Jaén, 1975).

Correspondence . . . of the Priory of Coldingham (Surtees Society 12, 1841).

Crede mihi, ed. John T. Gilbert (Dublin, 1897).

Crónica de Juan II de Castilla, ed. Juan de Mata Carriazo (Madrid, 1982).

Cronica principum Saxonie, ed. O. Holder-Egger, *MGH*, *SS* 25 (Hanover, 1880), 472–80.

Cronica sancti Petri Erfordensis moderna, ed. Oswald Holder-Egger, in *Monumenta Erphesfurtensia* (*SRG*, Hanover and Leipzig, 1899), 117–369.

Dalimil chronicler, ed. Jiří Daňhelka et al., *Nejstarší česká rýmovaná kronika tak řečeného Dalimila* (Prague, 1958).

Depositions and Other Ecclesiastical Proceedings from the Courts of Durham (Surtees Society 21, 1845).

Description . . . of . . . the . . . Rites . . . of Durham (Surtees Society 15, 1842).

Dignitas decani, ed. Newport B. White (Dublin, 1957).

Dioghluim Dána, ed. Lambert McKenna (MacCionaith) (Dublin, 1938).

Diplomatorio andaluz de Alfonso X, ed. Manuel González Jiménez (in press).

Documentos arábigo-granadinos, ed. Luis Seco de Lucena Paredes (Madrid, 1961).

Documents Illustrative of the History of Scotland, ed. Joseph Stevenson (2 vols., Edinburgh, 1870).

Documents on the Affairs of Ireland before the King's Council, ed. G. O. Sayles (IMC, Dublin, 1979).

Domesday Book, ed. Abraham Farley (2 vols., London, 1783).

Dowdall Deeds, ed. Charles McNeill and A. J. Otway-Ruthven (IMC, Dublin, 1960).

EBO, *Vita sancti Ottonis episcopi Babenbergensis*, ed. Jan Wikarjak and Kazimierz Liman, *MPH*, NS 7/2 (Warsaw, 1969).

EUGENIUS III, *Epistolae*, in *Patrologia latina*, clxxx, ed. J. P. Migne (Paris, 1855), cols. 1014–1614.

Extracts from the Records of the Merchant Adventurers of Newcastle-upon-Tyne, i (Surtees Society 93, 1895 for 1894).

FLAŠKA, SMIL, *Nová rada*, ed. Jiří Daňhelka (Prague, 1950).

Foedera, 2, pt. I (Record Commission, London, 1818).

FROISSART, JEAN, *Chronicles*, selected and trans. Geoffrey Brereton (Harmondsworth, 1968).

Fuero de Cuenca, ed. Rafael de Ureña y Smenjaud (Madrid, 1935).

Fueros de Sepúlveda, ed. Emilio Sáez (Segovia, 1953).

Fuero sobre el fecho de las cabalgadas, in *Memorial histórico español*, 2 (1851), 437–506.

GALÍNDEZ DE CARVAJAL, LORENZO, *Crónica de Enrique IV*, ed. Juan Torres Fontes, *Estudio sobre la 'Crónica de Enrique IV' del Dr. Galíndez de Carvajal* (Murcia, 1946), 67–543.

Galli chronicon, ed. August Bielowski, *MPH* I (Lwów, 1864), repr. Warsaw, 1966), 379–484; ed. Karol Maleczyński, *MPH* NS 2 (Cracow, 1952).

GEARÓID IARLA (i.e. Gerald fitz Maurice fitzGerland, earl of Desmond), 'Duanaire Ghearóid Iarla', ed. Gearóid MacNiocaill, *Studia Hibernica*, 3 (1963), 7–59.

GERALD OF WALES (Giraldus Cambrensis), *Expugnatio Hibernica*, ed. A. B. Scott and F. X. Martin (Dublin, 1978).

—— *The History and Topography of Ireland*, trans. J. J. O'Meara (Harmondsworth, 1982).

GONZÁLEZ DÁVILA, GIL, *Historia de la vida y hechos del rey don Henrique III de Castilla* (Madrid, 1638).

GRATIAN, *Decretum, Corpus iuris canonici*, i, ed. E. Friedberg (Leipzig, 1879).

Hamilton Papers, ed. Joseph Bain (2 vols., Edinburgh, 1890–2).

Hechos del condestable don Miguel Lucas de Iranzo, ed. Juan de Mata Carriazo (Madrid, 1940).

HELBIG, HERBERT, and WEINRICH, LORENZ (eds.), *Urkunden und erzählende Quellen zur deutschen Ostsiedlung im Mittelalter* (2 vols., Darmstadt, 1968–70).

HELMOLD of BOSAU, *Cronica Slavorum*, ed. Bernhard Schmeidler (*SRG*, Hanover, 1937).

HERBORD, *Dialogus de vita sancti Ottonis episcopi Babenbergensis*, ed. Jan Wikarjak and Kazimierz Liman, *MPH*, NS 7/3 (Warsaw, 1974).

Historia de los hechos del Marqués de Cádiz (1443–1488), in *Colección de documentos inéditos para la historia de España*, cvi (Madrid, 1893), 143–317.

Historia et cartularium monasterii sancti Petri Gloucestriae, ed. William Henry Hart (3 vols., RS, 1863–7).

Historic and Municipal Documents of Ireland, ed. John T. Gilbert (RS, 1870).

HOLINSHED, RAPHAEL, *Holinshed's Irish Chronicle*, ed. Liam Miller and Eileen Power (Dublin, 1979).

Holyrood Ordinale (The Book of the Old Edinburgh Club 7, 1914).

HORE, HERBERT, and GRAVES, JAMES (eds.), *The Social State of the Southern and Eastern Counties of Ireland in the Sixteenth Century* (Dublin, 1870).

IBN MARZUQ, *El 'Musnad': Hechos memorables de Abū-l-Ḥasan, sultán de los benimerines*, ed. and trans. María J. Viguera Molíns (Madrid, 1977).

AL-IDRISI, *Geografía de España*, ed. Antonio Ubieto Arteta (Valencia, 1974).

Iomarbhágh na bhFileadh: The Contention of the Bards, ed. Lambert McKenna (2 vols., ITS 20–1, London, 1920 for 1918–19).

Irish Cartularies of Llanthony prima and secunda, ed. Eric St John Brooks (IMC, Dublin, 1953).

'Irish Pipe Roll of 14 John, 1211–12', ed. Oliver Davies and David B. Quinn, *Ulster Journal of Archaeology*, 4, Supplement (July 1941).

John of Gaunt's Register 1379–83, ii, ed. Eleanor C. Lodge and Robert Somerville (Camden 3rd ser., 57, London, 1937).

JUAN LOVERA, CARMEN, 'Catálogo de la colección diplomática de Alcalá la Real', *Boletín del Instituto de Estudios Giennenses*, 91 (1977), 9–45.

JUAN MANUEL, Don, *Obras completas*, ed. José M. Blecua (2 vols., Madrid, 1982–3).

LAWLOR, H. J., 'A Calendar of the *Liber Niger* and *Liber Albus* of Christ Church, Dublin', *PRIA* 27 C (1908–9), 1–93.

Laws of the Marches, ed. Thomas Thomson and Cosmo Innes, *Acts of the*

Parliaments of Scotland, i (Edinburgh, 1844), 413–16 (red); trans.
George Neilson, *Miscellany of the Stair Society*, i (Stair Society 26,
1971), 11–77.

Leabhar Breac (facsimile, Dublin, 1872–6).

Lebor na Huidre, ed. R. I. Best and Osborn Bergin (Dublin, 1929).

LESLIE, JOHN, *The Historie of Scotland*, trans. James Dalrymple, ed.
E. G. Cody (Scottish Text Society 5, 14, Edinburgh and London, 1888).

Letters and Papers Foreign and Domestic of the Reign of Henry VIII, iv,
pt. I, ed. J. S. Brewer (London, 1870).

LEVI DELLA VIDA, G., 'Il regno di Granata nel 1465–1466 nei ricordi di un
viaggiatore egiziano', *Al Andalus*, 1 (1933), 307–34.

Libelle of Englyshe Polycye, ed. George Warner (Oxford, 1926).

Liber cartarum Sancte Crucis, ed. Cosmo Innes (Bannatyne Club,
Edinburgh, 1840).

Liber Pluscardensis, ii, ed. Felix J. H. Skene (The Historians of Scotland
10, Edinburgh, 1880).

Liber sancte Marie de Calchou, ed. Cosmo Innes (2 vols., Bannatyne
Club, Edinburgh, 1846).

Liber sancte Marie de Melros, ed. Cosmo Innes (2 vols., Bannatyne Club,
Edinburgh, 1837).

Libro del repartimiento de Jerez de la Frontera: Estudio y edición,
ed. Manuel González Jiménez and Antonio González Gómez (Cádiz,
1980).

Libro del repartimiento de Medina Sidonia: Estudio y edición, ed. A. M.
Anasagasti and L. Rodríguez (Cádiz, 1987).

Life of St Kentigern, ed. A. P. Forbes, *Lives of St Ninian and St Kentigern*
(The Historians of Scotland 5, Edinburgh, 1874).

Littere Wallie, ed. John Goronwy Edwards (Cardiff, 1940).

LÓPEZ DE AYALA, PERO, *Corónica del rey don Pedro*, ed. Constance L.
and Heanon M. Wilkins (Madison, 1985).

'Lord Chancellor Gerrard's Notes of his Report on Ireland', ed. Charles
McNeill, *Analecta Hibernica*, 2 (1931), 93–291.

LUNA, ALVARO DE, *Crónica de don Alvaro de Luna*, ed. Juan de Mata
Carriazo (Madrid, 1940).

MAC CON MIDHE, GIOLLA BRIGHDE, *Poems*, ed. N. J. A. Williams (ITS 51,
Dublin, 1980).

Macfarlane's Geographical Collections, iii, ed. Arthur Mitchell and James
T. Clark (Scottish History Society 53, 1908).

MACNIOCAILL, GEARÓID, *Na buirgéisí* (2 vols., Dublin, 1964).

MALDONADO, ALONSO DE, *Hechos de don Alonso de Monroy*, in *Memorial
histórico español*, vi (Madrid, 1853), 1–110.

MEDINA, PEDRO DE, *Libro de grandezas y cosas memorables de España*,
ed. Ángel González Palencia (Madrid, 1944).

Memoranda de Parliamento, ed. Frederick W. Maitland (RS, 1893).

MENÉNDEZ PELAYO, MARCELINO, *Antología de poetas líricos castellanos*, viii–ix (rev. edn., Madrid, 1945).

MENÉNDEZ PIDAL, RAMÓN, *Flor nueva de romances viejos* (22nd edn., Madrid, 1968).

Miscellaneous Irish Annals, ed. and trans. Séamus Ó hInnse (Dublin, 1947).

Monumenta Poloniae Vaticana, iii: *Analecta Vaticana*, ed. Jan Ptaśnik (Cracow, 1914).

'North Country Deeds', in *Miscellanea*, 2 (Surtees Society 127, 1916), 107–29.

Northumberland Lay Subsidy Roll of 1296, ed. Constance M. Fraser (Society of Antiquaries of Newcastle-upon-Tyne Record series 1, 1968).

NUGENT, WILLIAM, 'Poems of Exile by Uilliam Nuinseann mac Barúin Dealbhna', ed. Gerard Murphy, *Éigse*, 6 (1948), 8–15.

O'Clery Book of Genealogies, ed. Séamus Pender (*Analecta Hibernica*, 18, Dublin, 1951).

Ó DUBHAGÁIN, SEAÁN MÓR, and Ó HUIDHRÍN, GIOLLA-NA-NAOMH, *The Topographical Poems of John O'Dubhagáin and Giolla na naomh O'Huidhrin*, ed. John O'Donovan (Dublin, 1862), ed. James Carney (Dublin, 1943).

Ó HUIGINN, TADHG DALL, *Bardic Poems*, ed. Eleanor Knott (2 vols., ITS 22–3, London, 1922–6).

Ó RAGHALLAIGH, T. (ed.), 'Senchus na mBúrcach', *Journal of the Galway Archaeological and Historical Society*, 13 (1924–7), 50–60, 101–38; 14 (1928–9), 30–51, 142–67.

Origines parochiales Scotiae, ed. Cosmo Innes *et al.* (2 vols. in 3, Bannatyne Club, Edinburgh, 1850–5).

Oude vlaemsche lideren, ed. J. F. Willems (Ghent, 1848).

PARIS, MATTHEW, *Chronica majora*, ed. Henry Richards Luard (7 vols., RS, 1872–83).

Parliaments and Councils of Mediaeval Ireland, ed. H. G. Richardson and G. O. Sayles (IMC, Dublin, 1947).

Pipe Roll, 22 Henry II (Pipe Roll Society 25, 1904).

Placitorum abbreviatio (Record Commission, London, 1811).

Poems on Marcher Lords, ed. Anne O'Sullivan and Pádraig Ó Riain (ITS 53, London, 1987).

Poems on the Butlers, ed. James Carney (Dublin, 1945).

Pommersches Urkundenbuch, i, ed. Klaus Conrad (2nd edn., Cologne and Vienna, 1970).

Primera crónica general de España, ed. Ramón Menéndez Pidal (2 vols., Madrid, 1955).

Proceedings and Ordinances of the Privy Council of England, ed. Harris Nicolas (7 vols., London, 1834–7).

PUGH, T. B. (ed.), *The Marcher Lordships of South Wales 1415–1536: Select Documents* (Cardiff, 1963).

Red Book of the Earls of Kildare, ed. Gearóid MacNiocaill (IMC, Dublin, 1964).

Red Book of the Exchequer, ed. Hubert Hall (3 vols., RS, 1896).

REGINO OF PRÜM, *Epistula ad Hathonem archiepiscopum missa*, ed. Friedrich Kurze, *Reginonis . . . chronicon* (SRG, Hanover, 1890), pp. xix–xx.

Register of Ministers and Readers in the Kirk of Scotland, from the Book of Assignation of Stipends, 1574, in *The Miscellany of the Wodrow Society*, i, ed. David Laing (Edinburgh, 1844), 319–96.

Register of Richard Fox . . . 1494–1501, ed. Marjorie Peers Howden (Surtees Society 147, 1932).

Register of the Abbey of St Thomas Dublin, ed. John T. Gilbert (RS, 1889).

Register of the Hospital of St John the Baptist Dublin, ed. Eric St J. Brooks (Dublin, 1936).

Register of the Privy Council of Scotland, iv: *1585–1592*; vii: *1604–7*, ed. David Masson (Edinburgh, 1881, 1885).

Register of Thomas Langley, Bishop of Durham, 1406–1437, iii–iv, ed. Robin L. Storey (Surtees Society 169–70, 1959–61 for 1954–5).

Registrum sancte Marie de Neubotle, ed. Cosmo Innes (Bannatyne Club, Edinburgh, 1849).

Reports of the Deputy Keeper of the Public Records of Ireland 1–55 (Dublin, 1869–1923).

RILEY-SMITH, LOUISE and JONATHAN, *The Crusades: Idea and Reality 1095–1274* (London, 1981).

ROBERT THE MONK, *Historia Iherosolimitana*, *Recueils des historiens des croisades, Historiens occidentaux*, iii (Paris, 1866), 717–882.

Roll of the Shropshire Eyre of 1256, ed. Alan Harding (Selden Society 96, 1981 for 1980).

Rotuli chartarum in turri Londinensi asservati (1199–1216), ed. T. D. Hardy (London, 1837).

Rotuli curiae regis (1194–1200), ed. Francis Palgrave (2 vols., London, 1835).

Rotuli litterarum clausarum in turri Londinensi asservati (1204–27), ed. T. D. Hardy (2 vols., London, 1833–44).

Rotuli litterarum patentium in turri Londinensi asservati (1201–1216), ed. T. D. Hardy (London, 1835).

Rotuli Parliamentorum (6 vols., London, 1767–77).

Rotulorum patentium et clausorum cancellariae Hiberniae calendarium, i (Irish Record Commission, Dublin, 1828).

SAN PEDRO, DIEGO DE, *Cárcel de Amor*, ed. Keith Whinnom (Madrid, 1971).

SAXO GRAMMATICUS, *Gesta Danorum*, ed. J. Olrik and H. Raeder (2 vols., Copenhagen, 1931–57).

SAYLES, G. O. (ed.), 'The Legal Proceedings against the First Earl of Desmond', *Analecta Hibernica*, 23 (1966), 1–47.

Schlesisches Urkundenbuch, i, ed. Heinrich Appelt (Vienna, Cologne, and Graz, 1963–71), iii, ed. Winfried Irgang (Cologne and Vienna, 1984).

SMITH, COLIN C., *Spanish Ballads* (London, 1964).

Song of Dermot and the Earl, ed. and trans. Goddard H. Orpen (Oxford, 1892).

Staročeské satiry Hradeckého rukopisu a Smilovy školy, ed. Josef Hrabák (Prague, 1962).

Staročeské skladby dramatické původu liturgického, ed. Jan Máchal (Prague, 1908).

State Papers: Henry VIII, iv (Record Commission, London, 1836).

Statute Rolls of the Parliament of Ireland: Henry VI, I–XII Edward IV, ed. Henry F. Berry (Dublin, 1910, 1914); *XII–XXII Edward IV*, ed. James F. Morrissey (Dublin, 1939).

Statutes . . . of the Parliament of Ireland: King John to Henry V, ed. Henry F. Berry (Dublin, 1907).

STONES, E. L. G. (ed.), *Anglo-Scottish Relations 1174–1328* (Oxford, 1965).

STUBBS, WILLIAM, *Select Charters* (9th edn., Oxford, 1913).

SUÁREZ FERNÁNDEZ, LUIS, *Historia del reinado de Juan I de Castilla*, ii: *Registro documental, 1371–1383* (Madrid, 1982).

Taxatio ecclesiastica (Record Commission, London, 1802).

THEINER, AUGUSTIN (ed.), *Vetera monumenta Hibernorum et Scotorum historiam illustrantia* (Rome, 1864).

THIETMAR OF MERSEBURG, *Chronicon*, ed. Robert Holtzmann (*SRG*, Berlin, 1935).

Tkadleček, ed. Hynek Hrubý and František Šimek (Prague, 1923).

TOMÁŠ OF ŠTÍTNÝ, *Knížky šestery*, ed. Karel Jaromír Erben (Prague, 1852)

ULRICH VON ESCHENBACH, *Alexander*, ed. Wendelin Toischler (Tübingen, 1888).

Urkundenbuch des Erzstifts Magdeburg, i, ed. Friedrich Israël and Walter Möllenberg (Magdeburg, 1937).

VALERA, DIEGO DE, *Memorial de diversas hazañas*, ed. Juan de Mata Carriazo (Madrid, 1941).

Valor ecclesiasticus (6 vols., Record Commission, London, 1810–34).

VINCENT OF PRAGUE, *Annales*, ed. Wilhelm Wattenbach, *MGH, SS* 1 (Hanover, 1861), 658–83.

Vita (major) sancti Stanislai Cracoviensis episcopi, ed. Wojciech Kętrzyński, *MPH* 4 (Lwów, 1884, repr. Warsaw, 1961), 319–438.

Vita Prieflingensis, i.e. Sancti Ottonis episcopi Babenbergensis vita

Prieflingensis, ed. Jan Wikarjak and Kazimierz Liman, *MPH*, NS 7/1 (Warsaw, 1966).

Výbor z české literatury doby husitské, i, ed. Bohuslav Havránek *et al.* (Prague, 1963).

Welsh Assize Roll 1277–84, ed. James Conway Davies (Cardiff, 1940).

Westminster Chronicle 1381–1394, ed. and trans. L. C. Hector and Barbara Harvey (Oxford, 1982).

WILLIAM OF NEWBURGH, *Historia rerum Anglicarum*, ed. Richard Howlett, *Chronicles of the Reigns of Stephen, Henry II and Richard I* (4 vols., RS, 1884–9), i–ii.

WRIGHT, ROGER, *Spanish Ballads (with English Verse translations)* (Warminster, 1987).

SECONDARY LITERATURE

Abraham, Władysław, *Organizacja Kościoła w Polsce do połowy wieku XII* (3rd edn., Poznań, 1962).

—— 'Sprawa Muskaty', *Rozprawy Akademii Umiejętności: Wydział historyczno-filozoficzny*, 30 (1894), 122–80.

ACIÉN ALMANSA, MANUEL, *Ronda y su serranía en tiempo de los Reyes Católicos* (3 vols., Málaga, 1979).

ALBA, RAMÓN, *Acerca de algunas particularidades de las Comunidades de Castilla tal vez relacionadas con el supuesto acaecer terreno del Milenio Igualitario* (Madrid, 1975).

ALLMAND, C. T., *Lancastrian Normandy 1415–1450: The History of a Medieval Occupation* (Oxford, 1983).

ALPHANDÉRY, PAUL, and DUPRONT, ALPHONSE, *La Chrétienté et l'idée de croisade* (2 vols., Paris, 1954–9).

AMADOR DE LOS RÍOS, JOSÉ, *Memoria histórico-crítica de las treguas celebradas en 1439 entre los reyes de Castilla y Granada* (Madrid, 1879).

APPLEBOME, PETER, 'Some Say Frontier Is Still There', *New York Times* (12 Dec. 1987), 11.

ARGOTE DE MOLINA, GONZALO, *Nobleza de Andalucía* (Seville, 1588).

ARIÉ, RACHEL, *L'Espagne musulmane aux temps des Nasrides, 1232–1492* (Paris, 1973).

ARMISTEAD, SAMUEL G., and MONROE, JAMES T., 'A New Version of *La Morica de Antequera*', *La corónica*, 12 (1984), 228–40.

—— and SILVERMAN, JOSEPH H., '*La Sanjuanada*: ¿Huellas de una harǧa en la tradición actual?', in their *En torno al romancero sefardí (Hispanismo y balcanismo de la tradición judeo-española)* (Madrid, 1982), 13–22.

ARMSTRONG, ROBERT B., *The History of Liddesdale . . .* (Edinburgh, 1883).

ARRIBAS PALAU, MARIANO, *Las treguas entre Castilla y Granada firmadas por Fernando I de Aragón* (Tetuan, 1956).

BAGWELL, RICHARD, *Ireland under the Tudors* (3 vols., London, 1885–90).

BAILYN, BERNARD, *The Peopling of British North America: An Introduction* (New York, 1986).

—— *Voyagers to the West: A Passage in the Peopling of America on the Eve of the Revolution* (New York, 1986).

BALON, J., 'L'Organisation judiciaire des marches féodales', *Annales de la société archéologique de Namur*, 46 (1951), 5–72.

BALZER, OSWALD, 'Polonia, Poloni, gens Polonica w świetle źródeł drugiej połowy wieku XIII', in *Księga pamiątkowa ku czci Bolesława Orzechowicza* (2 vols., Lwów, 1916), i. 71–93.

BARKAI, RON, *Cristianos y musulmanes en la España medieval: El enemigo en el espejo* (Madrid, 1984).

BARRIOS GARCÍA, ÁNGEL, *Estructuras agrarias y de poder en Castilla: El ejemplo de Ávila (1085–1320)* (2 vols., Salamanca, 1983–4).

BARROW, GEOFFREY, *Robert Bruce and the Community of the Realm of Scotland* (rev. edn., Edinburgh, 1982).

—— *The Anglo-Norman Era in Scottish History* (Oxford, 1980).

—— *The Kingdom of the Scots* (London, 1973).

—— 'A Note on Falstone', *Archaeologia Aeliana*, 5th ser., 2 (1974), 149–52.

—— 'Northern English Society in the Early Middle Ages', *Northern History*, 4 (1969), 1–28.

—— 'The Pattern of Lordship and Feudal Settlement in Cumbria', *Journal of Medieval History*, 1 (1975), 117–38.

BARTELS, KARL, *Deutsche Krieger in polnischen Diensten von Misika I. bis Kasimir dem Grossen, c.963–1370* (Berlin, 1922).

BARTLETT, ROBERT, *Gerald of Wales 1146–1223* (Oxford, 1982).

—— 'Technique militaire et pouvoir politique, 900–1300', *Annales: Économies, sociétés, civilisations*, 41 (1986), 1135–59.

—— 'The Conversion of a Pagan Society in the Middle Ages', *History*, 70 (1985), 185–201.

BASZKIEWICZ, JAN, *Powstanie zjednoczonego państwa polskiego (na przełomie XIII i XIV wieku)* (Warsaw, 1954).

BATES, CADWALLADER, *The Border Holds of Northumberland* (Newcastle upon Tyne, 1891).

BATESON, MARY, 'The Laws of Breteuil', *EHR* 15 (1900), 73–8, 302–18, 496–523, 754–7; 16 (1901), 92–110, 332–45.

BAUMANN, WINFRIED, *Die Sage von Heinrich dem Löwen bei den Slaven* (Slavistische Beiträge 83, Munich, 1975).

BÉNICHOU, PAUL, *Creación poética en el romancero tradicional* (Madrid, 1968).

BEUMANN, HELMUT, 'Die Gründung des Bistums Oldenburg und die Missionspolitik Ottos des Großen', in his *Ausgewählte Aufsätze 1966–1986* (Sigmaringen, 1987), 177–92.

BIENIAK, JANUSZ, *Wielkopolska, Kujawy, Ziemie Łęczycka i Sieradzka wobec problemu zjednoczenia państwowego w latach 1300–1306 (Roczniki Towarzystwa Naukowego w Toruniu*, 74/2, Toruń, 1969).

—— 'Rola Kujaw w Polsce piastowskiej', *Ziemia Kujawska*, I (1963), 27–71.

—— 'Zjednoczenie państwa polskiego', in Aleksander Gieysztor (ed.), *Polska dzielnicowa i zjednoczona: Państwo—społeczeństwo—kultura* (Warsaw, 1972), 202–78.

BILLINGTON, RAY ALLEN, *America's Frontier Heritage* (New York, 1966).

—— *Frederick Jackson Turner: Historian, Scholar, Teacher* (New York, 1973).

—— *Genesis of the Frontier Thesis: A Study in Historical Creativity* (San Marino, 1971).

—— *The American Frontier Thesis: Attack and Defense* (American Historical Association pamphlet 101, Washington, 1971).

—— *Westward Expansion: A History of the American Frontier* (New York, 1949; 5th edn., 1982).

BISHKO, CHARLES J., 'The Castilian as Plainsman: The Medieval Ranching Frontier in La Mancha and Extremadura', in Archibald R. Lewis and Thomas F. McGann (eds.), *The New World Looks at its History: Proceedings of the Second International Congress of Historians of the United States and Mexico* (Austin, 1963), 47–69.

—— 'The Spanish and Portuguese Reconquest, 1095–1492', in Kenneth Setton (ed.), *A History of the Crusades*, iii: *The Fourteenth and Fifteenth Centuries*, ed. Harry W. Hazard (Madison, 1975), 396–456.

BISSON, THOMAS N., *The Medieval Crown of Aragon: A Short History* (Oxford, 1986).

BITTNER, KONRAD, *Deutsche und Tschechen: Zur Geistesgeschichte des böhmischen Raumes*, i (Brno, 1936).

BLAIR, PETER HUNTER, *Roman Britain and Early England* (Edinburgh and London, 1963).

BOGUCKA, MARIA, and SAMSONOWICZ, HENRYK, *Dzieje miast i mieszczaństwa w Polsce przedrozbiorowej* (Wrocław, 1986).

BONILLA, J. A., and TOVAL, E., *El tratado de paz de 1481 entre Castilla y Granada* (Jaén, 1982).

BORKOWSKA, URSZULA, 'La Reconstruction et le développement: Fin du XIe et XIIe siècle', in Jerzy Kłoczowski (ed.), *Histoire religieuse de la Pologne* (Paris, 1987), 56–67.

BOSSY, JOHN, 'Blood and Baptism: Kinship, Community and Christianity in Western Europe from the Fourteenth to the Seventeenth Centuries', in Derek Baker (ed.), *Studies in Church History*, 10 (Oxford, 1973), 129–43.

BOWEN, E. G., *Saints, Seaways and Settlements in the Celtic Lands* (Cardiff, 1969, repr. 1977).

BOYCE, GRAY, et al., 'S. Harrison Thomson', *Speculum*, 51 (1976), 578–80.

BRANKAČK, JAN, *Studien zur Wirtschaft und Sozialstruktur der Westslawen zwischen Elbe–Saale und Oder aus der Zeit vom 9. bis zum 12. Jahrhundert* (Bautzen, 1964).

BRAND, PAUL, 'Ireland and the Literature of the Early Common Law', *Irish Jurist*, NS 16 (1981), 95–113.

BREATNACH, PÁDRAIG A., 'The Chief's Poet', *PRIA* 83 C (1983), 3–79.

BREATNACH, R. A., 'The Book of Uí Mhaine', in *Great Books of Ireland* (Thomas Davis Lectures 1964, Dublin, 1967), 77–89.

BROOKS, ERIC ST JOHN, *Knights' Fees in Counties Wexford, Carlow and Kilkenny* (IMC, Dublin, 1950).

BROWN, A. L., 'The Priory of Coldingham in the Late Fourteenth Century', *Innes Review*, 23 (1972), 91–101.

BROWN, KEITH, *Bloodfeud in Scotland 1573–1625* (Edinburgh, 1986).

BROWING, ROBERT, *Byzantium and Bulgaria: A Comparative Study Across the Early Medieval Frontier* (Berkeley, 1975).

BRUNDAGE, JAMES A., *Medieval Canon Law and the Crusader* (Madison, 1969).

BRÜSKE, WOLFGANG, *Untersuchungen zur Geschichte des Liutizenbundes* (MF 3, Münster and Cologne, 1955).

BRYANT, W. N., 'The Financial Dealings of Edward III with the County Communities, 1330–1360', *EHR* 83 (1968), 760–71.

BUCZEK, DANIEL, 'Archbishop Jakub Świnka, 1283–1314', in Damian S. Wandycz (ed.), *Studies in Polish Civilization* (New York, n.d. (1971?)), 54–65.

BUCZEK, KAROL, 'Gospodarcze funkcje organizacji grodowej w Polsce wczesnofeudalnej (wiek X–XIII)', *Kwartalnik Historyczny*, 86 (1979), 363–84.

—— 'Z badań nad organizacją grodową w Polsce wczesnofeudalnej: Problem terytorialności grodów kasztelańskich', *Kwartalnik Historyczny*, 77 (1970), 3–29.

Bulletin of the Society for the Study of the Crusades and the Latin East, 7 (1987).

BUNTZ, HERWIG, *Die deutsche Alexanderdichtung des Mittelalters* (Stuttgart, 1973).

BURNS, ROBERT I., *Islam under the Crusaders: Colonial Survival in the Thirteenth-Century Kingdom of Valencia* (Princeton, 1973).

—— *Jaume I i els valencians del segle XIII* (Valencia, 1981).

—— *Medieval Colonialism: Postcrusade Exploitation of Islamic Valencia* (Princeton, 1975).

—— *Moors and Crusaders in Mediterranean Spain* (London, 1978).

—— *Muslims, Christians and Jews in the Crusader Kingdom of Valencia* (Cambridge, 1984).

—— *Society and Documentation in Crusader Valencia* (Princeton, 1985).

—— *The Crusader Kingdom of Valencia: Reconstruction on a Thirteenth-century Frontier* (2 vols., Cambridge, Mass., 1967).

—— *The Jesuits and the Indian Wars of the Northwest* (New Haven, 1966, repr., Moscow, Idaho, 1986).

—— 'The Missionary Syndrome: Crusader and Pacific Northwest Religious Expansionism', *Comparative Studies in Society and History* (forthcoming).

—— (ed.), *The Worlds of Alfonso the Learned and James the Conqueror* (Princeton, 1985).

BURRUS, ERNEST J., SJ, 'Alonso de Vera Cruz (+ 1584), Pioneer Defender of the American Indians', *Catholic Historical Review*, 70 (1984), 531–46.

BUTLER, RICHARD, *Some Notices of the Castle and of the Ecclesiastical Buildings of Trim* (Trim, 1835).

BYRNE, FRANCIS J., *Irish Kings and High Kings* (London and New York, 1973).

CABANELAS, DARÍO, 'Un franciscano heterodoxo en la Granada nasrí: Fray Alonso de Mella', *Al Andalus*, 15 (1950), 233–50.

CABRERA MUÑOZ, EMILIO, 'Del Tajo a Sierra Morena', in José A. García de Cortázar *et al.*, *La organización social del espacio en la España medieval: La Corona de Castilla en los siglos VIII a XV* (Barcelona, 1985), 123–61.

CAMPBELL, JAMES, 'England, Scotland and the Hundred Years War', in J. R. Hale, J. R. L. Highfield, and Beryl Smalley (eds.), *Europe in the Late Middle Ages* (London, 1965), 184–216.

ČAPEK, JAN B., 'Vznik a funkce Nové rady', *Věstník*, 1 (1938), 1–100.

CARDAILLAC, LOUIS, *Morisques et chrétiens: Un affrontement polémique (1492–1640)* (Paris, 1977).

CARDEW, ANNE A., 'A Study of Society in the Anglo-Scottish Borders 1455–1502' (Ph.D. thesis, St Andrews University, 1974).

CARRIAZO, JUAN DE MATA, 'Las últimas treguas con Granada', *Boletín del Instituto de Estudios Giennenses*, 3 (1954), 11–43.

—— 'Los moros de Granada en las actas del concejo de Jaén de 1479', *Miscelánea de estudios árabes y hebraicos*, 4 (1955), 81–125, repr. in *Homenaje al profesor Carriazo* (3 vols., Seville, 1971–3), i. 265–310.

—— 'Relaciones fronterizas entre Jaén y Granada: El año 1479', *Revista de archivos, bibliotecas y museos*, 61 (1955), 23–51.

—— 'Un alcalde entre los cristianos y los moros, en la frontera de Granada', *Al Andalus*, 13 (1948), 34–96.

CARSTEN, F. L., 'Slavs in North-Eastern Germany', *Economic History Review*, 11 (1941), 61–76.

CARY, GEORGE, *The Medieval Alexander* (Cambridge, 1956).

CASTRO, AMÉRICO, *The Structure of Spanish History* (Eng. trans., Princeton, 1954).

ČERNÝ, VÁCLAV, *Staročeský Mastičkář* (*Rozpravy československé akademie věd*, 65, řada SV, 7, 1955).

CHAUNU, PIERRE, *L'Expansion européenne du XIIIᵉ au XVᵉ siècle* (Paris, 1969).

CHRISTIANSEN, ERIC, *The Northern Crusades* (London, 1980).

CLANCHY, MICHAEL T., 'Law and Love in the Middle Ages', in John Bossy (ed.), *Disputes and Settlements: Law and Human Relations in the West* (Cambridge, 1983), 47–69.

CLARE, LUCIEN, 'Fêtes, jeux et divertissements à la cour du connétable de Castille, Miguel Lucas de Iranzo (1460–1470): Les Exercices physiques', in *La Fête et l'écriture: Théâtre de cour, cour-théâtre en Espagne et en Italie, 1450–1530 (Colloque international: France–Espagne–Italie, 1985)* (Aix-en-Provence, 1987), 5–32.

—— and HEERS, JACQUES (eds.), *Colloque sur les 'bandos' et querelles dynastiques en Espagne à la fin du Moyen Âge* (Paris, in press).

CLAUDE, DIETRICH, *Geschichte des Erzbistums Magdeburg bis in das 12. Jahrhundert* (2 vols., MF 67, Cologne, 1972–5).

COBLENZ, W., 'Das Sorbengebiet zur Zeit des Liutizenaufstandes', *Zeitschrift für Archäologie*, 18 (1984), 33–40.

CONNOLLY, PHILOMENA, 'An Account of Military Expenditure in Leinster, 1308', *Analecta Hibernica*, 30 (1982), 1–5.

—— 'The Financing of English Expeditions to Ireland, 1361–76', in James F. Lydon (ed.), *England and Ireland in the Later Middle Ages: Essays in Honour of Jocelyn Otway-Ruthven* (Dublin, 1981), 104–21.

CONSTABLE, GILES, 'The Second Crusade as Seen by Contemporaries', *Traditio*, 9 (1953), 213–79.

COSGROVE, ART (ed.), *New History of Ireland*, ii: *Medieval Ireland, 1169–1534* (Oxford, 1987).

COSSÍO, JOSÉ MARÍA DE, 'Cautivos de moros en el siglo XIII: El texto de Pero Marín', *Al Andalus*, 7 (1942), 49–112.

COWAN, IAN B., *The Parishes of Medieval Scotland* (Scottish Record Society 93, Edinburgh, 1967).

—— *The Scottish Reformation* (London, 1982).

COWDREY, H. E. J., 'Pope Urban II's Preaching of the First Crusade', *History*, 55 (1970), 177–88.

CRAMER, HELGA, 'Die Herren von Wedel im Lande über der Oder: Besitz und Herrschaftsbildung bis 1402', *Jahrbuch für die Geschichte Mittel- und Ostdeutschlands*, 18 (1969), 63–129.

CRONON, WILLIAM, 'Revisiting the Vanishing Frontier: The Legacy of Frederick Jackson Turner', *Western Historical Quarterly*, 18 (1987), 157–76.

CURTIS, EDMUND, *A History of Medieval Ireland* (Dublin, 1923).

—— 'The Clan System among English Settlers in Ireland', *EHR* 25 (1910), 116–20.

CURWEN, J. F., *The Castles and Fortified Towers of Cumberland, Westmorland and Lancashire North-of-the-sands* (Cumberland and Westmorland Antiquarian and Archaeological Society, extra series 13, 1913).

DĄBROWSKI, HENRYK, *Rozwój gospodarki rolnej w Polsce od XII do połowy XIV wieku* (*Studia z dziejów gospodarstwa wiejskiego* 5/1; *Studia i Materiały z Historii Kultury Materialnej*, 11, Warsaw, 1962).

DĄBROWSKI, JAN, *Dawne Dziejopisarstwo polskie (do roku 1480)* (Wrocław, 1964).

—— *Korona królestwa polskiego w XIV wieku: Studium z dziejów rozwoju polskiej monarchii stanowej* (Wrocław, 1956).

—— 'Die Krone des polnischen Königtums im 14 Jh.: Eine Studie aus der Geschichte der Entwicklung der polnischen ständischen Monarchie', in Manfred Hellmann (ed.), *Corona regni: Studien über die Krone als Symbol des Staates im späteren Mittelalter* (Darmstadt, 1961), 399–548.

DAVIES, REES, *Conquest, Coexistence and Change: Wales 1063–1415* (Oxford, 1987).

—— *Lordship and Society in the March of Wales 1282–1400* (Oxford, 1978).

—— 'Kings, Lords and Liberties in the March of Wales, 1066–1272', *TRHS*, 5th ser., 29 (1979), 41–61.

—— 'Race Relations in Post-Conquest Wales', *Transactions of the Honourable Society of Cymmrodorion* (1974–5), 32–56.

—— 'The Law of the March', *Welsh History Review*, 5 (1970–1), 1–30,

DELARUELLE, ÉTIENNE, 'L'Idée de croisade chez S. Bernard', in *Mélanges Saint Bernard* (Dijon, 1954), 53–67.

DÉRUMAUX, PIERRRE, 'S. Bernard et les infidèles', in *Mélanges Saint Bernard* (Dijon, 1954), 68–79.

DEWEY, H. W., 'Agriculture and Nutrition iv: The Slavic World', in Joseph R. Strayer (ed.), *The Dictionary of the Middle Ages*, i (New York, 1982), 96–103.

DILLON, MYLES, 'Laud Misc. 610', *Celtica*, 5 (1960), 64–76.

—— 'Laud Misc. 610 (cont.)', *Celtica*, 6 (1963), 135–55.

DLUGOPOLSKI, EDMUND, *Władysław Lokietek na tle swoich czasów* (Wrocław, 1951).

—— 'Bunt wójta Alberta', *Rocznik Krakowski*, 7 (1905), 135–86.

DOBSON, R. B., 'Cathedral Chapters and Cathedral Cities: York, Durham and Carlisle in the Fifteenth Century', *Northern History*, 19 (1983), 15–44.

—— 'The Last English Monks on Scottish Soil', *Scottish Historical Review*, 46 (1967), 1–25.

DODDS, JERRILYNN D., 'The Paintings in the *Sala de Justicia* of the Alhambra: Iconography and Iconology', *Art Bulletin*, 61 (1979), 186–97.

DODGSHON, R. A., *Land and Society in Early Scotland* (Oxford, 1981).

DONALDSON-HUDSON, R., 'Liddel Strength in Cumberland', *History of the Berwickshire Naturalists' Club*, 37/1 (1965), 50–3.

DOWIAT, JERZY, *Polska—państwem średniowiecznej Europy* (Warsaw, 1968).

DUBY, GEORGES, *The Chivalrous Society* (London and Berkeley, 1977).

DUFFY, P. J., 'The Nature of the Medieval Frontier in Ireland', *Studia Hibernica*, 22–3 (1982–3), 21–38.

DUFOURCQ, CHARLES-EMMANUEL, 'Chrétiens et musulmans durant les derniers siècles du Moyen Âge', *Anuario de estudios medievales*, 10 (1980), 207–25.

DVORNIK, FRANCIS, *The Making of Central and Eastern Europe* (London, 1949).

—— *The Slavs in European History and Civilization* (New Brunswick, 1962).

DYSON, STEPHEN, *The Creation of the Roman Frontier* (Princeton, 1985).

EDWARDS, JOHN GORONWY, 'The Normans and the Welsh March', *Proceedings of the British Academy*, 42 (1956), 155–77.

ELLIS, STEVEN G., 'Nationalist Historiography and the English and Gaelic Worlds in the Late Middle Ages', *Irish Historical Studies*, 25 (1986), 1–18.

—— 'Taxation and Defence in Late Medieval Ireland: The Survival of Scutage', *RSAIJn* 107 (1977), 5–28.

EMPEY, C. A., 'Conquest and Settlement: Patterns of Anglo-Norman Settlement in North Munster and South Leinster', *Irish Social and Economic History Journal*, 13 (1986), 5–31.

—— 'The Norman Period, 1185–1500', in William Nolan (ed.), *Tipperary: History and Society: Interdisciplinary Essays on the History of an Irish County* (Dublin, 1985), 71–92.

—— and Simms, Katharine, 'The Ordinances of the White Earl and the Problem of Coign in the Later Middle Ages', *PRIA* 75 C (1975), 161–87.

EPALZA, MÍKEL DE, *Jésus otage: Juifs, chrétiens et musulmans en Espagne (VIe–XVIIe siècle)* (Paris, 1987).

EPPERLEIN, SIEGFRIED, *Bauernbedrückung und Bauernwiderstand im hohen Mittelalter: Zur Erforschung der Ursachen bäuerlichen Abwanderung nach Osten im 12. und 13. Jh.* (Berlin, 1960).

ERDMANN, CARL, *A ideia de cruzada em Portugal* (Coimbra, 1940).

ESCALONA, R. F., *Historia del real monasterio de Sahagún* (facsimile edn., Madrid, 1982).

EYTON, ROBERT W., *Antiquities of Shropshire* (12 vols., London, 1853–60).

FEDOROWICZ, J. K. (ed.), *A Republic of Nobles: Studies in Polish History to 1864* (Cambridge, 1982).

FENRYCH, WIKTOR, *Nowa Marchia w dziejach politycznych Polski w XIII i w XIV wieku* (Zielona Góra and Poznań, 1959).

FLANAGAN, MARIE-THÉRÈSE, 'Monastic Charters from Irish Kings of the Twelfth and Thirteenth Centuries' (unpublished MA thesis, University College, Dublin, 1972).

FLORES, LEANDRO JOSÉ DE, *Memorias históricas de la villa de Alcalá* (Seville, 1833, new edn., Alcalá, 1983).

FLOWER, ROBIN, *Catalogue of Irish Manuscripts in the British Museum*, ii (London, 1926).

FRAME, ROBIN, *Colonial Ireland 1169–1369* (Dublin, 1981).

—— *English Lordship in Ireland, 1318–1361* (Oxford, 1982).

—— 'English Officials and Irish Chiefs in the Fourteenth Century', *EHR* 90 (1975), 748–77.

—— 'Power and Society in the Lordship of Ireland, 1272–1377', *Past and Present*, 76 (1977), 3–33.

—— 'Select Documents xxxvii: The Campaign against the Scots in Munster, 1317', *Irish Historical Studies*, 24 (1984–5), 361–72.

—— 'The Judicial Powers of the Medieval Irish Keepers of the Peace', *Irish Jurist*, NS 2 (1967), 308–26.

—— 'The Justiciarship of Ralph Ufford: Warfare and Politics in Fourteenth-Century Ireland', *Studia Hibernica*, 13 (1973), 7–47.

—— 'War and Peace in the Medieval Lordship of Ireland', in James F. Lydon (ed.), *The English in Medieval Ireland* (Dublin, 1984), 118–41.

FRASER, CONSTANCE M., 'The Pattern of Trade in the North-east of England, 1265–1350', *Northern History*, 4 (1969), 44–66.

FRASER, GEORGE M., *The Steel Bonnets* (London, 1971).

FRITZE, WOLFGANG H., 'Das Vordringen deutscher Herrschaft in Teltow und Barnim', in his *Frühzeit zwischen Ostsee und Donau*, ed. Ludolf Kuchenbuch and Winfried Schich (Berlin, 1982), 297–374.

—— 'Der slawische Aufstand von 983: Eine Schicksalswende', in Eckart Henning and Walter Vogel (eds.), *Festschrift der Landesgeschichtlichen Vereinigung für die Mark Brandenburg* (Berlin, 1984), 9–55.

—— 'Probleme der abodritischen Stammes- und Reichsverfassung und ihrer Entwicklung von Stammesstaat zum Herrschaftsstaat', in Herbert Ludat (ed.), *Siedlung und Verfassung der Slawen zwischen Elbe, Saale und Oder* (Giessen, 1960), 141–219.

GARCÍA ARIAS, LUIS, *El concepto de guerra y la denominada 'guerra fría'* (Saragossa, 1956).

GARCÍA DE CORTÁZAR, JOSÉ A., *et al.*, *La organización social del espacio en la España medieval: La Corona de Castilla en los siglos VIII a XV* (Barcelona, 1985).

GARCÍA FERNÁNDEZ, MANUEL, *Andalucía en tiempos de Alfonso XI* (microfiche edn., Seville, 1987).

GARCÍA FIGUERAS, TOMÁS, 'Relaciones fronterizas de Jerez y los musulmanes de las serranías de Cádiz y Málaga', in *Actas del Primer Congreso de Estudios Árabes e Islámicos* (Madrid, 1964), 277–84.

GARCÍA GUZMÁN, MARÍA DEL MAR, *El Adelantamiento de Cazorla en la Baja Edad Media* (Cádiz, 1985).

GAUTIER-DALCHÉ, JEAN, *Historia urbana de León y Castilla (siglos IX–XIII)* (Madrid, 1979).

GIEYSZTOR, ALEKSANDER, *et al.*, *History of Poland* (Warsaw, 1968).

—— (ed.), *Polska dzielnicowa i zjednoczona: Państwo—społeczeństwo—kultura* (Warsaw, 1972).

GIEYSZTOROWA, IRENA, 'Badania nad historią zaludnienia Polski', *Kwartalnik Historii Kultury Materialnej*, 11 (1963), 523–62.

—— 'Research into the Demographic History of Poland: A Provisional Summing-up', *Acta Poloniae historica*, 18 (1968), 5–17.

GIMÉNEZ SOLER, ANDRÉS, *La Corona de Aragón y Granada* (Barcelona, 1909).

GONZÁLEZ, JULIO, *Repoblación de Castilla la Nueva* (2 vols., Madrid, 1975–6).

—— 'Las conquistas de Fernando III en Andalucía', *Hispania*, 24 (1946), 545–631.

GONZÁLEZ GARCÍA, MANUEL, *Salamanca: La repoblación y la ciudad en la Baja Edad Media* (Salamanca, 1973).

GONZÁLEZ JIMÉNEZ, MANUEL, *En torno a los orígenes de Andalucia: La repoblación del siglo XIII* (Seville, 1980).

—— *La repoblación de la zona de Sevilla durante el siglo XIV* (Seville, 1975).

—— 'Alcalá de Guadaira en el siglo XIII: Conquista y repoblación', in *Actas de las I Jornadas de Historia de Alcalá de Guadaira* (Alcalá, 1987), 45–52.

—— 'La caballería popular en Andalucía (siglos XIII–XV)', *Anuario de estudios medievales*, 15 (1985), 315–29.

—— 'Los mudéjares andaluces (siglos XIII–XV)', in *Actas del V Coloquio de Historia Medieval Andaluza* (Córdoba, in press).

—— 'Reconquista y repoblación del Occidente Peninsular (siglos XI–XIII)', in *Actas del II Congreso Luso-Español de Historia Medieval*, ii (Oporto, in press).

GOODMAN, ANTHONY, 'The Anglo-Scottish Marches in the Fifteenth Century: A Frontier Society?', in Roger A. Mason (ed.), *Scotland and England 1286–1815* (Edinburgh, 1987), 18–33.

GÓRECKI, PIOTR, '*Viator* to *Ascriptitius*: Rural Economy, Lordship, and the Origins of Serfdom in Medieval Poland', *Slavic Review*, 42 (1983), 14–35.

GÓRSKI, KAROL, *Zakon Krzyżacki a powstanie państwa pruskiego* (Wrocław, 1977).

GRAHAM, BRIAN, 'The Mottes of the Anglo-Norman Liberty of Trim', in Harman Murtagh (ed.), *Irish Midland Studies: Essays in Commemoration of N. W. English* (Athlone, 1980), 39–56.

GRAHAM, T. H. B., *The Barony of Gilsland* (Cumberland and Westmorland Antiquarian and Archaeological Society, extra series 16, 1934).

GRANT, ALEXANDER, *Independence and Nationhood: Scotland 1306–1469* (London, 1984).

GRASSOTTI, HILDA, 'Un abulense en Beaucaire', *Cuadernos de historia de España*, 43–4 (1967), 133–53.

GRAUS, FRANTIŠEK, *Die Nationenbildung der Westslawen im Mittelalter* (Nationes 3, Sigmaringen, 1980).

GREENE, DAVID, 'The Professional Poets', in Brian Ó Cuív (ed.), *Seven Centuries of Irish Learning* (Dublin, 1961), 45–57.

GUERRERO LOVILLO, JOSÉ, *Las Cántigas: Estudio arqueológico de sus miniaturas* (Madrid, 1949).

GULLEY, J. L. M., 'The Turnerian Frontier: A Study in the Migration of Ideas', *Tijdschrift voor economische en sociale geographie*, 50 (1959), 65–72, 81–91.

HALPERIN, CHARLES, 'The Ideology of Silence: Prejudice and Pragmatism on the Medieval Religious Frontier', *Comparative Studies in Society and History*, 26 (1984), 442–66.

HAND, GEOFFREY J., *English Law in Ireland 1290–1324* (Cambridge, 1967).

HARDING, ALAN, 'The Origins and Early History of the Keeper of the Peace', *TRHS*, 5th ser., 10 (1960), 85–109.

HARRISS, G. L., *King, Parliament and Public Finance in Medieval England to 1369* (Oxford, 1975).

HARVEY, LEONARD P., 'Oral Composition and the Performance of Novels of Chivalry in Spain', *Forum for Modern Language Studies*, 10 (1974), 270–86.

HAWS, C. H., *Scottish Parish Clergy at the Reformation 1540–1574* (Scottish Record Society, NS 3, Edinburgh, 1972).

Hay, Denys, 'England, Scotland and Europe: The Problem of the Frontier', *TRHS*, 5th ser., 25 (1975), 77–93.

Heck, Roman, 'Historiography and Polish Medieval National Consciousness', *Quaestiones Medii Aevi*, 3 (1986), 93–110.

Hedley, William Percy, *Northumberland Families* (2 vols., Newcastle upon Tyne, 1968–70).

Heers, Jacques, *Le clan familial au Moyen Âge* (Paris, 1974).

Henneman, John B., *Royal Taxation in Fourteenth-Century France: The Captivity and Ransom of John II, 1356–1370* (Philadelphia, 1976).

—— *Royal Taxation in Fourteenth-Century France: The Development of War Financing 1322–1356* (Princeton, 1971).

Hensel, Witold, *Anfänge der Städte bei den Ost- und Westslawen* (Bautzen, 1967).

—— *Słowiańszczyzna wczesnośredniowieczna: Zarys kultury materialnej* (4th edn., Warsaw, 1987).

—— 'The Origins of Western and Eastern European Slav Towns', in M. W. Barley (ed.), *European Towns: Their Archaeology and Early History* (London and New York, 1977), 373–90.

Herrmann, Joachim (ed.), *Die Slawen in Deutschland: Ein Handbuch* (Berlin, 1972; rev. edn., 1985).

Hess, Andrew, *Forgotten Frontier: A History of the Sixteenth-Century Ibero-African Frontier* (Chicago, 1978).

Hewitt, Herbert J., *The Organization of War under Edward III 1338–62* (Manchester, 1966).

Higounet, Charles, *Die deutsche Ostsiedlung im Mittelalter* (Berlin, 1986).

Hillgarth, Jocelyn N., *The Spanish Kingdoms, 1250–1516* (2 vols., Oxford, 1976–8).

Historia de Andalucia, ii (Madrid and Barcelona, 1980).

History of Northumberland (15 vols., London and Newcastle upon Tyne, 1893–1940).

Holt, James C., *Robin Hood* (London, 1982).

—— *The Northerners* (Oxford, 1961).

—— 'Feudal Society and the Family in Early Medieval England', *TRHS*, 5th ser., 32 (1982), 193–212; 33 (1983), 193–220; 34 (1984), 1–25; 35 (1985), 1–28.

Hopkins, John F. P., *Medieval Muslim Government in Barbary until the Sixth Century of the Hijra* (London, 1958).

Horrent, Jacques, 'L'Histoire légendaire de Charlemagne en Espagne', *Actes du VIIᵉ Congrès International de la Société Rencesvals* (2 vols., Paris, 1978), i. 125–56.

Hrabák, Josef, *Studie ze starší české literatury* (Prague, 1956).

—— 'Česká středověká rytířská epika', in *Československé přednášky pro*

VII. mezinárodní sjezd slavistů ve Varšavě (2 vols., Prague, 1973), i. 159–67.

HRUBÝ, ANTONÍN, *Der Ackermann und seine Vorlage* (Munich, 1971).

HUGILL, ROBERT, *Borderland Castles and Peles* (Newcastle upon Tyne, 1970).

JACKSON, KENNETH H., 'The Sources for the Life of St Kentigern', in Nora K. Chadwick *et al.* (eds.), *Studies in the Early British Church* (Cambridge, 1958), 273–357.

JACKSON, W. TURRENTINE, 'A Brief Message for the Young and/or Ambitious: Comparative Frontiers as a Field for Investigation', *Western Historical Quarterly*, 9 (1978), 4–18.

JACOBS, WILBUR, 'Frederick Jackson Turner: Master Teacher', *Pacific Historical Review*, 23 (1954), 49–58.

—— (ed.), *The Historical World of Frederick Jackson Turner* (New Haven, 1968).

JAKOBSON, ROMAN, *Moudrost starých Čechů: Odvěké základy národního odboje* (New York, 1943).

JAMES, MERVYN, *Family, Lineage and Civil Society* (Oxford, 1974).

JIMENO, ESTHER, 'La población de Soria y su término en 1270', *Boletín de la Real Academia de la Historia*, 142 (1958), 207–74 and 365–494.

JOLLIFFE, J. E. A., 'Northumbrian Institutions', *EHR* 41 (1926), 1–42.

JONES, GLANVILLE R. J., 'Basic Patterns of Settlement Distribution in Northern England', *Advancement of Science*, 71 (1961), 192–200.

—— 'Early Territorial Organization in Northern England', in Alan Small (ed.), *The Fourth Viking Congress* (Edinburgh and London, 1965), 67–84.

JORDAN, KARL, *Die Bistumsgründungen Heinrichs des Löwen* (*MGH* Schriften 3, Leipzig, 1939).

—— *Henry the Lion* (Eng. trans., Oxford, 1986).

KAHL, HANS-DIETRICH, *Slawen und Deutsche in der brandenburgischen Geschichte des zwölften Jahrhunderts* (2 vols., MF 30, Cologne and Graz, 1964).

—— 'Christianisierungsvorstellungen im Kreuzzugsprogramm Bernhards von Clairvaux', *Przeglad Historyczny*, 75 (1984), 453–61.

—— 'Compellere intrare: Die Wendenpolitik Bruns von Querfurt', in Helmut Beumann (ed.), *Heidenmission und Kreuzzugsgedanke in der deutschen Ostpolitik des Mittelalters* (Wege der Forschung 7, Darmstadt, 1963), 177–274.

—— 'Die Ableitung des Missionskreuzzugs aus sibyllinischer Eschatologie', in Z. H. Nowak (ed.), *Die Rolle der Ritterorden in der Christianisierung und Kolonisierung des Ostseegebietes* (Colloquia Torunensia 1, Toruń, 1983), 129–39.

—— 'Einige Beobachtungen zum Sprachgebrauch von *Natio*', in Helmut

Beumann and Werner Schröder (eds.), *Aspekte der Nationenbildung im Mittelalter* (Nationes 1, Sigmaringen, 1978).

—— 'Fides cum Ydolatria', in *Festschrift für Berent Schwineköper* (Sigmaringen, 1982), 291–307.

—— 'Wie kam es zum Wendenkreuzzug?', in Klaus-Detlev Grothusen and Klaus Zernack (eds.), *Europa slavica–Europa orientalis: Festschrift für Herbert Ludat* (Berlin, 1980), 286–96.

KAPELLE, WILLIAM, *The Norman Conquest of the North* (Chapel Hill, 1979).

KARASIEWICZ, WLADYSLAW, *Jakub II Świnka arcybiskup gnieźnieński 1283–1314* (Poznań, 1948).

KEELING, SUSAN, M., 'Church and Religion in the Anglo-Scottish Border Counties, 1534–72' (Ph.D. thesis, Durham University, 1975).

KEPPIE, LAWRENCE, *Scotland's Roman Remains* (Edinburgh, 1986).

KHADDURI, MAJID, *War and Peace in the Law of Islam* (Baltimore, 1955).

KILGOUR, R. L., *The Decline of Chivalry as Shown in the French Literature of the Late Middle Ages* (Cambridge, Mass., 1937).

KIRBY, D. P., 'Strathclyde and Cumbria: A Survey of Historical Development to 1092', *Transactions of the Cumberland and Westmorland Antiquarian and Archaeological Society*, NS 62 (1962), 77–94.

KNOCH, PETER, 'Kreuzzug und Siedlung: Studien zum Aufruf der Magdeburger Kirche vom 1108', *Jahrbuch für die Geschichte Mittel- und Ostdeutschlands*, 23 (1974), 1–33.

KNOLL, PAUL, *The Rise of the Polish Monarchy: Piast Poland in East Central Europe 1320–1370* (Chicago, 1972).

—— 'Feudal Poland: Division and Reunion', *Polish Review*, 23/2 (1978), 40–52.

—— 'Poland', in Joseph R. Strayer (ed.), *The Dictionary of the Middle Ages*, ix (New York, 1987), 716–31.

—— 'The Urban Development of Medieval Poland, with Particular Reference to Kraków', in Bariša Krekić (ed.), *Urban Society of Eastern Europe in Pre-Modern Times* (Berkeley, Los Angeles, and London, 1987), 63–136.

—— 'Władysław Lokietek and the Restoration of the *Regnum Poloniae*', *Medievalia et humanistica*, 17 (1966), 51–78.

KNOTT, ELEANOR, *Irish Classical Poetry* (Dublin, 1957).

KOEBNER, RICHARD, '*Locatio*: Zur Begriffssprache und Geschichte der deutschen Kolonisation', *Zeitschrift des Vereins für Geschichte Schlesiens*, 63 (1929), 1–32.

KOSSMANN, OSKAR, *Polen im Mittelalter*, ii: *Staat, Gesellschaft, Wirtschaft im Bannkreis des Westens* (Marburg/Lahn, 1985).

KÖTZSCHKE, RUDOLF, 'Die deutschen Marken im Sorbenland', in his *Deutsche und Slawen im mitteldeutschen Osten: Ausgewählte Aufsätze* (Darmstadt, 1961).

Bibliography 355

KUHN, WALTER, 'Die deutschrechtlichen Städte in Schlesien und Polen in der ersten Hälfte des 13. Jahrhunderts', *Zeitschrift für Ostforschung*, 15 (1966), 278–337, 457–510, 704–43.

—— 'Die Siedlerzahlen der deutschen Ostsiedlung', in Karl Gustav Specht *et al.* (eds.), *Studium sociale: Karl Valentin Müller dargebracht* (Cologne and Opladen, 1963), 131–54.

LABUDA, GERARD, 'Geneza przysłowia "Jak świat światem, nie będzie Niemiec Polakowi bratem"', *Zeszyty Naukowe Uniwersytetu im. A. Mickiewicza (Poznań): Historia*, 8 (1968), 17–32.

—— 'Początki państwa polskiego w historiografii polskiej i niemieckiej', in *Stosunki polsko-niemieckie w historiografii* (Poznań, 1974), 150–217.

LACARRA, JOSÉ M., 'Aspectos económicos de la sumisión de los reinos de Taifas (1010–1102)', in *Homenaje a Jaime Vicens Vives*, i (Barcelona, 1965), 255–77.

—— 'Les Villes-frontières dans l'Espagne des XIᵉ et XIIᵉ siècles', *Le Moyen Âge*, 69 (1963), 205–22.

LADERO QUESADA, MIGUEL ÁNGEL, *Granada: Historia de un país islámico (1232–1571)* (2nd edn., Madrid, 1979).

—— *La Hacienda Real de Castilla en el siglo XV* (La Laguna, 1973).

—— 'Almojarifazgo sevillano y comercio exterior de Andalucía en el siglo XV', *Anuario de historia económica y social*, 2 (1969), 69–115.

——, and GONZÁLEZ JIMÉNEZ, MANUEL, 'La población en la frontera de Gibraltar y el repartimiento de Vejer (siglos XIII–XIV)', *Historia, instituciones, documentos*, 4 (1977), 199–316.

LALIK, TADEUSZ, 'Organizacja grodowo-prowincjonalna w Polsce XI i początków XII wieku', *Studia z Dziejów Osadnictwa*, 5 (1967), 5–51.

LAMBTON, ANNE K. S., *State and Government in Medieval Islam: An Introduction to the Study of Islamic Political Theory: The Jurists* (Oxford, 1981).

LAMMERS, WALTER, *Geschichte Schleswig-Holsteins*, iv/1: *Das Hochmittelalter bis zur Schlacht von Bornhöved* (Neumünster, 1981).

LAPIDUS, IRA M., *Muslim Cities in the Later Middle Ages* (Cambridge, Mass., 1967).

LAPSLEY, GAILLARD T., *The County Palatine of Durham* (Cambridge, Mass., 1900).

LATTIMORE, OWEN, *Studies in Frontier History: Collected Papers, 1928–1958* (London, 1962).

LEMARIGNIER, JEAN-FRANÇOIS, *Recherches sur l'hommage en marche et les frontières féodales* (Lille, 1945).

LEWIS, ARCHIBALD R., 'James the Conqueror: Montpellier and Southern France', in Robert I. Burns (ed.), *The Worlds of Alfonso the Learned and James the Conqueror* (Princeton, 1985), ch. 6, pp. 130–49.

—— 'The Closing of the Medieval Frontier, 1250–1350', *Speculum*, 33 (1958), 475–83.

LEWIS, N. B., 'The Organization of Indentured Retinues in Fourteenth-Century England', *TRHS*, 4th ser., 27 (1945), 29–39.

—— 'The Summons of the English Feudal Levy, 5 April 1327', in T. A. Sandquist and M. R. Powicke (eds.), *Essays in Medieval History Presented to Bertie Wilkinson* (Toronto, 1969), 236–49.

LEYSER, KARL, 'The German Aristocracy from the Ninth to the Early Twelfth Century: A Historical and Cultural Sketch', *Past and Present*, 41 (1968), 25–53, repr. in his *Medieval Germany and its Neighbours* (London, 1982), 161–89.

LITAK, STANISLAW, 'Le Temps des réformes et des luttes religeuses (XVIᵉ siècle–milieu du XVIIᵉ)', in Jerzy Kłoczowski (ed.), *Histoire religieuse de la Pologne* (Paris, 1987), 173–220.

LOMAX, DEREK W., *Las órdenes militares en la Península Ibérica durante la Edad Media* (Salamanca, 1976).

—— *The Reconquest of Spain* (London, 1978).

LOOMIS, ROGER S., 'A Phantom Tale of Female Ingratitude', *Modern Philology*, 14 (1916–17), 175–9.

LÓPEZ DAPENA, A., 'Cautiverio y rescate de D. Juan Manrique, capitán de la frontera castellana, 1456–1457', *Cuadernos de estudios medievales*, 12–13 (1984), 243–53.

LÓPEZ DE COCA CASTAÑER, JOSÉ ENRIQUE, 'Comercio exterior del reino de Granada', in *Actas del II Coloquio de Historia Medieval Andaluza* (Seville, 1982), 335–77.

—— 'De nuevo sobre la historicidad del romance "Río Verde, Río Verde"', in *Actas del I Coloquio de Historia Medieval Andaluza* (Córdoba, 1982), 11–19.

—— 'El reino de Granada, 1354–1501', in *Historia de Andalucía*, iii (2nd edn., Madrid, 1981), 327–497.

—— 'Esclavos, alfaqueques y mercaderes en la frontera del mar de Alborán, 1490–1516', *Hispania*, 38 (1978), 275–300.

—— 'Granada bajo la casa de Abū Naṣr Saʻd', in *Seis lecciones sobre la guerra de Granada* (Granada, 1983), 59–73.

—— 'Poblamiento y frontera en el obispado de Málaga a fines del siglo XV', *Cuadernos de estudios medievales*, 2–3 (1974–5), 367–407.

—— 'Privilegios fiscales y repoblación en el reino de Granada, 1485–1520', *Baetica*, 2 (1979), 205–23.

—— 'Revisión de una década de la historia granadina, 1446–1455', *Miscelánea de estudios árabes y hebraicos*, 29–30 (1980–1), 61–90.

—— 'Sobre historia económica y social del reino nazarí de Granada: Problemas de fuentes y método', in *Actas del I Congreso de Historia de Andalucía*, 1–2: *Andalucía medieval* (2 vols., Córdoba, 1978), ii. 395–404.

—— and ACIÉN ALMANSA, MANUEL, 'Los mudéjares del obispado

de Málaga (1485–1501)', in *Actas del I Simposio Internacional de Mudejarismo* (Madrid and Teruel, 1981), 307–47.

LÓPEZ ORTIZ, JOSÉ, 'Fatwàs granadinas de los siglos XIV y XV', *Al Andalus*, 6 (1941), 73–127.

LOTTER, FRIEDRICH, *Die Konzeption des Wendenkreuzzugs* (Vorträge und Forschungen, Sonderband 23, Sigmaringen, 1977).

—— 'Bemerkungen zur Christianisierung der Abodriten', in Helmut Beumann (ed.), *Festschrift für Walter Schlesinger* (2 vols., MF 74, Cologne, 1973–4), ii. 395–442.

—— 'Die Vorstellungen von Heidenkrieg und Wendenmission bei Heinrich dem Löwen', in Wolf-Dieter Mohrmann (ed.), *Heinrich der Löwe* (Göttingen, 1980), 11–43.

LOURIE, ELENA, 'A Society Organized for War: Medieval Spain', *Past and Present*, 35 (1966), 54–76.

—— 'The Confraternity of Belchite, the Ribat and the Temple', *Viator*, 13 (1982), 159–76.

LOWMIAŃSKI, HENRYK, *Początki Polski* (6 vols., Warsaw, 1964–85).

—— (ed.), *Polska w okresie rozdrobnienia feudalnego* (Wrocław, etc. 1973).

LOYD, LEWIS C., *The Origins of Some Anglo-Norman Families*, ed. C. T. Clay and D. C. Douglas (Harleian Society Publications 103, 1951).

LUCHT, DIETMAR, *Die Städtepolitik Herzog Barnims I. von Pommern 1220–1278* (Veröffentlichungen der historischen Kommission für Pommern 5/10, Cologne and Graz, 1965).

LUDAT, HERBERT, *An Elbe und Oder um das Jahr 1000: Skizzen zur Politik des Ottonenreiches und der slavischen Mächte in Mitteleuropa* (Cologne and Vienna, 1971).

—— *Die Anfänge des polnischen Staates* (Cracow, 1942).

LYDON, JAMES F., *Ireland in the Later Middle Ages* (Dublin, 1973).

—— 'Richard II's Expeditions to Ireland', *RSAIJn.* 93 (1963), 135–49.

—— 'The Braganstown Massacre, 1329', *Journal of the County Louth Archaeological and Historical Society*, 19 (1977), 5–16.

—— 'The Hobelar: An Irish Contribution to Medieval Warfare', *Irish Sword*, 2 (1954–6), 12–16.

—— 'The Problem of the Frontier in Medieval Ireland', *Topic: A Journal of the Liberal Arts*, 13 (1967), 5–22.

—— 'William of Windsor and the Irish Parliament', *EHR* 80 (1965), 252–67.

LYNCH, WILLIAM, *A View of the Legal Institutions . . . in Ireland . . .* (London, 1830).

McCRANK, LAWRENCE J., 'Cistercians as Frontiersmen', in *Estudios en homenaje a don Claudio Sánchez Albornoz en sus 90 años* (*Cuadernos de historia de España: Anexos*, 3 vols., Buenos Aires, 1983), ii, 313–60.

McGINN, BERNARD, 'St Bernard and Eschatology', in *Bernard of Clairvaux: Studies Presented to Dom Jean Leclercq* (Cistercian Studies Series 23, Washington, 1973), 161–85.

MACK, JAMES L., *The Border Line* (rev. edn., Edinburgh and London, 1926).

MACKAY, ANGUS, *Anatomía de una revuelta urbana: Alcaraz en 1458* (Albacete, 1985).

—— *Spain in the Middle Ages: From Frontier to Empire, 1000–1500* (London, 1977).

—— 'Andalucía como factor dinámico de la historia entre Oriente y Occidente' in *Actas del V Coloquio de Historia Medieval Andaluza* (Córdoba, in press).

—— 'Los romances fronterizos como fuente histórica', in *Actas del IV Coloquio de Historia Medieval Andaluza* (Almería, in press).

—— 'The Ballad and the Frontier in Late Medieval Spain', *Bulletin of Hispanic Studies*, 53 (1976), 15–33.

MACKINLAY, JAMES M., *Ancient Church Dedications in Scotland* (2 vols., Edinburgh, 1910–14).

MACKINNON, DONALD, *A Descriptive Catalogue of Gaelic Manuscripts* (Edinburgh, 1912).

McNAB, BRUCE, 'Obligations of the Church in English Society: Military Arrays of the Clergy, 1369–1418', in William C. Jordan, Bruce McNab, and Teófilo F. Ruiz (eds.), *Order and Innovation in the Middle Ages* (Princeton, 1976), 293–314.

MacNIOCAILL, GEARÓID, 'The Interaction of Laws', in James F. Lydon (ed.), *The English in Medieval Ireland* (Dublin, 1984), 105–17.

MARAVALL, JOSÉ ANTONIO, *El concepto de España en la Edad Media* (3rd edn. Madrid, 1981).

MARGARY, IVAN D., *Roman Roads in Britain* (rev. edn., London, 1967).

MARKHAM, JAMES M., 'Paris Journal: A French Thinker Who Declines a Guru Mantle', *New York Times* (21 Dec. 1987), 4.

MARTIN, F. X., *No Hero in the House: Diarmait Mac Murchada and the Coming of the Normans to Ireland* (Dublin, 1976).

MATTOSO, JOSÉ, *Identificação de um país: Ensaio sobre as origens de Portugal, 1096–1325*, i (Lisbon, 1985).

MAYER, HANS EBERHARD, *The Crusades* (Eng. trans., Oxford, 1972).

MELBIN, MURRAY, *Night as Frontier: Colonizing the World after Dark* (New York, 1987).

MENDOZA DÍAZ-MAROTO, FRANCISCO, 'Un nuevo manuscrito emparedado de fines del siglo XVI', *Al-Basit*, 9 (1983), 27–45.

MILHOU, ALAIN, *Colón y su mentalidad mesiánica en el ambiente franciscanista español* (Valladolid, 1983).

—— 'La Chauve-souris, le Nouveau David et le roi caché: Trois Images de l'empereur des derniers temps dans le monde ibérique: XIIe–XVIIe siècles', *Mélanges de la Casa de Velázquez*, 18 (1982), 61–78.

MILLER, DAVID H., and STEFFEN, JEROME (eds.), *The Frontier: Comparative Studies*, i (Norman, Okla., 1977).

MILLER, STEUART N. (ed.), *The Roman Occupation of South-Western Scotland* (Glasgow, 1952).

MILLMAN, R. N., *The Making of the Scottish Landscape* (London, 1975).

MIRRER-SINGER, LOUISE, 'Revaluating the *Fronterizo* Ballad: The *Romance de la morilla burlada* as a Pro-Christian Text', *La corónica*, 12 (1985), 157–67.

MITRE FERNÁNDEZ, EMILIO, 'De la toma de Algeciras a la campaña de Antequera', *Hispania*, 32 (1972), 77–122.

MODRZEWSKA, HALINA, 'Jeńcy i ich osady w Polsce wcześniejszego średniowiecza' (Ph.D. dissertation, Warsaw, 1977).

—— 'Osadnictwo jenieckie we wcześniejszym średniowieczu polskim', *Kwartalnik Historii Kultury Materialnej*, 17 (1969), 345–83.

MODZELEWSKI, KAROL, *Organizacja gospodarcza państwa piastowskiego: X–XIII wiek* (Wrocław, 1975).

—— 'The System of the *Ius Ducale* and the Idea of Feudalism', *Quaestiones Medii Aevi*, 1 (1977), 71–99.

MOFFAT, ALISTAIR, *Kelsae* (Edinburgh, 1985).

MOXÓ, SALVADOR DE, *Repoblación y sociedad en la España cristiana medieval* (Madrid, 1979).

MULDOON, JAMES, *Popes, Lawyers and Infidels: The Church and the Non-Christian World, 1250–1550* (Philadelphia, 1979).

—— *The Expansion of Europe: The First Phase* (Philadelphia, 1977).

MUÑOZ FERNÁNDEZ, ÁNGELA, 'Cultos, devociones y advocaciones religiosas en los orígenes de la organización eclesiástica cordobesa (siglos XIII–XIV)' in *Actas del V Coloquio de Historia Medieval Andaluza* (Córdoba, in press).

NASH, GERALD D., 'The Census of 1890 and the Closing of the Frontier', *Pacific Northwest Quarterly*, 71 (1980), 98–100.

—— 'Where's the West?', *Historian*, 49 (1986–7), 1–9.

NICHOLLS, KENNETH, *Gaelic and Gaelicised Ireland in the Middle Ages* (Dublin, 1972).

NICOLSON, JOSEPH, and BURN, RICHARD, *The History and Antiquities of Westmorland and Cumberland* (2 vols., London, 1777).

Ó CONCHEANAINN, TOMÁS, 'The Book of Ballymote', *Celtica*, 14 (1981), 15–25.

Ó CORRÁIN, DONNCHÁ, 'Nationality and Kingship in Pre-Norman Ireland', in T. W. Moody (ed.), *Nationality and the Pursuit of National Independence* (Historical Studies 11, Belfast, 1978), 1–35.

Ó Cuív, Brian, 'Bunús Mhuintir Dhíolún', *Éigse*, 11 (1964), 65–6.
—— 'Eachtra Muireadhaigh Í Dhálaigh', *Studia Hibernica*, 1 (1961), 56–69.
O'Grady, Standish H., *Catalogue of Irish Manuscripts in the British Museum*, i (London, 1926).
Orpen, Goddard H., *Ireland under the Normans, 1169–1333* (4 vols., Oxford, 1911–20).
Oskamp, H. P. A., 'The Yellow Book of Lecan Proper', *Ériu*, 26 (1975), 102–21.
O'Sullivan, William, 'Ciothruadh's Yellow Book of Lecan', *Éigse*, 18 (1981), 177–81.
Otway-Ruthven, A. J., *A History of Medieval Ireland* (London, 1968; rev. edn., 1980).
—— 'Knight Service in Ireland', *RSAIJn.* 89 (1959), 1–15.
—— 'Royal Service in Ireland', *RSAIJn.* 98 (1968), 37–46.
—— 'The Constitutional Position of the Great Lordships in South Wales', *TRHS*, 5th ser., 8 (1958), 1–20.
Owen, George, *The Description of Pembrokeshire*, ed. Henry Owen (4 vols., Cymmrodorion Record Ser. 1, 1892–1936).
Palliser, David, 'Richard III and York', in Rosemary Horrox (ed.), *Richard III and the North* (Hull, 1986), 51–81.
Palmer, J. J. N., 'The Last Summons of the Feudal Army in England (1385)', *EHR* 83 (1968), 771–5.
Parry, M. L., and Slater, T. R. (eds.), *The Making of the Scottish Countryside* (London, 1980).
Paul, James Balfour (ed.), *Scots Peerage* (9 vols., Edinburgh, 1904–14).
Pérez Prendes, José M., 'El origen de los caballeros de cuantía y los cuantiosos de Jaén en el siglo XV', *Revista española de derecho militar*, 9 (1962), 111–75.
Pescador del Hoyo, Carmela, 'La caballería popular en Castilla y León', *Cuadernos de historia de España*, 33–4 (1961), 101–238.
Peters, F. E., *Jerusalem: The Holy City in the Eyes of Chroniclers, Visitors, Pilgrims, and Prophets from the Days of Abraham to the Beginnings of Modern Times* (Princeton, 1985).
Petersohn, Jürgen, *Der südliche Ostseeraum im kirchlich-politischen Kräftespiel des Reichs, Polens und Dänemarks vom 10. bis 13. Jahrhundert* (Cologne and Vienna, 1979).
Petrů, Eduard, 'Specifičnost rytířské epiky ve slovanských literaturách', *Slavia*, 52 (1983), 250–8.
Pevsner, Nikolaus, *Cumberland and Westmorland* (The Buildings of England, Harmondsworth, 1967).
Piekarczyk, Stanislaw, *Studia z dziejów miast polskich w XIII–XIV wieku* (Warsaw, 1955).

PODWIŃSKA, ZOFIA, *Technika uprawy roli w Polsce średniowiecznej* (Wrocław, 1962).

—— *Zmiany form osadnictwa wiejskiego na ziemiach polskich we wcześniejszym średniowieczu: Źreb, wieś, opole* (Wrocław, 1971).

POPIOL-SZYMAŃSKA, ALEKSANDRA, 'Poglądy szlachty i mieszczan na handel wewnętrzny w Polsce od końca XV wieku do połowy XVII wieku', *Roczniki Historyczne*, 37 (1971), 39–83.

PORRAS ARBOLEDAS, PEDRO A., 'El comercio fronterizo entre Andalucía y el reino de Granada a través de sus gravámenes fiscales', *Baetica*, 7 (1984), 245–53.

POSTAN, M. M. (ed.), *Cambridge Economic History of Europe*, i: *The Agrarian Life of the Middle Ages* (2nd edn., Cambridge, 1966).

POWERS, JAMES F., 'The Origins and Development of Municipal Service in the Leonese and Castilian Reconquest, 800–1250', *Traditio*, 16 (1970), 91–113.

—— 'Townsmen and Soldiers: The Interaction of Urban and Military Organization in the Militias of Medieval Castile', *Speculum*, 46 (1971), 641–55.

POWICKE, MICHAEL, *Military Obligation in Medieval England* (Oxford, 1962).

PRAŽÁK, ALBERT, *Staročeská báseň o Alexandru Velikém* (Prague, 1946).

PRESTWICH, MICHAEL, *War, Politics and Finance under Edward I* (London, 1972).

—— 'Cavalry Service in Early Fourteenth-Century England', in John Gillingham and James C. Holt (eds.), *War and Government in the Middle Ages: Essays in Honour of J. O. Prestwich* (Woodbridge, 1984), 147–58.

PRINCE, ALBERT E., 'The Army and the Navy', in James F. Willard and William A. Morris (eds.), *The English Government at Work 1327–1336*, i (Cambridge, Mass., 1940), 332–93.

—— 'The Strength of English Armies in the Reign of Edward III', *EHR* 46 (1931), 353–71.

Priory of Hexham (Surtees Society 44, 1864 for 1863).

PRYCE, HUW, 'In Search of a Medieval Society: Deheubarth in the Writings of Gerald of Wales', *Welsh History Review*, 13 (1986–7), 265–81.

PUGH, T. B. (ed.), *Glamorgan County History*, iii: *The Middle Ages* (Cardiff, 1971).

PUTNAM, BERTHA H., 'The Transformation of the Keepers of the Peace into the Justices of the Peace, 1327–1380', *TRHS*, 4th ser., 12 (1929), 19–48.

QUINTANILLA RASO, MARÍA C., *Nobleza y señoríos en el reino de Córdoba: La casa de Aguilar (siglos XIV y XV)* (Córdoba, 1979).

—— 'Consideraciones sobre la vida en la frontera de Granada', in *Actas del III Coloquio de Historia Medieval Andaluza* (Jaén, 1984), 501–19.

—— 'Estructuras sociales y familiares y papel político de la nobleza cordobesa (siglos XIV–XV)', *En la España medieval*, 3 (1982), 331–52.

RÁDL, EMANUEL, *Válka Čechů s Němci* (Prague, 1928).

RAE, THOMAS I., *The Administration of the Scottish Frontier, 1513–1603* (Edinburgh, 1966).

REDDAWAY, W. F., *et al.* (eds.), *Cambridge History of Poland*, i (Cambridge, 1950).

REED, JAMES, *The Border Ballads* (London, 1973).

RICHARDSON, H. G., and SAYLES, G. O., *The Irish Parliament in the Middle Ages* (Philadelphia, 1952).

—— 'Irish Revenue, 1278–1384', *PRIA* 62 C (1962), 87–100.

RICHMOND, IAN A. (ed.), *Roman and Native in North Britain* (Edinburgh and London, 1958).

RIVERA GARRETAS, M., *La encomienda, el priorato y la villa de Uclés en la Edad Media (1174–1310)* (Madrid and Barcelona, 1985).

RIVET, A. L. F., and SMITH, COLIN, *The Place Names of Roman Britain* (London and Princeton, 1979).

RODRÍGUEZ LLOPIS, MIGUEL, *Señorío y feudalismo en el reino de Murcia* (Murcia, 1986).

RODRÍGUEZ MOLINA, JOSÉ, 'Las órdenes militares de Calatrava y Santiago en el Alto Guadalquivir (siglos XIII–XV)', *Cuadernos de estudios medievales*, 2–3 (1974–5), 59–83.

ROSE, RICHARD K., 'The Bishops and Diocese of Carlisle: Church and Society in the Anglo-Scottish Borders, 1292–1395' (Ph.D. thesis, Edinburgh University, 1984).

ROSENFELD, HANS FRIEDRICH, 'Ulrich von Eschenbach', in Wolfgang Stammler and Karl Langosch (eds.), *Die deutsche Literatur des Mittelalters: Verfasserlexicon* (5 vols., Berlin and Leipzig, 1933–55), iv, cols. 572–9.

ROSENFELD, HELLMUT, 'Der alttschechische *Tkadleček* in neuer Sicht. Ackermann-Vorlage, Walldenserallegorie oder höfische Dichtung?', *Welt der Slaven*, 26/2 (1981), 357–78.

RUSSELL, FREDERICK H., *The Just War in the Middle Ages* (Cambridge, 1975).

SÁEZ RIVERA, C., 'El derecho de represalia en el Adelantamiento de Cazorla durante el siglo XV' (unpublished paper).

SÁNCHEZ-ALBORNOZ, CLAUDIO, *Despoblación y repoblación del valle del Duero* (Buenos Aires, 1966).

SANCHO DE SOPRANIS, HIPÓLITO, *Historia social de Jerez de la Frontera al fin de la Edad Media* (2 vols., Jerez, 1959).

—— 'Jerez y el reino de Granada a mediados del siglo XV', *Tamuda*, 2 (1954), 287–308.

Bibliography 363

SANDERS, IVOR J. *Feudal Military Service in England* (Oxford, 1956).

SAVAGE, WILLIAM W., jun., and THOMPSON, STEPHEN I. (eds.), *The Frontier: Comparative Studies*, ii (Norman, Okla. 1979).

SAYLES, G. O., 'The Vindication of the Earl of Kildare from Treason, 1496', *Irish Historical Studies*, 7 (1950), 39–47.

SCAMMELL, JEAN, 'Robert I and the North of England', *EHR* 73 (1958), 385–403.

SCHIEDER, THEODOR (ed.), *Handbuch der europäischen Geschichte*, i (Stuttgart, 1976).

SCHMID, KARL, 'The Structure of the Nobility in the Earlier Middle Ages', in Timothy Reuter (ed.), *The Medieval Nobility* (Amsterdam, etc., 1978), 37–59.

SCHMIDT, EBERHARD, *Die Mark Brandenburg unter den Askaniern (1134–1320)* (MF 71, Cologne and Vienna, 1973).

SCHULTZE, JOHANNES, *Die Mark Brandenburg*, i: *Entstehung und Entwicklung unter den askanischen Markgrafen (bis 1319)* (Berlin, 1961).

SCHULZE, HANS K., *Adelsherrschaft und Landesherrschaft: Studien zur Verfassungs- und Besitzgeschichte der Altmark, des ostsächsischen Raumes und des hannoverschen Wendlandes im hohen Mittelalter* (MF 29, Cologne and Graz, 1963).

SCOTT, CHARLES ROCHFORT, *Excursions in the Mountains of Ronda and Granada with Characteristic Sketches of the Inhabitants of the South of Spain* (2 vols., London, 1838).

SCOTT, WALTER, *Minstrelsy of the Scottish Border* (5th edn., 3 vols., Edinburgh, 1821).

SECO DE LUCENA PAREDES, LUIS, *Muḥammad IX, sultán de Granada* (Granada, 1978).

—— 'El juez de frontera y los fieles del rastro', *Miscelánea de estudios árabes y hebraicos*, 7 (1958), 137–40.

—— 'La historicidad del romance "Río Verde, Río Verde"', *Al Andalus*, 23 (1958), 75–95.

—— 'Sobre el juez de frontera', *Miscelánea de estudios árabes y hebraicos*, 11 (1962), 107–9.

SEIBT, FERDINAND (ed.), *Handbuch der europäischen Geschichte*, ii (Stuttgart, 1987).

ŠEMBERA, A. V., 'Kdy a od koho jest sepsán Alexander český?', *Sitzungsberichte der königlichen böhmischen Gesellschaft der Wissenschaften* (1859), 30–6.

SILNICKI, TADEUSZ, and GOLĄB, KAZIMIERZ, *Arcybiskup Jakub Świnka i jego epoka* (Warsaw, 1956).

SIMMS, KATHARINE, *From Kings to Warlords: The Changing Political Structure of Gaelic Ireland in the Later Middle Ages* (Woodbridge, 1987).

—— 'Bardic Poetry as a Historical Source', in Tom Dunne (ed.), *The Writer as Witness* (Historical Studies 16, Cork, 1987), 60–7.

—— 'The Poet as Chieftain's Widow: Bardic Elegies', in L. Breatnach, K. McCone, and D. Ó Corráin (eds.), *Sages, Saints and Storytellers: Celtic Studies in Honour of Professor James Carney* (forthcoming).

—— 'Warfare in the Medieval Gaelic Lordships', *Irish Sword*, 12 (1975–6), 98–108.

SIMPSON, G. G., and WEBSTER, BRUCE, 'Charter Evidence and the Distribution of Mottes in Scotland', *Château Gaillard* (1972), 175–92.

SMITH, J. B., *Llywelyn ap Gruffudd: Tywysog Cymru* (Cardiff, 1986).

—— 'Cydfodau o'r Bymthegfed Ganrif', *Bulletin of the Board of Celtic Studies*, 21 (1965–6), 309–24; 25 (1972–4), 128–34.

—— 'Marcher Regality: *Quo Warranto* Proceedings Relating to Cantrefselyf in the Lordship of Brecon', *Bulletin of the Board of Celtic Studies*, 28 (1978–80), 267–88.

—— 'The Regulation of the Frontier of Meirionnydd in the Fifteenth Century', *Journal of the Merioneth Historical Society*, 5 (1965–6), 105–11.

SOLÀ-SOLÉ, JOSEP M., 'En torno al romance de la morilla burlada', *Hispanic Review*, 33 (1965), 135–46.

SONNLEITNER, KÄTHE, 'Die Slawenpolitik Heinrichs des Löwen im Spiegel einer Urkundenarenga', *Archiv für Diplomatik*, 26 (1980), 259–80.

STEFFEN, JEROME, *Comparative Frontiers: A Proposal for Studying the American West* (Norman, Okla., 1980).

STEWART-BROWN, RONALD, *The Sergeants of the Peace in Medieval England and Wales* (Manchester, 1936).

STOREY, R. L., *Thomas Langley and the Bishopric of Durham 1406–1437* (London, 1961).

STRAYER, JOSEPH R., and RUDISILL, GEORGE, jun., 'Taxation and Community in Wales and Ireland, 1272–1327', *Speculum*, 29 (1954), 410–16.

SUÁREZ FERNÁNDEZ, LUIS, *Juan II y la frontera de Granada* (Valladolid, 1954).

SULOWSKI, ZYGMUNT, 'L'Église polonaise à ses origines', in Jerzy Kłoczowski (ed.), *Histoire religieuse de la Pologne* (Paris, 1987), 17–51.

—— 'Początki Kościoła polskiego', in Jerzy Kłoczowski (ed.), *Kosciół w Polsce*, i. *Średniowiecze* (Cracow, 1966), 17–123.

SURTEES, ROBERT, *The History and Antiquities of the County Palatine of Durham* (4 vols., London, 1816–40).

ŠUSTA, JAN, 'Skládal Václav II milostné písně?', *Časopis české historie*, 21 (1915), 217–46.

ŠVÁB, MILOSLAV, *Prology a epilogy v české předhusitské literatuře* (Prague, 1966).

TAZBIR, JANUSZ, *Dzieje polskiej tolerancji* (Warsaw, 1973; German trans., *Geschichte der polnischen Toleranz* (Warsaw, 1977)).

—— *Państwo bez stosów* (Warsaw, 1967; Eng. trans., *A State without Stakes: Polish Religious Toleration in the Sixteenth and Seventeenth Centuries* (Warsaw and New York, 1973)).

—— 'Recherches sur la conscience nationale en Pologne au XVIᵉ et XVIIᵉ siècle', *Acta Poloniae historica*, 14 (1966), 5–22.

TEBRAKE, WILLIAM, *Medieval Frontier: Culture and Ecology in Rijnland* (College Station, Tex., 1985).

TERRASSE, HENRI, 'Le Royaume nasride dans la vie de l'Espagne du Moyen Âge: Indications et problèmes', *Mélanges offerts à Marcel Bataillon* (*Bulletin hispanique*, 64 bis, 1962), 253–60.

THOMPSON, E. A., *Romans and Barbarians: The Decline of the Western Empire* (Madison, 1982).

THOMPSON, JAMES WESTFALL, 'The German Church and the Conversion of the Baltic Slavs', *American Journal of Theology*, 20 (1916), 205–30, 372–89.

THOMSON, S. HARRISON, *Czechoslovakia in European History* (2nd edn., Princeton, 1953).

—— 'Czech and German: Action, Reaction and Interaction', *Journal of Central European Affairs*, 1 (1941), 306–24.

THUNDYIL, ZACHARIAS P., 'La Tradition de Charlemagne chez les chrétiens de Kerala (Inde)', *Actes du VIᵉ Congrès International de la Société Rencesvals* (Aix-en-Provence, 1974), 389–98.

TITZ, K. W., 'Ulrich von Eschenbach und der Alexander boëmicalis', *Jahresbericht der Lese- und Redehalle der deutschen Studenten in Prag* (1880–1), 13–22.

TOPOLSKI, JERZY, *An Outline History of Poland* (Warsaw, 1986).

TORRES FONTES, JUAN, *El monasterio de San Ginés de la Jara en la Edad Media* (Murcia, 1965).

—— *Fajardo el Bravo* (Murcia, 1944).

—— 'Don Fernando de Antequera y la romántica caballeresca', *Miscelánea medieval murciana*, 5 (1980), 83–120.

—— 'El alcalde entre moros y cristianos del reino de Murcia', *Hispania*, 20 (1960), 55–80.

—— 'El Fajardo del "Romance del juego de ajedrez"', *Revista bibliográfica y documental*, 2 (1948), 305–14.

—— 'La frontera de Granada en el siglo XV y sus repercusiones en Murcia y Oriehuela: Los cautivos', in *Homenaje a don José María Lacarra* (Saragossa, 1972), iv. 191–212.

—— 'La historicidad del romance "Abenámar, Abenámar"', *Anuario de estudios medievales*, 8 (1972–3), 225–56.

—— 'La Orden de Santa María de España', *Miscelánea medieval murciana*, 3 (1977), 75–118.

—— 'Las treguas con Granada de 1469 y 1472', *Cuadernos de estudios medievales*, 4–5 (1979), 211–36.

—— 'Los alfaqueques castellanos en la frontera de Granada', in *Homenaje a don Agustín Millares Carlo* (2 vols., Las Palmas, 1975), ii. 99–116.

—— 'Notas sobre los fieles del rastro y alfaqueques murcianos', *Miscelánea de estudios árabes y hebraicos*, 10 (1961), 89–105.

TOUGH, D. L. W., *The Last Years of a Frontier* (Oxford, 1928).

TRAWKOWSKI, STANISLAW, *Gospodarka wielkiej własności cysterskiej na Dolnym Śląsku w XIII wieku* (Warsaw, 1959).

—— 'Die Rolle der deutschen Dorfkolonisation und des deutschen Rechts in Polen im 13. Jahrhundert', in Walter Schlesinger (ed.), *Die deutsche Ostsiedlung des Mittelalters als Problem der europäischen Geschichte* (Vorträge und Forschungen 18, Sigmaringen, 1975), 349–68.

TUCK, J. A., 'War and Society in the Medieval North', *Northern History*, 21 (1985), 33–52.

URVOY, DOMINIQUE, 'Sur l'évolution de la notion de "ǧihād" dans l'Espagne musulmane', *Mélanges de la Casa de Velázquez*, 9 (1973), 335–71.

VCH Cumberland, i–ii (1901–5).

VCH Durham, i (1905).

VELTRUSKÝ, JARMILA F., *A Sacred Farce from Medieval Bohemia* (Ann Arbor, 1985).

VILLAR GARCÍA, LUIS-MIGUEL, *La Extremadura castellano-leonesa: Guerreros, clérigos y campesinos (711–1252)* (Valladolid, 1986).

VLASTO, A. P., *The Entry of the Slavs into Christendom* (Cambridge, 1970).

WALKER, DAVID, 'The Norman Settlement in Wales', in R. Allen Brown (ed.), *Proceedings of the Battle Conference on Anglo-Norman Studies*, i (Woodbridge, 1978), 131–43.

WALLACE-HADRILL, JOHN MICHAEL, *Early Germanic Kingship in England and on the Continent* (Oxford, 1971).

WALSH, MARGARET, *The American Frontier Revisited* (Atlantic Highlands, NJ, 1981).

WALSH, PAUL, *Mide magen Chloinne Cuinn* (Leaves of History series 1, Drogheda, 1930).

WARE, JAMES, *De Hibernia et antiquitatibus ejus disquisitiones* (2nd edn., London, 1658).

WASILEWSKI, TADEUSZ, 'Poland's Administrative Structure in Early Piast Times', *Acta Poloniae historica*, 44 (1981), 5–31.

WASSERSTEIN, DAVID, *The Rise and Fall of the Party-Kings: Politics and Society in Islamic Spain, 1002–1086* (Princeton, 1985).

WATSON, G., 'Wheel Kirk, Liddesdale', *Transactions of the Hawick Archaeological Society* (1914), 20–2.

WATT, JOHN A., *The Church and the Two Nations in Medieval Ireland* (Cambridge, 1970).

WEBER, DAVID J., 'Turner, the Boltonians, and the Borderlands', *American Historical Review*, 91 (1986), 66–81.

WECKMANN, LUIS, *La herencia medieval de México* (Mexico City, 1984).

WESTERMARCK, EDWARD, *Ritual and Belief in Morocco* (2 vols., London, 1926).

WHITE, LYNN T., *Medieval Religion and Technology* (Berkeley, 1978).

WIGHTMAN, W. E., *The Lacy Family in England and Normandy 1066–1194* (Oxford, 1966).

WILLARD, CHARITY C., 'Un écho de Roncevaux au nouveau monde', *Actes du IXe Congrès International de la Société Rencesvals* (2 vols., Modena, 1984), i. 203–10.

WILLARD, JAMES F., *Parliamentary Taxes on Personal Property 1290 to 1334* (Cambridge, Mass., 1934).

WINCHESTER, A. J. L., *Landscape and Society in Medieval Cumbria* (Edinburgh, 1987).

WIPPERMANN, WOLFGANG, *Der 'deutsche Drang nach Osten': Ideologie und Wirklichkeit eines politischen Schlagworts* (Darmstadt, 1981).

WOLF, KENNETH BAXTER, *Christian Martyrs in Muslim Spain* (Cambridge, 1988).

—— 'The Earliest Spanish Christian Views of Islam', *Church History*, 55 (1986), 281–93.

WORMALD, JENNY, *Lords and Men in Scotland: Bonds of Manrent 1442–1603* (Edinburgh, 1985).

WORSTER, DONALD, 'New West, True West: Interpreting the Region's History', *Western Historical Quarterly*, 18 (1987), 141–56.

WYNAR, LUBOMYR R., *S. Harrison Thomson: Bio-bibliography* (University of Colorado Bio-bibliographical Series 1, Boulder, 1963).

WYROZUMSKI, JERZY, *Histora Polski do roku 1505* (Warsaw, 1982).

ZAGRODZKI, TADEUSZ, 'Regularny plan miasta średniowiecznego a limiticja miernicza', *Studia Wczesnośredniowieczne*, 5 (1962), 1–101.

ZIENTARA, BENEDYKT, *Henryk Brodaty i jego czasy* (Warsaw, 1975).

—— 'Die deutschen Einwanderer in Polen vom 12. bis zum 14. Jahrhundert', in Walter Schlesinger (ed.), *Die deutsche Ostsiedlung des Mittelalters als Problem der europäischen Geschichte* (Vorträge und Forschungen 18, Sigmaringen, 1975), 333–48.

—— 'Foreigners in Poland in the 10th–15th Centuries: Their Role in the Opinion of Polish Medieval Community', *Acta Poloniae historica*, 29 (1974), 5–28.

—— '*Melioratio terrae*: The Thirteenth–Century Breakthrough in Polish History', in J. K. Fedorowicz (ed.), *A Republic of Nobles: Studies in Polish History to 1864* (Cambridge, 1982), 28–48.

—— 'Nationality Conflicts in the German–Slavic Borderland in the

13th–14th Centuries and their Social Scope', *Acta Poloniae historica*, 22 (1970), 207–25.

—— 'Przemiany społeczno-gospodarcze i przestrzenne miast w dobie lokacji', in Aleksander Gieysztor and Tadeusz Rosłanowski (eds.), *Miasta doby feudalnej w Europie środkowo-wschodniej* (Warsaw, 1976), 67–97.

—— 'Socio-Economic and Spatial Transformation of Polish Towns During the Period of Location', *Acta Poloniae historica*, 34 (1976), 57–83.

—— 'Walloons in Silesia in the 12th and 13th Centuries', *Quaestiones Medii Aevi*, 2 (1981), 127–50.

—— 'Zur Geschichte der planmäßigen Organisierung des Marktes im Mittelalter', in *Wirtschaftliche und soziale Strukturen im säkularen Wandel: Festschrift für Wilhelm Abel zum 70. Geburtstag* (3 vols., Hanover, 1974), ii. 345–65.

INDEX

Ellis, Steven 180
Ely O'Carroll 78
Emmethaugh 17
Embleton 14 n. 35
Emmehard, bp. of Mecklenburg 294
Empire ('Holy Roman') 155, 158, 167,
    201, 204
  see also Reich
England, English 3–21 *passim*, 25–7,
    30–1, 34–5, 39, 45, 46, 78–9, 81–2,
    85–7, 89–90, 92–4, 98, 101–17
    passim, 120–6, 128, 177, 180–91
    passim, 194, 196–7, 223, 245–66
    passim, 308, 312, 318, 320, 323;
    historians 100, 113
  kings of *see* Canute, Edward the
    Confessor, I, II and III, Henry I,
    II, III and IV, John, Richard II,
    Stephen, William II
  see also Anglo-Normans
Enyas 223
Eresma, r. 55
Erik the Proud 157
Erzgebirge 267
Eschenbach, Ulrich von 201
Escotot (family: Anketil, Gilbert,
    Hawisia, Isolde, Richard (bis),
    Robert, Roger, Walter, William)
    38–41
Esk, Eskdale 4, 21, 262
Essex 26
Estepa 67, 74
Ettleton 263
Ettrick 262
Eugenius III, pope 286–8, 291, 294
Europe 23, 33, 47, 50, 77, 80, 122,
    151–3, 173 n. 56, 181–2, 199, 205,
    208, 214, 230, 285, 288, 312–13,
    315, 317–18, 324–6, 329
Ewes, Ewesdale 248, 262
Extremadura (modern) 60–3
Extremaduras 53–5, 57, 60–1

Fadrique of Aragón 237
Fahrland 41
Fajardo, Alonso ('el Bravo') 218, 225,
    236–7; (family) 146
Fál, land of 193
Falstone 17
Father's Counsel to his Son see Flaška
Feipo, Adam de 37–8; (family) 39
Ferdinand of Antequera, kg. of Aragón
    128–30, 132 n. 13, 231–2, 240
Ferdinand the Catholic of Aragón 241–3

  see also Catholic Kings
Ferdinand I of Castile 53
Ferdinand III of Castile 64, 230, 231–2
Ferdinand IV of Castile 70, 72
Fermoy, lords of *see* Roche
Fernán González 234
Fernández de Córdoba (family) 73, 146
Fianna 182, 195
Fibonacci 311
Fionn MacCumhaill 182, 195
Filey 14 n. 36
Fir Bolg 190
Fir Dhomhnann 190
Fir Ghailian 190
Fitzalan of Oswestry 84
FitzGerald, Maurice 192; (family) 192,
    194
  see also Desmond, earls of; Kildare,
    earls of
FitzGodebert (family) 27
Fitzwarin of Whittington 84
Flanders, Flemings 11, 27, 30, 161, 275,
    277, 285, 302, 305
  ct. of *see* Robert
Flaška, Smil, of Pardubice 211–12
Flodden, btl. 256
Florence 232
Forestry Commission 17
Forth, Firth of 4, 6, 9
Four Courts, Dublin 101
Four Masters, Annals by 183
Fox, Richard, bp. of Durham 259–60
Frame, Robin 83
France, French 23–4, 26–7, 34, 53, 77,
    102, 113, 128, 152, 187, 191, 196,
    206, 209, 220, 223, 276 n. 27, 277,
    286, 318; historians 24
  kgs. of *see* Louis VII
Franciscans 42, 118, 168, 222, 327
Frankfurt/Main 287
Frankfurt/Oder 42
Franks 23, 50, 58, 190, 277, 302, 319
  see also Carolingians
Frederick I of Germany 294, 297,
    300
Frederick II Hohenstaufen 36
Freiberg, Heinrich von 210–11
Freudianism 213
Fribourg, Univ. of 316
Frisia 285
Froissart, Jean 183
Frowin of Drensen 24
Furness 8
Furnival, Lord *see* Talbot

Ormond 195; earls of 86, 106, 123, 192;
    James Butler, 'White Earl' 180–1,
    183–8, 189–90; Thomas 194
Osma, bp. of 229
Ossory, bp. of *see* Peter
Ostmark *see* Lusatia
Osuna 67
Oswestry *see* Fitzalan
Otterburn 8; btl. 254
Otto, bp. of Bamberg 278–81, 304
Otto I of Germany 267, 269, 284
Otto II of Germany 271
Otto III of Germany 155
Otto I of Brandenburg 302
Otto III of Brandenburg 42–3
Ottonians 269–70, 277, 303, 311
    see also Otto I, II, and III
Outremer 23, 317
Owain son of Dyfnwal 3

Pacific 32; North-west 316–17
Pale (Irish) 102, 117, 187, 196
Palestine 23, 276, 313
    see also Holy Land, Jerusalem
Pangermanism 303
Panslavism 303
Pardubice *see* Flaška
Paris, Matthew 36, 323
Partidas (of Alfonso X) 139
Party-kingdoms *see* taifas
Patrick, St 197
Patrick, earl of Dunbar 13
Paul, St 287, 299
Pecheneges 157
Peebles, Peeblesshire 8, 20
Peene, r. 279
Pelayo 234
Pembroke 27, 78; earl of 85–6
Penderleith 18
Pennines 4–6, 8, 19
Percy (family) 258, 264
Pérez de Guzmán (family) 73
Pernia, Luis de 235
Persante, r. 278
Persians 201, 205
Peter, bp. of Ossory 39–40
Peter I of Castile 128, 217–18, 223
Peter of Nysa 162
Petit, William 35–6; (family) 186
Phillip (name) 26
Piasts 24, 153, 155, 157–9, 165–6, 172–3
    see also Poland, rulers of
Picards 26
Picts 3

Pieczeniegi 157
Piekary 155
Pilltown, btl. 191
Pipard, Peter 36 n. 28
Play of the Merry Magdalene 209
Plön 283, 296
Poblet 314
Poer, Arnold le, seneschal of Kilkenny
    118; John 26; Robert 26
Pöhlde annalist 293
Polanes 153
Polabia, Polabians 270, 272, 282, 285,
    291, 304
Poland, Poles 29, 151–74, 270, 272,
    278–81, 284, 292, 293, 296, 301–4
    rulers of *see* Bolesław I, II and
        III, Casimir, Mieszko I and II,
        Przemyst, Wenceslas II and III
        Władysław Hermann,
        Władysław Lokietek
    see also Cujavia, Great Poland, Little
        Poland, Masovia, Silesia
Pomerania 24, 29, 41–2, 46, 157–8,
    166, 270, 278–81, 285, 291, 293–4,
    298–302, 304
    bps. of *see* Adalbert
    princes of *see* Barnim I, Bogislaw I,
        Casimar, Ratibor, Wartislaw
Pomerelia (east Pomerania) 278
    see also Gdańsk Pomerania
Pomorzany 157
Ponce de Léon, ct. Juan 235; Rodrigo,
    marquis of Cádiz 229–30, 231 n.
    60, 234–5, 240, 242
    see also *History of the Deeds of the
        Marquis of Cádiz*; (family) 73
Pontius Pilate 201–2
Poppo, bp. (of Cracow) 155
Porras, Pedro de 147–8
Porter, Robert 308
Portugal, Portugese 50, 53, 58, 60, 64,
    67 n. 54, 68 n. 55, 128, 148, 233,
    318
Potsdam 302
Powers, James 55, 57
Powys 84
Poznań, bp. of *see* Unger
Prague 199–200, 202 n. 9, 204, 207, 214
Premonstratensians 18, 46, 278, 300,
    302
Přemyslids 170–1, 200, 202
    see also Břetislav II, Přemysl Otakar
        I and II, Wenceslas I, and II, and
        III